Seasons Greetings
Wishes.

Vera & Marilyn

Doctrines of the Restoration

Sermons & Writings of Bruce R. McConkie

Doctrines of the Restoration

Sermons & Writings of Bruce R. McConkie

Edited & Arranged
by Mark L. McConkie

BOOKCRAFT
Salt Lake City, Utah

Library of Congress Catalog Card Number: 88–63583
ISBN 0–88494–644–4

2nd Printing, 1989

Printed in the United States of America

I can say with Nephi that the fulness of mine intent is to persuade men to come unto the God of Abraham and the God of Isaac and the God of Jacob and be saved—because the work is true, and because salvation is in Christ. And God being our witness, it is true.

—Bruce R. McConkie
General Conference
April 1972

CONTENTS

V: OVERCOMING THE WORLD

TO THE READER

The prospective reader deserves a friendly notice that *Doctrines of the Restoration*, as a title, may seem to imply more than this compilation seeks to achieve. This book is not intended to be a comprehensive examination of the gospel; neither does it aim at a comprehensive treatment of every subject it touches. Rather, it simply seeks to highlight significant issues from the variety of themes Elder McConkie touched upon in his ministry. What is compiled herein has never been encased together between the same two covers before, though significant portions of it have come from sources distantly available: *Church News, Improvement Era, Instructor, Ensign, New Era, Relief Society Magazine*, Conference Report, and speeches published by the BYU, for example.

This work seeks to do more, however, than simply catalog Elder McConkie's thinking on different gospel themes. He has some obvious spiritual gifts, the observation of which provide a lesson in gospel scholarship. His is the gift "to know that Jesus Christ is the Son of God, and that he was crucified for the sins of the world" (D&C 46:13). His is also the gift of knowledge, which he uses, as these pages testify, to bear witness of the Christ: every teaching contained herein, in one way or another, folds together to bear testimony of Jesus and of His doctrines. Elder McConkie's genius, however, if we are not too presumptuous in using the term, is in his use of the scriptures. They are the fountain from which he drinks, and the platform upon which he stands. He teaches only what he finds in the revelations—though through years of patient and plodding study he has earned the ability to read and see what we all seem to see, and then to go one step further, reading between the lines on occasion, showing relationships between different pieces of information and building therefrom a unified testimony of Jesus and of his prophets.

The reader should be further advised that this is not an official Church publication; the materials contained in this book come from the mind and experience of Elder McConkie. The notes and introductions, however, are mine. So also is the order and the form in which materials are presented; and in these arrangements I have sought wherever possible to retain the logical, step-by-step pattern so characteristic of Elder McConkie.

In the process of gathering and compiling these materials, I have incurred a number of debts, principally to my mother and to my brothers, Joseph, Stanford, and Stephen, for helping me to gather materials and advising me as to their use and worth; my sisters, Mary Donoho and Vivian Adams, also provided helpful materials; and Rebecca Pinegar and Sara Fenn have been equally supportive. Velma Harvey, for thirty-two years my father's very able secretary, was most helpful in helping to locate materials —particularly those which were difficult to find.

The process of compiling these materials has been self-rewarding. At the same time it has been a compelling witness that one of the greatest blessings of mortality is that of "having been born of goodly parents," and of therefore having been "taught somewhat in all the learning of my father" (1 Ne. 1:1).

MARK L. MCCONKIE

The Knowledge of God

INTRODUCTION TO PART I

"It is the first principle of the Gospel," said the Prophet Joseph Smith, "to know for a certainty the Character of God" (*Teachings of the Prophet Joseph Smith*, comp. Joseph Fielding Smith [Salt Lake City: Deseret Book Co., 1938], p. 345. Hereafter cited as *Teachings*). Consequently, the knowledge of God, to use the words of Elder McConkie, is the "rock foundation upon which all true religion is based," for when men learn and live in harmony with the truth about God, they grow spiritually, eventually becoming even as God is. This rock foundation was destroyed, however, during centuries of apostasy. Restored through the Prophet Joseph Smith, this knowledge has once again begun to lift men to celestial heights. These first selections from the sermons and writings of Elder McConkie are significant not simply because he crosses swords with the sophistries of the world, but also because he clarifies with Nephi-force misunderstandings and misinclinations that have arisen even within the Church. Seldom in our literature, for example, do we have such deliberate, forceful, and pointed expressions about the omniscience of God; and seldom do we find such simple and straightforward explanations of the omnipresence of God, the way in which God manifests himself through his Son, or what we properly mean by the phrase "God is a Spirit." Moreover, the doctrine here expounded constitutes a clear, unapologetic and knowledge-based expert witness that men and women can once again become even as are their eternal parents.

Elder McConkie further demonstrates the ability to "read between the lines," or, in the language of the Lord to Moses, to speak and write "after the tenor of" what the Lord has said — that is, after the sense, meaning, purport, or intent of the larger gospel picture. He thus takes a phrase from the Prophet Joseph Smith about "God the first, the Creator; God the second, the Redeemer; and God the third, the witness or Testator" (*Teachings*, p. 190), and sees in it the three greatest truths of eternity, each one corresponding to the mission of one member of the Godhead. He then takes those three composite truths, contrasts them with the three greatest heresies of eternity (the falsehoods which undermine the greatest truths), suggests the implications growing out of such knowledge, and illustrates again how this understanding bears testimony of the goodness of God and of the restoration of the gospel in our day.

This disciplined ability to speak "after the tenor of" what the Lord has revealed is again seen in his discussion of the divine sonship of Christ and the condescension of God. These are doctrines of the Restoration, but they are not often amplified or explored as done here. Moreover, Elder McConkie explains how, in the absence of these two doctrines, the doctrine of atonement is silenced and senseless. Once again, the Latter-day Saints stand apart from the world in their ability to teach and testify of Christ, for so much more has been revealed to them. The distance between the Latter-day Saints and the world is perhaps nowhere better dramatized than it is in the condescension of the Father, the condescension of the Son, and the fact that it not only enables Christ to atone, but makes that atonement, in Amulek's words, "infinite and eternal" (Alma 34:10, 12, 14). The expositions in chapter 2 are as pointed as any in our literature.

When Joseph Smith said that a man could get nearer to God through reading the Book of Mormon than through any other book (*History of the Church* 4:461), it was as if he had said one can know God more perfectly, more completely, more intimately, more thoroughly, and more profoundly, through the teachings and clarifications of the Book of Mormon than through those of any other book. Elder McConkie understood this truth, and applied it. Whenever he taught about God, his teachings were founded on the revelations of this dispensation; whenever he quoted from the Bible, he did so only in the interpretive and clarifying context which the Book of Mormon and other Latter-day revelations provide. His was not an effort to reach further and further back into some rabbinic past in order to gain some new insight. Rather, he had perfect faith in the revelations of this day, and consequently was able to win the instructive and interpretive guidance of the Holy Ghost in his analysis of the doctrines of Deity. For Elder McConkie, when the Lord said to Joseph Smith, "This generation shall have my word through you" (D&C 5:10), it was as if he had said, in effect, "This generation is appointed to receive my word through Joseph Smith and the revelations which I have given unto him. These revelations include, among other things, the Book of Mormon, the Doctrine and Covenants, the Pearl of Great Price, and the Joseph Smith Translation of the Bible. Previous generations were appointed to receive my word through Adam, Enoch, Abraham, Moses, Isaiah, Peter, Paul, and others. But this generation is to receive my word through Joseph Smith, for it is my eternal and unchanging practice that men always receive and understand the gospel through the ministration of living prophets."

In so speaking, we neither denigrate nor disregard the dead prophets; we simply view them from the divine perspective: living prophets teach the doctrines and administer the ordinances of salvation; dead prophets provide a supportive, corroborative testimony. One is a living voice, the other an ancient echo. Both are a necessary part of the plan of salvation, but there is an order of priority in which living prophets hold stewardship over those of their own day, while the dead prophets contribute to and support the living prophets by the teachings, traditions, example, and works which they have left behind.

Elder McConkie knew this, and had unfaltering faith and confidence in the revelations of this generation. He knew that we know the truth about God because of what God has said and done in our own day, and not because of the fragments of what he said thousands of years ago which have been passed through the generations to us. His confidence in the Restoration is reflected in all his teachings, though nowhere is it better illustrated than in his teachings about God.

The material in the first four chapters has been extracted from various sources, and each piece of information grouped according to topic. Two speeches ("Our Relationship with the Lord" and "What Think Ye of Salvation by Grace?"), however, appear almost in toto, in order to preserve the building-block, concept-upon-concept flow of logic. They are important because they join together to define the role and mission of the Christ and our relationship to him. In an age when major segments of the so-called Christian world have built upon the confusions of their fathers to misunderstand the Christ, and when they have either ignored the Father, or placed an unbalanced focus on the Son, it is helpful to have the steadying and certain hand of apostolic testimony as it draws a clear picture for our understanding. These two concluding speeches respond to some of the confusions of the day, bearing certain testimony of Jesus, and warning against the evils of distorting the scriptural view of who he is and what our relationship to him should be. Because Messiah's place is so central to the plan of salvation, and because salvation comes only in true worship, it is vital for Latter-day Saints, and others, to understand what the scriptures mean by the expression "salvation by grace." It is equally important to be able to trace the behavioral implications of this much-abused doctrine. These final two sections provide the platform for such understanding—and for the strengthening of faith which grows out of it.

In short, truth begets truth, and error begets error. One must understand correctly the nature and character of God if one is to understand correctly the mission and character of Apostles and prophets, for his testimony is their testimony, and their teachings are his. Therefore, Christ and his prophets are one. The understanding of the one comes only with the understanding of the other. And that is the point of chapter 4: to explain the relationship between God and his servants, and to show how both bear the identical testimony.

Chapter 1

GOD
THE ETERNAL FATHER

Importance of the Knowledge of God

The knowledge of God, the knowledge as to the nature and kind of being that he is, is the rock foundation upon which all true religion is based, and without that knowledge and without revelation from him, it is not possible for men to hope for or gain the blessings, honors, and glories of eternity.

The knowledge of God is the beginning of true religion. Without it there cannot be faith in God. The knowledge of God is the end of all true religion. If we have that knowledge and seek, as John says (John 3:3), to purify ourselves as he is pure, we can go on in eternal progression, having reached the blessings of peace and happiness here, and being assured of an eternal reward in the mansions that are prepared in the worlds to come.

The Master gave the key to this principle in his great intercessory prayer when he said, "And this is life eternal, that they might know thee the only true God, and Jesus Christ, whom thou hast sent" (John 17:3). The Prophet Joseph Smith said: "It is the first principle of the Gospel to know for a certainty the Character of God, and to know that we may converse with him as one man converses with another" (*Teachings*, p. 345). (Conference Report, April 1952.)

The Personality of God

The Godhead is composed of three members: God the Father, God the Son, and God the Holy Ghost.

Initially, however, in presenting the revealed knowledge of the personality of God, no attempt will be made where certain scriptures are concerned to distinguish between the Father and the Son.

Since they have the same personal characteristics, the same perfected attributes, the same personality (though they are separate personages), every such scripture cited does or could apply equally to each of them. Truth seekers can make the necessary distinctions later, showing the missions performed by each and their relationship to each other as members of the Godhead, or Trinity.

Now, since it is life eternal to know God, and since he desires that man gain this very salvation, he has revealed himself to man from time to time. This revelation began in the beginning with father Adam. While he was yet in the Garden, he walked and talked with God, saw his face, received instruction from him, and knew what kind of a being he was (Gen. 2:15–25; 3:1–24).

Then when the Lord revealed the account of the Creation, he was very express in teaching that he himself was a being in whose image and likeness man was created. That he was the pattern after which man was made physically and naturally upon the earth is very evident from the plain reading of the record. The language cannot be twisted to mean that man is merely in his spiritual likeness and image.

The account of man's creation as given in Genesis reads: "And God said, Let us make man *in our image,* after our likeness. . . . So God created man *in his own image,* in the image of God created he him; male and female created he them." (Gen. 1:26–27; italics added.) "This is the book of the generations of Adam. In the day that God created man, in the *likeness of God* made he him; Male and female created he them; and blessed them, and called their name Adam, in the day when they were created. And Adam lived an hundred and thirty years, and begat a son *in his own likeness,* after his image; and called his name Seth." (Gen. 5:1–3; italics added.)

Thus Adam was created in the image and likeness of God in the same way that Seth was created in the image and likeness of Adam. Paul gave the same literal meaning to these words by explaining that as man "is the image and glory of God," so "the woman is the glory of the man" (1 Cor. 11:7).

So man is in form like God, and God is in form like man. Both have size and dimensions. Both have a body. God is not an ethereal nothingness that is in all things, nor is he merely the powers and laws by which all things are governed.

Many Prophets Saw God

By faith many men have seen God and have left their testimonies as to the nature and kind of being he is. On one occasion, "as Moses," one of the greatest of these, "entered into the tabernacle, the cloudy pillar descended, and stood at the door of the tabernacle, and *the Lord talked with Moses.* . . . And the Lord spake unto Moses face to face, as a man speaketh unto his friend." On another occasion Moses was permitted to see the "back parts" of the Lord. (Ex. 33:9, 11, 23; italics added; 34:28–35.)

Moses was not alone as a witness of the Lord in his day. It was a period when by faith many great spiritual manifestations were given. "Then went up Moses, and Aaron, Nadab, and Abihu, and seventy of the elders of Israel: And *they saw the God of Israel*: and there was under his feet as it were a paved work of a sapphire stone, and as it were the body of heaven in his clearness. And upon the nobles of the children of Israel he laid not his hand: also *they saw God*, and did eat and drink." (Ex. 24:9–11; italics added.)

Isaiah has given us similar testimony. "*I saw also the Lord*," he said, "sitting upon a throne, high and lifted up, and his train filled the temple. Then said I, Woe is me! for I am undone; because I am a man of unclean lips, and I dwell in the midst of a people of unclean lips: *for mine eyes have seen the King*, the Lord of hosts." (Isa. 6:1, 5; italics added; 2 Ne. 16:1, 5.)

That Enoch (Gen. 5:24), Noah (Gen. 6:5–9), Abraham (Gen. 17:1; 18:1; Acts 7:2), Isaac (Gen. 26:2, 24), Jacob (Gen. 28:13; 32:30; 35:9; 46:2–3; 48:3), and many of the prophets had similar manifestations is almost too well known to require documentation. And that similar knowledge continued among God's elect in New Testament times is also commonly known by gospel students.

On the occasion of the martyrdom of Stephen, for instance, we find a plain illustration of the personalities of the members of the Godhead. For testifying of Christ to those whom he called "the betrayers and murderers" of the "Just One," Stephen was stoned to death.

"But he, being full of the Holy Ghost, looked up stedfastly into heaven, and *saw the glory of God, and Jesus standing on the right hand of God*, And said, Behold, I see the heavens opened, and the Son of man standing on the right hand of God" (Acts 7:55–56; italics added).

At that moment, Stephen, on earth, was receiving testimony from the Holy Ghost, one member of the Godhead, while the Father and the Son, the other two members, stood in heaven.[1]

In rejoicing over the testimony of the prophets, who through righteousness and by faith perfected themselves sufficiently to see the face of God, it is also worthy of note that the scriptures specifically promise that those who attain the celestial heaven shall yet see God, for "the throne of God and of the Lamb shall be in it; and his servants shall serve him: And they shall *see his face*; and his name shall be in their foreheads" (Rev. 22:3-4; italics added).

So we have the recorded testimonies of the prophets of old that they knew God, saw his face, stood in his presence, and heard his voice. We also know and testify that this same unchangeable being—this being who is the same yesterday, today, and forever; this being "with whom is no variableness, neither shadow of turning" (James 1:17) continues to speak and reveal himself to men.

The Fatherhood of God

Paul's method of proof to show the Athenians that the Godhead was not "like unto gold, or silver, or stone, graven by art and man's device," was to quote with approval their own poets who had taught that men are the offspring of God. That the poets had spoken truly Paul affirmed by making the positive declaration in his own right that "we are also the offspring of God." (Acts 17:29, 28.)

This same Apostle,[2] in exhorting the Hebrew Saints to endure the trials and chastenings of this mortal probation said: "We have had fathers of our flesh which corrected us, and we gave them reverence: shall we not much rather be in subjection unto the Father of spirits, and live?" (Heb. 12:9.)

And this same eternal truth—that we are the offspring of God—was made the basis of Christ's direction to his disciples that they should pray by addressing the Father as "Our Father which art in heaven" (Matt. 6:9). That is, God was not only the Father of Christ after the manner of the flesh (1 Ne. 11:18), but he is also the Father of the spirits of all men; all are his spirit offspring, born as his children before their mortal birth into this world.

This was reaffirmed by the Lord when, after his resurrection, Mary came rushing to embrace him, he restrained her by saying: "Touch me not; for I am not yet ascended to my Father: but go to my brethren, and say unto them, I ascend unto *my Father, and your Father*, and to *my God, and your God*" (John 20:17; italics added).

Many passages of scriptures shed light on this truth that men are the offspring of God, his spirit children, and that they lived with him in preexistence before their mortal birth.

It was during this preexistent era that "there was war in heaven," that Lucifer and one-third of the hosts of heaven were cast out for rebellion (Rev. 12:7-9), and have been known ever after as "the angels which kept not their first estate" (Jude 1:6).

It was of this period — "When the morning stars sang together, and all the sons of God shouted for joy" — that the Lord asked Job: "Where wast thou when I laid the foundations of the earth? declare, if thou hast understanding" (Job 38:1-7).

And it was God's foreknowledge, gained in this first estate, that enabled him to say to Jeremiah: "Before I formed thee in the belly I knew thee; and before thou camest forth out of the womb I sanctified thee, and I ordained thee a prophet unto the nations" (Jer. 1:5).

Now, if we are the sons of God the Father, the offspring of that same being to whom Christ ascended after his resurrection, if we are actually his spirit children, then we as his children are created in his image and likeness and he is a personal being. ("The Truth About God," missionary pamphlet, The Church of Jesus Christ of Latter-day Saints, n.d.)

Through Christ the Father Manifests Himself

Knowledge of God Comes Only by Revelation

The knowledge of God, always coming by revelation (Job 11:7; Jacob 4:8; Alma 26:22), has been had in every age of the earth's history when the gospel has been here. The prophets have known of him and have borne witness to the people concerning his attributes and his laws. He created Adam "in the image of his own body" (Moses 6:9) and then walked and talked with him, with the very man whom he had created in his own likeness (Gen. 3:8-22). He sent his firstborn spirit Son (Rom. 8:29; Col. 1:15; D&C 93:21), Jehovah, to commune with Moses "face to face, as a man speaketh unto his friend" (Ex. 33:11). And then in the meridian of time he sent this same Son, among other reasons, to manifest to the world the nature and kind of being that he is, so that men might know him and worship him. (Conference Report, April 1952.)

Four Gospels a Key to Understanding Deity

We now speak particularly of these wondrous books that we call the four Gospels. They contain hidden and unknown treasures. We haven't caught the vision and come to realize what we can get out of the four Gospels. Would it surprise you if I suggested that there is more knowledge in the four Gospels, more revealed truth relative to the nature and kind of being that God our Father is, than in all the rest of holy writ combined? All we need to do is learn how to get that knowledge out. We need guidance. We need the Spirit of the Lord to direct us as we study.

You remember that Philip met the eunuch from the Court of Candace. The eunuch was reading messianic prophecies in the book of Isaiah. Philip said unto him, "Understandest thou what thou readest?" And he said, "How can I, except some man should guide me?" (Acts 8:26–31.) Like the eunuch we need to be taught how to approach the standard works of the Church, and then, if we follow the simple, easy formulas that are provided, we shall have a new vision of doctrinal understanding, and new desires to live righteously will grow up in our hearts.

In Christ God Manifested Himself to the World

The Gospels show that God was, in Christ, manifesting himself to the world, teaching the nature and kind of being that he is. It is eternal life to know the Father and the Son (John 17:3) and to become like them. We know the Father by coming to an understanding of the Son. The Son is the revealer of God. No man cometh unto the Father except by him or by his word. (John 6:44; 14:6.) We want to know the Father and the Son, and the chief account is in the Gospels.

The Gospels' format is deliberate and straightforward. For instance, there is an account in which Jesus heals a man who was born blind. He does it on his own initiative. He does it for the purpose of assembling a congregation. Word of the deed is heralded through all Jerusalem. Hosts assemble to see what has been done. Then, to that great congregation, which knows very well that the Twenty-third Psalm identifies the Great Jehovah as Israel's Shepherd, he proceeds to teach, "I am the good shepherd," that is to say, "I am the Lord, Jehovah." In his sermon he says, "I and my Father are one." He preaches a glorious sermon on his own divine sonship. And his words are attested as being true because he opened the eyes of the man born blind. (John 9, 10.)

The same thing is illustrated in the raising of Lazarus from the dead. Jesus comes and preaches a sermon; he says, "I am the resurrection, and the life: he that believeth in me, though he were dead, yet shall he live." (John 11:25.) In other words, he says: "Immortality comes by me; eternal life is in and through me. I am the Son of God. I make these things possible." And lest there be any question about his doctrine, he commands them to roll the stone from the door of the tomb, and then he says, "Lazarus, come forth," whereupon the man whose body had started to decay rises and he comes out. This raising of Lazarus from the dead is thus a witness, for all the world and through all the eternities, that the Man who did it is the resurrection and the life; that immortality and eternal life come by him; that he is the Son of the Living God; that his testimony is true.

Let us take another illustration. After his resurrection, Jesus walks along the Emmaus road and converses with two of his disciples. He is made known to them in the breaking of bread. Soon thereafter he appears in the upper room to ten of the twelve (Thomas was absent)—and please note, it was to a congregation of Saints, which, without question, included the faithful sisters of that day—and to this entire group, not to ten men only, but to the entire group, he says, "Have ye here any meat?" They bring him a piece of broiled fish and of honeycomb and he takes it and eats before them. Then they feel the nail marks in his hands and in his feet and thrust their hands into his side. You talk about a teaching situation! That little episode that occurred on the Emmaus road and which was climaxed in the upper room is the paramount illustration in all the revelations that have ever been given as to what kind of a being a resurrected person is and how we, patterned after him, will yet become if we are true and faithful in all things. (See Luke 24.)

In reading the New Testament, and particularly the four Gospels, we have a marvelous opportunity to come to love the Lord and to get the desire to keep his commandments and consequently be inheritors of eternal life in the world to come. But it is not reading alone; it is reading, pondering, and praying so that the Spirit of the Almighty gets involved in the study and gives understanding. ("Drink from the Fountain," *Ensign,* April 1975, pp. 70–72.)

God Is Known by Knowing Man

Paul (Rom. 1:18–25) explains that God is revealed in man; that is, man as God's noblest creation, fashioned in fact in his image, is the most perfect earthly manifestation of God.

Thus to know God man has but to know himself. By introspective search in his own soul, man comes to a degree of understanding of God, including Deity's character, perfections, and attributes. As Joseph Smith said, "If men do not comprehend the character of God, they do not comprehend themselves" (*Teachings*, p. 343).

There is thus, Paul continues, no justification or excuse for man in his wisdom to worship false gods or to turn to idols, for when man lowers his standard of worship to that which is false and corruptible, his ethical standards fall also, and he is left to every evil lust.

"Because that which may be known of God is manifest in them"; he says, "for God hath shewed it unto them" (Rom. 1:19). In other words, that which may be known of God, to a degree at least, is manifest in man. That is, man has a body, is endowed with reason and intellect, possesses certain characteristics, enjoys certain attributes, exercises certain powers—and so it is in greater measure with Deity. God is like man because man is like God. (*Doctrinal New Testament Commentary*, 3 vols. [Salt Lake City: Bookcraft, 1973], 2:216-18, hereafter cited as *DNTC*; see also Acts 17:15-34.)

"He That Hath Seen Me Hath Seen the Father"

The resurrected Lord Jesus—having a tangible body of flesh and bones, a body which was felt and handled by Apostles in the upper room, a body that ate and digested food (Luke 24:36-43)—is in "the express image" of his Father's person (Heb. 1:13).

Thus, God was in Christ manifesting himself to the world—a gracious and condescending thing for the Eternal Father to do, for thereby men could come to know him and to gain that eternal life which such knowledge brings. The context in which these truths are unfolded is retold by John. In conversing with some of his disciples, Jesus said: "If ye had known me, ye should have known my Father also: and from henceforth ye know him, and have seen him. Philip saith unto him, Lord, shew us the Father, and it sufficeth us." (John 14:7-8.)

Jesus is saying, in effect, "If ye had known that as the Son of God, I am in the express image of his person, then ye should have known the Father, for he is manifesting himself to you through me; and you may now, therefore, say that ye know him, for he is in all respects as I am; and since ye have seen me, it is as though you had seen him."

Philip speaks for the others, and in effect says: "Lord, show us the Father himself so we may say we have seen him as well as his Prototype, and then we will be satisfied."

John's account then continues: "Jesus saith unto him, Have I been so long time with you, and yet hast thou not known me, Philip? he that hath seen me hath seen the Father; and how sayest thou then, Shew us the Father?" (John 14:9.)

In other words, "Jesus saith unto him, Philip, after all your association with me, have you not come to know that I am the Son of

God, and that the Father is manifesting himself to the world through me? Surely by this time you should know that he who hath seen me hath seen the Father, as it were, for I am so fully and completely like him. Why, then, do you ask for that which you are not now ready to receive, by saying, Show us the Father also?'' (See *DNTC* 1:730–31.)

The Father a Man of Holiness

We have a scripture that says, "The Father has a body of flesh and bones as tangible as man's; the Son also; but the Holy Ghost has not a body of flesh and bones, but is a personage of Spirit" (D&C 130:22). If we had lived in the beginning, in Adam's day, and had received the knowledge of God as taught by revelation from the mouth of Adam, the presiding high priest in the Church, we would have seen that the very name of the Father, literally interpreted, meant "Man of Holiness is his name, and the name of his Only Begotten is the Son of Man" (Moses 6:57).

When Christ repeatedly referred to himself as the Son of Man, he was certifying that Man of Holiness, God the Eternal Father, was his Father, and he had no reference to his immortality, his birth as the Son of Mary. (Conference Report, April 1952.)

Faithful Become Sons of God

All of us who have received the gospel have power given us to become the sons of God (John 1:12). We can do that by faith. And Paul says those that become, by adoption, sons of God are joint heirs with Jesus Christ (Rom. 8:13–17), entitled thereby to receive, inherit, and possess, as Christ has inherited before. The Apostle John, beloved disciple of the Lord, wrote these words: "Behold, what manner of love the Father hath bestowed upon us, that we should be called the sons of God; therefore the world knoweth us not, because it knew him not." And now, particularly note what he says: "Now are we the sons of God, and it doth not yet appear what we shall be: but we know that, when he shall appear, we shall be like him; for we shall see him as he is. And every man that hath this hope in him purifieth himself, even as he is pure." (1 John 3:1–3.)

To that same John, who had written these words as moved upon by the Holy Ghost, the Lord said: "He that overcometh shall inherit all things; and I will be his God, and he shall be my son" (Rev. 21:7). And then again: "To him that overcometh will I grant to sit with me in my throne, even as I also overcame, and am set down with my Father in his throne'' (Rev. 3:21).

These New Testament scriptures, and many others that could be cited, teach the doctrine of exaltation, a doctrine of eternal life and eternal lives, a doctrine of joint heirship with Christ the Son. And this knowledge has been given again, with more particulars, by revelation in this day (D&C 76:50–60; 84:33–38; 3 Ne. 28:10). We are taught that Christ received not the fulness at first but went from grace to grace, until he received all power both in heaven and on earth. After having this truth recorded in the revelation, the Lord says that he is doing it so we may know what we worship and know how to worship, and that if we keep his commandments, we can go from grace to grace until we become one in him as he is in the Father, that we may inherit a fulness of all things. (D&C 93:12–20.) (Conference Report, April 1952, pp. 56–57.)

God Revealed Through Joseph Smith

Wicked Deny True God

We live in a day of evil and wickedness. The generality of men are carnal, sensual, and devilish. They have forgotten God and are revelling in the lusts of the flesh. Crime, immorality, abortions, and homosexual abominations are fast becoming the norm of life among the wicked and ungodly. This world will soon be as corrupt as it was in the days of Noah.

The only way for men to escape the abomination of desolation (JS—H 1:12–20; D&C 84:114, 117; 88:84–85) to be poured out upon the wicked in the last days is for them to repent and live the gospel. The gospel is the message of peace and salvation for all men. And we have been commanded to proclaim its saving truths to all men everywhere (Mark 16:15–16; D&C 88:81).

True religion is found only where men worship the true and living God. False religion always results from the worship of false gods. Eternal life itself, which is the greatest of all the gifts of God (D&C 14:7), is available to those and those only who know God and Jesus Christ whom he hath sent.

It is all the rage in this modern world to worship false gods of every sort and kind. There are those who bow before idols of wood and stone, and others who lisp their petitions to icons and images. There are those who worship cows and crocodiles, and others who acclaim Adam or Allah or Buddha as their Supreme Being.

There are those who apply the names of Deity to some spirit essence that is immaterial, uncreated and unknowable and that fills the immensity of space and is everywhere and nowhere in particular present.

And there are even those who champion the almost unbelievable theory that God is an Eternal Student enrolled in the University of the Universe where he is busily engaged in learning new truths and amassing new and strange knowledge that he never before knew.

How belittling it is—it borders on blasphemy—to demean the Lord God Omnipotent by saying he is an idol, or an image, or an animal, or a spirit essence, or that he is ever learning but never able to come to a knowledge of all truth.

It is the first principle of revealed religion to know the nature and kind of being that God is. As for us: "We know [and testify] that there is a God in heaven, who is infinite and eternal, from everlasting to everlasting the same unchangeable God, the framer of heaven and earth, and all things which are in them" (D&C 20:17).

No Salvation in False Religion

There is no salvation in worshipping false gods; there is no salvation in false religion; there is no salvation in error in any form.

Man alone cannot save himself. No man can call forth his own crumbling dust from the grave and cause it to live again in immortal glory. No man can create splendor forever.

All the idols and icons and images combined, since the world began until the end of time, will never have power to cleanse and perfect a single human soul. Neither Adam, nor Allah, nor Buddha, nor any person real or imaginary will ever bring salvation to fallen man. An unknown, uncreated, immaterial spirit nothingness never has and never will endow men with the gifts of the Spirit or assure them of an eternal celestial home. And certainly a Student God, with finite powers, who is just experimenting in the Eternal Laboratories, is not a being in whom I at least would feel inclined to repose an infinite trust. (Conference Report, October 1980.)

We Can Develop Such Faith as Joseph Smith Had

I say, "Where is the Lord God of Joseph Smith?" Here we have the great prophet of the latter dispensation who saw angels, received visions, performed miracles in great number, and, in due course, was called home to his eternal reward. He laid the foundation; he taught the doctrine; he gave us what we need to know to chart our course toward eternal life in this final dispensation. One of the things that he said was this: "God hath not revealed anything to Joseph, but what He will make known unto the Twelve, and even the least Saint may know all things as fast as he is able to bear them" (*Teachings*, p. 149).

I ask, "Are we walking in the path that Joseph Smith trod? Are we receiving the revelations and visions and working the miracles —doing the things that he did?" If we are not, to the full measure that we should, well might we ask ourselves, "Where is the Lord God of Joseph Smith?"

I do not want to be understood to indicate that miracles and signs have ceased. They are with us. This is God's kingdom. There is not the slightest question or doubt about that. The sick are healed, and the dead are raised. The eyes of the blind are opened as much today as they were during the ministry of Joseph Smith. But I do think that this is more limited, in the sense that it has not spread among the generality of the people in the Church as fully as it should. So I would like—if I may so be led—to raise some questions about this and to make some expressions that will chart a course and indicate what we have to believe and what we have to do, if we are going to have in our lives, in full measure, the spirit and power of the religion that God has given us in this day.

The Nature of God

When we talk about the nature and kind of being that God is, we start with the proposition that it is life eternal to know him and that he is known by revelation. There is no other way. He is not found in a test tube or by research in the laboratory. God stands revealed, or he remains forever unknown. That is one principle. If I may be so led, I would like to teach and testify that there is a God in heaven who is everlasting and eternal (D&C 20:17; 39:1; 61:1; 76:4; Moses 6:66–67; Ps. 90:2; 102:26–27; 146:10; Heb. 13:8); who is infinite in all his powers and attributes; who has all wisdom, all knowledge (1 Ne. 9:6; 2 Ne. 9:20; W of M 1:7; Alma 26:35; Morm. 8:17; Moro. 7:22; D&C 38:1–2; Ps. 147:4–5), all might, all power (D&C 19:3, 14, 20; 20:24; 61:1; 93:17; Matt. 28:18; 1 Ne. 9:6; Mosiah 4:9; Alma 12:15; 26:35; Morm. 5:23; Ether 3:4), and all dominion; and who has given us the way and the means to advance, progress, and become like him.

God Revealed Through Joseph Smith

The Lord said to Joseph Smith: ''This generation shall have my word through you'' (D&C 5:10). What this means is that if we are going to receive the knowledge of God, the knowledge of truth, the knowledge of salvation, and know the things that we must do to work out our salvation with fear and trembling before the Lord, this must come in and through Joseph Smith and in no other way. He is the agent, the representative, the instrumentality that the Lord has appointed to give the truth about himself and his laws to all men in all the world in this age.

Of course, we are all acquainted with the First Vision in which the Prophet saw the Father and the Son standing above him in a pillar of light—holy beings, personages who defied description because of the glory and grandeur that attended them (JS—H 2:16–17). We are aware that they are personal beings (D&C 130:22–23). This First Vision is the beginning of the knowledge of God in this dispensation. In just a few moments of the opening of the heavens, the Lord swept away all the false concepts, the Apostasy, the cobwebs of the past, and once again there was one man on earth who knew that God was a personal being in whose image man is created. All of us are well acquainted with this proposition. We start out there, and we have no trouble. That is the beginning of the revelation of the knowledge of God in our day.

Then all of us are somewhat familiar with the crowning revelations and pronouncements that Joseph Smith made about Deity. These were made in two sermons—one on April 6, 1844, the King Follett Sermon (*Teachings*, pp. 342–62), and the second on June 16, 1844 (*Teachings*, pp. 369–76), just eleven days before Joseph Smith went to a martyr's death. These statements in the King Follett Sermon and its companion sermon are the ones that give us a little trouble.

The pronouncements, the vision, the glory, the truth, revealed in the First Vision, are in effect, by way of illustration, giving us some arithmetic. It is teaching us some basic, fundamental things. When we come to these crowning, concluding weeks of the Prophet's life, the knowledge that he gives us about God is in the realm of calculus. Our problem is that we take this calculus, and with a slight and restricted view about it, which sometimes gets us out of perspective, we do not recognize, understand, and know the importance of all the algebra, geometry, and fundamental principles that intervened and were taught between the time of the First Vision and the crowning pronouncements.

God Is an Exalted Man

In the King Follett Sermon, the Prophet said: "God himself was once as we are now, and is an exalted man, and sits enthroned in yonder heavens! That is the great secret. If the veil were rent today, and the great God who holds this world in its orbit, and who upholds all worlds and all things by his power, was to make himself visible,—I say, if you were to see him today, you would see him like a man in form—like yourselves in all the person, image, and very form as a man; for Adam was created in the very fashion, image, and likeness of God, and received instruction from, and walked, and talked and conversed with him, as one man talks and communes with another."

Then another sentence, "I am going to tell you how God came to be God." Here is where our problems start: "It is the first principle of the Gospel to know for a certainty the Character of God, and to know that we may converse with him as one man converses with another, and that he was once a man like us; yea, that God himself, the Father of us all, dwelt on an earth, the same as Jesus Christ himself did; and I will show it from the Bible."

He then proceeds with some great insight to do so: "Here, then, is eternal life—to know the only wise and true God; and you have got to learn how to be Gods yourselves, and to be kings and priests to God, the same as all Gods have done before you, namely, by going from one small degree to another, and from a small capacity to a great one; from grace to grace, from exaltation to exaltation, until you attain to the resurrection of the dead and are able to dwell in everlasting burnings, and to sit in glory, as do those who sit enthroned in everlasting power." (*Teachings*, pp. 345–47.)

This is eternal truth. In the June sixteenth sermon the Prophet added to what he had taught in the King Follett discourse, teaching that there are exalted beings above each other everlastingly. Let us not dwell on that until we can put it in perspective. Let us go back and pick up the great reservoir of eternal truth that the Prophet revealed about Deity. If we can comprehend it and envision what actually is, then this more mysterious or difficult thing that all of us are somewhat acquainted with will fall into position, and we shall discover that we have a view and a knowledge of Deity that will prepare us for eternal life in his kingdom.

These statements that I now read were in part written by the Prophet and in whole approved by him and taught by him in the School of the Prophets.[3] They are taken from the *Lectures on Faith*. He says: ''We here observe that God is the only supreme governor and independent being in whom all fullness and perfection dwell; who is omnipotent, omnipresent, and omniscient; without beginning of days or end of life; and that in him every good gift and every good principle dwell; and that he is the Father of lights; in him the principle of faith dwells independently, and he is the object in whom the faith of all other rational and accountable beings center for life and salvation.'' (N. B. Lundwall, comp., *A Compilation Containing the Lectures on Faith* . . . [Salt Lake City: Bookcraft, n.d.], p. 13. Hereafter cited as *Lectures on Faith*.)

Now I take a second one. This second, in effect, is a creed announcing who Deity is. In my judgment, it is one of the most comprehensive, intelligent, inspired utterances now existing in the English language which defines, interprets, expounds, announces, and testifies of the kind of being God is. It was written by the power of the Holy Ghost, by the spirit of inspiration. It is, in effect, eternal scripture; it is true. I will read only part of it, and even then, because of the deep content that is involved in the words, we cannot measure or fathom their full intent. We need to study and ponder and analyze the expressions that are made.

The Prophet says: ''There are two personages who constitute the great, matchless, governing, and supreme power over all things, by whom all things were created and made, that are created and made, whether visible or invisible, whether in heaven, on earth, or in the earth, under the earth, or throughout the immensity of space.''

Let us, to begin with, understand the concept that God Almighty created and upholds all things. When we say *all* things, we speak of the universe. There is nothing exempt. Does this not remind you of the language Enoch used? When talking to the Lord, he said, ''Were it possible that man could number the particles of the earth, yea, millions of earths like this, it would not be a beginning to the number of thy creations; and thy curtains are stretched out still'' (Moses 7:30). Let us get a concept instilled in our minds that God is omnipotent; that he is above all things; that the very universe itself is his creation and is subject to him; that he upholds, preserves, and governs it.

Continuing: ''They are the Father and the Son—the Father being a personage of spirit, glory, and power, possessing all perfection and fullness, the Son, who was in the bosom of the Father, a personage of tabernacle . . . he is also the express image and likeness of the personage of the Father, possessing all the fullness of the Father, or the same fullness with the Father. . . . And he being the Only Begotten of the Father, full of grace and truth, and having overcome, received a fullness of the glory of the Father, possessing the same mind with the Father, which mind is the Holy Spirit, that bears record of the Father and the Son, and these three are one; or, in other words, these three constitute the great, matchless, governing and supreme, power over all things; by whom all things were created and made that were created and made, and these three constitute the Godhead, and are one; the Father and the Son possessing the same mind, the same wisdom, glory, power, and fullness—filling all in all; the Son being filled with the fullness of the mind, glory, and power; or, in other words, the spirit, glory, and power, of the Father, possessing all knowledge and glory, and the same kingdom, sitting at the right hand of power, in the express image and likeness of the Father, mediator for man, being filled with the fullness of the mind of the Father; or, in other words, the Spirit of the Father, which Spirit is shed forth upon all who believe on his name and keep his commandments.'' (*Lectures on Faith*, pp. 48–49.)

The concluding part of this great creedal statement is the one that announces that we, as fallible, weak, mortal men—subject to all the ills, difficulties, and vicissitudes of life—have power to advance and progress and become like our exalted and Eternal Father and his Beloved Son. These next words, in effect, are the same doctrine that concludes, ''As God now is, man may become.'' This thing was announced, in principle, in the School of the Prophets and did not have to wait for the King Follett Sermon, although I suppose the Saints did not fully grasp what was involved in this language initially. But here it is: ''And all those who keep his commandments shall grow up from grace to grace, and become heirs of the heavenly kingdom, and joint heirs with Jesus Christ; possessing the same mind, being transformed into the same image or likeness, even the express image of him who fills all in all; being filled with the fullness of his glory, and become one in him, even as the Father, Son and Holy Spirit are one'' (*Lectures on Faith*, p. 49).

Does that remind you of what the Lord said to John about those who overcome—that they will sit with him in his throne even as he also overcame and now sits with his Father in his throne (see Rev. 3:21)? Does that remind you of what the resurrected Lord said to certain Nephites: ''Ye shall be even as I am, and I am even as the Father; and the Father and I are one'' (3 Ne. 28:10)? May I say that the whole purpose involved in the mind of God in revealing what kind of a being he is, is to enable us, his children, to chart a course and pursue it with the fidelity and devotion that will lead us to the same state of power and dominion and eminence that he possesses. The whole purpose and thrust of the plan of salvation is to enable us to advance and progress and become like God. The beginning of that advancement, the beginning of that eternal progression, is a knowledge of the nature and kind of being whom we worship.

The Character of God

With that much basic, fundamental truth before us, let me take up a little detail that is involved in the Prophet's presentation of the nature and kind of being that God is — the principles out of which faith grows, and without which faith cannot be perfected, and, therefore, without which no man can make the advancement and progression of which I speak, the advancement that leads to an eternal fulness in the presence of God, our Heavenly Father.

"[These] three things are necessary," the Prophet says, "in order that any rational and intelligent being may exercise faith in God unto life and salvation. First, the idea that he actually exists." There is no problem with us on that. That is the First Vision. "Secondly, a *correct* idea of his character, perfections, and attributes." Three things. We have a little problem, some of us, here. "Thirdly, an actual knowledge that the course of life which he is pursuing is according to his will." I guess if there is any field where we fall short, that is it. (*Lectures on Faith*, p. 33.)

Some of us do not so live that we can get in our hearts the assurance, born of the Spirit, that the course we are pursuing accords with divine standards. But now let us look at these three things: the character, perfections, and attributes of Deity. In the Prophet's language, here is God's character: "We learn the following things respecting the character of God: First, that he was God before the world was created, and the same God that he was after it was created. Second, that he is merciful and gracious, slow to anger, abundant in goodness, and that he was so from everlasting to everlasting (Ps. 103:6–8, 17, 18). Third, that he changes not, neither is there variableness with him; but that he is the same from everlasting to everlasting, being the same yesterday, today, and forever; and that his course is one eternal round, without variation (James 1:17; D&C 3:2; 35:1; Mal. 4:6; Morm. 9:9). Fourth, that he is a God of truth and cannot lie (Num. 23:19; Ps. 31:5; Deut. 32:4). Fifth, that he is no respecter of persons; but in every nation he that fears

God and works righteousness is accepted of him (Acts 10:34–35). Sixth, that he is love'' (1 John 4:8, 16; John 3:16; see also *Lectures on Faith*, pp. 35–36).

Those six things are the character of God, and as I say, there is so much meat in what is here expressed that we are not catching it by the mere recitation. We need to read it and study it and ponder it, and as we do we should get on our knees and ask the Lord for enlightenment and understanding so that we can know in our hearts and in our souls if it is true and what is meant by the expressions that the Prophet used.

Here is a paragraph from him as to why God must be all-powerful: ''An acquaintance with these attributes in the divine character, is essentially necessary, in order that the faith of any rational being can center in him for life and salvation. For if he did not, in the first instance, believe him to be God, that is, the Creator and upholder of all things, he could not *center* his faith in him for life and salvation, for fear there should be [one] greater than he who would thwart all his plans, and he like the gods of the heathen, would be unable to fulfill his promises; but seeing he is God over all, from everlasting to everlasting, the Creator and upholder of all things, no such fear can exist in the minds of those who put their trust in him, so that in this respect their faith can be without wavering.'' (*Lectures on Faith*, p. 35.)

The Omniscience of God

Let me come to the attributes of God. They are named simply as these—six in number: knowledge, faith or power, justice, judgment, mercy, and truth. Then a statement, illustrative of what is involved, is the Prophet's explanation of why God must know all things: ''Without the knowledge of all things, God would not be able to save any portion of his creatures; for it is by reason of the knowledge which he has of all things, from the beginning to the end, that enables him to give that understanding to his creatures by which they are made partakers of eternal life; and if it were not for the idea existing in the minds of men that God had all knowledge it would be impossible for them to exercise faith in him'' (*Lectures on Faith*, p. 43). (''The Lord God of Joseph Smith,'' BYU Devotional, 4 January 1972, pp. 1–6.)

There are those who say that God is progressing in knowledge and is learning new truths. This is a false teaching which grows out of a wholly twisted and incorrect view of the King Follett Sermon and of what is meant by eternal progression.

God progresses in the sense that his kingdoms increase and his dominions multiply — not in the sense that he learns new truths and discovers new laws. God is not a student. He is not a laboratory technician. He is not postulating new theories on the basis of past experiences. He has indeed graduated to that state of exaltation that consists of knowing all things and having all power.

The life that God lives is named eternal life. His name, one of them, is "Eternal" (Moses 7:35), using that word as a noun and not as an adjective, and he uses that name to identify the type of life that he lives. God's life is eternal life, and eternal life is God's life. They are one and the same. Eternal life is the goal we shall obtain if we believe and obey and walk uprightly before him. And eternal life consists of two things. It consists of life in the family unit, and, also, of inheriting, receiving, and possessing the fulness of the glory of the Father (D&C 132:19). Anyone who has each of these things is an inheritor and possessor of the greatest of all the gifts of God, which is eternal life (D&C 14:7).

Eternal progression consists of living the kind of life God lives and of increasing in kingdoms and dominions everlastingly. Why anyone should suppose that an infinite and eternal being, who made the sidereal heavens, whose creations are more numerous than the particles of the earth, and who is aware of the fall of every sparrow (Matt. 10:29; Luke 12:6-9) — why anyone would suppose that such a being has more to learn and new truths to discover in the laboratories of eternity is totally beyond my comprehension.

Will he one day learn something that will destroy the plan of salvation and turn men and the universe into an uncreated nothingness? Will he discover a better plan of salvation than the one he has already given to men in worlds without number?

The saving truth, as revealed to and taught, formally and officially, by the Prophet Joseph Smith in the *Lectures on Faith* is that God is omnipotent, omniscient, and omnipresent. He knows all things, he has all power, and he is everywhere present by the power of his Spirit. And unless we know and believe this doctrine we cannot gain faith unto life and salvation. ("The Seven Deadly Heresies," BYU Fourteen-Stake Fireside, 1 June 1980, pp. 4-5.)

The Perfections of God

Just a word about the perfections of God. The Prophet said: "What we mean by perfections is, the perfections which belong to all the attributes of his nature" (*Lectures on Faith*, p. 50).

In other words, where every attribute and every characteristic
is concerned, the Lord is perfect (Matt. 5:48; 3 Ne. 12:48) and in
him is embodied the totality of whatever is involved. Can anyone
suppose that God does not have all charity, that he falls short in integrity or honesty, or that there is any truth that he does not know?

I have not taken occasion here to read any of the revelations.
The revelations abound in these principles. They announce over
and over again, if we comprehend and understand them, that God
is almighty; that there is no power he does not possess, no wisdom
that does not reside in him, no infinite expanse of space or duration
of time where his influence and power are not felt. There is nothing
that the Lord God takes into his heart to do that he cannot do. (Gen.
18:14; Jer. 32:17; Matt. 19:26; Luke 1:37.) He has attained to a state
of glory and perfection where he is from everlasting to everlasting.
To be from everlasting to everlasting the same unchangeable, un-
varying being means, in effect, that he is from one preexistence to
the next—the same in knowledge, in power, in might, and in dominion. And yet he became such on the same system that you and I
have power so to attain. It is written expressly in our revelations
that if we advance and go forward in full measure according to the
divine plan, we also shall receive a fulness and a continuation of the
seeds forever: "Then shall they be gods, because they have no end;
therefore shall they be from everlasting to everlasting, because they
continue; then shall they be above all, because all things are subject
unto them. Then shall they be gods, because they have all power,
and the angels are subject unto them." (D&C 132:30.) ("The Lord
God of Joseph Smith," BYU Devotional, 4 January 1972.)

The Omnipresence of God

Men sometimes speak of the omnipresence of God as though
God himself filled the immensity of space and was everywhere
present. This is an utterly false and pagan notion. But there is a
sense in which God is omnipresent, and this term may be used to
describe him when properly understood and defined.

God is a personal being who is and can be in but one place at a
time. He is the possessor of all things, however. All power, all
wisdom, and all truth are his, and he has given laws to all things.
By his laws the earth was created and is controlled, all life exists
and grows, and the planets move in their orbits.

Because he has given laws to all things and because his power
of creation and control are in all things, it may be properly said that

he is omnipresent. He is a person; but the power, the agency, the influence, the spirit which proceeds from his person to govern and control all that he has created is everywhere present and does fill the immensity of space. But this is not God; it is the agency through which he works, the power that he has in all things.

Speaking in poetic language, David, accordingly, was led to exclaim: "Whither shall I go from thy spirit? or whither shall I flee from thy presence? If I ascend up into heaven, thou art there: . . . If I take the wings of the morning, and dwell in the uttermost parts of the sea; Even there shall thy hand lead me, and thy right hand shall hold me." (Ps. 139:7-10.)

In his famous Mars' hill speech Paul spoke in similar manner of the nearness of God. Men "should seek the Lord," he said, for he is "not far from every one of us: For in him [that is, in his presence] we live, and move, and have our being; as certain also of your own poets have said, For we are also his offspring" (Acts 17:27-28).

Again, both anciently and modernly, this doctrine of the omnipresence of God has been revealed in plainness. ("The Truth About God," missionary pamphlet.)

Testimony of Truths About God

I am simply announcing, as it were, a few basic, fundamental, eternal truths about the nature and kind of being that we worship. It is my pattern and custom simply to teach and testify. I do not debate and I do not argue. If someone wants to contend to the contrary, he is just as welcome as the day is long to do so. But let us understand this. When we deal with God and his laws, when we get in the realm of spiritual things, we are dealing with the things that save souls, and at our peril we are obligated to find the truth. The whole sectarian world sits out here, and they suppose that they have some truth and that they are pursuing a course that will save them. But God has restored the everlasting gospel to us. We have the power of God unto salvation in our hands, as it were. It is our obligation to come to an understanding of what is involved so that we can live in such a manner that the fulness of these blessings and rewards will come to us.

I am bold to testify that these doctrines are true; that God is all that the revelations say he is; that there is no power, no might, no omnipotence, that excels him; and that if you and I will advance and pursue the course that he has made available for us we can attain that state where we will be from everlasting to everlasting.

Then, as these revelations recite, we will know all things and have all power, and we will go on eternally in the same type and kind of existence that he lives.

Knowledge and Presence of God Available to Saints Today

God is just as available today as he has ever been. Just as assuredly as we center our hearts in him and believe in him with full purpose, we will stand as Elisha stood with reference to Elijah. We will stand where Joseph Smith stood, and we will have the visions, receive the revelations, work the miracles, and feel the sanctifying power of the Holy Spirit in our lives as he felt it in his. ("The Lord God of Joseph Smith," BYU Devotional, 4 January 1972.)

Some Attributes of Deity

How the Father and the Son Are One

"Be one!" Such is God's eternal command to his people. "Be one; and if ye are not one ye are not mine" (D&C 38:27). If and when perfect unity exists among the Saints, they accomplish the Lord's purposes on earth and gain their own exaltation in the life to come.

"Be one!" To keep this command ever before his people the Lord thunders it into their ears by using himself and the eternal Godhead as the illustration of what unity is and how it operates. "Be one, even as I and my Father are one; unite together as the Gods of heaven. Do not go your separate ways; rally round one standard. Believe the same doctrines; teach the same truths; testify of the same God; walk in the same path; live the same laws; hold the same priesthood; marry in the same celestial order; become one with me. Be one!"

Using himself as the perfect example, Deity is teaching unity to his people. Three mortal high priests comprise the First Presidency of the Church. Their goal is to be one as the three separate members of the eternal Godhead are one. Millions of weak and struggling mortals belong to the Church; Deity expects them all to be one as the Gods of heaven are one.

Since those who are one think and believe and act alike, they thus possess the same characteristics and attributes, or in other words, the same spirit dwells in them. Hence, in a figurative sense they are in each other, or they dwell in each other, even as God and Christ dwell in each other for the same reason.

To pretend that the Father and the Son are one in some mysterious and incomprehensible way so that the two designations are simply different manifestations of the same thing, is to wrest the scriptures, mangle the plain language they contain, and do away with some of the best symbolism and most perfect teaching known to man. Three Gods are one as endless millions of men should be one—and in no other sense.

Those who live the perfect law of unity "become the sons of God, even one in me as I am one in the Father, as the Father is one in me, that we may be one" (D&C 35:2). To Adam the Lord said: "Behold, thou art one in me, a son of God; and thus may all become my sons" (Moses 6:68).

This same oneness of the Godhead was taught by Jesus during his mortal ministry. In the great intercessory prayer in which he prayed for the Apostles and the Saints, he said: "Neither pray I for these alone, but for them also which shall believe on me through their word; That they all may be one; as thou, Father, art in me, and I in thee, that they also may be one in us: that the world may believe that thou hast sent me" (1 John 17:20-21).

He spoke similarly to the Nephites: "And now Father, I pray unto thee for them, and also for all those who shall believe on their words, that they may believe in me, that I may be in them as thou, Father, art in me, that we may be one" (3 Ne. 19:23). (*DNTC* 1:766-67.)

The Father Is Greater Than the Son

"For my Father is greater than I" (John 14:28), said Jesus. Yet we ask, are they not one? Do they not both possess all power, all wisdom, all knowledge, all truth? Have they not both gained all godly attributes in their fulness and perfection? Verily, yes, for the revelations so announce and the Prophets so taught. And yet our Lord's Father is greater than he, greater in kingdoms and dominions, greater in principalities and exaltations. One does and shall rule over the other everlastingly. Though Jesus himself is God, he is also the Son of God, and as such the Father is his God as he is ours. "I ascend unto my Father, and your Father; and to my God, and your God," he said (John 20:17).

Joseph Smith, with inspired insight, tells how Jesus is God's heir; how he receives and possesses all that the Father hath, and is therefore (as Paul said) "equal with God" (Philip. 2:16), and yet at the same time is subject to and less than the Father. These are his words: "What did Jesus do? Why, I do the things I saw my Father do when worlds came rolling into existence. My Father worked out his kingdom with fear and trembling, and I must do the same; and when I get my kingdom, I shall present it to my Father, so that he may obtain kingdom upon kingdom, and it will exalt him in glory. He will then take a higher exaltation, and I will take his place, and thereby become exalted myself. So that Jesus treads in the tracks of his Father, and inherits what God did before; and God is thus glorified and exalted in the salvation and exaltation of all his children." (*Teachings*, pp. 347–48.) (*DNTC* 1:743.)

God Is Love, Light, and a Consuming Fire

John wrote that "God is love" (1 John 4:8) and that "God is light" (1 John 1:5). Paul said, "Our God is a consuming fire" (Heb. 12:29). Similarly, God is also faith, hope, charity, righteousness, truth, virtue, temperance, patience, humility, and so forth. That is, God is the embodiment and personification of every good grace and godly attribute—all of which dwell in his person in perfection and in fulness. (*DNTC* 3:398.)

How God Is a Spirit

The views in the creeds of men were not formulated from and did not grow out of the scriptures. After these false beliefs were crystallized in the creeds, however, then certain scriptures were seized upon in a vain attempt to support the creeds and establish their verity.

The absurdity of selecting portions and fragments of the scriptures, tearing them from their contexts, and interpreting them without reference to the whole body of the revealed word, is generally recognized. Yet because this is the only way in which seeming support for false doctrines can be found in the scriptures, it becomes necessary to evaluate the claims made, and to study the passages in their proper perspective so that they may be seen to be in harmony with all of what the Lord has said on the subject.

Perhaps the most widely known such passage is gleaned from the conversation of our Lord with the Samaritan woman at the well. The selected words say: "God is a spirit," an expression that is neither confusing nor difficult to understand when rightly viewed.

Let us see the context. Our Lord was discussing with the woman of Samaria the place where the faithful should worship, it appearing the Samaritans worshipped in the mountain where they were then conversing, whereas the Jews designated Jerusalem as the central place of their worship.

Then our Lord said: "Ye worship ye know not what: we know what we worship: for salvation is of the Jews. But the hour cometh, and now is, when the true worshippers shall worship the Father in spirit and in truth: for the Father seeketh such to worship him. God is a Spirit: and they that worship him must worship him in spirit and in truth." Then the woman spoke of the promised Messiah, the Christ, who was to come, and the Lord replied: "I that speak unto thee am he." (John 4:22–24, 26.)

First, we should note that the Jews, those who were converted and had the knowledge of salvation, knew whom they worshipped. They were not professing to bestow their adoration upon an unknown, unknowable, incomprehensible spirit essence that is everywhere present. They knew who the Father was whom they worshipped.

Well, then, is God a spirit? Certainly he is; and on the same basis and within the same meaning of words, man is a spirit. But neither man nor God are spirit essences that are indefinably everywhere present. Both are spirit personages. Their respective spirits have form and size and dimensions, and are within their own bodies and within those bodies only.

Man is a spirit, but man is also a tangible body. God is a spirit, and God also is a tangible body.

A soul—either mortal or immortal—consists of a body and a spirit (D&C 88:15). The body is tangible and corporeal, and is made of a substance that can be felt and handled as the Apostles felt and handled the body of the resurrected Christ. The spirit also is an actual entity or being; however, the spirit body is made of a more pure and refined substance, so that it cannot be handled and felt by mortal men (D&C 129:1–7; 131:7–8).

Thus when the Apostles saw the resurrected Christ stand before them, "They were terrified and affrighted, and supposed that they had seen a spirit" (Luke 24:37). Christ comforted their fears and gave them the test whereby they could distinguish a spirit from a personage of tabernacle, one who had flesh and bones. They were to handle him, to feel the nail prints in his hands, and put their hands against the spear wound in his side.

The spirit of man is within his body. When he dies the spirit leaves the body, and the body goes to the grave. After his crucifixion Christ's body lay in the tomb, but his spirit went and preached to other spirits, the spirits of those men who "sometime were disobedient, when once the longsuffering of God waited in the days of Noah" (1 Pet. 3:20).

The third day his spirit entered the body again, the glorious resurrection took place, and he rose from the tomb, the first fruits of them that slept. Now he was immortal, not mortal, and now his body and spirit were inseparably connected, never again to be torn asunder by death.

And we have already seen that the resurrected Lord with his tangible body of flesh and bones was in the express image of the person of the Father who also had a tangible body of flesh and bones, one in which spirit and body are inseparably connected.

So man is body and spirit; Christ is body and spirit; and God is body and spirit. What impropriety is there, then, when a proper understanding of its meaning is had, of saying, "God is a spirit"? This is true in the same sense in which man and Christ also are spirits, and in no other.[4] ("The Truth About God," missionary pamphlet.)

Notes

1. The above list of prophets who have seen God is largely biblical. It might be expanded to include at least the following references: Abraham, Isaac, and Jacob (Ex. 6:3); Abimelech (Gen. 20:3); Balaam (Num. 22:9; 23:4, 16); Samuel (1 Sam. 3:10, 21); Solomon (1 Kgs. 3:3; 9:2; 2 Chr. 1:7; 7:12); David (2 Chr. 3:1); Micaiah (2 Chr. 18:18); Daniel (Dan. 7:13); Stephen (Acts 7:55-56); Paul (Acts 9:3-9, 17); Ananias (Acts 9:10); the ten Apostles (Luke 24:36-38); Peter (Luke 24:34; 1 Cor. 15:5); "of above five hundred brethren" James and Paul (1 Cor. 15:5); and Peter, James and John (2 Pet. 1:16). The Book of Mormon prophets had identical experiences: Lehi (1 Ne. 1:8-10); Nephi (1 Ne. 2:16; 11:7, 20-24; 12:6; 2 Ne. 1:15); Jacob (2 Ne. 2:4; 11:3); Lamoni (Alma 19:13); Alma (Alma 36:22); Mormon (Morm. 1:15); the brother of Jared (Ether 3:6-17); Emer (Ether 9:21-22); Moroni (Ether 12:39); and, of course, thousands of Nephites (3 Ne. 11-28). From the Pearl of Great Price we get an enlarged view of the experiences of Moses (Moses 1:1-11,

31), Enoch (Moses 7:4–11), and Abraham (Abr. 2:6–12, 19; 3:11). Elsewhere Joseph Smith (JS—H 1:16–20), Sidney Rigdon (D&C 76:22–23) and Oliver Cowdery (D&C 110:1–4) also saw God. All faithful Saints have the promise that they too may see him (D&C 93:1; John 14:23; D&C 130:3).

2. Protestant and Catholic theologians, and some within the Church, debate over the authorship of the Epistle to the Hebrews. Elsewhere Elder McConkie has written: "Speaking from the standpoint of uninspired biblical research, one of the so far unsolved mysteries of sectarian scholarship is: Who wrote the Epistle to the Hebrews?

"It is variously attributed to Paul, Barnabas, Apollos, Clement of Rome, Luke, and even the female Priscilla. 'Origen, the most learned of the early teachers, concluded his examination of the question with the words, "Who wrote the epistle God only knows" ' (Dummelow, p. 1012). So uncertain are the scholars that sometimes even Latter-day Saints choose to attribute quotations from it to, 'the author of the Epistle to the Hebrews,' rather than to Paul the Apostle.

"But the Prophet Joseph Smith says this Epistle was written 'by Paul . . . to the Hebrew brethren' (*Teachings*, p. 59), and repeatedly in his sermons he attributes statements from it to Paul. Peter, himself a Hebrew, whose ministry and teachings were directed in large part to his own people, seems to be identifying its authorship when he writes, 'Our beloved brother Paul . . . according to the wisdom given unto him hath written unto you [the Hebrews]; As also in all his [other] epistles, . . . some things hard to be understood' (2 Pet. 3:15–16). In any event, Paul did write Hebrews, and to those who accept Joseph Smith as an inspired witness of truth, the matter is at rest." (*DNTC* 3:133.)

3. Some have wondered as to the authorship of the *Lectures on Faith*, even questioning the Prophet's role and involvement, suggesting instead that they were written by Parley P. Pratt, Sidney Rigdon, or others. Nonetheless, Elder McConkie's expression here is precise and accurate. The *Lectures* were prepared by a committee presided over by the Prophet Joseph Smith—and, as with all matters of doctrine, his was the dominating and controlling influence.

Some of the difficulties arise in that the School of the Prophets, in which these lectures were presented, was conducted over a period of years. It met chiefly in Kirtland, though later in Jackson County, Missouri, and even, under the direction of Brigham Young, in Salt Lake City after the Saints arrived in the valley.

The Lord directed the setting up of the School of the Prophets (D&C 88:122, 127–41), also called "the school of mine apostles" (D&C 95:17). This particular school was organized in Kirtland in the winter of 1832–1833 with the Prophet Joseph Smith as its presiding officer (D&C 90:7, 13). That Joseph did preside over the school is important, for the revelation expressly states that the presiding officer also teach this school (D&C 88:128), which is where the *Lectures* were presented. B. H. Roberts noted that "these 'Lectures on Theology' . . . were . . . prepared by the Prophet (*History of the Church* 2:176), and Joseph Smith himself wrote that "during the month of January [1835], I was engaged in the school of the elders, and in preparing the lectures on theology for publication" (*History of the Church* 2:180).

4. In this analysis Elder McConkie had done what all gospel students should do—that is, seek harmony between different passages of scriptures. If we seek to harmonize a difficult-to-understand verse with what the rest of the revelations say, we invariably come upon correct answers; but if we isolate one difficult verse, and use it as the standard by which we judge the meaning of all others, confusion unavoidably follows.

The easiest way to explain the meaning of these verses in the fourth chapter of John is to note that they have fallen victim to mischievous translation, which has been corrected by the Prophet Joseph Smith. Hence, as the verse was actually written, it reads: "And the hour cometh, and now is, when true worshippers shall worship the Father in spirit and in truth; for the Father seeketh such to worship him. *For unto such hath God promised his Spirit.* And they who worship him, must worship in spirit and in truth." (Joseph Smith Translation John 4:25–26; italics added. The Joseph Smith Translation is hereafter cited as JST.)

Still, there is a sense, in addition to what Elder McConkie says in this section, in which it is proper to say that God is a spirit. God is a spirit in the same sense that a resurrected being is a spirit. Thus Paul notes that when resurrected, the body rises as "a spiritual body" (1 Cor. 15:44). The Lord said that because of the resurrection, "notwithstanding they die, they also shall rise again, a spiritual body" (D&C 88:27). To speak thus of a "spiritual body" is to speak of "the same body which was a natural body" (D&C 88:28) as a resurrected body. In shape and form this "spiritual body" is like the mortal body, except that it is glorified, has no blood, and has undergone some changes in the flesh, for "flesh and blood cannot inherit the kingdom of God" (1 Cor. 15:50). In this sense, God, a resurrected Personage, is a "spiritual body." In this same sense Amulek says resurrected beings become "spiritual and immortal" (Alma 11:45). Again, in this same sense, Joseph Smith speaks of God the Father as a "personage of spirit, glory, and power" (*Lectures on Faith*, p. 48). It is in this same sense that Paul speaks to the Hebrews of "all" angels (which includes resurrected beings) as "ministering spirits, sent forth to minister" (Heb. 1:13–14). Similarly, resurrected beings dwelling in the terrestrial kingdom are sent to minister to those in the telestial kingdom and are called ministering "spirits" (D&C 76:87–88).

God, a glorified, exalted, perfected and resurrected man, is a spirit in the same sense that all resurrected beings are spirits.

Chapter 2

THE DIVINE
SONSHIP OF CHRIST

The Condescension of God

Knowledge Makes Us Heirs of the Full Blessings

Of all the people in Christendom, we are the only ones in a position to reap the full blessings of the Spirit of Christ in our lives, to know what actually is involved in his ministry, to partake in full measure of that spirit which goes with the Christmas season. We have everything that the world has; we have the historical accounts of his coming onto the earth; we are aware of the traditions that have been woven around his birth, many of which have little substance in reality and fact. But the thing with which we are particularly blessed is the knowledge, gained by latter-day revelation, of his divine sonship. We know the doctrine of the divine sonship of our Lord, and it is this doctrine which we now consider. (BYU *Speeches of the Year*, 16 December 1969.)

The Vision of Nephi

This question, "Knowest thou the condescension of God?" which the angel asked of Nephi, is also an appropriate one for each of us to ask ourselves. What do we as individuals know about the condescension of God, and what feelings do we have in our hearts towards him because of it? The account that Nephi gave us is this: "And I beheld the city of Nazareth; and in the city of Nazareth I beheld a virgin, and she was exceedingly fair and white. And it came to pass that I saw the heavens open; and an angel came down and stood before me; and he said unto me: Nephi, what beholdest thou?

And I said unto him: A virgin, most beautiful and fair above all other virgins. And he said unto me: Knowest thou the condescension of God?'' (BYU *Speeches of the Year*, 15 August 1967.)

Now, Nephi, great and inspired as he was, had but a partial comprehension at that time on this point. And so he said: "And I said unto him: I know that he loveth his children; nevertheless, I do not know the meaning of all things.''

Well, what is the condescension of God as it pertains particularly to our Lord's birth and coming into mortality?

The next words in the account say: "And he said unto me: Behold, the virgin whom thou seest is the mother of the Son of God, after the manner of the flesh. And it came to pass that I beheld that she was carried away in the Spirit; and after she had been carried away in the Spirit for the space of a time the angel spake unto me, saying: Look! And I looked and beheld the virgin again, bearing a child in her arms. And the angel said unto me: Behold the Lamb of God, yea even the Son of the Eternal Father!'' (1 Ne. 11:13–21.)

We Must Understand God to Understand His Condescension

What, then, is the condescension of God? As I understand the definition of condescension, it is the act of descending to a lower and a less dignified state; or waiving the privileges of one's rank and status; of bestowing honors and favors upon one of lesser stature or status.

So if we are going to speak of the condescension of God, meaning of our Eternal Father, we must first know the nature and kind of being he is. We must come to know the dignity and majesty and glory that attend him, of the things that he has done and is doing for us and for all his children and in all eternity among all his creations.

We understand that God is a personal being in whose image man is created; that he is glorified, perfected, and exalted; that he has a body of flesh and bones as tangible as man's; that he has progressed and advanced through an infinite period until he has become the Creator of the universe and all things therein.

He has ordained the laws by which all things exist. He has established everything pertaining to this world and an infinite number of worlds that roll in space. In our infinite and temporal condition, we have no way of measuring, no way of understanding, no way of comprehending the majesty and glory and dominion and might and power and exaltation that attend him. We can read the words of the revelations and get a slight understanding, as far as mortal man quickened by the Spirit can, of what is involved. But his might and his dominion, his status and his position, are so far above anything that we can comprehend or understand, that we can but envision it slightly. With it all he has acquired the fulness of every good and godly attribute. He is the embodiment of charity and knowledge, of faith and power, of integrity and uprightness, of every attribute that is righteous and edifying.

The Condescension of the Father

When we think of the Father, we think of the most noble and exalted being there is. Then we read this question, "Knowest thou the condescension of God?" and discover that somehow it is associated with love for us, his children, his spirit children who are now dwelling as mortals here on earth. We discover in our text that he shall be the Father of a Son born "after the manner of the flesh"; that is, he condescends, in his infinite wisdom, to be the Father of a holy being who shall be born into mortality. He determines to fulfill what he decreed when he announced the plan of salvation in the premortal life, when, having explained the plan, he asked for a Redeemer and a Savior and said, "Whom shall I send [to be my Son]?" (Abr. 3:27.) Thus the condescension of God is that he is the Father literally of a Son born in mortality, in the language here, a Son born "after the manner of the flesh." (BYU *Speeches of the Year*, 16 December 1969.)

Oh, what a glorious and wondrous thing it is that our almighty, glorified, exalted Father comes down to mortal status, as it were — not literally, but in a sense — and becomes the parent, the Father of a Son "after the manner of the flesh," according to the language that we have just read; and that Holy Being who is thus born of Mary is literally the Son of God!

The mercy, the grace, the love, the condescension that is involved in the fact of the birth of Christ into the world is something that is beyond our comprehension. Yet it had to be, and it had to occur in the very manner in which it did occur, so that there would be a Personage here among men who on the one hand could lay down his life and on the other hand could take it up again. He could lay it down because Mary was his mother, and he could take it up again because God was his Father. (BYU *Speeches of the Year*, 15 August 1967.)

The Condescension of Christ

The angel, having manifested this truth about the condescension of God the Father to Nephi, then shows him added material, added vision, and comes again to the matter of divine condescension. He says: "Look and behold the condescension of God!" And this time he is talking about the condescension of Christ the Son and not God the Father.

Nephi says: "And I looked, and I beheld the Lamb of God going forth among the children of men. And I beheld multitudes of people who were sick, and who were afflicted with all manner of diseases, and with devils and unclean spirits; and the angel spake and showed all these things unto me. And they were healed by the power of the Lamb of God; and the devils and the unclean spirits were cast out. And it came to pass that the angel spake unto me again, saying: Look! And I looked and beheld the Lamb of God, that he was taken by the people; yea, the Son of the everlasting God was judged of the world; and I saw and bear record. And I, Nephi, saw that he was lifted up upon the cross and slain for the sins of the world." (1 Ne. 11:27, 31–33.)

Thus, we have a second matter relative to Deity's condescension. This time it is the fact that Christ elected, chose, and volunteered to come into the world and be born as God's Son, undergo the mortal probation and ministry assigned him, and then climax it with the working out of the infinite and eternal atoning sacrifice.

So when we think of Christ's condescension in this matter, we must think of the glory and dominion and exaltation that he possessed. We read in the revelations that he was "like unto God" (Abr. 3:24). We read the language of the Father where he says, "Worlds without number have I created; . . . and by the Son I created them, which is mine Only Begotten" (Moses 1:33).We discover that Christ was like the Father; that he was co-creator, that he had the might and power and dominion and omnipotence of the Father and that he acted under his direction in the regulating and the creating of the universe.

We read the words which an angel spake to King Benjamin, in which the angel described him as "the Lord Omnipotent who reigneth, who was, and is from all eternity to all eternity," and then said that he would come down and tabernacle in a body of clay and minister among men; that he would be the Son of God and that Mary would be his mother (see Mosiah 3:5, 8).

The Divine Sonship of Christ

The Atoning Sacrifice

Now, the greatest and most important single thing there is in all
eternity—the thing that transcends all others since the time of the
creation of man and of the worlds—is the fact of the atoning sacrifice of Christ the Lord. He came into the world to live and to die—to
live the perfect life and be the pattern, the similitude, the prototype
for all men, and to crown his ministry in death, in the working out
of the infinite and eternal atoning sacrifice. And by virtue of this
atonement, all things pertaining to life and immortality, to existence, to glory and salvation, to honor and rewards hereafter, all
things are given full force and efficacy and virtue. The Atonement is
the central thing in the whole gospel system. The Prophet said that
all other things pertaining to our religion are only appendages to it.
(*Teachings*, p. 121.)

The Atonement is made possible because of the doctrine of divine sonship; and if Christ had not been born into the world in the
express and particular manner in which he was, he would not have
inherited from his Father the power to work out this infinite and
eternal atoning sacrifice, in consequence of which the whole plan of
salvation would have been void and we never would have inherited or possessed the blessings of immortality or the glories of
eternal life.

We cannot now comprehend (nor can we expect to in our present state) how the effects of this infinite and eternal atoning sacrifice
passed upon all men. We cannot comprehend and understand how
creation works, where God came from, or how we came into being.
Someday these things will be within the comprehension and understanding of those who gain exaltation. But the fact that we cannot
explain them does not lessen the fact that we have been created,
that we do exist, that there is a resurrection, that in due course all
men will be raised in immortality, and that those who have believed and obeyed the gospel law will be raised in addition unto
eternal life in our Father's kingdom. And all of this is possible because of the divine sonship of Christ the Lord, because he inherited
in his birth the power of immortality from God his Father.

It is our custom and our practice to read in Luke and in Matthew the accounts that attended Christ's coming to earth. These are
historical events. Woven into them is some expression of the doctrine involved; but the historical events are of lesser import. It is the

doctrine that is of transcendent value and worth to us; out of it comes the great blessings that I have indicated. How glorious it is that Christ was born into the world as the Son of God! (BYU *Speeches of the Year*, 16 December 1969.)

Importance of the Doctrine of Divine Sonship

This matter of the divine sonship of the Lord is the heart and core of revealed religion. It is the very center of our system of worship; all things revolve around it; all things center in it. If anyone is going to investigate revealed religion, the focal point of the investigation should be this matter of the divine sonship of Christ.

If he was the Son of God, then the infinite and eternal atoning sacrifice is a reality—he worked it out, and as a consequence immortality is available for all men, and those who believe and obey have the hope of eternal life in his kingdom. But if he was not the Son of God, then he did not inherit from his Father the power of immortality—the power to work out the infinite and eternal atoning sacrifice. So, in the ultimate and final sense, in the last analysis, where the investigation of truth is concerned, it centers around the Lord Jesus and the ministry and mission he performed, and the sacrifice he wrought, commencing in the Garden of Gethsemane and climaxing upon the cross.

Saints Stand Alone in Knowledge of Sonship

Some of us assume there is a general feeling in Christendom that Jesus is the Son of God; at least there are hosts of people who give lip service to this concept. But there is a great deal more involved in being the Son of the Eternal Father than having rendered to him the lip service of the sectarian world!

Some of us heard and have also read the sermons of President Heber J. Grant. On a number of occasions (see G. Homer Durham, comp., *Gospel Standards: Selections from the Sermons and Writings of Heber J. Grant* [Salt Lake City: Deseret News Press, 1969], pp. 290–93) he referred to a book written by the late Senator Albert J. Beveridge of the state of Indiana, which recites a rather extensive survey made of sectarian ministers in which they were asked three basic and fundamental questions where God, Christ, and man are concerned.

In substance these questions went like this:

First: ''Do you believe in God? God a person, not a congeries of laws floating like a fog in the universe, but God a person in whose image you were created?'' There, of course, were no answers in the affirmative. Not a minister answered yes.

President Grant recited the second question to this effect: ''Do you believe that Jesus Christ is literally the Son of God as you are the son of your father? Now, I am not asking if you believe that He was the greatest moral teacher that ever lived—that is conceded by all—but as a minister of the gospel, yes, or no, was he literally the Son of God who came into the world with the definite appointed mission to die upon the cross for the sins of the world?'' Though there were some who hoped so, some who wished they had this concept, none had the knowledge or surety in their hearts; none answered in the affirmative without reservations.

The third question was: ''Do you believe that when you die you shall live again as a conscious entity, knowing and being known as you are?'' Again the answers were negative.

The world gives lip service to the divine sonship; they address God as *Father* and refer to Christ as *his Son.* But the question is one of whether they have the true concept of what is involved in this relationship. The fact that they profess to worship a god who is without body, parts, or passions, who fills the immensity of space, who is a spirit essence that in some indefinable way is everywhere and nowhere in particular present—the fact that they worship this kind of a being of itself is indicative of an inability to conceive that Christ is literally his Son as I am the son of my father; and that Christ thereby could actually receive by native endowment and inheritance the power to work out this infinite and eternal atoning sacrifice. Though sectarians give lip service to the concept that Christ is the Son of God, they have not envisioned the full reality of this doctrine to the extent that it must be the case if men are going to work out their salvation with fear and trembling before God. Thus we have a very large segment of the world giving lip service to the divine sonship without any real comprehension of the true doctrine.

What Think Ye of Christ?

I suppose also that among those who give lip service to the concept that Jesus is the Son of God there are many who in effect deny his divine sonship through the course of conduct they pursue. At least they reject him and instead follow the course of carnality, wickedness, and rebellion. Many people today are not much different from those to whom Christ preached when he said: ''What think ye of Christ? whose son is he?'' (Matt. 22:42.)

They responded that he was the Son of David (which was what their scripture taught) without being able to comprehend that he was also the Son of God. "He saith unto them, How then doth David in spirit call him Lord, saying, The Lord said unto my Lord, Sit thou on my right hand, till I make thine enemies thy footstool? If David then call him Lord, how is he his son? And no man was able to answer him a word." (Matt. 22:43-46.)

And so it is today. Who in the sectarian world can answer Jesus' question properly until they gain the concept and idea that he is actually and literally the Son of God? This is one of the most important questions in the religious world.

Four Suggestions to Know Christ

I desire to make some very simple suggestions as to how we can go about getting the knowledge that we ought to have of Jesus and of his mission and ministry and work. We must have this knowledge in order to bear witness to the world that God is our Father; that Christ is his Son; and that salvation and glory and honor and reward are available to us and all men because of their love and their condescension for us.

The first suggestion is this: *Become a student of the four Gospels;* fall in love with the Lord; see him in his birth situation, and in his growing up, and in the days of his ministry; sit with him in the privacy of a home in Bethany; go with him when he worked the many miracles; be among the multitude who ate the loaves and fishes when they were multiplied by divine power; stand at the tomb when Lazarus, dead for days and already decaying, was commanded to come forth; participate, vicariously as it were, to the extent of your abilities, in the acts and occurrences of the life of Jesus.

Number two: *Read the Book of Mormon* in the designated and prescribed way, that is, with faith in God and with real intent, asking Deity as to its truth. With reference to a conversation he had earlier in the day with the Twelve, the Prophet wrote in his journal: "I told the brethren that the Book of Mormon was the most correct of any book on earth, and the keystone of our religion, and a man would get nearer to God abiding by its precepts, than by any other book" (*History of the Church,* 4:461).

I would like to fall in love with Christ, and live and believe and think and do, insofar as possible, as he did; and the Book of Mormon is the volume that God has ordained in this day to get me in tune with the Spirit; to get me to feel that this work is divine; to have the Holy Spirit whisper to my soul. No man could have written that book; it is the voice and mind of God to the world; and Joseph Smith, who translated it, was the Lord's prophet. You can be in tune with the Lord; you can be in harmony with the Spirit more and better by a study of the Book of Mormon than anything that God has ever given in our day. The Book of Mormon is the portion of his word which he has preserved and segregated and set out by itself to introduce the gospel and to bring testimony into the hearts of the people.

Number three: *Listen to the witness of the living oracles.* Faith comes by hearing the word of God when it is taught by a legal administrator who has power from God (Rom. 10:17). This is the principle upon which Jesus operated. He said: "My sheep hear my voice" (John 10:27). So he, as the Son of God, bore testimony of his own divinity and taught the doctrines of salvation. And among his hearers were those who had advanced in spiritual talents to the point that they could understand and bear the message that then sank into their hearts. They knew, in a way that could not be defined and described, that the teachings were true.

The Lord's sheep still hear his voice. When the testimony of Jesus is borne by the power of the Holy Ghost, it sinks into the hearts of the righteous by that same power (2 Nephi 33:1). By way of illustration: If the Holy Spirit rests upon me and I stand here and I say to you that I know as I know that I live—which is the case —that Jesus is the Messiah, then, if the Holy Spirit also rests upon you, you feel in your heart that what I have said is true. You respond to the testimony and the witness that I bear, and as a consequence faith cometh by hearing—by hearing the word of God taught by the spirit of prophecy in power, by a legal administrator who speaks by authority of the Holy Ghost.

Number four: *Ask God in faith.* Let religion become a personal experience with you. Men do not get religion until they get the Holy Ghost. Anybody can read about religion and have an intellectual experience by learning what somebody else (insofar as they are able to understand it) knew or saw or felt; but religion does not come to the heart of an individual until God speaks to that soul by the power of his Holy Spirit.

Knowledge of Christ Not Intellectual Alone

Religion is not intellectual alone, although it meets all the standards of perfect intellectuality. Religion is a spiritual thing and people have to get the spiritual experience incident to it; religion comes from God. Men don't ordain it; men can ordain things in the intellectual field, but when you begin dealing with the things of God, no man knoweth the things of God, but by the Spirit of God which is in him (see 1 Cor. 2:11).

Paul said something that reads, in our King James Version, this way: "No man can *say* that Jesus is the Lord, but by the Holy Ghost" (1 Cor. 12:3; italics added). When the Prophet took that and put it in the Joseph Smith Translation, he improved on it so that it reads: "No man can *know* that Jesus is the Lord but by the Holy Ghost" (JST 1 Cor. 12:3; italics added).

This is the ultimate; this is the final thing. This is why the sectarians don't know about the divine sonship; they wish or believe or hope it might be so, but they don't know that it is true.

God has given the gift of the Holy Ghost again in our day so that we can know of the divine sonship. We can know that Jesus is the Lord. I think it is our obligation to follow the pattern that I have here indicated, or some equivalent pattern that we may work out, out of which there will come into our lives the personal assurance of the divine sonship of Jesus. It will come to us proportionately as we walk in the light and keep the standards that pertain to the gospel. (BYU *Speeches of the Year*, 15 August 1967.)

Fulness of Gospel Prerequisite to Perfect Testimony of Divine Sonship

There can be no perfect testimony of the divine sonship of Christ and his saving goodness unless and until we receive the fulness of his everlasting gospel. A testimony of the gospel comes by revelation from the Holy Ghost. When the Holy Spirit speaks to the spirit within us, we then know with an absolute conviction of the verity of the revealed message. (Conference Report, October 1974.)

Ours the Obligation to Testify of Christ

We have an especial and particular obligation to stand as witnesses of the truth to the world in this day. We live in the great era of darkness, spiritual darkness and apostasy, that is to precede the second coming of the Son of Man. He has called us and appointed us to stand as lights to the world. We are expected to be witnesses of the truth; to bear record of the divine sonship; to stand valiantly and courageously on the Lord's side of the line in defense of truth and righteousness and in proclaiming the gospel to his other children in the world.

This is not something we are particularly concerned with debating. We have ample evidence. The revelations are before us and the world. We can point to them. We can expound the doctrine involved. But the Lord has said this is a day of warning and not of many words (D&C 63:58); he has said that we who are in the Church are called to be witnesses of his name and that it becometh every man who hath been warned to warn his neighbor (D&C 88:81). (BYU *Speeches of the Year,* 16 December 1969.)

Chapter 3

THE EFFECTS FLOWING
FROM THE DIVINE SONSHIP

The Three Greatest Truths of Eternity

"Jesus Christ, and Him Crucified"

To lay an appropriate foundation I shall read three quotations. The first is from the Doctrine and Covenants; in it the Lord says: "Learn of me, and listen to my words; walk in the meekness of my Spirit, and you shall have peace in me" (D&C 19:23).

The second, Nephi writing, is from the Book of Mormon: "Believe in Christ, and . . . be reconciled to God; for we know that it is by grace that we are saved, after all we can do. And we talk of Christ, we rejoice in Christ, we preach of Christ, we prophesy of Christ, and we write according to our prophecies, that our children may know to what source they may look for a remission of their sins." And then, "Believe in Christ, and deny him not; and Christ is the Holy One of Israel; wherefore ye must bow down before him, and worship him with all your might, mind, and strength, and your whole soul; and if ye do this ye shall in nowise be cast out." (2 Ne. 25:23, 26, 29.)

The third quotation, from the Prophet Joseph Smith, gives us information that he learned by translating the papyrus, a portion of which is published as the book of Abraham: "Everlasting covenant was made between three personages before the organization of this earth, and relates to their dispensation of things to men on the earth; these personages, according to Abraham's record, are called God the first, the Creator; God the second, the Redeemer; and God the third, the witness or Testator" (*Teachings*, p. 190).

As members of The Church of Jesus Christ of Latter-day Saints, we have taken upon ourselves his name in the waters of baptism (2

Ne. 31:13; Mosiah 18:10). We renew the covenant therein made when we partake of the sacrament. If we have been born again, we have become the sons and daughters of the Lord Jesus Christ. We are members of his family. We are obligated and expected to live by the standards of the family. Because of that family membership, that close association, we have the privilege of an intimate association with him. We have been given the gift of the Holy Ghost, which is the constant companionship of that member of the Godhead based on faithfulness. And that Holy Spirit has as one of his chief missions to bear record of the Father and the Son, and to reveal to us, in a way that cannot be controverted or questioned, his divine sonship and the glorious truths that are in him.

Three Greatest Truths—and Heresies—of Eternity

We start with God, our Heavenly Father, who is here named God the first, the Creator. And we have to understand that he is a holy and perfected and exalted person (*Teachings*, pp. 345–46); that he is a being in whose image man is created (Gen. 1:26–27); that he has a body of flesh and bones as tangible as man's (D&C 130:22); and that we are literally his spirit children (Num. 16:22; Heb. 12:9), the Lord Jesus being the firstborn (D&C 93:21; Rom. 8:29; Col. 1:15). I suggest that the greatest truth in all eternity, bar none, is that there is a God in heaven who is a personal being, in whose image man is made, and that we are his spirit children. We must build on that rock foundation before any progression ever begins in the spiritual realm. We first believe in God our Heavenly Father.

I suggest also that the greatest heresy that was ever devised by an evil power was the heresy that defines the nature and kind of being that God is as a spirit essence that fills immensity; as a being without body, parts or passions; as something that is incomprehensible, uncreated, and unknowable. The greatest truth is God; the greatest heresy is the doctrine that recites the opposite of the truth as to God's person.

I suggest that the second greatest truth in all eternity is that Christ our Lord is the Redeemer; that he was foreordained in the councils of eternity to come down here and work out the infinite and eternal atoning sacrifice (Isa. 53; Rev. 13:8); that because of what he did we are ransomed from the effects of the temporal and spiritual death that came into the world by the fall of Adam (2 Ne. 2:19–25; 1 Cor. 15:21–22). And all of us have the hope, the potential, the possibility, to gain eternal life in addition to immortality, meaning that we can become like God our Heavenly Father (*Teachings*, pp. 346–48). That is the second greatest truth in all eternity.

The second greatest heresy in all eternity is the doctrine that denies the divine sonship, that sets up a system that says you can give lip service to the name of Christ, but you are saved by grace alone without efforts and without work on your part.

I suggest, conformable to what the Prophet said about God the third, who is the Witness or Testator, that the third greatest truth in all eternity is that the Holy Spirit of God, a personage of spirit, a member of the Godhead, has power to reveal eternal truth to the heart and soul and mind of man. And that revelation — known first as a testimony, and then known as the general receipt of truth in the spiritual field — that testimony is the great thing that man needs to lead him on a course back to our Father in Heaven.

Since that is the third greatest truth in all eternity, it follows that the third greatest and third most serious heresy in all eternity is the doctrine that denies that the Holy Spirit of God reveals truth to the human soul, and that denies that there are gifts of the Spirit, that there are miracles and powers and graces and good things that the Lord by his Spirit pours out upon mortal men.

Gratitude to the Father, Son, and Holy Ghost

We ought to have in our hearts an overflowing feeling of gratitude and thanksgiving. We praise the Lord our God, meaning the Father, because he created us (Alma 5:25; 19:32; Ps. 82:6). If he had not created us, we would not be; neither would the earth, or the sidereal heavens, or the universe, or anything else. If there had been no eternal God and no creation, there would be nothing. And because we exist, we ought in our souls to have an infinite degree of gratitude and thanksgiving to God our Heavenly Father.

Second, we ought to have an infinite degree of gratitude and thanksgiving to Christ the Lord, because he worked out the infinite and eternal atoning sacrifice and put into operation the terms and conditions of the Father's plan. If there had been no atonement of Christ, there would be no resurrection. And if there had been no atonement of Christ, there would be no eternal life, and hence our bodies would have lain forever in the dust and our spirits everlastingly been cast out from the presence of God, and we would have become like the devil and his angels. (2 Ne. 9:7–9.) What I am saying is that, through the atoning sacrifice of the Lord Jesus, the plan of the Father became operative.

Third, by virtue of obedience to the laws that are ordained and by becoming clean and spotless and pure, because the Spirit will not dwell in an unclean tabernacle (Mosiah 2:37; 1 Cor. 3:16-17), we get in a position to receive revelation by the power of the Holy Spirit. Once we are in tune, we become part of the family of the Lord Jesus. We partake of the same spirit that he possesses; we begin to believe as he believed, to act as he acted, to speak as he spoke. As a consequence, we get in a position to gain that glory and eternal life which he, as our prototype, has already gained. And so, third, we rejoice in what has come to us by the power of the Holy Ghost and have, again, an infinite gratitude where those things are concerned.

Christ Adopted the Father's Plan

God our Heavenly Father ordained and established the plan of salvation. Joseph Smith expressed it in these words. He said, "God himself, finding he was in the midst of spirits and glory, because he was more intelligent, saw proper to institute laws whereby the rest could have a privilege to advance like himself" (*Teachings*, p. 354). God is exalted and omnipotent and enthroned; he has all power, all might, and all dominion (Mosiah 3:5, 21; 4:9; 5:15; Alma 26:35; D&C 19:3, 14, 20; 63:1). He lives in the family unit (see Joseph Fielding Smith, *Man His Origin and Destiny* [Salt Lake City: Deseret Book Co., 1954], pp. 348-55), and the name of the kind of life that he lives is eternal life. And so, if we advance and progress and go forward until we become like him, we then become, like Christ, inheritors of eternal life in the kingdom of God (Rom. 8:13-17; D&C 76:50-62; 132:19-20). That is our aim and our goal. Hence, there is this thing which Paul calls "the gospel of God" (Rom. 1:1; 15:16; 1 Thes. 2:2, 8-9) meaning that the Father ordained and established the plan of salvation. But then Paul says, "Concerning his Son Jesus Christ our Lord, which was made of the seed of David according to the flesh" (Rom. 1:3), meaning that Christ adopted the Father's plan. He made it his own. He espoused it. He became the advocate of salvation, the leader in the cause of salvation—all because he was chosen to be born into the world as God's Son.

Our Premortal Knowledge and Experience

All of this was known and taught and understood in the great eternities that went before. We all heard the gospel preached. We knew its terms and conditions. We knew what would be involved in this mortal probation. We knew that it was necessary to come here and get a mortal body as a step toward gaining an immortal body, one of flesh and bones. We knew that when we came here we would need to be tried and examined and tested. We'd need to undergo probationary experiences when we were outside the presence of God, when we walked by faith rather than by sight, when the spirit was housed in a tabernacle of clay and subject to the lusts and appetites and passions of mortality. This we all knew. And then our Father sent forth the great decree through the councils of eternity, "Whom shall I send to be my son, to work out the infinite and eternal atoning sacrifice?" He got two volunteers. Christ the Lord said, "Father, thy will be done." (See Moses 4:1–3.) That is, "I will go down and do what thou hast ordained and sacrifice myself. I will be the Lamb slain from the foundation of the world." Lucifer wanted to modify the Father's plan so radically that we could almost say he offered a new system of salvation. He wanted to deny all men their agency, to save all men and, in return, receive the power and dignity and glory of the Father. He wanted to take the place of the Father. The decision was then made: "I will send the first" (Abr. 3:27).

The plan was put into operation. Part of it was the creation of this earth. Then came its peopling. We are all the sons and daughters of father Adam; all of us are eternal beings, offspring of Deity. Our mortal bodies have been made from the dust of the earth. We're here, having mortal bodies, being examined and tried and tested to see if we will walk uprightly and keep the commandments.

We Must First Believe in Christ

Our first obligation is to believe in Christ and accept him literally and completely and fully for what he is. We believe in Christ when we believe the doctrine he teaches, the words that he speaks, the message that he proclaims. When he came in the flesh as Mary's son, the account says that he "went about . . . preaching the gospel of the kingdom" (Matt. 9:35), meaning that his message was a revelation to people in that day of the plan of salvation, of the things that they had to do to overcome the world, to perfect their lives, and to qualify to go back with him to the presence of the everlasting Father.

So, first of all, we believe in Christ. And the test as to whether we believe in him is whether we believe his words and whether we believe those whom he hath sent—the Apostles and prophets of all

the ages (D&C 1:38; 84:36). And then, having believed, we have the
obligation of conforming to the truths that we have thus learned
(Mosiah 4:10; Matt. 7:21). If we do conform we begin to grow in
spiritual graces. We add to our faith virtue, and to our virtue knowledge, and to knowledge temperance and patience and godliness
and all of the other attributes and characteristics that are written in
the revelations (2 Pet. 1:5). So step by step and degree by degree we
begin to become like God our Heavenly Father.

Gaining Salvation a Process Not an Event

We do not work out our salvation in a moment; it doesn't come
to us in an instant, suddenly. Gaining salvation is a process. Paul
says, "Work out your own salvation with fear and trembling"
(Philip. 2:12). To some members of the Church who had been baptized and who were on the course leading to eternal life, he said,
"Now is our salvation nearer than when we believed" (Rom.
13:11). That is, "We have made some progress along the straight
and narrow path. We are going forward, and if we continue in that
direction, eternal life will be our everlasting reward."

We start out in the direction of eternal life when we join The
Church of Jesus Christ of Latter-day Saints. We enter in at a gate,
and the name of the gate is repentance and baptism. We thereby get
on a path, and the name of the path is the straight and narrow path.
And then if we endure to the end, meaning if we keep the commandments of God after baptism, we go up that straight and narrow path, and at its end is a reward that is named eternal life. All of
this is available because of the atoning sacrifice of Christ. If he had
not come, there would be no hope or no possibility under any circumstance for any man either to be resurrected or to have eternal
life. (2 Ne. 9:8-9.) Salvation comes by the mercy and the love and
the condescension of God. In other words, it comes by the grace of
God, meaning that our Lord made it available. But he has done his
work, and we must now do ours; and we have the obligation to endure to the end, to keep the commandments, to work out our salvation, and that is what we are in the process of doing in the Church
and the kingdom of God on earth.

Spiritual Rebirth a Process

We say that a man has to be born again, meaning that he has to
die as pertaining to the unrighteous things in the world. Paul told us

to "crucify the old man of sin and come forth in a newness of life" (Rom. 6:6). We are born again when we die as pertaining to unrighteousness and when we live as pertaining to the things of the Spirit. But that doesn't happen in an instant, suddenly. That also is a process. Being born again is a gradual thing, except in a few isolated instances that are so miraculous they get written up in the scriptures. As far as the generality of the members of the Church are concerned, we are born again by degrees, and we are born again to added light and added knowledge and added desires for righteousness as we keep the commandments.

Sanctification a Process

The same thing is true of being sanctified. Those who go to the celestial kingdom of heaven have to be sanctified, meaning that they become clean and pure and spotless. They have had evil and iniquity burned out of their souls as though by fire, giving rise to the figurative expression "the baptism of fire." Here again it is a process. Nobody is sanctified in an instant, suddenly. But if we keep the commandments and press forward with steadfastness after baptism, then degree by degree and step by step we sanctify our souls until that glorious day when we're qualified to go where God and angels are.

Spiritual Growth Gradual, Not Instantaneous

So it is with the plan of salvation. We have to become perfect to be saved in the celestial kingdom. But nobody becomes perfect in this life. Only the Lord Jesus attained that state, and he had an advantage that none of us has. He was the Son of God, and he came into this life with a spiritual capacity and a talent and an inheritance that exceeded beyond all comprehension what any of the rest of us was born with: Our revelations say that he was "like unto God" (Abr. 3:24) in the premortal life and he was, under the Father, creator of worlds without number (*Teachings*, p. 348). That Holy Being was the Holy One of Israel anciently and he was the Sinless One in mortality (1 Ne. 20:17; 21:7; 22:20–21; 2 Ne. 6:9; 9:11–12; 25:29). He lived a perfect life, and he set an ideal example. This shows that we can strive and go forward toward that goal, but no other mortal—not the greatest prophets nor the mightiest Apostles nor any of the righteous Saints of any of the ages—has ever been perfect, but we must become perfect to gain a celestial inheritance (3 Ne. 12:48;

Matt. 5:48; Moro. 10:32–33; D&C 67:13; 76:50–70, esp. v. 69; Heb. 6:1). As it is with being born again, and as it is with sanctifying our souls, so becoming perfect in Christ is a process.

We begin to keep the commandments today, and we keep more of them tomorrow, and we go from grace to grace, up the steps of the ladder, and we thus improve and perfect our souls. We can become perfect in some minor things. We can be perfect in the payment of tithing. If we pay one-tenth of our interest annually into the tithing funds of the Church, if we do it year in and year out, and desire to do it, and have no intent to withhold, and if we would do it regardless of what arose in our lives, then in that thing we are perfect. And in that thing and to that extent we are living the law as well as Moroni or the angels from heaven could live it. And so, degree by degree and step by step we start out in the course to perfection with the objective of becoming perfect as God our Heavenly Father is perfect, in which eventuality we become inheritors of eternal life in his kingdom.

As members of the Church, if we chart a course leading to eternal life; if we begin the process of spiritual rebirth, and are going in the right direction; if we chart a course of sanctifying our souls, and degree by degree are going in that direction; and if we chart a course of becoming perfect, and, step by step and phase by phase, are perfecting our souls by overcoming the world, then it is absolutely guaranteed—there is no question whatever about it—we shall gain eternal life. Even though we have spiritual rebirth ahead of us, perfection ahead of us, the full degree of sanctification ahead of us, if we chart a course and follow it to the best of our ability in this life, then when we go out of this life we'll continue in exactly that same course. We will no longer be subject to the passions and the appetites of the flesh. We will have passed successfully the tests of this mortal probation and in due course we'll get the fulness of our Father's kingdom—and that means eternal life in his everlasting presence.

Salvation Within Our Reach

We can talk about the principles of salvation and say how many there are and how people have to meet these standards. And it may thereby seem hard and difficult and beyond the capacity of mortals so to obtain. But we need not take that approach. We ought to realize that we have the same appetites and passions that all of the Saints and righteous people had in the dispensations that have gone before (see, e.g., James 5:17). They were no different than we are. They overcame the flesh. They gained the knowledge of God. They understood about Christ and salvation. They had the revelations of the Holy Spirit to their souls certifying of the divine sonship and of the prophetic ministry of whatever prophets ministered among them. And as a consequence they worked out their salvation.

Occasionally in the overall perspective someone came along who so lived that he was translated, but that's not particularly for our day and generation. When we die, our obligation is to go into the spirit world and continue to preach the gospel there. So, as far as people now living are concerned, our obligation is to believe and live the truth, and chart a course to eternal life. And if we do it, we get peace and joy and happiness in this life; and, when we go into the eternal realms ahead, we continue there to work in the cause of righteousness. And we will not fail! We go on to eternal reward.

The Prophet Joseph Smith said that no man can commit the unpardonable sin after he departs this life (*Teachings,* p. 357). Of course not; that is part of the testing of this mortal probation. And on that same basis, anybody who is living uprightly and has integrity and devotion, if he is doing all that he can here, when he leaves this sphere he is going to go into the paradise of God and have rest and peace, that is, rest and peace as far as the troubles and turmoils and vicissitudes and anxieties of this life are concerned. But he'll continue to labor and work on the Lord's errand, and eventually he'll come up in the resurrection of the just. He will get an immortal body, meaning that body and spirit will be inseparably connected. That soul will never again see corruption. Never again will there be death, but what is equally as glorious, or more so, that soul will go on to eternal life in the kingdom of God. And eternal life means the continuation of the family unit. Eternal life means inheriting, receiving, and possessing the fulness of the Father, the power and might and creative ability and all that he has that enabled him to create worlds without number and to be the progenitor of an infinite number of spirit progeny.

We cannot really conceive of how glorious and wondrous all these things are. We can get some glimmering; we can get a little understanding. We know that they are available because God the Creator established the plan of salvation. We know that they are available because God the Redeemer put into force and gave efficacy and validity to all of the terms and conditions of that eternal plan. And we know that they can be revealed and known to us because God the Witness or Testator bears witness, certifies, testifies to the spirit that is within us in a way that cannot be controverted, that the things of which we speak are true.

Personal Sanctification Available Through Atonement

The Atonement was worked out in a way that is totally beyond our comprehension. We do not understand how. We know some of the why. We know that it did occur. We know that, in a way incomprehensible to a finite intellect, the Son of God took upon himself the sins of all men on conditions of repentance. That is, he paid the penalty. He satisfied the demands of justice. He made mercy available to us. Mercy cometh because of the Atonement. Mercy is for the repentant. Everyone else has to suffer for his own sins and pay to the full extent the demands of justice. (D&C 19:16–19; Mosiah 15:26–27; 16:5–11; Alma 11:40–41.) But our Eternal Redeemer has done for us what no one else could, and he did it because he was God's Son and because he possessed the power of immortality. He has taken our sins upon him on conditions of repentance. Repentance means that we have faith in the Lord Jesus Christ, that we forsake our sins, that we come into the Church and kingdom of God on earth and receive the Holy Ghost. Repentance is far more than reformation. Repentance is a gift of God, and it comes to faithful members of the Church. We get it by the power of the Holy Ghost.

The cleansing process that occurs in our lives comes because we receive the cleansing power of the Holy Ghost. The Holy Ghost is a revelator and a sanctifier. The Holy Ghost reveals truth to every human soul that obeys the laws. Obedience qualifies us to know the truth. (John 7:16–17.) And then the Holy Ghost sanctifies the human soul, so that we become clean and spotless and eventually are qualified to go where God and Christ are. (BYU *Speeches of the Year*, 5 September 1976.)

Greatness of Creation, Atonement, and Divine Sonship

As I analyze and view the matter, it seems to me that the greatest miracle that ever occurred was the miracle of creation: the fact that God, our Heavenly Father, brought us into being; the fact that we exist; that we were born as his spirit children; and that now we are privileged to abide in mortal tabernacles and partake of a probationary experience.

It seems to me that the second greatest miracle that has ever occurred, in this or any of God's creations, is the atoning sacrifice of his Son; the fact that he came into the world to ransom men from the temporal and spiritual death brought into this existence by the fall of Adam; the fact that he is reconciling us again to God and making immortality and eternal life available to us. This atoning sacrifice of Christ is the greatest thing that has ever happened since the Creation.

The Prophet was once asked, "What are the fundamental principles of your religion?" He responded: "The fundamental principles of our religion are the testimony of the Apostles and Prophets, concerning Jesus Christ, that He died, was buried, and rose again the third day, and ascended into heaven; and all other things which pertain to our religion are only appendages to it." (*Teachings*, p. 121.)

The very heart and core and center of revealed religion is the atoning sacrifice of Christ. All things rest upon it, all things are operative because of it, and without it there would be nothing. Without it the purposes of creation would be void, they would vanish away, there would be neither immortality nor eternal life, and the ultimate destiny of all men would be to become as Lucifer and his followers are. (2 Ne. 9:9.)

The underlying foundation upon which the atoning sacrifice of Christ rests is the doctrine of the divine sonship. . . . Christ was the only person who has ever lived who had the power within himself to either live or die as he chose—and therefore the power to work out the infinite and eternal atoning sacrifice upon which all things rest. It seems appropriate . . . for us to talk about the doctrine of his coming into mortality. This is what I consider, in many respects, to be the third greatest miracle of eternity. ("Who Shall Declare His Generation?" BYU Devotional, 2 December 1975.)

Our Relationship with the Lord

Church Doctrine on Man's Relationship to Deity

I shall speak of our relationship with the Lord and of the true fellowship all Saints should have with the Father and the Son in order to gain eternal life.

I shall expound the doctrine of the Church relative to what our relationship should be to all members of the Godhead, and do so in plainness and simplicity so that none need misunderstand or be led astray by other voices.

I shall express the views of the Brethren, of the prophets and Apostles of old, and of all those who understand the scriptures and are in tune with the Holy Spirit.

These matters lie at the very foundation of revealed religion. In presenting them I am on my own ground and am at home with my subject. I shall not stoop to petty wranglings about semantics, but shall stay with matters of substance. I shall simply go back to basics and set forth fundamental doctrines of the kingdom, knowing that everyone who is sound spiritually and who has the guidance of the Holy Spirit will believe my words and follow my counsel.

Religious Falsehoods Abound

Please do not put too much stock in some of the current views and vagaries that are afloat, but rather, turn to the revealed word, get a sound understanding of the doctrines, and keep yourselves in the mainstream of the Church.

It is no secret that many false and vain and foolish things are being taught in the sectarian world and even among us about our need to gain a special relationship with the Lord Jesus. I shall summarize the true doctrine in this field and invite erring teachers and beguiled students to repent and believe the accepted gospel verities as I shall set them forth.

There is no salvation in believing any false doctrine, particularly a false or unwise view about the Godhead or any of its members. Eternal life is reserved for those who know God and the One whom he sent to work out the infinite and eternal atonement (John 17:3; D&C 132:24).

True and saving worship is found only among those who know the truth about God and the Godhead and who understand the true relationship men should have with each member of that Eternal Presidency.

It follows that the devil would rather spread false doctrine about God and the Godhead, and induce false feelings with reference to any one of them, than almost any other thing he could do. The creeds of Christendom illustrate perfectly what Lucifer wants so-called Christian people to believe about Deity in order to be damned.

These creeds codify what Jeremiah calls the lies about God (Jer. 16:19–21). They say he is unknown, uncreated, and incomprehensible. They say he is a spirit, without body, parts, or passions. They say he is everywhere and nowhere in particular present, that he fills the immensity of space and yet dwells in the hearts of men, and that he is an immaterial, incorporeal nothingness. They say he is one-god-in-three, and three-gods-in-one who neither hears nor sees nor speaks. Some even say he is dead, which he might as well be if their descriptions identify his being.

These concepts summarize the chief and greatest heresy of Christendom. Truly the most grievous and evil heresy ever imposed on an erring and wayward Christianity is their creedal concept about God and the Godhead! But none of this troubles us very much. God has revealed himself to us in this day even as he did to the prophets of old.

Truth About God

We know thereby that he is a personal being in whose image man was made. We know that he has a body of flesh and bones as tangible as man's; that he is a resurrected, glorified, and perfected being; and that he lives in the family unit. We know that we are his spirit children; that he endowed us with the divine gift of agency; and that he ordained the laws whereby we might advance and become like him. (*Teachings*, p. 354.)

We know that God is the only supreme and independent being in whom all fulness and perfection dwell and that he is omnipotent, omniscient, and, by the power of his spirit, omnipresent.

We know ''the Almighty God gave his Only Begotten Son'' (D&C 20:21), as the scriptures attest, to ransom man from the temporal and spiritual death brought into the world by the fall of Adam, and to put into operation all of the terms and conditions of the Father's plan.

We know that the Holy Ghost, as a personage of Spirit, is both a revelator and a sanctifier and that his chief mission is to bear record of the Father and the Son.

Thus there are, in the Eternal Godhead, three persons—God the first, the Creator; God the second, the Redeemer; and God the third, the Testator (*Teachings*, p. 190). These three are one—one God if you will—in purpose, in powers, and in perfections. But each has his own severable work to perform, and mankind has a defined and known and specific relationship to each one of them. It is of these relationships that we shall now speak.

Let us set forth those doctrines and concepts that a gracious God has given us in this day and which must be understood in order to gain eternal life. They are:

1. We worship the Father and him only and no one else. We do not worship the Son and we do not worship the Holy Ghost. I know perfectly well what the scriptures say about worshipping Christ and Jehovah, but they are speaking in an entirely different sense—the sense of standing in awe and being reverentially grateful to Him who has redeemed us. Worship in the true and saving sense is reserved for God the first, the Creator.

Our revelations say that the Father "is infinite and eternal," that he created mankind, "and gave unto them commandments that they should love and serve him, the only living and true God, and that he should be the only being whom they should worship." (D&C 20:17-19).

Jesus said: "True worshippers shall"—note that this is mandatory—"worship the Father in spirit and in truth; for the Father seeketh such to worship him. For unto such hath God promised his Spirit. And they who worship him, must worship in spirit and in truth." (JST John 4:25-26.) There is no other way, no other approved system of worship.

2. We love and serve both the Father and the Son. In the full, final, and ultimate sense of the word, the divine decree is: "Thou shalt love the Lord thy God with all thy heart, with all thy might, mind, and strength; and in the name of Jesus Christ thou shalt serve him" (D&C 59:5). And Jesus also said: "If ye love me, keep my commandments" (John 14:15).

These, then, are the commandments of commandments. They tie the Father and the Son together as one, so that both receive our love and service.

3. Christ himself loves, serves, and worships the Father. Though Christ is God, yet there is a Deity above him, a Deity whom he worships. That God is the Father. To Mary Magdalene, the first mortal to see a resurrected person, Jesus said: "I ascend unto my Father, and your Father; and to my God, and your God" (John 20:17).

All of us, Christ included, are the spirit children of the Father; all of us, Christ included, seek to become like the Father. In this sense the Firstborn, our Elder Brother, goes forward as we do.

4. The plan of salvation is the gospel of the Father. The plan of salvation originated with the Father; he is the author and finisher of our faith in the final sense; he ordained the laws by obedience to which both we and Christ can become like him.

The Father did *not* ask for volunteers to propose a plan whereby man might be saved. What he did was ask whom he should send to be the Redeemer in the plan he devised. Christ and Lucifer both volunteered and the Lord chose his Firstborn and rejected the amendatory offer of the son of the morning.

Thus Paul speaks of "the gospel of God, . . . concerning his Son Jesus Christ our Lord, which was made of the seed of David according to the flesh" (Rom. 1:1-3). It is the Father's gospel, it became the gospel of the Son by adoption, and we call it after Christ's name because his atoning sacrifice put all of its terms and conditions into operation.

5. Christ worked out his own salvation by worshipping the Father. After the Firstborn of the Father, while yet a spirit being, had gained power and intelligence that made him like unto God; after he had become, under the Father, the Creator of worlds without number; after he had reigned on the throne of eternal power as the Lord Omnipotent—after all this he yet had to gain a mortal and then an immortal body.

After the Son of God "made flesh" his "tabernacle," and while he "dwelt among the sons of men"; after he left his preexistent glory as we all do at birth; after he was born of Mary in Bethlehem of Judea—after all this he was called upon to work out his own salvation.

Of our Lord's life while in this mortal probation the scripture says: "He received not of the fulness at the first, but received grace for grace; And he received not of the fulness at first, but continued from grace to grace, until he received a fulness." Finally, after his resurrection, "he received a fulness of the glory of the Father; And he received all power, both in heaven and on earth, and the glory of the Father was with him, for he dwelt in him." (D&C 93:12-13, 16-17.)

Note it, please; the Lord Jesus worked out his own salvation while in this mortal probation by going from grace to grace until, having overcome the world and being raised in immortal glory, he became like the Father in the full, complete, and eternal sense.

6. All men must worship the Father in the same way Christ did in order to gain salvation. Thus saith the Lord: "I give unto you these sayings" —those we have just quoted which tell how Christ gained his salvation by worshipping the Father—"I give unto you these sayings," saith the Lord, "that you may understand and know *how* to worship, and know *what* you worship, that you may come unto the Father in my name, and in due course receive of his fulness."

What a wondrous concept this is! We too can become like the Father: "For if you keep my commandments," the Lord continues, "you shall receive of his fulness, and be glorified in me as I am in the Father; therefore, I say unto you, you shall receive grace for grace." (D&C 93:19-20; italics added.)

7. *The Father sent the Son to work out the infinite and eternal atonement.* As temporal and spiritual death came by the fall of Adam, so immortality and eternal life come by the atonement of Christ. Such was and is and ever shall be the plan of the Father. Adam was sent to earth to fall and Christ came to ransom men from the Fall.

Thus the Father sent forth this call in the councils of eternity: "Whom shall I send to be my Son, to ransom men from temporal and spiritual death, to bring to pass the immortality and eternal life of man, to put into full operation all the terms and conditions of my eternal plan of redemption and salvation?"

Christ is the Redeemer of men and the Savior of the world because his Father sent him and gave him power to do the assigned work. He said he had power to lay down his life and to take it again because he had been so commanded by the Father. Lehi says he rose from the dead "by the power of the Spirit" (2 Ne. 2:8).

The great and eternal redemption, in all its phases, was wrought by Christ using the power of the Father.

8. *The Son came to do the will of the Father in all things.* Jesus said: "I came down from heaven, not to do mine own will, but the will of him that sent me" (John 6:38). Also: "I came into the world to do the will of my Father, because my Father sent me. And my Father sent me that I might be lifted up upon the cross." (3 Ne. 27:13-14.) And Paul said of him: He "made himself of no reputation, and took upon him the form of a servant, and was made in the likeness of men: And being found in fashion as a man, he humbled himself, and became obedient unto death, even the death of the cross" (Philip. 2:7-8).

How better could his relationship with his Father be stated?

9. *God, through Christ, is reconciling men to himself.* Fallen man is carnal, sensual, and devilish by nature; he is spiritually dead; he is out of harmony with the Father. Thus, as Paul says, "All things are of God, who hath reconciled us to himself by Jesus Christ, and hath given to us the ministry of reconciliation; To wit, that God was in Christ reconciling the world unto himself." We have "the word of reconciliation," which is the gospel, and our preaching is: "Be ye reconciled to God," that is, to the Father. (2 Cor. 5:18-20.)

10. *Christ is the Mediator between God and man.* Because all men must be reconciled to God in order to be saved, he, in his goodness and grace, has provided a mediator for them. Paul tells us: "There is one God, and one mediator between God and men, the man Christ

Jesus; Who gave himself a ransom for all'' (1 Tim. 2:5–6). To this we add: If there were no Mediator we could never be reconciled to the Father and hence there would be no salvation.

11. Christ is our Intercessor with the Father, our Advocate in the courts above. In the process of mediating between us and our Maker, in the process of reconciling sin-ridden men with a sin-free God, Christ makes intercession for all who repent. He advocates the cause of those who believe in him. ''Father,'' he pleads, ''spare these my brethren that believe on my name, that they may come unto me and have everlasting life.'' (D&C 45:5.)

12. Our eternal fellowship is with the Father and the Son. John says: ''Our fellowship is with the Father, and with his Son Jesus Christ.'' If we keep the commandments, ''we have fellowship'' with the Father—which is the object and end of our existence. And in the very nature of things we also have eternal fellowship with Christ, because he walked in the light and became and is one with the Father. (See 1 John 1:3–7.)

13. God was in Christ manifesting himself to the world. The Son, Paul tells us, is in ''the express image of his [Father's] person'' (Heb. 1:3). ''I and my Father are one,'' Jesus said (John 10:30). Thus, in his appearance, in his person, and in his attributes, the Son is the image and likeness of the Father. ''He that hath seen me hath seen the Father,'' Jesus said (John 14:9). The four Gospels are a treasure house of knowledge concerning the Father because they set forth what the Son is like, and he is like the Father.

14. Christ is the revealer of the Father. God is and can be known only by revelation; he stands revealed or he remains forever unknown. Jesus said: ''No man knoweth . . . who the Father is, but the Son, and he to whom the Son will reveal him'' (Luke 10:22).

15. Christ is the way to the Father. ''I am the way,'' he said. ''No man cometh unto the Father, but by me.'' (John 14:6.) Who can doubt that Christ's mission is to reveal the Father, to lead men to the Father, to teach them how to worship the Father, to reconcile them to the Father?

16. Christ proclaims the gospel of the Father. In the ultimate sense the word of salvation comes from the Father. ''God, who at sundry times and in divers manners spake in time past unto the fathers by the prophets,'' Paul says, ''Hath in these last days spoken unto us by his Son.'' (Heb. 1:1, 2.)

The Father sent the prophets; they represented him, and they spoke his word. When Jesus quoted the Old Testament prophets to the Nephites, he attributed their words to the Father.

Though the revelations came from the Son, yet in the ultimate sense the truths taught were those of the Father. We are also aware of many instances in which Jesus, acting by divine investiture of authority, speaks in the first person as though he were the Father. Thus Jesus said: "My doctrine is not mine, but his that sent me. If any man will do his will, he shall know of the doctrine, whether it be of God, or whether I speak of myself." (John 7:16–17.)

17. *Christ glorifies the Father and so must we.* "Glorify thy Son," Jesus prayed to the Father, "that thy Son also may glorify thee. I have glorified thee on the earth: I have finished the work which thou gavest me to do." (John 17:1, 4.)

As Christ, our pattern, by obedience and by doing his appointed labors, glorified the Father, so must we. Acting in his Father's name, Jesus ascribed the honor and glory in all things to the Father. The very pattern of prayer that he gave us directs that we go and do likewise (see Matt. 6:9).

Now, we might continue on and list added concepts, all of which would bear the same witness and accord with what we have said. Let us instead, based on these present concepts, discuss the problem at hand and draw some conclusions.

Perfect Unity Among the Deities

What is and should be our relationship to the members of the Godhead?

First, be it remembered that most scriptures that speak of God or of the Lord do not even bother to distinguish the Father from the Son, simply because it doesn't make any difference which God is involved. They are one. The words or deeds of either of them would be the words and deeds of the other in the same circumstance.

Further, if a revelation comes from or by the power of the Holy Ghost, ordinarily the words will be those of the Son, though what the Son says will be what the Father would say, and the words may thus be considered as the Father's. And thus any feelings of love, praise, awe, or worship that may fill our hearts when we receive the divine word will be the same no matter who is thought or known to be the author of them.

And yet we do have a proper relationship to each member of the Godhead, in part at least because there are separate and severable functions which each performs, and also because of what they as one Godhead have done for us.

Our Relationship with the Father

Our relationship with the Father is supreme, paramount, and preeminent over all others. He is the God we worship. It is his gospel that saves and exalts. He ordained and established the plan of salvation. He is the one who was once as we are now. The life he lives is eternal life, and if we are to gain this greatest of all the gifts of God, it will be because we become like him.

Our relationship with the Father is one of parent and child. He is the one who gave us our agency. It was his plan that provided for a fall and an atonement. And it is to him that we must be reconciled if we are to gain salvation. He is the one to whom we have direct access by prayer, and if there were some need—which there is not—to single out one member of the Godhead for a special relationship, the Father, not the Son, would be the one to choose.

Our Relationship with the Son

Our relationship with the Son is one of brother or sister in the premortal life and one of being led to the Father by him while in this mortal sphere. He is the Lord Jehovah who championed our cause before the foundations of the earth were laid. He is the God of Israel, the promised Messiah, and the Redeemer of the world.

By faith we are adopted into his family and become his children. We take upon ourselves his name, keep his commandments, and rejoice in the cleansing power of his blood. Salvation comes by him. From creation's dawn, as long as eternity endures, there neither has been nor will be any act of such transcendent power and import as his atoning sacrifice.

We do not have a fraction of the power we need to properly praise his holy name and ascribe unto him the honor and power and might and glory and dominion that are his. He is our Lord, our God, and our King.

Our Relationship with the Holy Spirit

Our relationship with the Holy Spirit is quite another thing. This holy personage is a revelator and a sanctifier. He bears record of the Father and the Son. He dispenses spiritual gifts to the faithful. Those of us who had received the gift of the Holy Ghost have the right to his constant companionship.

And again, if it were proper—and I repeat, it is not!—to single out one member of the Godhead for some special attention, we might well conclude that member should be the Holy Ghost. We might well adopt as a slogan: Seek the Spirit. The reason of course is that the sanctifying power of the Spirit would assure us of reconciliation with the Father. And any person who enjoys the constant companionship of the Holy Spirit will be in complete harmony with the divine will in all things.

Dangers in Misguided Belief

Now, in spite of all these truths, which ought to be obvious to every spiritually enlightened person, heresies rear their ugly heads among us from time to time. There are those deluded cultists, and others who, unless they repent, are on the road to becoming cultists, who choose to believe we should worship Adam. These have or should find their way out of the Church. There are others—in the main they are intellectuals without strong testimonies—who postulate that God does not know all things but is progressing in truth and knowledge and will do so everlastingly. These, unless they repent, will live and die weak in the faith and will fall short of inheriting what might have been theirs in eternity. There are yet others who have an excessive zeal which causes them to go beyond the mark. Their desire for excellence is inordinate. In an effort to be truer than true they devote themselves to gaining a special, personal relationship with Christ that is both improper and perilous.

I say perilous because this course, particularly in the lives of some who are spiritually immature, is a gospel hobby which creates an unwholesome holier-than-thou attitude. In other instances it leads to despondency because the seeker after perfection knows he is not living the way he supposes he should.

Another peril is that those so involved often begin to pray directly to Christ because of some special friendship they feel has been developed. In this connection a current and unwise book, which advocates gaining a special relationship with Jesus, contains this sentence: "Because the Savior is our mediator, our prayers go through Christ to the Father, and the Father answers our prayers through his Son."

This is plain sectarian nonsense. Our prayers are addressed to the Father, and to him only. They do not go through Christ, or the Blessed Virgin, or St. Genevieve or along the beads of a rosary. We are entitled to "come boldly unto the throne of grace, that we may obtain mercy, and find grace to help in time of need" (Heb. 4:6).

And I rather suppose that he who sitteth upon the throne will choose his own ways to answer his children, and that they are numerous. Perfect prayer is addressed to the Father, in the name of the Son (3 Ne. 18:19–21); it is uttered by the power of the Holy Ghost; and it is answered in whatever way seems proper by him whose ear is attuned to the needs of his children.

Follow Church Leaders

Now, I know that some may be offended at the counsel that they should not strive for a special and personal relationship with Christ. It will seem to them as though I am speaking out against mother love, or Americanism, or the little red schoolhouse. But I am not. There is a fine line here over which true worshippers will not step.

It is true that there may, with propriety, be a special relationship with a wife, with children, with friends, with teachers, with the beasts of the field and the fowls of the sky and the lilies of the valley. But the very moment anyone singles out one member of the Godhead as the almost sole recipient of his devotion, to the exclusion of the others, that is the moment when spiritual instability begins to replace sense and reason.

The proper course for all of us is to stay in the mainstream of the Church. This is the Lord's Church, and it is led by the spirit of inspiration, and the practice of the Church constitutes the interpretation of the scripture. And you have never heard one of the First Presidency or the Twelve, who hold the keys of the kingdom, and who are appointed to see that we are not "tossed to and fro, and carried about with every wind of doctrine" (Eph. 4:14), you have never heard one of them advocate this excessive zeal that calls for gaining a so-called special and personal relationship with Christ.

You have heard them teach and testify of the ministry and mission of the Lord Jesus, using the most persuasive and powerful language at their command. But never, never at any time have they taught or endorsed the inordinate and intemperate zeal that encourages endless, sometimes day-long, prayers in order to gain a personal relationship with the Savior.

Those who truly love the Lord and who worship the Father in the name of the Son by the power of the Spirit, according to the approved patterns, maintain a reverential barrier between themselves and all the members of the Godhead.

Seeking Special Relationships Characteristic of Sectarianism

I am well aware that some who have prayed for endless hours feel they have a special and personal relationship with Christ that they never had before. I wonder if this is any or much different, however, from the feelings of fanatical sectarians who with glassy eyes and fiery tongues assure us they have been saved by grace and are assured of a place with the Lord in a heavenly abode, when in fact they have never even received the fulness of the gospel.

I wonder if it is not part of Lucifer's system to make people feel they are special friends of Jesus when in fact they are not following the normal and usual pattern of worship found in the true Church.

Let me remind you to stay in the course charted by the Church. It is the Lord's Church, and he will not permit it to be led astray. If we take the counsel that comes from the prophets and seers we will pursue the course that is pleasing to the Lord.

Respectful Distance Separates Man from God

Would it be amiss if I reminded you that Jesus maintained a reserve between him and his disciples and that he did not allow them the same intimacy with him that they had with each other? This was particularly true after his resurrection. For instance, when Mary Magdalene, in a great outpouring of love and devotion, sought to embrace the risen Lord, her hands were stayed. "Touch me not," he said (John 20:17). Between her and him, no matter the degree of their love, there was a line over which she could not pass. And yet, almost immediately thereafter, a whole group of faithful women held that same Lord by the feet and, we cannot doubt, bathed his wounded feet with their tears (Matt. 28:9).

It is a fine and sacred line, but clearly there is a difference between a personal and intimate relationship with the Lord, which is improper, and one of worshipful adoration, which yet maintains the required reserve between us and him who has bought us with his blood.

Respect for the Savior

I sincerely hope that no one will imagine that I have in the slightest degree downgraded the Lord Jesus in the scheme of things.

I have not done so. As far as I know there is not a man on earth who thinks more highly of him than I do. It just may be that I have preached more sermons, taught more doctrine, and written more words about the Lord Jesus Christ than any man now living. I have ten large volumes in print, seven of which deal almost entirely with Christ, and the other three with him and his doctrine.

Avoid Doctrinal Controversy

I do not suppose that what I have here said will be an end to controversy or to the spread of false views and doctrines. The devil is not dead and he delights in controversy (3 Ne. 11:29). But you have been warned, and you have heard the true doctrine taught. ("Our Relationship with the Lord," BYU Devotional, 2 March 1982.)

What Think Ye of Salvation by Grace?

The "New" Reformation

I wonder how many of us are aware of one of the great religious phenomenon of the ages, one that is now sweeping through Protestant Christianity, as only one other thing has ever done in the whole Christian Era?

We are silent witnesses of an almost worldwide religious craze that had its birth in the minds of a few great religious reformers nearly five hundred years ago and which is now receiving a new birth of freedom and influence.

May I divorce myself for the moment from the mainstream of present-day evangelical Christanity, swim upstream as it were, and give forth some rather plain and pointed expressions on this supposedly marvelous means of being saved with very slight effort?

But before zeroing in on this religious mania that has now taken possession of millions of devout but deluded people, and as a means of keeping all things in perspective, let me first identify the original heresy that did more than anything else to destroy primitive Christianity.

This first and chief heresy of a now fallen and decadent Christianity — and truly it is the father of all heresies — swept through all of the congregations of true believers in the early centuries of the Christian era; it pertained then and pertains now to the nature and kind of being that God is.

It was the doctrine, adapted from Gnosticism, that changed Christianity from the religion in which men worshipped a personal God, in whose image man is made (Gen. 1:26–27; James 3:9; Mosiah 7:27; Ether 3:15; D&C 20:18; Moses 6:8–9), into a religion in which men worshipped a spirit essence called the Trinity. This new God, no longer a personal Father, no longer a personage of tabernacle (D&C 130:22), became an incomprehensible three-in-one spirit essence that filled the immensity of space.

The adoption of this false doctrine about God effectively destroyed true worship among men and ushered in the age of universal apostasy. The dominant church then became a political power, ruling autocratically over kingdoms and empires as well as over her own congregations (1 Ne. 13, 14). Salvation, as was then supposed, was administered by the church through the seven sacraments.

Nearly a millennium and a half later, during the sixteenth century, as the Reformation grew out of the Renaissance, as a means of breaking the hold of the dominant church, the great Christian reformers lit a new doctrinal fire. That fire, burning wildly over the dry and arid prairies of religious autocracy, is what really prepared the way for the restoration of the gospel in modern times.

"Salvation by Grace Alone" Negates Atonement

It was nonetheless the doctrinal fire—the burning, flaming, heretical fire—that became the second greatest heresy of Christendom, because it effectively destroyed the efficacy and power of the atonement of the Lord Jesus Christ by whom salvation comes.

The first great heresy, sweeping like a prairie fire through the struggling branches of a newborn Christianity, destroyed the worship of the true God. And the second, a heresy originating in the same courts of darkness, destroyed the very atonement of God's only Son.

This second heresy—and it is the prevailing delusion and mania that prevails to this day in the great evangelical body of Protestantism—is the doctrine that we are justified by faith alone, without the works of the law. It is the doctrine that we are saved by grace alone, without works. It is the doctrine that we may be born again simply by confessing the Lord Jesus with our lips while we continue to live in our sins.[1]

We have all listened to sermons by the great revivalists and self-appointed prophets of the various radio and television ministries. Whatever the subjects of their sermons may be, they invariably end with an invitation and a plea for people to come forward and confess the Lord and receive the cleansing power of his blood.

Television broadcasts of these sermons always show arenas or colosseums or stadiums filled with people, scores and hundreds and thousands of whom go forward to make their confessions, to become born-again Christians, to be saved with all they suppose this includes.

While driving along a highway in my car I was listening to the radio sermon of one of these evangelists who was preaching of salvation by grace alone. He said all anyone had to do to be saved was to believe in Christ and perform an affirmative act of confession. Among other things he said: "If you are travelling in a car, simply reach forth your hand and touch your car radio, thus making contact with me, and then say, 'Lord Jesus, I believe,' and you will be saved."

Interwoven with this concept is the doctrine that the elect of God are predestined to be saved regardless of any act on their part, which, as I suppose, is part of the reason a Lutheran minister once said to me: "I was saved two thousand years ago, and there is nothing I can do about it one way or the other now," meaning that he thought he was saved by the blood of Christ shed on Calvary, without any works or effort on his part.

Luther's Motive in Accepting "Grace Alone"

Here is an account of how Martin Luther himself came to believe the doctrine of justification by faith alone; it is an ideal illustration of why this doctrine has such wide appeal.

A friendly biographer tells us: Luther "was much concerned about his personal salvation and given to gloomy reflections over his sinful condition," so much so that "he fell dangerously ill, and was seized with a fit of despair."

Also: "No one surpassed him in prayer, fasting, night watches, self-mortification. He was . . . a model of sanctity. But . . . he found no peace and rest in all his pious exercises. . . . He saw sin everywhere. . . . He could not trust in God as a reconciled Father, as a God of love and mercy, but trembled before him, as a God of wrath, as a consuming fire. . . . It was sin as an all-pervading power and vitiating principle, sin as a corruption of nature, sin as an alienation from God and hostility to God, that weighed on his mind like an incubus and brought him to the brink of despair."

While in this state he gained "the conviction that the sinner is justified by faith alone, without the works of the law. . . . This experience acted like a new revelation on Luther. It shed light upon the whole Bible and made it to him a book of life and comfort. He felt relieved of the terrible load of guilt by an act of free grace. He was led out of the dark prison house of self-inflicted penance into the daylight and fresh air of God's redeeming love. Justification broke the fetters of legalistic slavery, and filled him with the joy and peace of the state of adoption; it opened to him the very gates of heaven." (Philip Schaff, *History of the Christian Church* [New York: Charles Scribner's & Sons, reprinted, 1980], 7:111, 116–17, 122–24.) So says Luther's biographer.

It should be perfectly clear to all of us that Luther's break with Catholicism was part of the divine program; it came as an Elias preparing the way for the Restoration. But this does not in any sense put a stamp of divine approval on the doctrine he devised to justify the break in his own mind.

Few Accept "Strait and Narrow Way"

Now, let us reason together on this matter of being saved without the need to do the works of righteousness. Did you ever wonder why our missionaries convert one of a city and two of a family while the preachers of this doctrine of salvation by grace alone gain millions of converts? (Jer. 3:14; 1 Ne. 14:12.)

Does it seem strange to you that we wear out our lives in bringing one soul unto Christ, that we may have joy with him in the kingdom of the Father, while our evangelist colleagues cannot even count their converts so great is their number? Why are those who come to hear the message of the Restoration numbered in the hundreds *and* thousands, rather than in the hundreds *of* thousands?

May I suggest that the difference is between the strait and narrow way,[2] which few find, and the broad way, "that leadeth unto destruction, and many there be which go in thereat" (Matt. 7:13).

All men must have and do have some way of worship—call it Christianity or communism or Buddhism or atheism, or the wandering ways of Islam. I repeat: All men must and do worship; this inclination is given them by their Creator as a natural gift and endowment. The Light of Christ is shed forth upon all mankind (D&C 84:44–46; 88:7–13; 93:2; John 1:9); all men have a conscience and know by instinct the difference between good and evil (Moro.

7:12–19); it is inherent in the human personality to seek and worship a divine being of some sort.

As we are aware, since the Fall all men have become carnal, sensual, and devilish by nature; they have become worldly; and their inclination is to live after the manner of the flesh and satisfy their lusts and appetites (Mosiah 3:19; 16:3; 1 Cor. 2:11–14; Gal. 5:19–21). Accordingly, anytime men can devise a system of worship that will let them continue to live after the manner of the world, to live in their carnal and fallen state, and at the same time one which will satisfy their innate and instinctive desires to worship, such, to them, is a marvelous achievement.

True Doctrine of Salvation by Grace

Now, there is a true doctrine of salvation by grace—a salvation by grace alone and without works, as the scriptures say. To understand this doctrine we must define our terms as they are defined in holy writ.

1. What is salvation? It is both immortality and eternal life (D&C 29:43; 2 Ne. 9:22–24). It is an inheritance in the highest heaven of the celestial world (D&C 131:1–4; 132). It consists of the fulness of the glory of the Father and is reserved for those for whom the family unit continues in eternity (D&C 132:19). Those who are saved become as God is and live as he lives (Rom. 8:13–18; Rev. 21:7; 3 Ne. 28:10; D&C 84:31–38; 132:18–20).

2. What is the plan of salvation? It is the system ordained by the Father to enable his spirit children to advance and progress and become like him (Moses 4:1–4; Abr. 3:22–28). It consists of three great and eternal verities—the Creation, the Fall, and the Atonement—without any one of which there could be no salvation.

3. What is the grace of God? It is his mercy, his love, and his condescension—all manifest for the benefit and blessing of his children, all operating to bring to pass the immortality and eternal life of man.

We rejoice in the heavenly condescension that enabled Mary to become "the mother of the Son of God, after the manner of the flesh" (1 Ne. 11:18). We bask in the eternal love that sent the Only Begotten into the world, "that whosoever believeth in him should not perish, but have everlasting life" (John 3:16). We are profoundly grateful for that mercy which endureth forever (1 Chr. 16:34, 41; 2 Chr. 5:13; 7:3, 6; Ezra 3:11; Ps. 106:11; 107:1; 118:1–4; 136) and through which salvation is offered to erring mortals.

How Salvation Is a Free Gift

In his goodness and grace the great God ordained and established the plan of salvation. No works on our part were required. In his goodness and grace he created this earth and all that it is (Col. 1:16–17; Heb. 2:10; D&C 93:9–10), with man as the crowning creature of his creating—without which creation his spirit children could not obtain immortality and eternal life. No works on our part were required. In his goodness and grace he provided for the fall of man, thus bringing mortality and death and a probationary estate into being—without all of which there would be no immortality and eternal life (2 Ne. 2; 9; Alma 42; D&C 29:40–42). And again no works on our part were required. In his goodness and grace—and this above all—he gave his Only Begotten Son to ransom man and all life from the temporal and spiritual death brought into the world by the fall of Adam. He sent his Son to redeem mankind, to atone for the sins of the world, to bring to pass the immortality and eternal life of man (3 Ne. 27:13–16). And again, all this comes to us as a free gift and without works.

There is nothing any man could do to create himself. This was the work of the Lord God. Nor did we have any part in the fall of man, without which there would be no salvation. The Lord provided the way and Adam and Eve put the system into operation. And finally, there neither has been, nor is, nor can be any way or means by which man alone, by any power he possesses, can redeem himself.

We cannot resurrect ourselves anymore than we can create ourselves. We cannot create a heavenly abode for the Saints, or make provision for the continuation of the family unit in eternity, or bring salvation and exaltation into being. All these things are ordained and established by that God who is the Father of us all. And they all came into being, and are made available to us, as free gifts, without works, because of the infinite goodness and grace of him whose children we are.

Truly, there is no way to overstate the goodness and grandeurs and glories of the grace of God which bringeth salvation. Such wondrous love, such unending mercy, such infinite compassion and condescension—all these can come only from the Eternal God who lives in eternal life and who desires all of his children to live as he lives and be inheritors of eternal life.

Paul's Context for "Salvation by Grace"

Knowing these things, as did Paul and our fellow Apostles of old, let us put ourselves in their position. What words shall we choose, to offer to the world the blessings of a freely given atoning sacrifice?

On the one hand we are preaching to Jews who in their lost and fallen state have rejected their Messiah and who believe they are saved by the works and performances of the Mosaic law (Gal. 2:15–16).

On the other hand we are preaching to pagans—Romans, Greeks, those in every nation—who know nothing whatever about the messianic word, or of the need for a Redeemer, or of the working out of the infinite and eternal atonement. They worship idols, the forces of nature, the heavenly bodies, or whatever suits their fancy. As with the Jews, they assume that this or that sacrifice or appeasing act will please the deity of their choice and some vague and unspecified blessings will result.

Can either the Jews or the pagans be left to assume that the works they do will save them? Or must they forget their little grovelling acts of petty worship, gain faith in Christ, and rely on the cleansing power of his blood for salvation?

They must be taught faith in the Lord Jesus Christ and to forsake their traditions and performances. Surely we must tell them they cannot be saved by the works they are doing, for man cannot save himself. Instead they must turn to Christ and rely on his merits and mercy and grace.

Book of Mormon Clarifies Teachings on Salvation by Grace

Abinadi struggled with this same problem in his contentions with the priests and people of Noah. They had the law of Moses, with its various rites and performances, but they knew nothing of the Atoning One. And so Abinadi asked: "Doth salvation come by the law of Moses? What say ye? And they answered and said that salvation did come by the law of Moses." (Mosiah 12:31–32.)

After teaching them some of the great truths of salvation, Abinadi answered his own question: "Salvation doth not come by the law alone," he said; "and were it not for the atonement, which God himself shall make for the sins and iniquities of his people, that they must unavoidably perish, notwithstanding the law of Moses"

(Mosiah 13:28). Salvation is not in works—not even in those revealed of God—but in Christ and his atonement.

A Modern Application

Now let us suppose a modern case. Suppose we have the scriptures, the gospel, the priesthood, the Church, the ordinances, the organization, even the keys of the kingdom—everything that now is, down to the last jot and tittle—and yet there is no atonement of Christ. What then? Can we be saved? Will all our good works save us? Will we be rewarded for all our righteousness?

Most assuredly we will not. We are not saved by works alone, no matter how good; we are saved because God sent his Son to shed his blood in Gethsemane and on Calvary that all through him might ransomed be. We are saved by the blood of Christ (Acts 20:28; 1 Cor. 6:20).

To paraphrase Abinadi: "Salvation doth not come by the Church alone; and were it not for the atonement, given by the grace of God as a free gift, all men must unavoidably perish, and this notwithstanding the Church and all that appertains to it."

True Doctrine of Grace and Works

Let us now come to the matter of whether we must do something to gain the blessings of the Atonement in our lives. And we find the answer written in words of fire and emblazoned across the whole heavens; we hear a voice speaking with the sound of ten thousand trumpets; the very heavens and the earth are moved out of their place, so powerful is the word that goes forth. It is a message that neither men nor angels nor the Gods themselves can proclaim with an undue emphasis.

This is the word: Man cannot be saved by grace alone; as the Lord lives, man must keep the commandments (Eccl. 12:13; Matt. 19:17; 1 Ne. 22:31; D&C 93:20); he must work the works of righteousness (Matt. 7:21; James 2:18–26; D&C 78:5–7); he must work out his salvation with fear and trembling before the Lord (Philip. 2:12); he must have faith like the ancients—the faith that brings with it gifts and signs and miracles.

Does it suffice to believe and be baptized without more? The answer is no, in every language and tongue. Rather, after belief, after repentance, after baptism, "Ye must press forward with a steadfastness in Christ, having a perfect brightness of hope, and a love of God and of all men. Wherefore, if ye shall press forward, feasting upon the word of Christ, and endure to the end, behold, thus saith the Father: Ye shall have eternal life. And now, behold, . . . this is the way; and there is none other way nor name given under heaven whereby man can be saved in the kingdom of God." (2 Ne. 31:20–21.)

John the Beloved Apostle promises the Saints eternal life with the Father on this condition: "If we walk in the light, as he is in the light, we have fellowship one with another, and the blood of Jesus Christ his Son cleanseth us from all sin" (1 John 1:7). The blood of Christ was shed as a free gift of wondrous grace, but the Saints are cleansed by the blood after they keep the commandments.

Nowhere has this ever been taught better than in these words of the risen Lord to his Nephite brethren: "And no unclean thing can enter into his kingdom; therefore nothing entereth into his rest save it be those who have washed their garments in my blood, because of their faith, and the repentance of all their sins, and their faithfulness unto the end. Now this is the commandment: Repent, all ye ends of the earth, and come unto me and be baptized in my name, that ye may be sanctified by the reception of the Holy Ghost, that ye may stand spotless before me at the last day. Verily, verily, I say unto you, this is my gospel; and ye know the things that ye must do in my church; for the works which ye have seen me do that shall ye also do; for that which ye have seen me do even that shall ye do; Therefore, if ye do these things blessed are ye, for ye shall be lifted up at the last day." (3 Ne. 27:19–22.)

Men must be doers of the word, not hearers only; they must do the very works that Christ did (2 Ne. 31:10; 3 Ne. 27:21–22); and those who have true and saving faith in him accomplish this very end.

In our day, among other Christians at least, we are not faced with the problems of our predecessors. They had to show that any works then being performed were of no avail without the Atonement; that salvation was in Christ and his spilt blood; and that all men must come unto him to be saved.

Our need in today's world, in which Christians assume there was an atonement, is to interpret the scripture properly and to call upon men to keep the commandments so as to become worthy of the cleansing power of the blood of the Lamb.

Hear then the word of the Lord Jesus: "Not every one that saith unto me, Lord, Lord, shall enter into the kingdom of heaven; but he that doeth the will of my Father which is in heaven" (Matt. 7:21).

And it is the will of the Father — as a great many scriptures attest — that all men everywhere must endure to the end, must keep the commandments, must work out their salvation with fear and trembling before the Lord, or they can in no wise enter into the kingdom of heaven.

How well Nephi said: "Believe in Christ, and . . . be reconciled to God; for we know that it is by grace that we are saved, after all we can do" (2 Ne. 25:23).

Sectarian Notions of "Grace Alone" Pervert Divine Intent

Salvation by grace alone and without works, as it is taught in large segments of Christendom today, is akin to what Lucifer proposed in the preexistence — that he would save all mankind, and one soul should not be lost. He would save them without agency, without works, without any act on their part. (Moses 1:1; D&C 29:36.)

As with the proposal of Lucifer in preexistence to save all mankind, so with the doctrine of salvation by grace alone, without works, as it is taught in modern Christendom — both concepts are false. There is no salvation in either of them. They both come from the same source; they are not of God.

We believe and proclaim that it is life eternal to know the only wise and true God and Jesus Christ whom he has sent (John 17:3). Let men worship whomsoever they will, but there is no salvation in worshipping any God but the true God.

We believe and proclaim that salvation is in Christ, in his gospel, in his atoning sacrifice (2 Ne. 31:21; Mosiah 4:8; Acts 4:12). We are bold to say it comes by the goodness and grace of the Father and the Son. No people on earth praise the Lord with greater faith and fervor than we do because of this goodness and grace.

As the Lord's agents, as his servants, as ambassadors of Christ — sent by him; sent to speak in his place and stead; sent to say what he would say if he personally were here — we testify that no man, as long as the earth shall stand, or the heavens endure, or God continues as God, no man shall ever be saved in the kingdom of God, in the celestial kingdom of heaven, without doing the works of righteousness.

What We Must Do to Be Saved

As far as man is concerned, the great and eternal plan of salvation is:

1. Faith in the Lord Jesus Christ; faith in him as the Son of God; faith in him as the Savior and Redeemer who shed his blood for us in Gethsemane and on Calvary.
2. Repentance of all our sins—thus forsaking the world and its carnal course; thus turning from the broad way that leads to destruction; thus preparing for the spiritual rebirth into the kingdom of God;
3. Baptism by immersion for the remission of sins; baptism under the hands of a legal administrator who has power to bind on earth and seal in heaven—thus planting our feet firmly on the strait and narrow path leading to eternal life;
4. Receiving the gift of the Holy Ghost—thus enabling us to be baptized with fire; to have sin and evil burned out of our souls as though by fire; to be sanctified so as to stand pure and spotless before the Lord at the last day; and
5. Enduring to the end in righteousness, keeping the commandments, and living by every word that proceedeth forth from the mouth of God.

Thus saith the Lord: "He who doeth the works of righteousness shall receive his reward, even peace in this world, and eternal life in the world to come" (D&C 59:23).

As God is true, as Christ is the Savior, and the Holy Ghost is their minister and witness, such is the plan of salvation, and there is not nor ever shall be any other.

Let those in the world think and act as they please; let us, the Saints of God who know better, together with all who are willing to live by the higher standard of the gospel, praise the Lord for his goodness and grace and do so by keeping his commandments, thereby becoming heirs of eternal life. ("What Think Ye of Salvation by Grace?" BYU Devotional, 10 January 1984.)

Notes

1. One reason why a man may not be born again by the simple confession that Jesus is Lord is that the process of spiritual rebirth includes receiving the ordinances of salvation. Joseph Smith said: "Being born again, comes by the Spirit of God through ordinances" (*Teachings*, p. 162). One sign which the Lord gave the early brethren by which they would know if people were accepted of God was

whether or not they accepted and obeyed his ordinances (D&C 52:15–16). "The question is frequently asked," said Joseph Smith, " 'Can we not be saved without going through with all the ordinances?' I would answer, No, not the fulness of salvation." (*Teachings*, p. 331.) Indeed, baptism is the initiatory ordinance betokening repentance and a willingness to keep the commandments; nevertheless, no one is saved without additional ordinances, such as, for example, the endowment and temple marriage.

2. Elder McConkie's words here are well chosen. As he himself has noted: "The course leading to eternal life is both *strait* and *straight*. It is *straight* because it has an invariable direction — always it is the same. There are no diversions, crooked paths, or tangents leading to the kingdom of God. It is *strait* because it is narrow and restricted, a course where full obedience to the full law is required. Straightness has reference to direction, straitness to width. The gate is *strait*; the path is both *strait* and *straight*. (2 Ne. 9:41; 31:9, 17–18; 33:9; Alma 37:44–45; Hel. 3:29–30; 3 Ne. 14:13–14; 27:33; D&C 22; 132:22; Matt. 7:13–14; Luke 13:23–24; Heb. 12:13; Jer. 31:9.)" (*Mormon Doctrine*, p. 769.)

Chapter 4

CHRIST REVEALED
THROUGH HIS PROPHETS

Christ and His Prophets Are One

To Accept Christ, We Must Accept His Servants

Christ and his prophets go together. They cannot be separated. It is utterly and completely impossible to believe in Christ without also believing in and accepting the divine commission of the prophets sent to reveal him and to carry his saving truths to the world. (D&C 1:38; 21:4–5; 84:36; 3 Ne. 28:34; Ether 4:10; Matt. 10:40–41.)

No one today would say: "I will believe in Christ, but will not believe in Peter, James, and John and their testimony of him." In the very nature of things belief in Christ is more than accepting him as a single person standing alone, as one person independent of any other. Belief in Christ presupposes and includes within it the acceptance of the prophets who reveal him to the world.

Jesus said: "He that receiveth whomsoever I send receiveth me" (John 13:20). Also: "He that heareth you heareth me; and he that despiseth you despiseth me" (Luke 10:16).

To believe in Christ we must not only accept the prophets who reveal him, but we must also believe the scriptural accounts recorded by those prophets. Jesus said to a Book of Mormon prophet: "He that will not believe my words will not believe me—that I am" (Ether 4:12), meaning that he will not believe that I exist and am the Son of God.

Nephi, another Book of Mormon prophet, invited all men to "believe in Christ. And if ye shall believe in Christ," he said, "ye will believe in these words [that is, the Book of Mormon account], for they are the words of Christ, and he hath given them unto me." (2 Ne. 33:10.)

But even the very scriptures themselves can only be interpreted with surety when the spirit of prophecy is present, as Peter said: "No prophecy of the scripture is of any private interpretation. For the prophecy came not in old time by the will of man; but holy men of God spake as they were moved by the Holy Ghost." (2 Pet. 1:20–21.)

Prophets gave the scripture, and prophets must interpret it. Holy men of old received revelation from the Holy Ghost, which they recorded as scripture; now men must have the same Holy Spirit to reveal what is meant by the scripture—otherwise there will be a host of private interpretations and consequently many different and disagreeing churches, which is precisely the condition in the religious world today. (Conference Report, October 1964.)

We could not believe in Christ if there were not prophets to declare Christ and his saving truths unto us. The Apostle Paul reasoned on this subject, and he said: "How shall they believe in him of whom they have not heard? and how shall they hear without a preacher? And how shall they preach, except they be sent?" (Rom. 10:14–15.)

Except for Christ, there would be no salvation. Except for the prophets of God, sent in the various ages of the earth's history, the testimony of Christ would not be borne, the message of salvation would not be taught, and there would be no legal administrators who could perform the ordinances of salvation for men, that is, perform them so they will be binding on earth and sealed eternally in the heavens.

So it is that the Lord has sent prophets. No one would suppose that he could believe in Christ and reject the prophets. The Lord and his prophets go hand in hand. Christ said: "I am the true vine, and my Father is the husbandman"; then he said to his Apostles, "Ye are the branches." (John 15:1, 5.) The branches and the vine are connected. He also taught that if the branches were torn away from him, they would wither and die and be cast into the fire. If people in the world would pick the fruit of eternal life off the branches, they have to accept the prophets, for the branches are the prophets.

Saints Acknowledge God's Prophets in Every Dispensation

This has been the system that the Lord has had from the days of father Adam to the present moment, and it will continue eternally. The Lord sent Adam in the beginning to teach the principles of salvation (Moses 5:58–59; 6:1). Adam had a dispensation of the gospel, that is, the Lord revealed direct from heaven to Adam, dispensed to him the saving truths; and anybody that lived in the days of Adam, to be saved in the celestial kingdom, had to accept Jesus Christ in whom salvation lay, and also had to accept Adam as the revealer, the prophet, the legal administrator who taught the laws of salvation and administered the ordinances thereof. It went in just that manner in every succeeding dispensation.

In the days of Enoch, if a man would be saved in the celestial kingdom, he accepted Christ as the Savior of the world and Enoch as his prophet. And so in the days of Abraham, of Moses, of Peter, James and John, and of this day.

I suppose that the Church procedure was not too different in former days. They had testimony meetings then, and when people stood up in them, as they were moved upon by the Holy Ghost, they bore witness that Jesus Christ was the Son of God who would come, and that Adam was his prophet, or Enoch, or the head of whatever dispensation was involved; and that is the way it is today. We certify of Jesus Christ, and we certify of Joseph Smith, and they are one. They are unified perfectly. (D&C 84:36–38.) (Conference Report, October 1951.)

God Operates Through Prophets

In other words, if we "call upon the name of the Lord," if we confess the Lord Jesus with the mouth, if we believe in our hearts "that God hath raised him from the dead," it is because we first believe and accept the testimony of the Apostle or prophet who is sent of God to give us the knowledge of salvation.

It is not the Lord's program to appear personally to every man and to tell him what to believe and how to act to be saved. But it is the Lord's program to send legal administrators endowed with power from on high, to send prophets and Apostles to teach his truths and perform the ordinances of salvation.

Paul was one of these. Since he was sent to the Romans, that nation was required to accept him as an Apostle in order to accept Christ as the Savior. If they believed in Paul's divine commission, they could then believe his testimony about Christ and the saving truths of his gospel. If they believed in Christ and accepted him as the Son of God, they of necessity had to believe that Paul was an Apostle, for he was the preacher sent to them to reveal the truth about Christ and the gospel. (Conference Report, October 1964.)

Abraham Saw God's Prophets

Now may I mention the great vision that the patriarch Abraham had? You recall that the Lord showed him the preexistent hosts and, more particularly, the noble and great in that world. Abraham saw them, the intelligences, the spirit sons of God our Father, the noble and great spirits who were among them, and the Lord said to him, "Abraham, thou art one of them; thou wast chosen before thou wast born" (Abr. 3:23).

The Place of Joseph Smith in the Eternal Schema

As with Abraham, so with all the prophets of God. Sometimes someone may wonder (that is, someone in the world) how is it that the Father and the Son would appear to a fourteen-and-a-half-year-old boy in the spring of 1820, to usher in, as we express it, the dispensation of the fulness of times?

Joseph Smith sat with father Abraham in the councils of eternity, and Joseph Smith was ordained as Abraham was ordained to come down and be the head of a gospel dispensation here. He had ascended by virtue of obedience, intelligence, progression, and righteousness to a high state of spiritual perfection in that world. When he came here, he brought with him the talents and abilities, the deep spirituality, and the innate righteousness that he developed back there under the tutelage of God the Father.

In the eternal worlds, the firstborn spirit offspring of the Father was Jehovah, who is Christ (Abr. 2:7-8; JST Ex. 6:3; Ps. 83:18; Isa. 12:2; 26:4, 19; D&C 110:1-10; Moro. 10:34). He was preeminent (Abr. 3:24, 27). Standing next to Christ was the great spirit, Michael (*Teachings*, p. 157). Christ was ordained as a lamb slain from the foundation of the world (Rev. 13:8), chosen to come here and be the Redeemer. Michael was prepared and chosen and sent here as father Adam, the first man of all men, the first flesh upon the earth (Moses 3:7), the head of the human race, and the presiding high priest, under Christ, over all the earth.

The spirit men who were associated with Christ and with Adam in all the preexistent eternities, and who were more valiant than all their fellows, were the ones chosen to head the various dispensations of the gospel. One of these was the Prophet Joseph Smith. It doesn't take much reflection then, . . . for us to know that Joseph Smith was one of the dozen greatest spirits that God the Eternal Father had in all the councils of eternity; that he came so as to be here at the appointed time and at the express hour and at the very moment that the Lord designed to open this dispensation. He was here to take part in that event.

I do not think that the Father and the Son would have appeared to an ordinary fourteen-and-a-half-year-old boy, if he had gone out into that grove of trees to ask the Lord which of all the churches was right. . . . The Lord had been preparing Joseph Smith for that event from all eternity. . . . Joseph Smith had the spiritual stature, the strength for righteousness that enabled him to endure the vision; he had the talent and ability to press forward in righteousness in the kingdom of God on earth: first, to establish it; and then, somewhat, to perfect its organization before he was taken home, before he sealed his testimony with his blood.

Christ and his prophets are one; and salvation in this day is, first, through Christ and his atoning sacrifice, and it is, second, through accepting the atoning sacrifice and the doctrines of Christ as they have been revealed by the Prophet Joseph Smith, and as they are taught by the living oracles who wear the mantle of the Prophet and stand at this moment at the head of the kingdom of God on earth.

Personal Knowledge of Living Prophets

May I just tell you one experience that I had? I have never told this to any person before, except my wife. Six months ago [April, 1951] in the solemn assembly, when the First Presidency of the Church were sustained, as I sat down here behind one of these lower pulpits, the voice of the Lord came into my mind as certainly, I am sure, as the voice of the Lord came into the mind of Enos, and the very words were formed, and it said: "These are they whom I have chosen as the First Presidency of my Church. Follow them" — those few words.

I have had a testimony of the divinity of this work from my youth. I was reared in a home where love was the motive force, where my parents taught me righteousness, and I have grown up with a testimony. But that witness was an added assurance. It meant to me that this is the Lord's Church; that his hand is over it; that he organized it; that these men who preside are called of him; that they are his anointed; that if we will follow them as they follow Christ, we will have eternal life. (Conference Report, October 1951.)

False Prophets Proclaim False Christs

People everywhere today are hearing voices, strange voices enticing them to follow bye and forbidden paths which lead to destruction. Nowhere is this more evident than in the pleading tones of that chorus of discordant voices which speak of the Savior of the world himself.

There are voices crying, "Lo, here is Christ" or "Lo there" — meaning that various preachers are saying: "Believe in Christ, and be saved according to this system" or "according to that system."

A voice from the Koran acclaims Jesus as a prophet like Abraham and Moses, but sweeps aside the divine sonship with the declaration that Allah has no need for a son to redeem men; rather, he has but to speak and a thing is done.

A voice from one sect, looking back to the cross, says: "We were saved two thousand years ago, and there is nothing we can do about it one way or the other now."

Another voice proclaims: "Baptism is of no moment: simply believe; confess the Lord with your lips; no more is needed; Christ did it all."

Another sect sets aside the need for good works with the assertion that there will be a final harmony of all souls with God—all will be saved.

Another sings out about confession, and penance, and purgatory, and the ritualistic rites of a priestly hierarchy. Another says our Lord was a great moral teacher, nothing more. Others believe the virgin birth was only a pious fiction fabricated by simple disciples who also made up the accounts of the miracles.

And so it goes; all sects, parties, and denominations acclaim a Christ molded to fit their diverse theological idiosyncrasies. And as we know, this very babble of voices crying out that salvation comes through Christ, according to this or that conflicting system, is itself one of the signs of the times.

Jesus foretold that in our day there would be false Christs and false prophets, meaning that false religions bearing his name would arise, and that false doctrines and false teachers would be everywhere (Matt. 24:5, 11, 23–24; JS—M 1:5–6, 9, 21–22).

Ours the Lone Voice of Truth

Amid it may we raise the one voice which echoes the mind and will and voice of the Lord. Our voice is one which testifies of a true and living Christ; it is one which says that the Lord Jesus has revealed himself and his gospel anew in modern times; it is a voice which invites all men to come to him who died on Calvary, and to live his laws as he has given them to modern prophets. (Conference Report, April 1977.)

Our Commission to Testify of Christ

Our Mission One of Testimony

As I understand it, our mission to the world in this day is to testify of Jesus Christ. Our mission is to bear record that he is the Son of the Living God and that he was crucified for the sins of the world; that salvation was, and is, and is to come, in and through his atoning blood; that by virtue of his atonement all men will be raised in immortality, and those who believe and obey the gospel law both in immortality and eternal life.

And the position which Joseph Smith holds in the scheme of things is that he is the chiefest witness of Christ that there has been in this world since the Son of God personally walked among men and bore record of himself saying, "I am the Son of God" (Matt. 27:43; John 10:36).

All Facets of Gospel Testify of Christ

We believe, and I certify, that Jesus Christ is the Firstborn spirit child of Elohim who is God, our Heavenly Father. We believe that while he lived in the preexistent world, by virtue of his superior intelligence, progression, and obedience, he attained unto the station of a God. And he then became, under the Father, the creator of this world and all things that are in it, as also the creator of worlds without number.

We believe that he was the Jehovah of the Old Testament; that it was through him that God the Father dealt with all the ancient prophets, revealing his mind and his will and the plan of salvation to them.

Christ gave the gospel to the ancients beginning with Adam and going on down, dispensation after dispensation, until this present time. And everything that has been given in the gospel and everything that has been in any way connected with it has been designed for the express purpose of bearing record of Christ and certifying as to his divine mission.

Sacrifices in Similitude of Son of God

From Adam to Moses and from Moses to Christ, God's prophets and priests offered sacrifices. Such were in the similitude of the
sacrifice of the Only Begotten of the Father who was to come. (Ex.
12; Moses 5:5-8; Alma 34:10-14.) When Moses lifted the serpent
on the pole in ancient Israel and told the Israelites that those who
would look would live when they were bitten by poisonous serpents, it was in similitude of the fact that the Son of God would be
lifted up on the cross and that all who would look to him might live
eternally (Num. 21:8-9; John 3:14; Alma 33:19-22).

Gospel Ordinances Center Attention in Christ

Every ordinance of the gospel is designed to point and center
the attention of men in Christ. We are baptized in similitude of the
death, burial, and resurrection. (Rom. 6:3-5.) We honor Sunday as
the Sabbath because it was on that day when he arose from the
grave (Acts 20:7), breaking the bands of death and becoming the
first fruits of them that slept (1 Cor. 15:20). The ancients honored
the seventh day as one of rest and worship because it was on that
day that he rested from his labors after working under the direction
of his Father in the creation of this world (Ex. 20:8-11). In fact,
Jacob says: "All things which have been given of God from the beginning of the world, unto man, are the typifying of him" (2 Ne.
11:4).

Every prophet that there has been in the world has borne record that he is the Son of God (Acts 10:43), because in its very nature
that is the chief calling of a prophet. The testimony of Jesus is
synonymous with the spirit of prophecy (Rev. 19:10).

By Covenant We Are His Witnesses

When Latter-day Saints pass through the waters of baptism, it
is with a covenant that we will stand as witnesses of Christ at all
times and in all things, and in all places that we may be in, even
until death, that we may be redeemed of God, numbered with
those of the first resurrection, and gain eternal life, by which we
mean life in the celestial kingdom of heaven. One of our revelations
says that it becometh every man who hath been warned to warn
his neighbor (D&C 88:81). That is our responsibility.

We Testify Through Word and Deed

It is not always a matter of just saying in so many words that these things are true. First of all, I think we bear witness of Christ in the life we live, by letting our light shine and by letting the gospel principles speak through us (Matt. 5:13–16; 2 Tim. 4:12). If we can get the love, charity, integrity, humility, and virtue that are part of the gospel into our lives so that others may see our good works, we are by that fact testifying of the fruits of Mormonism, of the fact of the restoration of the gospel, and of the divinity of Jesus Christ whose hand is in this work. (Conference Report, October 1948.)

The Mission of the Holy Ghost

INTRODUCTION TO PART II

The witness of the Holy Ghost is central to our entire religious structure: we measure our doctrine, perform our ordinances, judge our worthiness, make our decisions and our covenants, and exercise spiritual gifts, all by the power of the Holy Ghost. The quality of our worship—the very quality of our lives!—depends on our ability to receive and respond to the promptings and whisperings of the Holy Ghost. Indeed, faith itself is a gift which comes from and is nourished by the Holy Ghost (1 Cor. 12:9); similarly, repentance is a gift of the Holy Ghost, no baptism is acceptable to God unless sealed and accepted by the Holy Ghost, and the divine command, in effect, is to live by the power of the Holy Ghost, which is the power of revelation, and of testimony, and is the ability to live not "by bread alone, but by every word that proceedeth out of the mouth of God" (Matt. 4:4). To walk "in holiness before the Lord" (D&C 20:69) is to live by the spirit of inspiration; it is to receive revelation.

Obviously, to understand the mission of the Holy Ghost we must distinguish between the different meanings attached to the phrases "the Holy Ghost," "the Holy Spirit," "the Spirit of God," "the Spirit of Christ," "the Light of Christ," and other expressions. Chapter 5 begins with such definitional clarifications, and shows that in order to understand what the Lord means, we must understand the scriptural context in which he speaks and have a basic understanding of the principles involved in the mission of the Holy Ghost and of the Light of Christ so that we read no improper meanings into the words and phrases used in the scriptures.

But it is still not enough to have an intellectual understanding of the meaning of the words and the phrases which the Lord uses. The purpose of mortality is to see if we will live so as to experience the companionship—that is, hear the voice—of the Holy Ghost, for, as

Elder McConkie notes, His voice is the voice of the Lord. Thus Elder McConkie testifies that because of the Restoration, the Holy Ghost speaks again in our day, endowing men with the same powers, gifts, understanding, and experiences possessed by any of the ancient Saints. This is the great evidence that the work is true.

Of all the revelations given by the Holy Ghost, the most important is that which enables one "to know that Jesus Christ is the Son of God, and that he was crucified for the sins of the world" (D&C 46:13). This is the testimony of Jesus, and comes only by the power of the Holy Ghost. Since the days of the Prophet Joseph Smith, we have known that it was upon the rock of revelation that Jesus built his kingdom (see *Teachings*, p. 274); Elder McConkie adds that this means more than Apostles and prophets receiving revelation to guide the affairs of the Church. In addition, it means, specifically, individuals obtaining the testimony of Jesus in the same way Peter did: by the power of the Holy Ghost. This knowledge is the rock foundation upon which the kingdom is built. Chapter 6, then, illustrates the importance of this particular testimony: men and women can be saved if they have never spoken in tongues, raised the dead, discerned an evil spirit or performed some particular miracle. But none will be saved without the testimony of Jesus. And again, how do we prove that our testimony is true, that Jesus is the Christ, that Joseph Smith was a Prophet, or that any other spiritual reality is in fact true? By the power of the Holy Ghost; by the power of Spirit-borne testimony.

The experiences of Peter illustrate this truth. They also illustrate that spiritual growth and development, like being born again, becoming sanctified and becoming converted, are processes which take place over time; they are not events which happen of a sudden.

The Lord ordained prayer (chapter 7) for many reasons, none more important than that of bringing the Holy Ghost into our lives. But *how* do we pray? Joseph Smith taught that if you want to be saved, you do what a saved person did, and he pointed to Christ as "the prototype or standard of . . . a saved being" (*Lectures on Faith*, p. 63). Thus we study how Jesus prayed, and we imitate the same process in our own prayers. "Follow thou me," (2 Ne. 31:10) Jesus commanded, and added: "The works which ye have seen me do that shall ye also do; for that which ye have seen me do even that shall ye do" (3 Ne. 27:21).

How could we do better than to pray as Jesus prayed? Elder McConkie analyzes, in part, the great intercessory prayer, and then weaves together other scriptural counsel in explaining "why the Lord ordained prayer." He provides ten guidelines, which, when followed, will help us pray more as Jesus prayed.

Chapters 8 and 9 deal with obtaining answers to prayer—that is, with obtaining revelation. In chapter 8 Elder McConkie expands upon a "spiritual formula" for obtaining revelation, provides illustrations from the lives and testimonies of those who have received revelation, emphasizes that spirituality is not an office to which we are called but is the result of righteous living and that therefore all can and should receive personal revelation.

One of the most significant revelations given in this dispensation came on June 1, 1978, to President Spencer W. Kimball, in which the Lord instructed that the criteria for receiving the holy priesthood be personal worthiness, and that those of every race might be given the priesthood, conditioned only on personal worthiness. In chapter 9 we have one of the few accounts, or testimonies, written by one who was present when the voice of the Lord spoke. This account is important because it provides an apostolic view of the context into which the Lord spoke.

The pentecostal outpouring here discussed, which in importance ranks with the revelation preceding the issuance of the Manifesto in 1890 and which changes the operations of the Church both here on earth and in the spirit world, is one of the signs of the times and a renewed testimony that the Church is divinely guided. It also provides the perfect illustration of how to receive revelation. This revelation came to the President of the Church for the benefit of the Church, but the principles involved, and the things which he did to receive it, are the same as must be applied by individuals seeking personal revelation.

In reciting the events surrounding this revelation, and in providing a doctrinal context for its significance, Elder McConkie illustrates how President Kimball, his counselors, and the Twelve complied perfectly with the guidelines given in chapter 8, in compliance with which revelation comes. Thirteen faithful men—Apostles, prophets and seers—all deliberately and consistently keeping the commandments, motivated by a spirit of love, met in perfect unity of purpose, spirit, and faith, to speak with the Lord on a problem over which they had struggled for an extended period of time. They came in a spirit of worship, fasting, with a willingness to accept whatever the Lord said, pleading first for a forgiveness of sins for all. They had been involved in counsel, in testimony, in teaching one another, and in renewing their covenants in the sacrament. They had separated themselves from the thoughts, cares, and concerns of the world. They came with pure desire, and with a humble prophet as voice, offered a fervent, inspired prayer. In this setting the voice of God spoke, changing the course of history and providing an unblemished illustration of how to obtain revelation.

Chapter 5

THE MISSION
OF THE HOLY GHOST

What Is Meant by "The Holy Spirit"?

One of the most difficult of all problems of scriptural interpretation is to determine, in each instance, what is meant by the designations "Holy Spirit," "the Spirit of the Lord," "Holy Ghost," and related terms.

Scriptures using these various terms have reference to one of the following:

1. *The Holy Ghost*—a personage of spirit, a member of the Godhead; or
2. *The gift of the Holy Ghost*—the right, bestowed at the time of baptism, to receive personal revelation from and enjoy the companionship of the Holy Ghost; or
3. *The Light of Christ*—the spirit which fills the immensity of space and is everywhere present, the light which "enlighteneth" every man born into the world (D&C 84:45–47), "the influence of God's intelligence . . . the substance of his power . . . the spirit of intelligence that permeates the universe," as President Joseph F. Smith has said. (*Gospel Doctrine: Selections from the Sermons and Writings of Joseph F. Smith*, 12th ed. [Salt Lake City: Deseret News Press, 1961], p. 61. Hereafter cited as *Gospel Doctrine*.)

In some passages the term "Holy Ghost" means the Spirit entity who is one of three persons in the Godhead; in others, the inference is to the gift and not the personage.

Both the expressions "Holy Spirit" and "Spirit of the Lord" can refer to the Holy Ghost or to the Light of Christ, depending on what is intended and meant in the particular passage.

As a personage of spirit, a being in form like man, the Holy Ghost is one with the Father and the Son—one in plan and purpose, one in character, perfection, and attributes. Joseph Smith said: "The Holy Ghost is a revelator." Also: "No man can receive the Holy Ghost without receiving revelations." (*Teachings*, p. 328.)

As a revelator, the Holy Ghost has the responsibility to bear witness of the Father and the Son. He is to reveal the truth and divinity of the Lord's work to all men whether they are members of the Church or not. Thus Moroni made the promise to all men— those in the Church and those in the world—that if they would read the Book of Mormon and ask the Father in the name of Christ whether it was true, they would learn by the power of the Holy Ghost that it was (Moro. 10:3–5).

When people learn by the power of the Holy Ghost that the Lord has revealed his gospel anew, they are obligated, at the peril of losing their inheritance in the celestial kingdom, to join the Church by baptism and receive the gift of the Holy Ghost by the laying on of hands.

"There is a difference between the Holy Ghost and the gift of the Holy Ghost," the Prophet said. "Cornelius received the Holy Ghost before he was baptized, which was the convincing power of God unto him of the truth of the gospel, but he could not receive the gift of the Holy Ghost until after he was baptized" (*Teachings*, p. 199).

The gift is bestowed only by the laying on of hands. A legal administrator, who actually represents Deity, promises the newly baptized person that he, on certain terms and conditions, can gain the constant companionship of the Spirit. The gift is reserved for the Saints.

The Holy Ghost may give a flash of revelation to anyone who sincerely seeks truth, a flash comparable to lightning breaking into the darkness of a night storm. But the constant companionship of the Spirit, comparable to walking in the full blaze of the noonday sun, is reserved for those who join the Church and keep the commandments.

Those who enjoy the gift of the Holy Ghost are in the process of sanctifying their lives. The Holy Ghost is a sanctifier; when men receive the baptism of fire, evil and iniquity are burned out of their souls as though by fire.

In distinguishing between the Holy Ghost and Light of Christ, President Joseph F. Smith says: "The Holy Ghost as a personage of

Spirit can no more be omnipresent in person than can the Father or the Son, but by his intelligence, his knowledge, his power and influence, over and through the laws of nature, he is and can be omnipresent throughout all the works of God. It is not the Holy Ghost who in person lighteth every man who is born into the world, but it is the light of Christ, the Spirit of Truth, which proceeds from the source of intelligence, which permeates all nature, which lighteth every man and fills the immensity of space.'' (*Gospel Doctrine*, p. 61.)

Speaking from the perspective of eternity, eternal life is the greatest of all the gifts of God. But narrowing the perspective to this life only, the gift of the Holy Ghost is the greatest gift a mortal can enjoy.

And this gift all members of the Church are entitled to have, such endowment coming because of the covenant made in the waters of baptism. There can be no greater achievement than to live so as to enjoy the guidance and gift of the Holy Ghost. (''What Is Meant by 'The Holy Spirit'? *Instructor*, February 1965, vol. 100, No. 2, pp. 56–57.)

The Holy Ghost Is a Revelator

The Holy Ghost ''is the gift of God unto all those who diligently seek him, as well in times of old as in the time that he should manifest himself unto the children of men. For he is the same yesterday, to-day, and forever; and the way is prepared for all men from the foundation of the world, if it so be that they repent and come unto him. For he that diligently seeketh shall find; and the mysteries of God shall be unfolded unto them, by the power of the Holy Ghost, as well in these times as in times of old, and as well in times of old as in times to come; wherefore, the course of the Lord is one eternal round.'' (1 Ne. 10:17–19.)

The Father, a personage of tabernacle having flesh and bones, begat us as spirits in the beginning and ordained the plan whereby we might have power to grow in intelligence and knowledge and become like him.

The Son, his Firstborn in the spirit and Only Begotten in the flesh, under his direction became the Creator and Redeemer of the earth and all things that are on it. From time to time he has revealed to men the plan of salvation, the gospel of Jesus Christ.

The Holy Ghost, a personage of spirit, is their minister, who has been given the power and assigned the functions of bearing record of the Father and the Son, of revealing the truths of salvation to men on earth, and, in due course, of revealing to them all truth. (Conference Report, April 1953.)

The Holy Ghost the Perfect Voice of Father and Son

Just as Jesus and the Father are so much alike in appearance, and so completely united in doctrine and in all the attributes of godliness that he who has seen one has in effect seen the other, so there is a similar unity between Jesus and the Holy Ghost. They are one in that they both would say and do the same thing under the same circumstances. Hence, as long as Jesus was with the disciples in person, there was not the full need for them to have the constant companionship of the Spirit that there would be after Jesus left. The disciples had, on occasion, felt the promptings of the Spirit. Peter, for one, had received a revelation from the Father, given by the power of the Holy Ghost, certifying that Jesus was "the Christ, the Son of the living God" (Matt. 16:16). But the enjoyment of the gift of the Holy Ghost, that is, the actual and continuing companionship of that holy being, was yet future. (*DNTC* 1:753–54.)

The Holy Ghost a Revelator Even After Death

When Christ was here in his ministry, he told his Apostles that when he went away, he would send them another Comforter (John 14:16–28; 15:26–27; 16:7–14)—that is, a Comforter other than he, himself, for he was a comfort unto them—and that this Comforter would recall to their minds all things that he had told them, and would guide them into all truth. And when he said they would be guided into all truth, I believe that he meant it literally, and that in due course—not in time, but in eternity—they would obtain a fulness of truth, even as Christ himself, having gone from grace to grace, has received a fulness of truth, and a fulness of the glory of the Father.

The Holy Ghost the Greatest Gift in This Life

You will recall that in ancient Israel after Eldad and Medad had been called of God to a high calling, that his Spirit fell upon them and they prophesied in the camp. Then Joshua came before Moses and said, "My Lord Moses, forbid them." But Moses who himself had this gift of the Holy Ghost, this spirit of revelation and of prophecy—and it was by this power that he had led Israel through the Red Sea—said: "Enviest thou for my sake? would God that all the Lord's people were prophets, and that the Lord would put his spirit upon them!" (Num. 11:28-29).

There is no greater gift that a person can enjoy for himself in mortality than the gift of the Holy Ghost, which gift is the right to the constant companionship of that member of the Godhead, and which is actually enjoyed only on conditions of individual righteousness. (Conference Report, April 1953.)

The Holy Ghost Speaks the Voice of God

The Holy Ghost is a revelator. He speaks and his voice is the voice of the Lord. He is Christ's minister, his agent, his representative. He says what the Lord Jesus would say if he were personally present.

Speaking "unto all those who" are "ordained unto" his "priesthood," the Lord says: "And whatsoever they shall speak when moved upon by the Holy Ghost shall be scripture, shall be the will of the Lord, shall be the mind of the Lord, shall be the word of the Lord, shall be the voice of the Lord, and the power of God unto salvation" (D&C 68:2-4).

Truly this is that promised day when "every man might speak in the name of God the Lord, even the Savior of the world" (D&C 1:20). If all Latter-day Saints lived as they should, then Moses' petition would be granted: "Would God that all the Lord's people were prophets, and that the Lord would put his spirit upon them!" (Num. 11:29). This is the promised day when "God shall give unto" us "knowledge by his Holy Spirit," when, "by the unspeakable gift of the Holy Ghost," we shall gain knowledge "that has not been revealed since the world was until now" (D&C 121:26).

This is the day of which Joseph Smith said: "God hath not revealed anything to Joseph, but what He will make known unto the Twelve, and even the least Saint may know all things as fast as he is able to bear them" (*Teachings*, p. 149). And we look forward to that glorious millennial day when "they shall teach no more every man his neighbour, and every man his brother, saying, Know the Lord: for they shall all know me, from the least of them unto the greatest of them, saith the Lord" (Jer. 31:34). (Conference Report, October 1978.)

The Holy Ghost Speaks to Spirit of Man

The intelligent part of the human personality is the spirit that is within. As far as this body is concerned, it does not know a thing, but my spirit knows whatever it is I happen to know. The Prophet said that the mind of man is in the spirit (see *Teachings,* pp. 352–54). So any knowledge or any intelligence or any revelation that I receive has to be lodged in the spirit. I can get knowledge to my mind, or my spirit, through my senses, through touch and taste and smell. Or, I can get knowledge to my spirit through my reason, through the ability to evaluate and sort things out. My senses—my touch and my taste and my smell—can be deceived. One thing can be involved and I can think it is something else. My reason can be deluded; I can be in error in the conclusions that I reach. But there is one provision that is made for getting knowledge to the mind of man which cannot be deceived, and that is to get it by revelation from the Holy Spirit. The Holy Spirit is a personage of spirit, and the intelligent, sentient, believing, understanding part of men is a spirit entity, a child of God, to whom the Holy Spirit can speak. ("Last Message Series," University of Utah, 22 January 1971, pp. 4–5.)

Revelations Come in Many Ways

Revelations come in many ways, but they are always manifest by the power of the Holy Ghost. Jesus' promise to the ancient Apostles was: "The Comforter, which is the Holy Ghost, whom the Father will send in my name, he shall teach you all things" (John 14:26). Our modern scriptures say: "The Comforter knoweth all things, and beareth record of the Father and of the Son" (D&C 42:17). They also give us this promise: "By the power of the Holy Ghost ye may know the truth of all things" (Moro. 10:5).

When men are quickened by the power of the Spirit, the Lord can reveal his truths to them in whatever way he chooses.

The Holy Ghost Speaks Again

Seeking Knowledge About the Holy Ghost

Every religiously inclined person has at some time or other asked himself: Am I on the path to salvation? Have I been born again, born of the Spirit? Have I gained the promised baptism of fire and of the Holy Ghost?

As a matter of fact, few things are less understood in the world today than who the Holy Ghost is and how he operates upon the souls of men. Confusion about the personality of God is so prevalent that most people do not even have a clear understanding of what is meant by the Holy Spirit. And as to the gifts of the Spirit — revelation, prophecy, visions, healings, tongues, and all the rest — these are neither sought after nor accepted by most of the Christian world.

The Father and the Son, as the scriptures teach, are personages of tabernacle, exalted and perfected beings in whose images men are created. The Holy Ghost — united as one with them in plan, purpose, and perfections — is a personage of Spirit, a personage who has power to impress his will and influence upon the righteous everywhere.

Gaining the new birth of the Spirit is a personal matter. Gaining light and truth is a personal matter. Gaining the gifts of the Spirit is a personal matter. Gaining salvation itself is a personal matter. Yet to gain all of these things, a man must conform to the laws of the Lord which govern them, and an unchangeable God has decreed that these laws are the same for all people and all ages.

It is well known that the God-fearing and righteous people of Old and New Testament times conformed to the laws of the Lord and gained the gifts of the Spirit. Consequently, we now turn to those ancient scriptures for much of our knowledge about spiritual gifts and the manner in which they can be obtained.

And our search into the realm of spiritual gifts will be of transcendent importance to us, for out of it we will learn how to gain the greatest of all the gifts of God — peace in this life, and eternal life in the world to come.

The Holy Spirit Promised the Saints

In the meridian of time many devout persons gave heed to the teachings of John the Baptist, repented, and were baptized by him for the remission of sins. "I indeed baptize you with water unto repentance," he proclaimed to those who brought forth fruits meet for repentance, "but he that cometh after me is mightier than I, whose shoes I am not worthy to bear: he shall baptize you with the Holy Ghost, and with fire" (Matt. 3:11).

Later Christ said: "Except a man be born again, he cannot see the kingdom of God. . . . Except a man be born of water and of the Spirit, he cannot enter into the kingdom of God." (John 3:3-5.)

Our search for the truth about the Holy Ghost and his mission, then, begins with this proposition: The baptism of the Holy Ghost, the baptism of fire, the new birth of the Spirit is essential to salvation in the kingdom of God. Those who receive this endowment are on the path leading to eternal life, while those not so blessed must yet find the path before they can gain peace in this world and eternal life in the world to come.

Still later in his mortal ministry, our Lord gave renewed and specific assurance that he would fulfill John's promise of a baptism of fire and the Holy Ghost, and that the faithful would be born of the Spirit.

While Christ ministered personally among his disciples, he taught and comforted them, and also promised that they would continue to be taught from on high and receive the comfort afforded by spirituality even after his return to his Father.

"I will pray the Father," he said, "and he shall give you another Comforter, that he may abide with you for ever; Even the Spirit of truth; whom the world cannot receive, because it seeth him not, neither knoweth him: but ye know him; for he dwelleth with you, and shall be in you. But the Comforter, which is the Holy Ghost, whom the Father will send in my name, he shall teach you all things, and bring all things to your remembrance, whatsoever I have said unto you." (John 14:16–17, 26.)

Further: "When the Comforter is come, whom I will send unto you from the Father, even the Spirit of truth, which proceedeth from the Father, he shall testify of me" (John 15:26).

"It is expedient for you that I go away; for if I go not away, the Comforter will not come unto you; but if I depart, I will send him unto you. I have yet many things to say unto you, but ye cannot bear them now. Howbeit when he, the Spirit of truth, is come, he will guide you into all truth: for he shall not speak of himself; but whatsoever he shall hear, that shall he speak: and he will shew you things to come. He shall glorify me: for he shall receive of mine, and shall shew it unto you." (John 16:7, 12–14.)

Now, let us be sure we catch the full vision of these glorious promises:

1. Christ, the Son (one member of the Godhead), would ask the Father (another member), to send the disciples the Comforter, the Spirit of Truth, the Holy Ghost (the third member of the Godhead).

2. The world could not receive this Comforter, for he would not come to men except on conditions of righteousness. The dis-

ciples were "not of the world," even as Christ was "not of the world" (John 15:19; 17:14-16).

3. But with those who had forsaken the world, the Comforter was to abide forever, not just in the early days of the Christian faith, but *forever*.

4. He would teach them all things, guide them into all truth, and bring all the Master's teachings to their remembrance.

5. Further, he would reveal the future to them, show them things to come, truths which they were not then prepared to receive.

6. He would testify of Christ and glorify him in the eyes of all who would receive that witness.

That these same blessings of inspiration and revelation from the Holy Spirit had been enjoyed by righteous men of Old Testament times we learn from Peter's pronouncement "that no prophecy of the scripture is of any private interpretation. For the prophecy came not in old time by the will of man: but holy men of God spake as they were moved by the Holy Ghost." (2 Pet. 1:20-21.)

Pentecostal Outpouring of the Spirit

Our Lord's promise to the disciples that they should receive the Holy Ghost—a promise made first during his mortal ministry and then renewed after his resurrection (John 20:22)—was destined to receive the fulfillment only after his ascension to his Father.

"Behold, I send the promise of my Father upon you," he assured them, "but tarry ye in the city of Jerusalem, until ye be endued with power from on high" (Luke 24:49). Then the very last recorded sentence spoken by him before his ascension contained the promise: "Ye shall receive power, after that the Holy Ghost is come upon you: and ye shall be witnesses unto me . . . unto the uttermost part of the earth" (Acts 1:8).

Soon after the Apostles, by revelation, had chosen Matthias to fill the vacancy left by Judas in the Twelve, they received the promised endowment from on high in a miraculous manner.

"Suddenly there came a sound from heaven as of a rushing mighty wind, and it filled all the house where they were sitting. And there appeared unto them cloven tongues like as of fire, and it sat upon each of them. And they were all filled with the Holy Ghost, and began to speak with other tongues, as the Spirit gave them utterance.

"And there were dwelling at Jerusalem Jews, devout men, out of every nation under heaven. Now when this was noised abroad, the multitude came together, and were confounded, because that every man heard them speak in his own language. And they were all amazed and marvelled, saying one to another, Behold are not all these which speak Galilaeans? And how hear we every man in our own tongue, wherein we were born?" (Acts 2:2–8.)

Here, then, is something marvelous almost beyond belief. The promised gift of the Holy Ghost, the Comforter, the Spirit of Truth, the endowment of power from on high now rested with the Apostles. As with their Lord before them, now they had power to gain knowledge of all things, to read the future, to prophesy, to interpret the ancient scriptures. They had the gift of the Holy Ghost, and immediately "many wonders and signs were done by" them (Acts 2:44).

Because of this gift, Peter arose before the marvelling multitude on the day of Pentecost, bore testimony to them of Christ, and told them what they must do to be saved. The miraculous manifestations they had just witnessed had come, he explained, because Christ "having received of the Father the promise of the Holy Ghost, he hath shed forth this, which ye now see and hear" (Acts 2:33).

Fortunately the assembled host consisted of "devout men" who believed the witness of Peter, who manifested faith in Christ, and who desired to be saved. To Peter and the rest of the Apostles they cried out: "Men and brethren, what shall we do?"

Peter, speaking as the Spirit gave utterance, replied: "Repent, and be baptized every one of you in the name of Jesus Christ for the remission of sins, and ye shall receive the gift of the Holy Ghost. For the promise is unto you, and to your children, and to all that are afar off, even as many as the Lord our God shall call." (Acts 2:37–39.)

In this answer we find the literal application of the truth that God is no respecter of persons. All have equal power to come unto him and receive his blessings and approbations.

That the Apostles had the gift of the Holy Ghost, all will agree. But now we see that the same gift, the same Comforter, the same Spirit of Truth, the same endowment from on high is promised to all who will forsake the world and accept it. "The promise is unto you, and to your children, and to all that are afar off." Wherever there are true disciples, the Comforter will abide forever. The enjoyment of the spiritual gifts is the conclusive test of the divinity of any so-called Christian church.

Laying on of Hands for Gift of the Holy Ghost

Peter's teachings on the day of Pentecost, coupled with many other passages of scripture, outline the steps which must be taken to gain salvation. These are:

1. Faith in the Lord Jesus Christ.
2. Repentance.
3. Baptism by immersion under the hands of a legal administrator for the remission of sins.
4. The actual enjoyment of the Holy Ghost, also given by a legal administrator by the laying on of hands.
5. Continued righteousness and good works by means of which those desiring salvation endure to the end.

Now, the actual enjoyment of the gift of the Holy Ghost is conditioned upon the personal worthiness of the individual and upon his compliance with the ordinances of the Lord. Receipt of the gift, accordingly, follows faith, repentance, baptism, and the laying on of hands by a legal administrator, one who has power to authorize the receipt of the gift.

One of the strange things about nearly every modern so-called Christian church is that no ordinance is performed for the present bestowal of the gift of the Holy Ghost, and no claim is made for the resultant enjoyment of the spiritual gifts. It is true that some prayers are offered which petition that the Holy Ghost may come, but there are no authoritative attempts to make a present bestowal of that gift. Further, the evidence of the receipt of the gift, that is, the actual manifestations of the spiritual gifts, is not to be found among the various sects.

What did the Apostles do to confer this gift following the baptism of the convert? Few answers are recorded with greater plainness in the scriptures than that which pertains to the present bestowal of the gift of the Holy Ghost. For instance:

"Now when the apostles which were at Jerusalem heard that Samaria had received the word of God, they sent unto them Peter and John: Who, when they were come down, prayed for them, that they might receive the Holy Ghost: (For as yet he was fallen upon none of them: only they were baptized in the name of the Lord Jesus.) Then laid they their hands on them, and they received the Holy Ghost." (Acts 8:14–17.)

Paul had a similar experience with certain disciples at Ephesus. "Have ye received the Holy Ghost since ye believed?" he asked them. They answered: "We have not so much as heard whether there be any Holy Ghost.

"And he said unto them, Unto what then were ye baptized?
And they said, Unto John's baptism. Then said Paul, John verily
baptized with the baptism of repentance, saying unto the people,
that they should believe on him which should come after him, that
is, on Christ Jesus."

These Ephesians had not learned that John was a forerunner
who prepared the way for the coming of Christ and the setting up of
the Church and kingdom on earth. They had not learned that the
preparatory work was past and that now the fulness of the kingdom
had come, with the keys thereof centering in the Apostles.

But "when they heard this, they were baptized in the name of
the Lord Jesus. And when Paul had laid his hands upon them, the
Holy Ghost came on them; and they spake with tongues, and
prophesied." (Acts 19:1–6.)

This, then, is the procedure: after a man has gained faith, has
repented of his sins, has been baptized in the name of the Lord, he
must then receive the laying on of hands for the gift of the Holy
Ghost. This gift is the right to receive personal revelation from and
have the constant companionship of the Holy Ghost based on faithfulness.

Where is this either taught, attempted, or accomplished among
the churches in the world? If there are those who have power to
confer the Holy Ghost, a power which he who baptized the Savior
did not have, where are the manifestations of the gifts of the Spirit
which always followed this holy endowment in days of old?

Signs Follow Believers

After his resurrection, our Lord appeared to the Apostles and
gave them this command: "Go ye into all the world, and preach to
the gospel to every creature. He that believeth and is baptized shall
be saved; but he that believeth not shall be damned." (Mark 16:15–
16.)

This command, given specifically to the Apostles, has been
greatly misconstrued. After their day many who had no direct commission from the Lord assumed the prerogative of preaching what
they supposed was the gospel, and then of attempting to perform
the saving ordinance of baptism. There were to be false apostles,
false prophets, false Christs, false teachers, false ministers of religion
(Matt. 24:23–24; Acts 20:28–30; 2 Pet. 2:1–2; 1 John 2:18; 4:1;

Jude 1:4; Rev. 2:2) as well as true ones. And so that the honest in heart might discern between the true and false, our Lord gave those original apostles the sign whereby the wheat and the chaff might be separated.

"And these signs shall follow them that believe," he continued. "In my name shall they cast out devils; they shall speak with new tongues; They shall take up serpents; and if they drink any deadly thing, it shall not hurt them; they shall lay hands on the sick, and they shall recover." (Mark 16:17–18.)

There is nothing permissive in this. It is an eternal decree of the Almighty. "Signs shall follow them that believe." If there are no signs, there is no belief in the true doctrines of salvation. When men come to a knowledge of the truth, when they believe it with that fervency which was evidenced by the Saints of old, signs will follow.

The Apostles, so commissioned, "went forth, and preached every where, the Lord working with them, and confirming the word with signs following" (Mark 16:20). What was true anciently is true today.

These plain Bible teachings should be enough to make all Christendom stop, take warning, and seek for the pure Christianity of old. They are the proof conclusive that men have transgressed the laws, changed the ordinances, broken the gospel covenant (Isa. 24:5).

These teachings ought to cause sincere truth seekers to search their own hearts and ask: What signs follow me? Have I really believed the same gospel taught by the Apostles of old? Or have I followed the false creeds and philosophies of the day? Where can I find the pure truths of primitive Christianity? And where can I find a legal administrator who has power from on high to baptize and lay hands on for the gift of the Holy Ghost?

Gifts of the Spirit

Paul sets forth the doctrine of spiritual gifts in great plainness in chapters 12, 13, and 14 of 1 Corinthians. Every truth seeker should study these and similar scriptures (Moro. 10; D&C 46) carefully and prayerfully. It will be readily apparent to such investigators that the gospel of Paul is *not* the gospel of modern Christianity.

Briefly, he teaches that no man can know that "Jesus is the Lord, but by the Holy Ghost" (1 Cor. 12:3; see, in addition, *Teach-*

ings, p. 223), and that different Church members receive different spiritual gifts.

"The manifestation of the Spirit is given to every man to profit withal. For to one is given by the Spirit the word of wisdom; to another the word of knowledge by the same Spirit; To another faith by the same Spirit; to another the gifts of healing by the same Spirit; To another the working of miracles; to another prophecy; to another discerning of spirits; to another divers kinds of tongues; to another the interpretation of tongues: But all these worketh that one and the selfsame Spirit, dividing to every man severally as he will."

Here, then, is a partial list, at least, of the gifts of the Spirit. All of them are to be found in the true Church of Jesus Christ, but the various members of the Church are to be endowed with various of the gifts according to their talents, faith, and personal righteousness.

Again sincere Christians can use Paul's measuring rod in determining the divinity of their church and the power in their beliefs, by asking: Are all these gifts manifest in my church? Where are the miracles, healings, prophecies, tongues? Which of these gifts do I have? Or how can I gain them?

After comparing the Church to the human body, and showing that the gifts are analogous to the different parts of the body, and after teaching that one part of the body cannot say to another part, "I have no need of thee," Paul says: "Now ye are the body of Christ, and members in particular. And God hath set some in the church, first apostles, secondarily prophets, thirdly teachers, after that miracles, then gifts of healings, helps, governments, diversities of tongues. Are all apostles? are all prophets? are all teachers? are all workers of miracles? Have all the gifts of healing? do all speak with tongues? do all interpret? But covet earnestly the best gifts."

Then Paul records his glorious teachings on faith, hope, and charity, and comes up with this conclusion: "Follow after charity, and desire spiritual gifts, but rather that ye may prophesy."

He follows this with a searching comparison of the value of prophecy and tongues, indicating that it is better to speak "by revelation, or by knowledge, or by prophesying, or by doctrine," than by tongues.

"Forasmuch as ye are zealous of spiritual gifts, seek that ye may excel to the edifying of the church."

"Let the prophets speak two or three, and let the other judge. If any thing be revealed to another that sitteth by, let the first hold his peace. For ye may all prophesy one by one, that all may learn, and all may be comforted. And the spirits of the prophets are subject to the prophets. For God is not the author of confusion, but of peace, as in all the churches of the saints.''

''If any man think himself to be a prophet, or spiritual, let him acknowledge that the things that I write unto you are the commandments of the Lord. But if any man be ignorant, let him be ignorant. Wherefore, brethren, covet to prophesy, and forbid not to speak with tongues. Let all things be done decently and in order.'' (1 Cor. 14:12, 29–33.)

Now, which shall we believe, the teachings of the sects of the day which say there is neither revelation, nor prophecy, nor miracles, nor gifts of the Spirit, or the word of the Lord as found in the Bible?

In seeking out the true Church, shall we find one that has Apostles, prophets, miracles, healings, and all the gifts which Paul says God hath set in the Church, or shall we follow the traditions of men which deny the Bible teachings?

Revelation from the Holy Ghost

The Holy Ghost is a revelator. His mission is to bear record of the Father and the Son and of all truth. He teaches the truths of salvation to the righteous until they, eventually, ''have the mind of Christ.''

With a power of expression seldom equalled, Paul has left us this record of the teaching power of the Holy Ghost: ''My speech and my preaching,'' he says, ''was not with enticing words of man's wisdom, but in demonstration of the Spirit and of power: That your faith should not stand in the wisdom of men, but in the power of God.

''As it is written, Eye hath not seen, nor ear heard, neither have entered into the heart of man, the things which God hath prepared for them that love him.

''But God hath revealed them unto us by his Spirit: for the Spirit searcheth all things, yea, the deep things of God. For what man knoweth the things of a man, save the spirit of man which is in him? even so the things of God knoweth no man, but the Spirit of God.

''Now we have received, not the spirit of the world, but the spirit which is of God; that we might know the things that are freely given to us of God. Which things also we speak, not in the words which man's wisdom teacheth, but which the Holy Ghost teacheth; comparing spiritual things with spiritual.

"But the natural man receiveth not the things of the Spirit of God: for they are foolishness unto him: neither can he know them, because they are spiritually discerned. But he that is spiritual judgeth all things, yet he himself is judged of no man. For who hath known the mind of the Lord, that he may instruct him? But we have the mind of Christ." (1 Cor. 2:4-5, 9-16.)

One whose mind is open, who is willing to prove all things and hold fast that which is good (1 Thes. 5:21), who really believes these inspired words of Paul mean what they say, will want to know: Where among the churches of the day are there ministers who teach "in demonstration of the Spirit and of power"? Or do the various professors of religion "teach with their learning, and deny the Holy Ghost, which giveth utterance" (2 Ne. 28:4)?

Where do we find those to whom the Spirit hath revealed the deep things of God, the things which eye hath not seen, nor ear heard, neither have entered into the heart of man?

Where do we find a people who have the mind of Christ? A people who know by the revelations of the Spirit to them what Christ thinks about salvation, about latter-day visions, prophecies, and miracles?

Either an unchangeable God has changed or these things are still revealed to those who believe the same gospel that Paul believed.

A Nephite Pentecost

We have seen what the Bible teaches about the gift of the Holy Ghost, and the spiritual gifts enjoyed by those who have this gift. Will it be amiss now to see how that God who loves all men of every nation has manifest the same gifts among other peoples?

When the resurrected Lord ministered among the ancient Nephite inhabitants of the American continent, he gave them also the fulness of his gospel, organized a church among them, and called twelve disciples to administer its affairs. Of these Twelve the Book of Mormon records:

"They did pray for that which they most desired; and they desired that the Holy Ghost should be given unto them. And it came to pass when they were all baptized and had come up out of the water, the Holy Ghost did fall upon them, and they were filled with the Holy Ghost and with fire. And behold, they were encircled about as if it were by fire; and it came down from heaven, and the multitude did witness it, and did bear record; and angels did come down out of heaven and did minister unto them.''

In gratitude to his Father, Jesus then said: ''Father, I thank thee that thou hast given the Holy Ghost unto these whom I have chosen; and it is because of their belief in me that I have chosen them out of the world. Father, I pray thee that thou wilt give the Holy Ghost unto all them that shall believe in their words. Father, thou hast given them the Holy Ghost because they believe in me.'' (3 Ne. 19:9, 13–14, 20–22.)

The Plan of Salvation

We have also seen the Bible record of what men must do to be saved, as Peter himself outlined it. Now let us turn to the Nephite record and, in language that surpasses even that of Peter, find how our Lord summarized the same truths:

''No unclean thing can enter into his [the Father's] kingdom; therefore nothing entereth into his rest save it be those who have washed their garments in my blood, because of their faith, and the repentance of all their sins, and their faithfulness unto the end. Now this is the commandment: Repent, all ye ends of the earth, and come unto me and be baptized in my name, that ye may be sanctified by the reception of the Holy Ghost, that ye may stand spotless before me at the last day.'' (3 Ne. 27:19–20.)

After setting up his Church in modern times, after again giving men power to baptize and confer the Holy Ghost, and after decreeing again that signs should follow believers, the Lord said: ''Verily, verily, I say unto you, they who believe not on your words, and are not baptized in water in my name, for the remission of their sins, that they may receive the Holy Ghost, shall be damned, and shall not come into my Father's kingdom where my Father and I am'' (D&C 84:74). (''The Holy Ghost Speaks Again,'' missionary pamphlet, The Church of Jesus Christ of Latter-day Saints, n.d.)

Chapter 6

THE HOLY GHOST
REVEALS CHRIST

The Holy Ghost Testifies of Christ

Let us look in upon a sweet and tender scene that took place near Caesarea Philippi up north of the Sea of Galilee and near Mount Hermon. Multitudes who but recently sought to crown Jesus king and whose clamoring for earthly bread brought forth the rebuff in the sermon on the bread of life—these multitudes have turned away. (John 6; note particularly v. 66.)

The little remaining group of true and valiant believers upon whom our gaze falls are in need of spiritual refreshment. First they have prayers. Then Jesus testifies of his own divine sonship as he so often did during the days of his flesh. He asked his disciples who men said that he, the Son of Man, was. The very question was itself a witness of his godhood, for he knew and they knew that his Father's name was Man of Holiness (Moses 6:57) and that the name of his Only Begotten was the Son of Man of Holiness.

Their answers set forth the fantasies and delusions of an apostate people. Some, they said, accepted the expressed views of evil Antipas who had slain the blessed Baptist whom he now thought had risen from the dead. Others, they said, thought he was Elias who should restore all things; or Elijah who should come before the great and dreadful day; or Jeremiah who, according to their traditions, had hidden the ark of the covenant in a cave on Mount Nebo and would prepare the way for the Messiah by restoring it and the Urim and Thummim to the Holy of Holies.

Then came the question to which every living soul must give proper answer if he is to gain salvation: "But whom say ye that I am?" Ye Apostles of the Lord Jesus Christ, ye saints of the Most

High, ye devout souls who seek salvation: What think ye? Is salvation in Christ or look we for another? Let every man speak for himself!

On this occasion, first Simon Peter, then all the rest acclaimed: "Thou art the Christ, the Son of the living God." (Matt. 16:13-20.) Thou art the promised Messiah; thou art the Only Begotten in the flesh; God is thy Father.

What a wondrous, awesome thing this is! As Paul said: "Great is the mystery of godliness: God was manifest in the flesh, justified in the Spirit, seen of angels, preached unto the Gentiles, believed on in the world, received up into glory" (1 Tim. 3:16).

And now, here near the foot of that mountain in which he will soon be transfigured, the Son of Man, whose Father is divine, accepts and approves the solemn testimonies of his friends.

To Peter, Jesus said: "Blessed art thou, Simon Bar-jona." How carefully and aptly Jesus preserves the distinction between him and all men. He is the Son of God; Peter is the son of Jonah. The Father of Jesus is the immortal Man of Holiness; Peter's sire is a mortal man.

The Rock of Revelation

But why is Peter so blessed? It is because he knows by the power of the Holy Ghost that Jesus is the Lord; the Holy Spirit has spoken to the spirit housed in Simon's body telling the chief Apostle of the divine sonship of this Jesus of Nazareth of Galilee.

"Blessed art thou, Simon Bar-jona," Jesus says: "for flesh and blood hath not revealed it unto thee, but my Father which is in heaven."

Then again Jesus alluded to the difference in paternal ancestry between him and Peter and continued his words of blessing and doctrine by saying: "And upon this rock"—the rock of revelation —"I will build my church; and the gates of hell shall not prevail against it." (Matt. 16:13-18.)

And how could it be otherwise? There is no other foundation upon which the Lord could build his Church and kingdom. The things of God are known only by the power of his Spirit (1 Cor. 2:11). God stands revealed or he remains forever unknown. No man can know that Jesus is the Lord but by the Holy Ghost (1 Cor. 12:3).

Revelation: Pure, perfect, personal revelation—this is the rock!

Revelation that Jesus is the Christ: the plain, wondrous word that comes from God in heaven to man on earth, the word that affirms the divine sonship of our Lord—this is the rock!

The divine sonship of our Lord: the sure, heaven-sent word that God is his Father and that he has brought life and immortality to light through the gospel (2 Tim. 1:10)—this is the rock!

The testimony of our Lord: the testimony of Jesus which is the spirit of prophecy (Rev. 19:10)—this is the rock!

All this is the rock, and yet there is more. Christ is the rock (1 Cor. 10:4): the Rock of Ages, the Stone of Israel, the Sure Foundation—the Lord is our rock!

Again we hear Paul's voice: "Other foundation can no man lay than that is laid, which is Jesus Christ" (1 Cor. 3:11). And also: Ye "are built upon the foundation of the apostles and prophets, Jesus Christ himself being the chief corner stone" (Eph. 2:20).

As we ponder all these things, and as their full meaning dawns upon us, we hear anew the exhortation of our ancient apostolic friend which says: "Examine yourselves, whether ye be in the faith; prove your own selves" (2 Cor. 13:5). And so we ask ourselves: Shall the gates of hell prevail against us?

If we build our house of salvation on the rock of personal revelation; if we build it on the revealed reality that Jesus is the Lord; if we build it on him who is the eternal rock—it will stand forever. If we are guided by the spirit of inspiration while here in mortality, we will be able to withstand all the floods and storms that beat upon us. If we are founded upon a rock, we worship the Father in the name of the Son by the power of the Holy Ghost.

If we are founded upon a rock, we know that salvation comes by the grace of God to those who believe the gospel and keep the commandments. If we are founded upon a rock, we forsake the world, flee from carnal things, and live upright and godly lives.

If we are founded upon a rock, the gates of hell shall not prevail against us. As long as we remain in our house of faith we shall be preserved when the rains of evil fall, when the winds of false doctrine blow, and when the floods of carnality beat upon us.

Thanks be to God that we, as Latter-day Saints, are founded upon a rock. And so it is that the faithful among us hear a calm voice of quiet certainty saying: "If you shall build up my church, upon the foundation of my gospel and my rock, the gates of hell shall not prevail against you. Behold, you have my gospel before you, and my rock, and my salvation." (D&C 18:5, 17.) (Conference Report, April 1981.)

Gaining a Testimony of Jesus Christ

For some years I have sought to learn all that a mortal can of the life of Jesus Christ—the greatest life ever lived—of his words and works in the days of his flesh, the Atonement he wrought, and the glory that was his in life, and in death, and in living again.

I stand in awe. The glorious Majesty from on high has dwelt among men. He has made flesh his tabernacle; he was born of woman; he took upon himself the form of a servant; he condescended to leave his eternal throne that he might abolish death and bring life and immortality to life through the gospel. The Great God, the Eternal Jehovah, the Lord Omnipotent came among us as a man, as Mary's son, as the Son of David, as the Suffering Servant, as the perfect manifestation of the father.

Two Great Truths: Atonement and Restoration

In 1935, on the one-hundredth anniversary of the organization of the first quorum of Apostles in our dispensation, the First Presidency of the Church—Presidents Heber J. Grant, J. Reuben Clark, Jr., and David O. McKay—issued a statement: "Two great truths must be accepted by mankind if they shall save themselves; first, that Jesus is the Christ, the Messiah, the Only Begotten, the very Son of God, whose atoning blood and resurrection save us from the physical and spiritual death brought to us by the Fall; and next, that God has again restored to the earth, in these last days, through the Prophet Joseph, His holy Priesthood with the fulness of the everlasting Gospel, for the salvation of all men on the earth. Without these truths man may not hope for the riches of the life hereafter." ("A Testimony to the World," *Improvement Era*, April 1935, p. 205.)

We Prove Spiritual Truth by Testimony

We have a glorious message to take to the world. It is a message of salvation, a message of joy and hope and glad tidings. It is in the spiritual realm. And immediately the question arises as to how you establish the truth and divinity of a spiritual message.

How do you prove spiritual truths? How do you prove the resurrection of Jesus Christ? How do you prove that the Father and the Son appeared to Joseph Smith, or that any of the angelic ministrants came who gave him keys and power and authorities as the Church was established?

We stand in exactly the same situation the ancient Apostles were in. They, too, had a proclamation to take to the world. They had to proclaim, first, the divine sonship of the Lord Jesus, that he was in literal reality God's Son, that he had come into the world and worked out the infinite and eternal atoning sacrifice whereby all men are raised in immortality, while those who believe and obey may be raised unto eternal life. And they had to proclaim, second, that they themselves—Peter, James, and John, and all of the Twelve, and the seventies, and the others—were legal administrators called of God, empowered by him, given the keys of the kingdom, the right to proclaim the truths of the gospel, and the power to administer its ordinances. Now, how could eleven men and their auxiliary associates—eleven Galileans who had no rabbinical training, who were not scholars in the eyes of the world—go out and do the thing that Jesus laid upon their shoulders, which was to take the message of salvation to every creature.

I shall take a segment of Christ's life and use it as an illustration, a pattern, an indication. It sets the principle, showing how the message of salvation was proclaimed in that day. And if we can envision what is here involved, we will know what we have to do in principle in our day to take the equivalent message to our Father's other children.

I believe that a testimony of Jesus Christ hinges on a belief in the Resurrection. If Jesus rose from the dead, he is the Son of God. If he is the Son of God, his gospel is true. If his gospel is true, men must believe or disobey at their peril. They must accept his truths and be baptized and live the law, or they will be damned. What this comes down to is that if the Apostles in that day had the power and ability to convince men that Jesus rose from the dead, they had established the truth and divinity of the work. And how do you prove the Resurrection? As we are going to see, you prove it by testimony.

Paul testified that Jesus Christ was "declared to be the Son of God with power, according to the spirit of holiness, by the resurrection from the dead" (Rom. 1:4).

Resurrection: The Key to Testimony of Christ

The Resurrection proves that Jesus was the Son of God. Now these words also from Paul: "Moreover, brethren, I declare unto you the gospel which I preached unto you, which also ye have received, and wherein ye stand [Now, this is the very heart and core of the gospel]; By which also ye are saved, if ye keep in memory what I preached unto you, unless ye have believed in vain. For I delivered unto you first of all that which I also received, how that Christ died for our sins according to the scriptures; And that he was buried, and that he rose again the third day according to the scriptures: And that he was seen of Cephas, then of the twelve: After that, he was seen of above five hundred brethren at once; of whom the greater part remain unto this present, but some are fallen asleep. After that, he was seen of James; then of all the apostles." (1 Cor. 15:1–7.)

Resurrected Christ Proves Resurrection

Now, the segment of the life of the Lord Jesus which we will consider:

We'll begin after the supper and the sermons in the upper room, after the incomprehensible agony in the Garden of Gethsemane, after the trials, and after the Crucifixion. The body of Jesus was placed in a tomb before sunset on Friday, and his spirit was in the spirit world for thirty-eight or forty hours.

Sometime early Sunday morning, Jesus rose from the dead. We do not know the time, but the record says that "when it was yet dark" (John 20:1), Mary Magdalene came to the tomb. Of all the women of the New Testament, Mary Magdalene is preeminent save only Mary, the Lord's mother. Mary Magdalene is the one alone who is named as having traveled with Jesus and the Twelve as they went on their missionary journeys in all the villages and cities of Galilee. When she arrived at the tomb, she found not the body of the Lord Jesus. She was told by the angels to tell Peter that Christ was risen, and that he was going before them into Galilee, according to the promise that he had made.

We can't tell exactly the sequence, but we can be reasonably certain. Either she went back and told Peter and came again, or she went out of the tomb then and saw the risen Lord. In any event, she was the first mortal to see a resurrected person. In her sorrow and in her tears and in her anxiety, she sensed a presence, supposed it was the gardener, and said with perfect proprietary right, "Sir, if you have taken him, show me where that I may take him." (See John 20:15.) The Personage said one word, "Mary." Immediately she recognized the Lord. She said, "Rabboni," which is the reverential form of the word *Rabbi*, and means "my Lord" or "my Master." And at that point, she attempted to throw her arms around the Lord Jesus, and he said, "Hold, touch me not; I have not

yet ascended to my Father which is in Heaven.'' (See JST John
20:17.)

Now, either there is more that is not there recorded, or between
that episode and one that immediately followed, the Lord did ascend to his Father, because very shortly, and the record says, ''As it
began to dawn'' (Matt. 28:1), other women arrived, apparently in a
group, and they went into the tomb and were told various things by
the angelic ministrants. But when they came out, the account says,
they met Jesus and they threw their arms around his feet. Now,
that has to mean that they felt the nail marks in his hands and perhaps more. We do not know what transpired there, other than that
Jesus directed again the same message the angels had given the
woman from Magdala. Jesus said, ''Tell Peter and the brethren that
I am going before them into Galilee.'' (See Matt. 28:10.) That is two
appearances of the risen Lord on Easter morning.

The next appearance, although we cannot document this with
accuracy—we do not know the total chronology—was to Peter and
we suppose it was because Peter was to be the President of the
Church; he held the keys of the kingdom. The Lord appeared to
him, obviously to renew and reaffirm the relationship and the
power and authority that he had, and to recommission him, as it
were, to do the work that he had been appointed to do.

The next appearance, the details of which we know, occurred
on the Emmaus road. Emmaus, whose location is lost to us, was
some seven or eight miles from Jerusalem. On the afternoon of that
day, two disciples were walking from Jerusalem to Emmaus. One
of them was named Cleopas; we assume the other one was Luke,
since he alone records what took place. As they walked along, a
stranger joined them and asked them what they were discussing
and considering. They were a little put out that someone would
come and interfere with their sacred communication, and, in effect,
they said to him: ''Art thou a stranger here? Don't you know what's
happened in Jerusalem? Haven't you heard that Jesus was crucified
at the Passover time and that he promised to rise again the third
day?'' (See Luke 24:18–21.) And they told him that certain women
had been in their group and had made reports of his rising.

Then he said to them, ''O fools, and slow of heart to believe all
that the prophets have spoken'' (Luke 24:25), and he proceeded
from Moses and the prophets and the Psalms to talk about the messianic sayings concerning himself. It may be that this conversation
lasted as long as two hours. In any event, they arrived at the place
in Emmaus where the two disciples were going to camp, and they

invited him to stay: "Abide with us: 'tis eventide." (See Luke 24:29.) He made as though he would go on, but he accepted the invitation. And then he broke bread and blessed it. He must have done it in a way that was familiar to them, or something else happened to remove the veil from their eyes, because they immediately recognized him. Then he vanished out of their sight.

That's four appearances. Those two disciples returned immediately from Emmaus to Jerusalem. They went to a place that is called the upper room. We are quite secure in speculating that this was the same upper room in which the Last Supper was held. It was a large and commodious place; there was quite a congregation present. The only ones we usually talk about are the ten Apostles, but there were others. In any event, the two disciples went and began to recite to the group what had occurred to them. When they entered the room, someone was bearing testimony that the Lord had appeared to Simon, showing that that appearance had preceded this hour at least.

As they were going forward with their meal and their testimonies, the account says Jesus himself stood in the midst of them. Then it says "they were terrified and affrighted, and supposed that they had seen a spirit" (Luke 24:37), which is a natural conclusion because they were in a barred room, the door was closed, and here someone had materialized who had come either through the ceiling or the wall. And he said to them: "Why are ye troubled? and why do thoughts arise in your hearts? Behold my hands and my feet, that it is I myself: handle me, and see; for a spirit hath not flesh and bones, as ye see me have." (Luke 24:38–39.)

And without any question, they then felt the nail marks in his hands and his feet, and they thrust their hands into the spear wound in his side. We know by express declaration that that is precisely what the Nephite believers did when he appeared during the latter part of that year in the Americas. Then he said to those in the upper room, "Have ye here any meat?" (Luke 24:41) which was a rhetorical question—they were eating and he knew it. They brought "him a piece of a broiled fish, and of an honeycomb. And he took it, and did eat before them." (Luke 24:42–43.) And some other conversation ensued.

Ten of the Twelve were there. For what reason we do not know, Thomas was absent. When they told Thomas what had happened, he said, "Except I shall see with my eyes and handle with my hands and feel the prints of the nails, I will not believe." (See John 20:25.) Now, we've come to suppose that this was doubt on his part, which it was, but it was no more material or substantial than the doubt in the minds of the other ten when they supposed Jesus was a spirit. Thomas was simply indicating that he had not yet envisioned the corporeal, literal nature of the Resurrection, though he should have accepted the testimony of the Apostles. Thomas, in fact, was one of the most valiant of the Twelve—he was the only one of the Twelve who said, "I will go and die with thee," when Jesus was going to raise Lazarus from the dead, and when the others said the Jews in that area sought to kill the Lord (see John 11:16).

These men were valiant and capable and devoted and able, but they were learning degree by degree and step by step.

One week later, again on a Sabbath day—and this is setting the pattern for worship on Sunday as the Sabbath—apparently in the upper room, the same or a similar group assembled. Jesus appeared, and he said to Thomas, "Stretch forth thine hand, and feel the prints of the nails in my hands and in my feet, and be not faithless, but believing." (See John 20:27.) Then Thomas apparently fell on his knees and said, "My Lord and my God" (John 20:28). And we suppose that he accepted the invitation and felt and handled as the others had felt and handled the previous week. Then came the words about him being blessed for believing when he saw but others being more blessed who believed without seeing.

The next appearance chronologically of which we have record was on the shore of the lake of Tiberias (the Sea of Galilee). Some time must have elapsed. The scene is early in the morning. Only seven of the Twelve were present, five of whom are named. They had been fishing all night and had caught nothing. Jesus stood on the shore of the lake and called out to them and said, "Children, have ye any meat?" They had not. He said, "Cast your net on the other side" which they did. (See John 21:5–6.) And immediately the nets were full to the breaking point, which is reminiscent of the same miracle that occurred in his mortal life with the sons of Zebedee.

John, with a little more spiritual insight than the others, said, "It is the Lord" (John 21:7). And Peter, in his impetuous nature, cast off the fisherman's robe and swam to shore to be the first to greet the Lord. They brought the fish in. When they got on the shore, they found that Jesus had a fire on which he was broiling fish and baking bread, and he also asked them for fish from their supply, which he added to what was being already cooked. And they ate, and the presumption is—and I'll indicate a reason why later—that Jesus also on that occasion ate.

That's the time when Jesus asked Peter three times if he loved him and gave the great decree to feed his sheep. That's the occasion when he told John that he would live to bear testimony before nations and kingdoms before he would see the Lord returning in his glory.

The next appearance was on that mountain in Galilee. We know very little of this, but quite obviously it was a great and glorious and grand appearance—more than five hundred brethren were there. This leads us to assume that there must have been women present also. We suppose that he would follow the same pattern that he followed among the Nephites and that for a select group of that sort he would preach more doctrine and do more things than he had otherwise done. In any event, that's the occasion when he issued the decree that the Twelve should go into all the world and preach the gospel to every creature. And many other things, without question, were said.

Now, that's eight appearances. After that he appeared to James (see 1 Cor. 15:7).

The tenth appearance of which the New Testament speaks is the Ascension. With reference to that, we know only that forty days after his resurrection he appeared to the eleven. They apparently walked out to the Mount of Olives; and while they were on the Mount of Olives they had the conversation about the restoration of the kingdom to Israel. And then he ascended. The account says that two angels stood by and said, "Ye men of Galilee, why stand ye gazing up into heaven? this same Jesus, which is taken up from you into heaven, shall so come in like manner as ye have seen him go into heaven." (Acts 1:11.)

The Conduct of Resurrected Beings

From this brief review we learn several important things: we know that resurrected beings, containing their glory within themselves, can walk as mortals do on earth; that they can converse and reason and teach as they once did in mortality; that they can both withhold and manifest their true identities; that they can pass with corporeal bodies through solid walls; that they have bodies of flesh and bones which can be felt and handled; that if need be (and at special times) they can retain the scars and wounds of the flesh; that they can eat and digest food; that they can vanish from mortal eyes and transport themselves by means unknown to us.

Inspired Testimony Establishes or Proves Truth

How do you prove that the Father and the Son appeared to Joseph Smith? How do you prove the message of salvation that Jesus gave to those Apostles? Here is an illustration, and the words are part of the sermon that Peter preached when he went to the home of Cornelius, who had been visited by an angel, and who had found special favor in the Lord's sight. Peter said, "We are witnesses of all things which [Jesus of Nazareth] did both in the land of the Jews, and in Jerusalem; whom they slew and hanged on a tree: Him God raised up the third day, and shewed him openly; Not to all people, but unto witnesses chosen before of God, even to us, *who did eat and drink with him after he rose from the dead.* And he commanded us to preach unto the people, and to testify that it is he which was ordained of God to be the Judge of quick and dead. To him give all the prophets witness, that through his name whosoever believeth in him shall receive remission of sins." (Acts 10:39–43; italics added.)

The way that Peter and the ancients proved that Jesus was the Son of God, and therefore that the gospel which he taught was the plan of salvation, was to establish that he rose from the dead. And the way you prove that a man rises from the dead, because it is in the spiritual realm, is to bear witness by the power of the Spirit of knowledge that is personal and real and literal to you. Peter could have gone into a congregation and said, "I know that Jesus is the Lord because Isaiah said this and this with reference to him. Or one of the other prophets said this." And he did that, for a reason, I suppose. But the great crowning thing that Peter could do was to stand before the people and say, "I know he was the Son of God. I stood in the upper room. I recognized him. He is the man who ministered among us for more than three years. I felt the nail marks in his hands and in his feet. I thrust my hand into the spear wound in his side. I saw him eat food—he ate fish and an honeycomb. He has a body. He said his body was flesh and bone. I know he is the Son of God. I am his witness!"

The message of salvation is proclaimed by witnesses, and this segment of the life of the Lord Jesus set a pattern and shows what we have to do when we carry the message of the Restoration to our Father's other children.

Prove the Restoration by Testimony

How do you prove the message of the Restoration? Well, you preach the gospel. You have to teach the doctrines of salvation, or else people will not have a judgment or be in an intelligent position to weigh the merit and proof of your testimony. First, you teach what God has done in wondrous glory in the day in which we live. You teach how the heavens have been opened and how he has spoken again and how he has restored the fulness of his everlasting gospel, sending angelic ministrants to give keys and powers and authorities to men. And after you have taught the truth and used the holy scriptures to do it, and made the message as plain and as easy and as simple as in your power lies, then the crowning and convincing and convicting thing that is left is that you bear testimony.

We as members of the Church and kingdom of God on earth have received what is called the gift of the Holy Ghost. And the gift of the Holy Ghost is the right to the constant companionship of that member of the Godhead based on faithfulness. And that means that the Holy Spirit of God, who is a personage of Spirit, in harmony with eternal laws that have been ordained, will speak to the spirit that is within us, giving us eternal proof. And we call the receipt of that proof *testimony*. It comes by revelation from the Holy Spirit of God.

Components of Testimony

A testimony in our day consists of three things: It consists of the knowledge that Jesus is the Lord, that he is the Son of the living God who was crucified for the sins of the world; it consists of the fact that Joseph Smith was a prophet of God called to restore the gospel truth and be the revealer of the knowledge of Christ for our day; and it consists of knowing that The Church of Jesus Christ of Latter-day Saints is the only true and living Church upon the face of the whole earth, the one place where salvation is found, the organization which administers the gospel and therefore administers salvation to the sons of men.

Teach by Testimony

We teach the gospel. And after we have taught in plainness to the best of our ability, then we bear witness, and we say, ''I know.'' We say the Holy Spirit of God has revealed to me, to us, to the Latter-day Saints, that this work is true. And after we have taught and borne testimony, every individual who is in tune, every individual who has prepared himself spiritually to receive the truth, will feel in his heart that what we have said is true. And it will not be a matter of argument; it will not be a matter of debate; it will not be an intellectual conversion. It will be a revelation from the Holy Spirit of God.

I think this same pattern has been followed in every age and dispensation. I think also that we have something in our day that is over and above and beyond what was had in any other day. The Lord has given us the Book of Mormon as a witness of the truth, and the Book of Mormon is "to the convincing of the Jew and Gentile that Jesus is the Christ, the Eternal God, manifesting himself unto all nations" (Title page, Book of Mormon). And the Book of Mormon came forth to prove "to the world that the holy scriptures are true, and that God does inspire men and call them . . . in this age and generation, as well as in generations of old" (D&C 20:11).

If we do not get something out of the life of Jesus that applies to us, we do not get the benefit that we ought. We should take his life and pattern our lives after the way he lived. We should take the episodes of his life and learn from them the concepts and principles that will enable us in similar situations to do what we have been called upon to do in our day.

When the Lord himself bore testimony of the truth of the Book of Mormon, he used the most solemn language known to mankind. He swore with an oath. He said with reference to Joseph Smith, "He has translated the book, even that part which I have commanded him, and as your Lord and your God liveth it is true" (D&C 17:6).

If we are properly in tune and understand what is involved in the eternal realities of which we speak, we ought to be able to bear that same kind of witness with reference to the restoration of eternal truth in our day. We ought to be able to say: "The Lord has restored again and set up his kingdom among men." And God being our witness, it is true. ("Gaining a Testimony of Jesus Christ," *Ensign*, December 1980, pp. 11–15.)

The Holy Ghost, Testimony, and Conversion: The Case of Simon Peter

Saints Distinguished by Testimony

One of the great, unique, and distinctive things about Latter-day Saints is that they have testimonies; they know the work in which they are engaged is true. Other people argue and wrangle about theological matters. They entangle themselves in academic fields and in the fields of reason. Where we are concerned, however, we have all that is good academically; we desire and do reason to the extent of our abilities, which is the equivalent or better than that of other people in the world. But what we have that is singular, that is unique and distinctive, is the personal knowledge, born of the Spirit, resident in the hearts of all of us, that the work is true. We have what is called a testimony of the divinity of the work.

Satan Desires Peter's Soul

I shall take a text from Luke: "And the Lord said, Simon, Simon, behold, Satan hath desired to have you, that he may sift you as wheat" (Luke 22:31).

This is an idiomatic expression which was clear to the people in that day, more so than to people in our day. In essence and thought content Jesus is saying, "Peter, Satan wants you in his harvest. He wants to harvest your soul, and bring you into his granary, into his garner, where he will have you as his disciple." It is the same figure that we use when we say that the field is white, already to harvest. And we go out and preach the gospel and harvest the souls of men. Well, Satan wanted Peter; he wanted to sift him as wheat or to harvest his soul.

"But [Jesus says] I have prayed for thee, that thy faith fail not: and when thou are converted, strengthen thy brethren. And he [that is, Peter] said unto him, Lord, I am ready to go with thee, both into prison, and to death. And he said, I tell thee, Peter, the cock shall not crow this day, before that thou shalt thrice deny that thou knowest me." (Luke 22:32–34.)

Nature of Peter's Conversion

The setting for the fulfillment of this is the occasion in the outer court of the high priest's abode the night before Jesus is to be taken away and crucified. This is the occasion when Peter denies that he knows who the Lord is. So here we have a situation which occurs almost at the end of Jesus' ministry, and yet Jesus speaks of some future time when Peter is going to be converted.

This makes us wonder, "What kind of a state was Peter in?" After all the experience he had had, after all the testimonies that he had borne, how is it he could not yet be classified as a convert? We talk about the people joining the Church through the missionary effort today, and sometimes we call them "convert baptisms." We say that of them the minute they come into the Church. Yet, here is a man who has been with Jesus for three and a half years in his ministry; who has eaten and slept and lived with him; who has been sent out on a mission; who has been ordained, undoubtedly an elder, but surely an Apostle; who has had power to work miracles, and who has in fact worked them; who has been a mighty and valiant and effective preacher in the cause of righteousness. And still the Lord says to him, "When thou are converted, do such and such," meaning that there was something more that was going to come into the life of Peter to convert him, something more than already had come, in spite of all the marvelous things that he had seen and in which he had participated.

Peter was converted in the sense of joining the Church in the early days of Jesus' ministry, but not converted in the full and acceptable and total sense that Saints must be converted. He first heard about the gospel from his brother Andrew. Andrew and John, who is known to us as John the Revelator, had both been disciples of John the Baptist, who had been preparing the way before the face of the Lord, and had been baptizing people for the remission of sins with the promise that there came one after him who would baptize with fire and with the Holy Ghost. John the Baptist had baptized the Lord. He has assembled a measurable group of disciples; he knew that his ministry was drawing to a close, and he wanted his disciples—among whom were John, soon to be the Revelator; and Andrew, Peter's brother—to follow Jesus. And so he climaxed his ministry by bearing testimony of the divine sonship of the Lord and introducing Jesus to his disciples. He bore those fervent testimonies, that are summarized in this language: "Behold the Lamb of God, which taketh away the sin of the world" (John 1:29).

John the Baptist invited his disciples to forsake him, because he was now to diminish and decrease, and to follow Jesus who was to increase and whose cause was to multiply and be perfected. And Andrew and John the disciple got the message; they forsook the

Baptist and began to follow Jesus, and, apparently, immediately had the assurance in their souls that Jesus was the Lamb of God. Andrew then did what almost every new convert, so-called, to the Church does; he started out to get the members of his family, his friends, his kindred, and let them come and receive the blessings that had been given him.

Peter Taught by Jesus

Andrew found Peter and said, ''We have found the Messias'' (John 1:41). And he had Peter come to meet Jesus. We do not know the teaching and the conversation that took place, except in very fragmentary form, but when Peter came he was taught the gospel, obviously, by Jesus. He was told that he would have the title and the designation of Cephas, a stone. He began immediately to follow Jesus. We do not have the record, but there is no question but that he was baptized. He became a disciple; he joined, as it were, the Church.

Now, Jesus' ministry lasted three and a half years and Peter was with him virtually all that time. Initially, apparently, he did not spend his full time at it; he went off with his partners James and John into the fishing enterprise that they ran. He must have been ordained an elder somewhere along the line. But in any event, when the time came for the call of the Twelve and for him to come and devote his full time to the ministry, Jesus met him and his two partners on the shore of the Sea of Galilee, and said: ''Come ye after me, and I will make you to become fishers of men'' (Mark 1:17).

Peter Ordained an Apostle

This was the occasion when he ordained them Apostles. Then he took them up on a high plateau above the city of Capernaum, where the multitude followed, and preached the sermon which was an ordination sermon; we call it the Sermon on the Mount.

At least from that time on, Peter and the others devoted virtually full time to the ministry. They were with Jesus continually. It would have been in the home of Peter that Jesus spent his time when he was in Capernaum. Capernaum was known as the city of our Lord; that was where he dwelt. Peter lived there.

There is not much question but that it was in the home of Peter in which he was preaching on that day when they lowered the paralytic down through the tile on the roof, because they could not otherwise get him into his presence. This was the occasion when Jesus said to the paralytic, "Son, thy sins be forgiven thee." Then when the disbelieving Jews began to reason in their hearts that such an act was blasphemous, Jesus said: "Whether is it easier to say to the sick of the palsy, Thy sins be forgiven thee; or to say, Arise, and take up thy bed and walk? But that ye may know that the Son of Man hath power on earth to forgive sins, (he saith to the sick of the palsy,) I say unto thee, Arise, and take up thy bed, and go thy way into thine house." (Mark 2:5–11.)

And the man did so.

Jesus Testifies of His Own Divine Sonship

Jesus deliberately used the occasion to prove his divine sonship. The fact that he forgave sins would have been blasphemy if he had not been the Son of God. And the fact that the paralyzed man was able to walk showed that Jesus was the Son of God, because no one unclean and without divine power and authority could have performed such a miracle.

I recite this much to indicate the kind of experiences Peter was having. Peter was with the Lord when these miracles transpired. He was taken with James and John into the room alone when Jesus raised the young maiden from death. He was with the Lord at the tomb of Lazarus when that man had been dead for four days, had started to decay, and had been called forth by Jesus. So Peter had enjoyed a host of rich spiritual experiences.

And of course Peter had borne testimony of the divine sonship. On that occasion when the disciples were in the coasts of Caesarea Philippi and Jesus asked, "Whom do men say that I the Son of man am?" and had received the various answers, it was Peter who answered the query, "But whom say ye that I am?" with the declaration, "Thou art the Christ, the Son of the living God." It was on that occasion that Jesus said: "Blessed art thou, Simon Bar-jona: for flesh and blood hath not revealed it unto thee, but my Father which is in heaven." (Matt. 16:13, 15–17.)

Thus Peter, on that occasion, in the presence of the Lord, by revelation from the Holy Ghost, had received in his soul the assurance that Jesus was the Lord.

Testimony Defined

Now, we call that a testimony. It is a perfect example of a testimony. A testimony is *to know by personal revelation from the Holy Spirit that Jesus is the Son of God.* The spirit of prophecy is synonymous with the testimony of Jesus (Rev. 19:10). Peter had had the prophetic spirit resting upon him, and he knew—not by reason, not by argument, not from a theological sense, but by the promptings and whisperings and voice of the Spirit—he knew that this man Jesus was literally the Son of God; he was a witness.

Undoubtedly he bore his witness on many occasions. We have another very dramatic occasion when he did, which followed the sermon on the bread of life. Jesus had fed the five thousand, provided bread for them, in order to get a congregation and in order to have a setting in which he could preach in this sermon that he was the bread of life, to teach them that he gave them spiritual food, even as he had given them this temporal food. This sermon was severe and harsh; it contained difficult doctrine; and the multitudes began to fall away.

Jesus said to his disciples, "Will ye also go away?" and Peter, mouth for the group, said: "Lord, to whom shall we go? thou hast the words of eternal life. And we believe and are sure that thou art that Christ, the Son of the living God." (John 6:67–69.)

Peter knew; Peter had a testimony. Peter had worked miracles; he had been in the ministry. Now we come to this occasion when Jesus is going to be tried and in due course crucified, and we discover the Lord saying to him, in effect, "Peter, you have got a testimony of the gospel; you have borne record that I am the Son of God. I have certified to you previously that your testimony was true, but you are not converted."

Testimony and Conversion Differ

There is a difference, as is evident from this, between having a testimony and being converted. It is only fair, and it is also essential to the story, to say that the reason Peter was not converted in the full sense is that the time had not then arrived when the Holy Spirit was poured out upon the people. As long as Jesus was with them, for some reasons that are only partially understood by us, they did not need the full and constant companionship of the Holy Spirit. This came later; it was the promised endowment that they got on the day of Pentecost.

Gift of the Holy Ghost Defined

This does not mean that they did not have the Spirit on occasion. We have already shown that they did. They had the Spirit that certified truth to them from time to time, but they did not have the constant companionship; the full sanctifying power had not yet come into their lives. Here is an analogy that shows what was involved: They had been walking through a world of darkness, a world that was stormy and tumultuous; in the midst of storm there had been flashes of lightning from time to time to chart the course. These flashes of lightning had been revelation from the Holy Ghost. Peter had one of those in the presence of Jesus, as we have recited. But the time had not come — it was future — when they would walk in the full light of the sun all the time. That would be when the gift of the Holy Ghost was given. The gift of the Holy Ghost, by definition, is the right to the constant companionship of that member of the Godhead based on faithfulness. Peter had yet to receive that gift.

After the Crucifixion the disciples, the sheep, were scattered. Peter said to his associates, "I go a fishing" (John 21:3). And he did it literally; but what it symbolizes is that he left the ministry to go off after the things of this world.

There were a number of appearances of Jesus; the one that concerns us is on the seashore that morning when Jesus appeared and called out to the disciples who were fishing, commanding them to cast their nets on the other side. This they did, and the nets were so filled that the record marvels that they did not break.

John recognized him, and he said, "It is the Lord!" (John 21:7). Peter then jumped out of the boat and swam to shore to be the first to greet him.

Measuring Degree of Conversion

Jesus prepared a fish over the fire; they ate it in silence; and then this conversation took place. Jesus said: "Simon, son of Jonas, lovest thou me more than these? [That is, these fish that symbolized the things of the world, the things that Peter was seeking instead of being in the ministry where he belonged.] He saith unto him, Yea, Lord; thou knowest that I love thee. He saith unto him, Feed my lambs.

"He saith to him again the second time, Simon, . . . lovest thou me? He saith unto him, Yea, Lord; thou knowest that I love thee. He saith unto him, Feed my sheep.

"He saith unto him the third time, Simon, . . . lovest thou me? Peter was grieved because he said unto him the third time, Lovest thou me? And he said unto him, Lord, thou knowest all things;

thou knowest that I love thee. Jesus saith unto him, Feed my sheep." (John 21:15–17.)

We now have two statements. One says, "When thou art converted, strengthen thy brethren." After this one was made, Peter denied three times that he knew who Christ was. "I do not know the man" (Matt. 26:72), he said to the maid who accused him of having been with Him. Now, this other statement says, "Feed my sheep." These are the two statements that are a measuring rod to indicate the degree of conversion a person has. The test is whether he is out strengthening his brethren and whether he is out feeding the Lord's sheep.

Receiving Holy Ghost at Pentecost

On the day of Pentecost, Peter and the others were together; he was preaching. The promised endowment came; the Holy Ghost fell upon them; the gift of tongues was manifest; cloven tongues of fire rested upon them, which is the language that is used to describe the miraculous things that transpired in their hearts. There really is no language that it is possible to use to tell what happened in the hearts of the disciples on that occasion, which is the one when they became fully converted. And so they did the best they could to get some language, and they said "cloven tongues like as of fire" rested upon them.

So this was the day of conversion. And after this day of conversion there was a total and complete change in the life of Peter, a change that made him a different kind of man than he was even when he ate and lived and walked with Jesus in the course of his mortal ministry.

Peter Preaches in Apostolic Power

Now, one little episode that dramatizes what happened in the life of Peter after the day of Pentecost is this: He and John were walking into the gate of the temple which is called Beautiful. They met a man who was asking alms who had been lame from his mother's womb. He begged of them and supposed that he was going to get something when they spoke. Peter said: "Silver and gold have I none; but such as I have give I thee: In the name of Jesus Christ of Nazareth rise up and walk" (Acts 3:6).

And he reached forth his right hand and he lifted up the beggar by the right hand. Immediately strength came into his feet and his ankles, and he began leaping and praising God, and went and showed himself to the people in the temple.

The result was that Peter and John were arrested and put in prison. They were brought out at a subsequent occasion to be interrogated. Part of the conversation was this; Peter said: "If we this day be examined of the good deed done to the impotent man, by what means he is made whole; Be it known unto you all, and to all the people of Israel, that by the name of Jesus Christ of Nazareth, whom ye crucified, whom God raised from the dead, even by him doth this man stand here before you whole. Neither is there salvation in any other . . . name." (Acts 4:9–10, 12.)

Peter Converted Gradually

The story of Peter is a story of conversion, and it shows that a process was involved. Peter heard about the gospel from Andrew. He came to Christ and he joined the Church; he began to get experience in the Church, to grow in grace and wisdom and understanding. He was ordained to offices in the priesthood, including the apostleship. He worked miracles, and the Holy Ghost spoke to him. He knew that the work was divine. He had a testimony; and then there came a day when he got the companionship of the Holy Spirit, and that was the day of his conversion. When he had a testimony, he yet said, "I do not know the man." In that day he said, "I go a fishing." But when the conversion occurred, instead of saying, "I do not know the man," he faced the people who had crucified Jesus, he faced those who thirsted for his own blood, and accused them of their murder and bore witness of the divine sonship.

Conversion Defined

What is conversion? It is just as simple as the meaning of the term. Conversion is to change something from one state into another state. In the chemical laboratory we change sugar into starch or the reverse. The same elements are present but there is some rearrangement so that the substance seems to be different than it was previously. In the world there are people who are unconverted and people who are converted. Outwardly they appear to be the same. Read the scriptural passages dealing with being born again.

Alma the Younger Born Again

Read particularly what is in Mosiah 27, which tells about the experience of Alma the younger, how he was visited by the angel, was smitten, went into a trance, stayed there for a couple of days while his father, the high priest, and the Saints fasted for his well-being and recovery. Then read how Alma the younger, who had obviously been baptized in his youth, came out of the trance and said, "I have been born again." Then he explains that the Lord says that all mankind—men, women, children—have to be born again or they cannot be saved in the kingdom of God. Note that he says men must be changed from their carnal and fallen state to a state of righteousness, being born again, becoming the Lord's sons and his daughters. Now, this is what is involved in conversion.

Every person who is in the world, who has ever been born into the world, who arrives at the years of accountability without being baptized, dies spiritually. Since the Fall of Adam, according to our revelations, all accountable men have become carnal, sensual, and devilish by nature. This is called the natural man. Now, what is required in conversion is to put off the natural man and to become a Saint by the power of the atoning sacrifice of Christ. And so people are born again. They are changed from a carnal and fallen state to a state of righteousness. Paul describes it by saying that we crucify the old man (Rom. 6:6). We die as to the things of the world and we become alive as to the things of righteousness, and it does not happen and cannot happen unless and until someone gets the sanctifying power of the Holy Ghost into their lives.

The Holy Ghost: A Witness and a Sanctifier

The Holy Ghost does two things in particular. On the one hand he is a witness to truth, and so he bears the testimony of the truth, and that is how we get a testimony, by revelation from the Holy Ghost. But on the other hand the Holy Spirit is a sanctifier, and he has the power to cleanse and perfect the human soul, to wash evil and iniquity out, and to replace it with righteousness. And that is the occasion when we are converted. We get a testimony from the Holy Spirit when that member of the Godhead tells us that the work is true, and his great function in that field is to bear testimony of the truth.

We are cleansed from sin and are born again and become converted to the truth when we get the constant companionship of that member of the Godhead, that is, get the *right* to the constant companionship. Nobody actually has that companionship all the time, because no one is perfect, no one lives in the ideal and perfect state. We do the best we can, and get sufficient of the companionship to have our sins burned out of us as though by fire. And that is what is involved when we use the expression "the baptism of fire," meaning the baptism of the Holy Ghost. That is a symbolism to mean that dross and evil are burned out of the human soul as though by fire, and as a consequence the individual becomes a new creature of the Holy Ghost, as Alma explained. So you become a new creature. There has been a change. There has been a conversion. In the past you walked after the manner of the world, but now you walk as becometh a Saint of God.

Latter-day Saints should obtain testimonies. We are a testimony-bearing people. Everywhere and always in our meetings somebody is saying, "I know that the work is true." This is sound and this is good; this is the way things ought to be. We ought to bear testimony nearly all the time, because when we bear testimony it strengthens the testimonies of other people. If we get the Spirit of the Lord in our soul, and certify by the power of the Holy Ghost that the work is true, then everybody that hears us who is in tune with the same Spirit knows also in his heart that the work is true. And so the spirit of the bearer is fed, and he is encouraged in faith and devotion.

The Importance of Testimony

Sometimes it is more important to bear testimony than it is to teach doctrine, although you need to teach the doctrine to have the foundation and the background laid so that the testimony itself will have more compelling effect on the hearts and souls of people. A testimony does not mean anything to them until they get enough doctrinal understanding to get their lives into that circumstance which would enable the Holy Ghost to tell them that the testimony being borne is true. We have, thus, testimony on the one hand, and conversion on the other hand.

Alma's Sudden and Miraculous Conversion

We may have testimonies without being converted. But all of us ought to be in the process of getting converted—and it is a process.

A person may get converted in a moment, miraculously. That is what happened to Alma the younger. He had been baptized in his youth, he had been promised the Holy Ghost, but he had never received it. He was too worldly wise; he went off with the sons of Mosiah to destroy the Church and to do away with the teachings of his father, who in effect was President of the Church. He was fighting, and in opposition to, the truth; he was like the college student who thinks he knows more than the Lord because he has learned a little science, and it does not seem to fit into what his parents have been telling him about the plan of salvation. Alma was in this state, and then this occasion occurred when a new light came into his soul, when he was changed from his fallen and carnal state to a state of righteousness. In his instance the conversion was miraculous, in the snap of a finger, almost. At least it was in that two-day period while he was in a trance.

The Step-by-Step Process of Conversion

But this is not the way it happens with most people. With most people, the conversion is a process; and it goes step by step, degree by degree, level by level, from a lower state to a higher, from grace to grace, until the time that the individual is wholly turned to the cause of righteousness. Now, this means that an individual overcomes one sin today and another sin tomorrow. He perfects his life in one field now, and in another field later on. And the conversion process goes on until it is completed, until we become, literally, as the Book of Mormon says, Saints of God instead of natural men (Mosiah 3:19).

Valiance in Testimony Required

What we are striving to do is to be converted. It is not enough to have a testimony. Do you want to know what happens to people who have a testimony who do not work at it? Read it in the vision of the degrees of glory (D&C 76:71–80); it is talking about the terrestrial kingdom. And it says that those who are not valiant in the testimony of Jesus, obtain not the crown in the kingdom of our God. That means members of the Church who are lukewarm. They are members of the Church who manage to get in tune on occasions, so that a flash of lightning comes to them, and they know in their hearts that the work is true. Maybe they work at it for a while. Maybe they go on a mission for a couple of years and then they fall away. They get into the state where they know the work is true, but they are not valiant. They do not endure in righteousness to the end.

There are many in the Church who know this work is true who do not do very much about it. But if you backed them into a corner and began to condemn the Church, they would stand up in wrath and ire and defend the kingdom. This is all to their credit and all to their advantage. But they "go fishing"; that is, they go off after the things of the world instead of putting first in their lives the things of God's kingdom, the things of righteousness. And hence they are lukewarm, they are not valiant.

If people who are not valiant in testimony go to the terrestrial kingdom, who is it that goes to the celestial, which is the kingdom of God, the one we are aspiring to? Obviously, the way you go to the celestial kingdom is to be valiant in testimony; that is, to be working at it, to make religion a working, living thing in your life. We have noted some passages that have told us two things that are involved in making religion a working, living thing in our lives. One of them said, "Strengthen thy brethren"; and the other one said, "Feed my sheep." And if we wanted to say a third thing that embraces the whole field, it would be "Keep my commandments." (See John 15:7-14; D&C 76:5-6.)

Examine Yourself

Try a little test on yourself. You know you have a testimony; that is not open to question. You already know the work is true. Are you converted? Have you been born again? Read the fifth chapter of Alma for the recitation of the tests that tell a person whether he has been born again and how he knows. You know if you have been born again, or you know the degree to which you have been born again; it is the measure to which you keep the commandments and feed the Lord's sheep and strengthen your brethren. In other words, it is the measure of your involvement in the things of the Spirit, in the things of the Church.

Religion is not just a theological matter. It is not just a matter of analyzing some passages of scripture and coming up with some conclusions. Religion is a matter of *doing* something.

"Pure religion and undefiled before God and the Father is this, To visit the fatherless and widows in their affliction, and to keep himself unspotted from the world" (James 1:27). That is two things. It is involvement and service, which means righteous living. It is visiting the fatherless and the widows; it is strengthening your brethren; it is keeping the commandments, being thereby unspotted from the world.

Religion is a thing that has to live in the lives of people, and hence all these expressions to the effect that we show our faith by our works (James 2:18), and that we are not hearers only, but doers (James 1:22), or should be. You can be a hearer if all that is involved in religion is this matter of theology, of studying and analyzing passages of scripture. But you are a doer if you get religion into operation in your life. You are a hearer, in part at least, if all that you have is testimony. But you become a doer when you add to a testimony this pure conversion of which we are speaking. Peter is the classical example, as long as we understand that in the experiences of his life he was as he was because the Holy Ghost had not yet been given in full.

The Holy Ghost has been given in full in our day in the sense that the companionship of that member of the Godhead is available to us.

We Seek Full Conversion

We want to be involved in the things of the Spirit. We do not want to sit on the sidelines and look in at some people who are converted. We want to be converted and participate in religion; we want to feel the promptings of the Spirit; we want to work miracles. We want to heal our sick; we want the gifts and graces that God gives the faithful. And they come when we get involved in the religion that he has so graciously and beneficently given us in this day. ("Be Ye Converted," BYU First Stake Conference, 11 February 1968.)

Chapter 7

WHY THE LORD ORDAINED PRAYER

Jesus' Prayer in Gethsemane

On the west wall of the Council of the Twelve room in the Salt Lake Temple hangs a picture of the Lord Jesus as he prays in Gethsemane to his Father.

In agony beyond compare, suffering both body and spirit to an extent incomprehensible to man—the coming torture of the cross paling into insignificance—our Lord is here pleading with his Father for strength to work out the infinite and eternal atonement.

Of all the prayers ever uttered, in time or in eternity—by gods, angels, or mortal men—this one stands supreme, above and apart, preeminent over all others.

In this garden called Gethsemane, outside Jerusalem's wall, the greatest member of Adam's race, the One whose every thought and word were perfect, pleaded with his Father to come off triumphant in the most torturous ordeal ever imposed on man or God.

There, amid the olive trees—the spirit of pure worship and perfect prayer—Mary's son struggled under the most crushing burden ever borne by mortal man.

There, in the quiet of the Judean night, while Peter, James, and John slept—with prayer on his lips—God's own Son took upon himself the sins of all men on conditions of repentance.

Upon his Suffering Servant, the great Elohim there and then placed the weight of all the sins of all men of all ages who believe in Christ and seek his face. And the Son, who bore the image of the Father, pleaded with his divine progenitor for power to fulfill the chief purpose for which he had come to earth.

This was the hour when all eternity hung in the balance. So great was the sin-created agony—laid on him who knew no sin—

that he sweat great drops of blood from every pore, and "would," within himself, that he "might not drink the bitter cup" (D&C 19:18). From creation's dawn to this supreme hour, and from this atoning night through all the endless ages of eternity there neither had been nor would be again such a struggle as this.

"The Lord Omnipotent who reigneth, who was, and is from all eternity to all eternity," who had "come down from heaven among the children of men" (Mosiah 3:5); the Great Creator, Upholder, and Preserver of all things from the beginning, who had made clay his tabernacle; the one person born into the world who had God as his father; the very Son of God himself—in a way beyond mortal comprehension—did then and there work out the infinite and eternal atonement, whereby all men are raised in immortality, while those who believe and obey come forth also to an inheritance of eternal life. God the Redeemer ransomed men from the temporal and spiritual death brought upon them by Adam's fall.

And it was at this hour that he, who then bought us with his blood (Acts 20:25), offered the most pleading and poignant personal prayer ever to fall from mortal lips. God the Son prayed to God the Father, that the will of the one might be swallowed up in the will of the other, and that he might fulfill the promise made by him when he was chosen to be the Redeemer: "Father, thy will be done, and the glory be thine forever" (Moses 4:4).

True, as an obedient son whose sole desire was to do the will of the Father who sent him, our Lord prayed always and often during his mortal probation. By natural inheritance, because God was his father, Jesus was endowed with greater powers of intellect and spiritual insight than anyone else has ever possessed. But in spite of his superlative natural powers and endowments—or, shall we not rather say, because of them (for truly the more spiritually perfected and intellectually gifted a person is, the more he recognizes his place in the infinite scheme of things and knows thereby his need for help and guidance from Him who truly is infinite)—and so by virtue of his superlative powers and endowments, Jesus above all men felt the need for constant communion with the source of all power, all intelligence, and all goodness.

When the time came to choose the twelve special witnesses who should bear record of him and his law unto the ends of the earth, and who should sit with him on twelve thrones judging the whole house of Israel, how did he make the choice? The inspired account says: "He went out into a mountain to pray, and continued all night in prayer to God." Having thus come to know the mind and will of Him whose offspring he was, "when it was day, . . . he chose twelve, whom also he named apostles." (Luke 6:12–13.)

When the hour of his arrest and passion were at hand; when there remained one more great truth to be impressed on the Twelve —that if they were to succeed in the assigned work and merit eternal reward with him and his Father, they must be one even as he and the Father were one—at this hour of supreme import, he taught the truth involved as part of his great intercessory prayer, fragments of which are preserved for us in John 17.

When he, after his resurrection—note it well: after his resurrection, he was still praying to the Father!—when he, glorified and perfected, sought to give the Nephites the most transcendent spiritual experience they were able to bear, he did it, not in a sermon, but in a prayer. "The things which he prayed cannot be written," the record says, but those who heard bore this testimony:

"The eye hath never seen, neither hath the ear heard, before, so great and marvelous things as we saw and heard Jesus speak unto the Father; And no tongue can speak, neither can there be written by any man, neither can the hearts of men conceive so great and marvelous things as we both saw and heard Jesus speak; and no one can conceive of the joy which filled our souls at the time we heard him pray for us unto the Father." (3 Ne. 17:15–17.)

But here in Gethsemane—as a pattern for all suffering, burdened, agonizing men—he poured out his soul to his Father with pleadings never equaled. What petitions he made, what expressions of doctrine he uttered, what words of glory and adoration he then spoke we do not know. Perhaps like his coming prayer among the Nephites the words could not be written, but could be understood only by the power of the Spirit. We do know that on three separate occasions in his prayer he said in substance and thought content: "Oh my Father, if it be possible, let this cup pass from me: nevertheless not as I will, but as thou wilt" (Matt. 26:39).

Here in Gethsemane, as he said to his Father, "Not my will, but thine, be done," the inspired record says, "There appeared an angel unto him from heaven, strengthening him. And being in an agony he prayed more earnestly: and his sweat was as it were great drops of blood falling to the ground." (Luke 22:42–44.)

Now, here is a marvelous thing. Note it well. The Son of God "prayed more earnestly"! He who did all things well, whose every word was right, whose every emphasis was proper; he to whom the Father gave his Spirit without measure; he who was the only perfect being ever to walk the dusty paths of planet earth—the Son of God "prayed more earnestly," teaching us, his brethren, that all prayers, his included, are not alike, and that a greater need calls forth more earnest and faith-filled pleadings before the throne of him to whom the prayers of the Saints are a sweet savor.

In this setting, then, seeking to learn and live the law of prayer so that we, like him, can go where he and his Father are, let us summarize what is truly involved in the glorious privilege of approaching the throne of grace. Let us learn how to do so boldly and efficaciously, not in word only but in spirit and in power, so that we may pull down upon ourselves, even as he did upon himself, the very power of heaven. Perhaps the following ten items will enable us to crystallize our thinking and will guide us in perfecting our personal prayers.

1. What Prayer Is

Once we dwelt in our Father's presence, saw his face, and knew his will. We spoke to him, heard his voice, and received counsel and direction from him. Such was our status as spirit children in the premortal life. We then walked by sight.

Now we are far removed from the divine presence; we no longer see his face and hear his voice as we then did. We now walk by faith. But we need his counsel and direction as much or more than we needed it when we mingled with all the seraphic hosts of heaven before the world was. In his infinite wisdom, knowing our needs, a gracious Father has provided prayer as the means of continuing to communicate with him. As I have written elsewhere:

"To pray is to speak with God, either vocally or by forming the thoughts involved in the mind. Prayers may properly include expressions of praise, thanksgiving, and adoration; they are the solemn occasions during which the children of God petition their Eternal Father for those things, both temporal and spiritual, which they feel are needed to sustain them in all the varied tests of this mortal probation. Prayers are occasions of confession—occasions when in humility and contrition, having broken hearts and contrite spirits, the Saints confess their sins to Deity and implore him to grant his cleansing forgiveness." (*Mormon Doctrine*, 2nd ed., p. 581.)

2. Why We Pray

There are three basic and fundamental reasons why we pray:

a. *We are commanded to do so.* Prayer is not something of relative insignificance which we may choose to do if the fancy strikes us. Rather, it is an eternal decree of Deity. "Thou shalt repent and call upon God in the name of the Son forevermore,'' was his word in the first dispensation. ''And Adam and Eve, his wife, ceased not to call upon God.'' (Moses 5:8, 16.) In our day we are instructed: ''Ask, and ye shall receive; knock, and it shall be opened unto you'' (D&C 4:7). Home teachers are appointed in the Church to ''visit the house of each member, and exhort them to pray vocally and in secret'' (D&C 20:47). And speaking by way of ''commandment'' to his Latter-day people, the Lord says: ''He that observeth not his prayers before the Lord in the season thereof, let him be had in remembrance before the judge of my people'' (D&C 68:33).

b. *Temporal and spiritual blessings follow proper prayer.* As all the revelations show, the portals of heaven swing wide open to those who pray in faith; the Lord rains down righteousness upon them; they are preserved in perilous circumstances; the earth yields her fruits to them; and the joys of the gospel dwell in their hearts.

c. *Prayer is essential to salvation.* No accountable person ever has or ever will gain celestial rest unless he learns to communicate with the Master of that realm. And ''how knoweth a man the master whom he has not served, and who is a stranger unto him, and is far from the thoughts and intents of his heart?'' (Mosiah 5:13).

3. Pray to the Father

We are commanded to pray to the Father (Elohim) in the name of the Son (Jehovah). The revelations are perfectly clear on this. ''Ye must always pray unto the Father in my name,'' the Lord Jesus said to the Nephites (3 Ne. 18:19). And yet there is an amazing mass of false doctrine and false practice in the churches of Christendom and occasionally even among the true Saints.

There are those who pray to so-called saints and plead with them to intercede with Christ on their behalf. The official prayer books of the various sects have some prayers addressed to the Father, others to the Son, and others to the Holy Spirit, and it is the exception rather than the rule in some quarters when prayers are offered in the name of Christ. There are those who feel they gain some special relationship with our Lord by addressing petitions directly to him.

It is true that when we pray to the Father, the answer comes from the Son, because ''there is . . . one mediator between God and men, the man Christ Jesus'' (1 Tim. 2:5). Joseph Smith, for instance, asked the Father, in the name of the Son, for answers to questions, and the answering voice was not that of the Father but of the Son, because Christ is our advocate, our intercessor, the God (under the Father) who rules and regulates this earth.

And it is true that sometimes in his answers Christ assumes the prerogative of speaking by divine investiture of authority as though he were the Father; that is, he speaks in the first person and uses the name of the Father because the Father has placed his own name on the Son. For a full explanation of this see the official pronouncement "The Father and the Son: A Doctrinal Exposition by the First Presidency and the Twelve," beginning on page 465 of the *Articles of Faith* by Elder James E. Talmage.

It is true that we and all the prophets can with propriety shout praises to the Lord Jehovah (Christ). We can properly sing unto his holy name, as in the cry, "Hallelujah," which means praise Jah, or praise Jehovah. But what we must have perfectly clear is that we *always* pray to the Father, not the Son, and we *always* pray in the name of the Son.

4. Ask for Temporal and Spiritual Blessings

We are entitled and expected to pray for all things properly needed, whether temporal or spiritual. We do not have the right of unlimited petition; our requests must be based on righteousness. "Ye ask, and receive not, because ye ask amiss, that ye may consume it upon your lusts" (James 4:3).

Amulek speaks of crops and herds, of fields and flocks, as well as of mercy and salvation, when he lists those things for which we should pray (see Alma 34:17–29). The Lord's Prayer speaks of "our daily bread" (Matt. 6:11), and James urges us to seek for wisdom (see James 1:5) which in principle means we should seek all of the attributes of godliness. Our revelation says, "Ye are commanded in all things to ask of God" (D&C 46:7). Nephi says, "Ye must not perform any thing unto the Lord save in the first place ye shall pray unto the Father in the name of Christ, that he will consecrate thy performance unto thee, that thy performance may be for the welfare of thy soul" (2 Ne. 32:9). And the Lord's promise to all the faithful is: "If thou shalt ask, thou shalt receive revelation upon revelation, knowledge upon knowledge, that thou mayest know the mysteries and peaceable things—that which bringeth joy, that which bringeth life eternal" (D&C 42:61).

It is clear that we should pray for all that in wisdom and righteousness we should have. Certainly we should seek for a testimony, for revelations, for all of the gifts of the Spirit, including the

fulfillment of the promise in Doctrine and Covenants 93:1 of seeing
the face of the Lord. But above all our other petitions, we should
plead for the companionship of the Holy Ghost in this life and for
eternal life in the world to come. When the Nephite Twelve "did
pray for that which they most desired," the Book of Mormon account records, "they desired that the Holy Ghost should be given
unto them" (3 Ne. 19:9). The greatest gift a man can receive in this
life is the gift of the Holy Ghost, even as the greatest gift he can gain
in eternity is eternal life (D&C 14:7).

5. *Pray for Others*

Our prayers are neither selfish nor self-centered. We seek the
spiritual well-being of all men. Some of our prayers are for the benefit and blessing of the Saints alone, others are for the enlightenment
and benefit of all our Father's children. "I pray not for the world,"
Jesus said in his great intercessory prayer, "but for them which
thou hast given me" (John 17:9). But he also commanded: "Love
your enemies, bless them that curse you, do good to them that hate
you, and pray for them which despitefully use you, and persecute
you" (Matt. 5:44).

And so, just as Christ "is the Saviour of all men, specially of
those that believe" (1 Tim. 4:10), so we pray for all men, but especially for ourselves, our families, the Saints in general, and those
who seek to believe and know the truth. Of especial concern to us
are the sick who belong to the household of faith and those who are
investigating the restored gospel. "Pray one for another, that ye
may be healed," James says, with reference to Church members,
for "the effectual fervent prayer of a righteous man availeth much"
(James 5:16). And as to those who attend our meetings and who
seek to learn the truth, the Lord Jesus says: "Ye shall pray for them
unto the Father, in my name," in the hope that they shall repent
and be baptized (3 Ne. 18:23; see also v. 30).

6. *When and Where to Pray*

"Pray always" (see 2 Ne. 32:9). So it is written—meaning:
Pray regularly, consistently, day in and day out; and also, live with
the spirit of prayer always in your heart, so that your thoughts,
words, and acts are always such as will please him who is Eternal.
Amulek speaks of praying "both morning, mid-day, and evening,"
and says we should pour out our souls to the Lord in our closets, in

our secret places, and in the wilderness (Alma 34:17–29). Jesus commanded both personal and family prayer: "Watch and pray always," he said; and also, "Pray in your families unto the Father, always in my name, that your wives and your children may be blessed." (3 Ne. 18:15, 21.)

The practice of the Church in our day is to have family prayer twice daily, plus our daily personal prayers, plus a blessing on our food at mealtimes (except in those public or other circumstances where it would be ostentatious or inappropriate to do so), plus proper prayers in our meetings.

7. How to Pray

Always address the Father; give thanks for your blessings; petition him for just and proper needs; and do it in the name of Jesus Christ.

As occasion and circumstances require and permit, confess your sins; counsel with the Lord relative to your personal problems; praise him for his goodness and grace; and utter such expressions of worship and doctrine as will bring you to a state of oneness with him whom you worship.

Two much-overlooked, underworked, and greatly needed guidelines for approved prayer are:

a. *Pray earnestly, sincerely, with real intent, and with all the energy and strength of your soul.* Mere words do not suffice. Vain repetitions are not enough. Literary excellence is of little worth. Indeed, true eloquence is not in excellence of language (although this should be sought for), but in the feeling that accompanies the words, however poorly they are chosen or phrased. Mormon said: "Pray unto the Father with all the energy of heart" (Moro. 7:48). Also, it is "counted evil unto a man, if he shall pray and not with real intent of heart; yea, and it profiteth him nothing, for God receiveth none such" (Moro. 7:9).

b. *Pray by the power of the Holy Ghost.* This is the supreme and ultimate achievement in prayer. The promise is: "The Spirit shall be given unto you by the prayer of faith" (D&C 42:14), "and if ye are purified and cleansed from all sin, ye shall ask whatsoever you will in the name of Jesus and it shall be done" (D&C 50:29). Of the coming millennial era, when prayers shall be perfected, the scripture says: "And in that day whatsoever any man shall ask, it shall be given unto him" (D&C 101:27).

8. *Use Both Agency and Prayer*

It is not, never has been, and never will be the design and purpose of the Lord—however much we seek him in prayer—to answer all our problems and concerns without struggle and effort on our part. This mortality is a probationary estate. In it we have our agency. We are being tested to see how we will respond in various situations; how we will decide issues; what course we will pursue while we are here walking, not by sight but by faith. Hence, we are to solve our own problems and then to counsel with the Lord in prayer and receive a spiritual confirmation that our decisions are correct.

As he set forth in his work of translating the Book of Mormon, Joseph Smith did not simply ask the Lord what the characters on the plates meant, rather he was required to study the matter out in his mind, make a decision of his own, and then ask the Lord if his conclusions were correct (see D&C 8, 9). So it is with us in all that we are called upon to do. Prayer and works go together. If and when we have done all we can, then in consultation with the Lord, through mighty and effectual prayer, we have power to come up with the right conclusions.

9. *Follow the Formalities of Prayer*

These (though many) are simple and easy and contribute to the spirit of worship that attends sincere and effectual prayers. Our Father is glorified and exalted; he is an omnipotent being. We are as the dust of the earth in comparison, and yet we are his children with access, through prayer, to his presence. Any act of obeisance which gets us in the proper frame of mind when we pray is all to the good.

We seek the guidance of the Holy Spirit in our prayers. We ponder the solemnities of eternity in our hearts. We approach Deity in the spirit of awe, reverence, and worship. We speak in hushed and solemn tones. We listen for his answer. We are at our best in prayer. We are in the divine presence.

Almost by instinct, therefore, we do such things as bow our heads and close our eyes; fold our arms, or kneel, or fall on our faces. We use the sacred language of prayer (that of the King James Version of the Bible—thee, thou, thine, not you and your). And we say Amen when others pray, thus making their utterances ours, their prayers our prayers.

10. Live as You Pray

There is an old saying to this effect: ''If you can't pray about a thing, don't do it,'' which is intended to tie our prayers and acts together. And true it is that our deeds, in large measure, are children of our prayers. Having prayed, we act; our proper petitions have the effect of charting a righteous course of conduct for us. The boy that prays (earnestly and devoutly and in faith) that he may go on a mission, will then prepare himself for his mission, and in fact receive his call to service. The young people who pray always, in faith, to marry in the temple, and then act accordingly, are never satisfied with worldly marriage. So intertwined are prayer and works that having recited the law of prayer in detail, Amulek then concludes:

''After ye have done all these things, if ye turn away the needy, and the naked, and visit not the sick and afflicted, and impart of your substance, if ye have, to those who stand in need—I say unto you, if ye do not any of these things, behold, your prayer is vain, and availeth you nothing, and ye are as hypocrites who do deny the faith'' (Alma 34:28).

We have now spoken, briefly and in imperfect fashion, of prayer and some of the great and eternal principles which attend it. There remains now but one thing more—to testify that these doctrines are sound and that prayer is a living reality which leads to eternal life.

Prayer may be gibberish and nonsense to the carnal mind; but to the Saints of God it is the avenue of communications with the Unseen.

To the unbelieving and rebellious it may seem as an act of senseless piety born of mental instability; but to those who have tasted its fruits it becomes an anchor to the soul through all the storms of life.

Prayer is of God—not the vain repetitions of the heathen, not the rhetoric of the prayer books, not the insincere lispings of lustful men—but that prayer which is born of knowledge, which is nurtured by faith in Christ, which is offered in spirit and in truth.

Prayer opens the door to peace in this life and eternal life in the world to come. Prayer is essential to salvation. Unless and until we make it a living part of us so that we speak to our Father and have his voice answer, by the power of his Spirit, we are yet in our sins.

Oh, thou by whom we come to God,
The Life, the Truth, the Way!
The path of prayer thyself hast trod;
Lord, teach us how to pray.
("Prayer Is the Soul's Sincere Desire," *Hymns of The Church of Jesus Christ of Latter-day Saints*, 1985, No. 145. Hereafter cited as *LDS Hymns* No.)

Of all these things I testify, and pray to the Father in the name of the Son, that all of the Latter-day Saints, as well as all those in the world who will join with them, may — through prayer and that righteous living which results therefrom — gain peace and joy here and an eternal fulness of all good things hereafter. Even so. Amen. ("Why the Lord Ordained Prayer," *Ensign*, January 1976, pp. 7–12.)

Chapter 8

HOW TO OBTAIN
PERSONAL REVELATION

Church Leaders Receive Revelation

As a people, we are in the habit of saying that we believe in
latter-day revelation. We announce quite boldly that the heavens
have been opened, that God has spoken in our day, that angels
have ministered to men, that there have been visions and revelations, and that no gift or grace possessed by the ancients has been
withheld—it has all been revealed anew in our day.

But ordinarily when we talk this way, we think of Joseph
Smith, Brigham Young, David O. McKay, or some other President
of the Church. We think of Apostles and prophets—men called,
selected or foreordained to hold the positions which they hold and
to do the ministerial service that is theirs. We think of them and of
the general principle of the Church itself operating by revelation.

Now, there is no question at all about this: The organization
that we belong to is literally the Lord's kingdom. It is the kingdom
of God on earth, and is designed to prepare and qualify us to go to
the kingdom of God in heaven which is the celestial kingdom. This
Church is guided by revelation. I have sat in meetings with the
Brethren on many occasions when the President of the Church,
who is the prophet of God on earth, has said in humility and with
fervent testimony that the veil is thin, that the Lord is guiding and
directing the affairs of the Church, and that it is His Church and He
is making His will manifest.

There *is* inspiration at the head, and the Church is in the line
and course of its duty; it is progressing in the way that the Lord
would have it progress. There is no question that the Church receives revelation all the time. Someone said to Brother John A.
Widtsoe, speaking derogatorily, "When did the Church get its last

revelation?'' He said, ''Well, this is Sunday, the last one came last Thursday.'' And this is just how simple it is. The Brethren get direction and revelation all the time, as they meet to direct the affairs of the Church.

Revelation Not Reserved to a Few

I desire to point attention, however, to the fact that revelation is not restricted to the prophet of God on earth. The visions of eternity are not reserved for Apostles — they are not reserved for the General Authorities. Revelation is something that should come to *every* individual. God is no respecter of persons (Acts 10:34), and every soul, in the ultimate sense, is just as precious in his sight as the souls of those that are called to positions of leadership. Because he operates on principles of eternal, universal and never-deviating law, any individual that abides the law which entitles him to get revelation can know exactly and precisely what any prophet knows, can entertain angels just as well as Joseph Smith entertained them, and can be in tune in full measure with all of the things of the Spirit. (Alma 26:21–22.) (BYU Devotional, 11 October 1966; published as ''How to Get Personal Revelation,'' *Ensign*, June 1980, pp. 46–50.)

Personal Revelation

Joseph Smith said: ''Reading the experience of others, or the revelations given to *them*, can never give *us* a comprehensive view of our condition and true relation to God. Knowledge of these things can only be obtained by experience through the ordinances of God set forth for that purpose. Could you gaze into heaven five minutes, you would know more than you would by reading all that ever was written on the subject.'' (*Teachings*, p. 324.)

Now note this statement: ''Could you gaze into heaven five minutes, you would know more than you would by reading all that ever was written on the subject.'' I think our concern is to get personal revelation, to know for ourselves, independent of any other individual or set of individuals, what the mind and the will of the Lord is as pertaining to his Church and as pertaining to us in our individual concerns.

Intellectual and Spiritual Fields

We can divide the realm of inquiry into an intellectual field and a spiritual field. In academic halls, we seek knowledge primarily in the intellectual field, which knowledge comes in most instances by reason and through the senses. Somehow, by ordained laws, we have power through reason and through the sense that God has given us, to convey knowledge to the spirit that is within us. "The mind of man," the Prophet said, in effect, "is in the spirit" (see *Teachings,* p. 353). So we say that we learn certain things—that we do this in an intellectual realm. Some knowledge comes to us in this way, and we spend a very great deal of time engaged in this pursuit.

This is tremendously vital and important—and we encourage and urge it upon all who desire progression, enlightenment, and advancement in their lives.

But we need to devote an increasingly large portion of our time in the actual pursuit of knowledge in the spiritual realm. When we deal with spiritual realities, we are not talking about gaining something by reason alone, we are not talking about conveying in some way knowledge to the mind or the spirit that is within us through the sense alone, but we are talking about revelation. We are talking about learning how to come to a knowledge of the things of God by attuning the spirit that we have to the eternal Spirit of God. Such a course, primarily, is the channel and way that revelation comes to an individual.

It does not concern me very much that somebody writes or evaluates or analyzes from an intellectual standpoint either a doctrinal or Church problem of any sort. No one questions that everything in the spiritual realm is in total and complete accord with the intellectual realities that we arrive at through reason, but when the two are compared and evaluated and weighed as to their relative merits, the things that are important are in the spiritual realm and not the intellectual. The things of God are known only by the Spirit of God (1 Cor. 12:3).

True Religion Requires Personal Involvement

It is true that you can reason about doctrinal matters, but you do not get religion into your life until it becomes a matter of *personal experience*—until you feel something in your soul, until there has been a change made in your heart, until you become a new creature of the Holy Ghost. Providentially, *every* member of the Church has the opportunity to do this because, in connection with baptism, every member of the Church has the hands of a legal administrator placed on his head, and he is given the promise, "Receive the Holy Ghost." He thus obtains "the gift of the Holy Ghost" which, by definition, means that he then has the right to the constant companionship of this member of the Godhead, based upon his personal righteousness and faithfulness.

Now, I say we are *entitled* to revelation. I say that every member of the Church, independent and irrespective of any position that he may hold, is entitled to get revelation from the Holy Ghost; he is entitled to entertain angels; he is entitled to view the visions of eternity; and if we would like to go the full measure, he is entitled to see God the same way that any prophet in literal and actual reality has seen the face of Deity (D&C 76:1–10; 93:1).

Each Man a Prophet to Himself

We talk about latter-day prophets; we think in terms of prophets who tell the future destiny of the Church and the world. But, in addition to that, the fact is that every person should be a prophet for himself and in his own concerns and in his own affairs. It was Moses who said: "Would God that all the Lord's people were prophets, and that the Lord would put his spirit upon them" (Num. 11:29). It was Paul who said we should "covet to prophesy" (1 Cor. 14:39).

A Doctrine of Personal Revelation

Let me take occasion to read a few statements from the revelations given to the Prophet Joseph Smith which, taken together, outline the formula, as it were, by which I as an individual can come to know the things of God by the power of the Spirit.

One thing the Lord said was this: "I will tell you in your mind and in your heart, by the Holy Ghost, which shall come upon you and which shall dwell in your heart. Now, behold, this is the spirit of revelation." (D&C 8:2–3.)

This revelation speaks of spirit speaking to spirit—the Holy Spirit speaking to the spirit within me and in a way incomprehensible to the mind, but plain and clear to spirit understanding—conveying knowledge, giving intelligence, giving truth and giving sure knowledge of the things of God.

Now, this applies to everyone: "God shall give unto you knowledge by his Holy Spirit, yea, by the unspeakable gift of the Holy Ghost, that has not been revealed since the world was until now; Which our forefathers have awaited with anxious expectations to be revealed in the last times" (D&C 121:26–27).

Here is another passage—a glorious one. This is *not* directed to the General Authorities. This is *not* directed to the prophets of God. This is directed to every living soul in the Church. In other words, it is a personal revelation to you:

"For thus saith the Lord—I, the Lord, am merciful and gracious unto those who fear me, and delight to honor those who serve me in righteousness and in truth unto the end.

"Great shall be their reward and eternal shall be their glory.

"And to them [the whole body of the kingdom] will I reveal all mysteries, yea, all the hidden mysteries of my kingdom from days of old, and for ages to come, will I make known unto them the good pleasure of my will concerning all things pertaining to my kingdom.

"Yea, even the wonders of eternity shall they know, and things to come will I show them, even the things of many generations.

"And their wisdom shall be great, and their understanding reach to heaven; and before them the wisdom of the wise shall perish, and the understanding of the prudent shall come to naught.

"For by my Spirit will I enlighten them, and by my power will I make known unto them the secrets of my will—yea, even those things which eye has not seen, nor ear heard, nor yet entered into the heart of man." (D&C 76:1–10.)

We can entertain angels, we can dream dreams, we can see visions, we can see the face of the Lord. Here is one promise in that field: "Verily, thus saith the Lord: It shall come to pass that every soul who forsaketh his sins and cometh unto me, and calleth on my name, and obeyeth my voice, and keepeth my commandments, shall see my face and know that I am (D&C 93:1).

No Salvation Without Revelation

The Prophet Joseph said that the veil might as well be rent today as any day, provided we come together as the elders of the kingdom in faith and in righteousness and qualify to have the visions of eternity (*Teachings*, p. 9).

Here is a statement from Joseph Smith:

"Salvation cannot come without revelation [and I am not now speaking about the revelation that gave the dispensation in which we live—I am speaking of personal revelation to individuals]; it is vain for anyone to minister without it. No man is a minister of Jesus Christ without being a Prophet. No man can be a minister of Jesus Christ except he has a testimony of Jesus; and this is the spirit of prophecy. Whenever salvation has been administered, it has been by testimony. Men of the present time testify of heaven and hell, and have never seen either; and I will say that no man knows these things without this.'' (*Teachings,* p. 160.)

We are entitled to revelation. Personal revelation is essential to our salvation. The scriptures abound with illustrations of what has happened. Here is one of the things Nephi said: ''If ye will not harden your hearts, and ask me in faith, believing that ye shall receive, with diligence in keeping my commandments, surely these things shall be made known unto you'' (1 Ne. 15:11).

There is a Book of Mormon statement about some tremendously successful missionaries, the sons of Mosiah: ''They were men of a sound understanding and they had searched the scriptures diligently, that they might know the word of God.

''But this is not all; they had given themselves to much prayer, and fasting; therefore they had the spirit of prophecy, and the spirit of revelation, and when they taught, they taught with power and authority of God.'' (Alma 17:2–3.)

I shall take time for one more quotation. This is the Prophet Joseph Smith:

''A person may profit by noticing the first intimation of the spirit of revelation; for instance, when you feel pure intelligence flowing into you, it may give you sudden strokes of ideas, so that by noticing it, you may find it fulfilled the same day or soon; (i.e.,) those things that were presented unto your minds by the Spirit of God, will come to pass; and thus by learning the Spirit of God and understanding it, you may grow into the principle of revelation, until you become perfect in Christ'' (*Teachings,* p. 151).

We Need Religious *Experience*

The scriptures say much about this. The Prophet and all of the prophets have said much about it. What it means to us is that we need religious experience; we need to become personally involved with God. Our concern is not to read what somebody has said *about* religion. I read frequently, but primarily for amusement or diversion, what somebody has said in a critical vein about the Church or what some professor of religion has said about the tenets of Christianity. Actually, such views are not of great importance. It is totally immaterial what someone has to say about the Church in a critical vein; or when someone is writing to evaluate from an intellectual standpoint a doctrine or a practice or a so-called program of the

Church—it is just totally inconsequential as far as the Church is concerned and as its spiritually inclined people are concerned. Religion is *not* a matter of the intellect.

What We Can Do

I repeat, the better the intellect, the more we are able to evaluate spiritual principles, and it is a marvelous thing to be learned and educated and have insight and mental capacity, because we can use these talents and abilities in the spiritual realm. But what counts in the field of religion is to become a personal participant in it. Instead of reading all that has been written and evaluating all that all the scholars of all the world have said about heaven and hell, we need to do what the Prophet said: gaze five minutes into heaven. As a consequence, we would know more than all that has ever been evaluated and written and analyzed on the subject.

Religion is a matter of getting the Holy Ghost into the life of an individual. We study, of course, and we need to evaluate. And by virtue of our study we come up with some foundations that get us into the frame of mind so that we *can* seek the things of the Spirit. But in the end the result is getting our souls touched by the Spirit of God.

A Formula for Obtaining Revelation

Would you like a formula to tell you how to get personal revelation? My formula is simply this:
1. Search the scriptures.
2. Keep the commandments.
3. Ask in faith.

Any person who will do this will get his heart so in tune with the Infinite that there will come into his being, from the "still small voice," the eternal realities of religion. And as he progresses and advances and comes nearer to God, there will be a day when he will entertain angels, when he will see visions, and the final end is to view the face of God.

Religion is a thing of the Spirit. Use your intellectuality to help you, but in the final analysis, you have to get in tune with the Lord.

The first great revelation that a person needs to get is to know of the divinity of the work. We call that a testimony. When a person gets a testimony, he has thereby learned how to get in tune with the Spirit and get revelation. So, repeating the connection—getting in tune anew—he can get knowledge to direct him in his personal affairs. Then ultimately enjoying and progressing in this gift, he can get all the revelations of eternity that the Prophet or all the prophets have had in all the ages.

A Testimony

To some extent I, along with you, have received revelation. I have received revelation that tells me that this work is true. And as a consequence, I *know* it. And I know it independent of any study and research, and I know it because the Holy Spirit has spoken to the spirit that is within me, and given me a testimony. As a consequence, I can stand as a legal administrator and say in verity that Jesus Christ is the Son of God, that Joseph Smith is his prophet, that the President of the Church wears the prophetic mantle today, and that The Church of Jesus Christ of Latter-day Saints is the only true and living Church upon the face of the whole earth.

And, further, in connection with the matter we are here considering, I can certify and testify that every living soul who will abide the law, search the scriptures, keep the commandments, and ask in faith, can have personal revelation from the Almighty to the great glory and satisfaction of his soul here and to his ultimate salvation in the mansion on high. (BYU Devotional, 11 October 1966; published as "How to Get Personal Revelation," *Ensign*, June 1980, pp. 46–50.)

Chapter 9

REVELATION
ON PRIESTHOOD

Personal Testimony of Revelation on Priesthood

I was present when the Lord revealed to President Spencer W. Kimball that the time had come, in His eternal providences, to offer the fulness of the gospel and the blessings of the holy priesthood to all men.

I was present, with my brethren of the Twelve and the counselors in the First Presidency, when all of us heard the same voice and received the same message from on high.

It was on a glorious June day in 1978. All of us were together in an upper room in the Salt Lake Temple. We were engaged in fervent prayer, pleading with the Lord to manifest his mind and will concerning those who are entitled to receive his holy priesthood. President Kimball himself was mouth, offering the desires of his heart and of our hearts to that God whose servants we are.

In his prayer President Kimball asked that all of us might be cleansed and made free from sin so that we might receive the Lord's word. He counseled freely and fully with the Lord, was given utterance by the power of the Spirit, and what he said was inspired from on high. It was one of those rare and seldom-experienced times when the disciples of the Lord are perfectly united, when every heart beats as one, and when the same Spirit burns in every bosom.

Perfect Unity Among Presidency and Twelve

I have thought since that our united prayer must have been like that of the Nephite disciples—the Lord's Twelve in that day and for that people—who "were gathered together and were united in mighty prayer and fasting" to learn the name that the Lord had given to his Church (3 Ne. 27:1–3). In their day the Lord came personally to answer their petition; in our day he sent his Spirit to deliver the message.

And as it was with our Nephite brethren of old, so it was with us. We too had come together in the spirit of true worship and with unity of desire. We were all fasting and had just concluded a meeting of some three hours' duration that was attended by nearly all of the General Authorities. That meeting was also held in the room of the First Presidency and the Twelve in the holy temple. In it we had been counseled by the First Presidency, had heard the messages and testimonies of about fifteen of the Brethren, had renewed our covenants, in the ordinance of sacrament, to serve God and keep his commandments that we might always have his Spirit to be with us, and, surrounding the holy altar, had offered up the desire of our hearts to the Lord. After this meeting, which was one of great spiritual uplift and enlightenment, all of the Brethren except those in the Presidency and the Twelve were excused.

President Kimball Directs

When we were alone by ourselves in that sacred place where we meet weekly to wait upon the Lord, to seek guidance from his Spirit, and to transact the affairs of his earthly kingdom, President Kimball brought up the matter of the possible conferral of the priesthood upon those of all races. This was a subject that the group of us had discussed at length on numerous occasions in the preceding weeks and months. The President restated the problem involved, reminded us of our prior discussions, and said he had spent many days alone in this upper room pleading with the Lord for an answer to our prayers. He said that if the answer was to continue our present course of denying the priesthood to the seed of Cain, as the Lord had theretofore directed, he was prepared to defend that decision to the death. But, he said, if the long-sought day had come in which the curse of the past was to be removed, he thought we might prevail upon the Lord so to indicate. He expressed the hope that we might receive a clear answer one way or the other so the matter might be laid to rest.

The Brethren Share Feelings

At this point President Kimball asked the Brethren if any of them desired to express their feelings and views as to the matter in hand. We all did so, freely and fluently and at considerable length, each person stating his views and manifesting the feelings of his heart. There was a marvelous outpouring of unity, oneness, and agreement in council. This session continued for somewhat more than two hours. Then President Kimball suggested that we unite in formal prayer and said, modestly, that if it was agreeable with the rest of us he would act as voice.

Brethren Unite in Prayer

It was during that prayer that the revelation came. The Spirit of the Lord rested mightily upon us all; we felt something akin to what happened on the day of Pentecost and at the dedication of the Kirtland Temple. From the midst of eternity, the voice of God, conveyed by the power of the Spirit, spoke to his prophet. The message was that the time had now come to offer the fulness of the everlasting gospel, including celestial marriage, and the priesthood, and the blessings of the temple, to all men, without reference to race or color, solely on the basis of personal worthiness. And we all heard the same voice, received the same message, and became personal witnesses that the word received was the mind and will and voice of the Lord.

President Kimball's prayer was answered and our prayers were answered. He heard the voice and we heard the same voice. All doubt and uncertainty fled. He knew the answer and we knew the answer. And we are all living witnesses of the truthfulness of the word so graciously sent from heaven.

Ancient Curse Removed

The ancient curse is no more. The seed of Cain and Ham and Canaan and Egyptus and Pharaoh (Abr. 1:20-27; Moses 5:16-41; 7:8, 22)—all these now have power to rise up and bless Abraham as their father. All these, Gentile in lineage, may now come and inherit by adoption all the blessings of Abraham, Isaac, and Jacob (Rom. 8:14-24; 9:4; Gal. 4:5; Eph. 1:5; *Teachings*, pp. 149-50). All these may now be numbered with those in the one fold of the one shepherd who is Lord of all.

A Powerful Witness

In the days that followed the receipt of the new revelation, President Kimball and President Ezra Taft Benson—the senior and most spiritually experienced ones among us—both said, expressing the feelings of us all, that neither of them had ever experienced anything of such spiritual magnitude and power as was poured out upon the Presidency and the Twelve that day in the upper room in the house of the Lord. And of it I say: I was there; I heard the voice; and the Lord be praised that it has come to pass in our day.

"All Are Alike unto God"

Not long after this revelation came, I was scheduled to address nearly a thousand seminary and institute teachers on a Book of Mormon subject. After I arrived on the stand, Brother Joe J. Christensen, under whose direction the symposium was going forward, asked me to depart from my prepared talk and give those assembled some guidance relative to the new revelation. He asked if I would take 2 Nephi 26:33 as a text. This I agreed to do, and, accordingly, spoke the following words:

I would like to say something about the new revelation relative to our taking the priesthood to those of all nations and races. "He [meaning Christ, who is the Lord God] inviteth them all to come unto him and partake of his goodness; and he denieth none that come unto him, black and white, bond and free, male and female; and he remembereth the heathen; and all are alike unto God, both Jew and Gentile" (2 Ne. 26:33).

These words have now taken on a new meaning. We have caught a new vision of their true significance. This also applies to a great number of other passages in the revelations. Since the Lord gave this revelation on the priesthood, our understanding of many passages has expanded. Many of us never imagined or supposed that they had the extensive and broad meaning that they do have.

I shall give you a few impressions relative to what has happened, and then attempt—if properly guided by the Spirit—to indicate to you the great significance that this event has in the Church, in the world, and where the rolling forth of the great gospel is concerned.

Gospel Preached on a Priority Basis

The gospel goes to various peoples and nations on a priority basis. We were commanded in the early days of this dispensation to preach the gospel to every nation, kindred, tongue, and people (see D&C 133:8, 16). Our revelations talk about its going to every creature (D&C 18:26–28; 58:64; 68:8; 80:1; 112:28–29; 124:128). There was, of course, no possible way for us to do all of this in the beginning days of our dispensation, nor can we now, in the full sense.

And so, guided by inspiration, we began to go from one nation and one culture to another. Someday, in the providences of the Lord, we shall get into Red China and Russia and the Middle East, and so on, until eventually the gospel will have been preached everywhere, to all people; and this will occur before the second coming of the Son of Man (Matt. 24:14; JS—M 1:31).

Not only is the gospel to go, on a priority basis and harmonious to a divine timetable, to one nation after another, but the whole history of God's dealings with men on earth indicates that such has been the case in the past; it has been restricted and limited where many people are concerned. For instance, in the day between Moses and Christ, the gospel went to the house of Israel almost exclusively. By the time of Jesus, the legal administrators and prophetic associates that he had were so fully indoctrinated with the concept of having the gospel go only to the house of Israel that they were totally unable to envision the true significance of his proclamation that after the Resurrection they should then go to all the world. They did not go to the gentile nations initially. In his own ministration, Jesus preached only to the lost sheep of the house of Israel, and had so commanded the Apostles (Matt. 10:6).

It is true that he made a few minor exceptions because of the faith and devotion of some gentile people. There was one woman who wanted to eat the crumbs that fell from the table of the children, causing him to say, "O woman, great is thy faith." (Matt. 15:28; see also Mark 7:27–28; Matt. 9:10; Luke 7:9.) With some minor exceptions, the gospel in that day went exclusively to Israel. The Lord had to give Peter the vision and revelation of the sheet coming down from heaven with the unclean meat on it, following which Cornelius sent the messenger to Peter to learn what he, Cornelius, and his gentile associates should do. The Lord commanded them that the gospel should go to the Gentiles, and so it was. (Acts 10:1–35.) There was about a quarter of a century, then, in New Testament times, when there were extreme difficulties among the Saints. They were weighing and evaluating, struggling with the problems of whether the gospel was to go only to the house of Israel or whether it now went to all men. Could all men come to him on an equal basis with the seed of Abraham?

There have been these problems, and the Lord has permitted them to arise. There is not any question about that. We do not envision the whole reason and purpose behind all of this; we can only suppose and reason that it is on the basis of preexistence and of our premortal devotion and faith.

You know this principle: God "hath made of one blood all nations of men for to dwell on all the face of the earth, and hath determined the times before appointed, and the bounds of their habitation; That they should seek the Lord, if haply they might feel after him, and find him" (Acts 17:26–27)—meaning that there is an appointed time for successive nations and peoples and races and cultures to be offered the saving truths of the gospel. There are nations today to whom we have not gone—notably Red China and Russia. But you can rest assured that we will fulfill the requirement of taking the gospel to those nations before the second coming of the Son of Man.

Gospel to Cover Earth Before Second Coming

And I have no hesitancy whatever in saying that before the Lord comes, in all those nations we will have congregations that are stable, secure, devoted, and sound. We will have stakes of Zion. We will have people who have progressed in spiritual things to the point where they have received all of the blessings of the house of the Lord. That is the destiny.

We have revelations that tell us that the gospel is to go to every nation, kindred, tongue, and people before the second coming of the Son of Man (Matt. 24:14; JS—M 1:31). And we have revelations that recite that when the Lord comes, he will find those who speak every tongue and are members of every nation and kindred, who will be kings and priests, who will live and reign on earth with him a thousand years (Rev. 5:9–10; 1 Ne. 14:12; D&C 90:11). That means, as you know, that people from all nations will have the blessings of the house of the Lord before the Second Coming.

We Follow Living *Prophets*

We have read these passages and their associated passages for many years. We have seen what the words say and have said to ourselves, "Yes, it says that, but we must read out of it the taking of the gospel and the blessings of the temple to the Negro people, because they are denied certain things." There are statements in our literature by the early Brethren that we have interpreted to mean that the Negroes would not receive the priesthood in mortality. I have said the same things, and people write me letters and say,

"You said such and such, and how is it now that we do such and such?" All I can say is that it is time disbelieving people repented and got in line and believed in a living, modern prophet. Forget everything that I have said, or what President Brigham Young or President George Q. Cannon or whoever has said in days past that is contrary to the present revelation. We spoke with a limited understanding and without the light and knowledge that now has come into the world.

We get our truth and light line upon line and precept upon precept (2 Ne. 28:30; Isa. 28:9–10; D&C 98:11–12; 128:21). We have now added a new flood of intelligence and light on this particular subject, and it erases all the darkness and all the views and all the thoughts of the past. They don't matter anymore.[1]

It doesn't make a particle of difference what anybody ever said about the Negro matter before the first day of June 1978. It is a new day and a new arrangement, and the Lord has now given the revelation that sheds light out into the world on this subject. As to any slivers of light or any particles of darkness of the past, we forget about them. We now do what meridian Israel did when the Lord said the gospel should go to the Gentiles. We forget all the statements that limited the gospel to the house of Israel, and we start going to the Gentiles.

Time Had Come in the Lord's Timetable

Obviously, the Brethren had had a great anxiety and concern about this problem for a long period of time, and President Spencer W. Kimball had been exercised and had sought the Lord in faith. When we seek the Lord on a matter, with sufficient faith and devotion, he gives us an answer. You will recall that the Book of Mormon teaches that if the Apostles in Jerusalem had asked the Lord, he would have told them about the Nephites (3 Ne. 15:18–24; 16:4). But they did not ask, and they did not manifest the faith — and they did not get an answer. One underlying reason for what happened to us is that the Brethren asked in faith; they petitioned and desired and wanted an answer — President Kimball in particular. And the other underlying principle is that in the eternal providences of the Lord, the time had come for extending the gospel to a race and a culture to whom it had previously been denied, at least as far as all of its blessings are concerned. So it was a matter of faith and righteousness and seeking on the one hand, and it was a matter of the divine timetable on the other hand. The time had arrived when the gospel, with all its blessings and obligations, should go to the Negro.

President Kimball Offers Inspired Prayer

Thus, in that setting, on the first day of June 1978, the First Presidency and the Twelve, after full discussions of the proposition and all the premises and principles that are involved, importuned the Lord for a revelation.

President Kimball was mouth, and he prayed with great faith and great fervor; this was one of those occasions when an inspired prayer was offered. You know the Doctrine and Covenants' statement that if we pray by the power of the Spirit we will receive answers to our prayers and it will be given us what we shall ask (D&C 50:30). It was given the President what he should ask. He prayed by the power of the Spirit, and there was a perfect unity, total and complete harmony, between the Presidency and the Twelve on the issue involved.

Revelation Came—and Comes—by Holy Ghost

And when President Kimball finished his prayer, the Lord gave a revelation by the power of the Holy Ghost. Revelation primarily comes by the power of the Holy Ghost. Always that member of the Godhead is involved. But most revelations, from the beginning to now, have come in that way. There have been revelations given in various ways on other occasions. The Father and the Son appeared in the Sacred Grove. Moroni, an angel from heaven, came relative to the Book of Mormon and the plates and relative to instructing the Prophet in the affairs that were destined to occur in this dispensation. There have been visions, notably the vision of the degrees of glory. There may be an infinite number of ways that God can ordain that revelations come. But, primarily, revelation comes by the power of the Holy Ghost. The principle is set forth in the Doctrine and Covenants (D&C 68:3–4), that whatever the elders of the Church speak, when moved upon by the power of the Holy Ghost, shall be scripture, shall be the mind and will and voice of the Lord.

Presidency and Twelve United Witnesses

On this occasion, because of the importuning and the faith, and because the hour and the time had arrived, the Lord in his providences poured out the Holy Ghost upon the First Presidency and the Twelve in a miraculous and marvelous manner, beyond anything that any then present had ever experienced. The revelation came to the President of the Church; it also came to each individual present. There were ten members of the Council of the Twelve and three of the First Presidency there assembled. The result was that President Kimball knew, and each one of us knew, independent of any other person, by direct and personal revelation to us, that the time had now come to extend the gospel and all its blessings and all its obligations, including the priesthood and the blessings of the house of the Lord, to those of every nation, culture, and race, including the black race. There was no question whatsoever as to what happened or as to the word and message that came.

The revelation came to the President of the Church, and in harmony with Church government, was announced by him; the announcement was made eight days later over the signature of the First Presidency. But in this instance, in addition to the revelation coming to the man who would announce it to the Church and to the world, and who was sustained as the mouthpiece of God on earth, the revelation came to every member of the body that I have named. They all knew it in the temple.

Eternal Import of This Revelation

In my judgment this was done by the Lord in this way because it was a revelation of such tremendous significance and import; one that would reverse the whole direction of the Church, procedurally and administratively; one that would affect the living and the dead; one that would affect the total relationship that we have with the world; one, I say, of such significance that the Lord wanted witnesses who could bear record that the thing had happened.

Now, if President Kimball had received the revelation and had asked for a sustaining vote, obviously he would have received it and the revelation would have been announced. But the Lord chose this other course, in my judgment, because of the tremendous import and the eternal significance of what was being revealed. This affects our missionary work and all of our preaching to the world. This affects our genealogical research and all of our temple ordinances. This affects what is going on in the spirit world, because the gospel is preached in the spirit world preparatory to men's receiving the vicarious ordinances that make them heirs to salvation and exaltation. This is a revelation of tremendous significance.

Revelation Affects Both Sides of the Veil

The vision of the degrees of glory begins by saying, "Hear, O ye heavens, and give ear, O earth" (D&C 76:1). In other words, in that revelation the Lord was announcing truth to heaven and to earth because those principles of salvation operate on both sides of the veil; and salvation is administered to an extent here to men, and it is administered to another extent in the spirit world. We correlate and combine our activities and do certain things for the salvation of men while we are in mortality, and then certain things are done for the salvation of men while they are in the spirit world awaiting the day of resurrection.

Saints Should Avoid Speculation and Exaggeration

Once again a revelation was given that affects this sphere of activity and the sphere that is to come. And so it has tremendous significance; the eternal import was such that it came in the way it did. The Lord could have sent messengers from the other side to deliver it, but he did not. He gave the revelation by the power of the Holy Ghost. Latter-day Saints have a complex: many of them desire to magnify and build upon what has occurred, and they delight to think of miraculous things. And maybe some of them would like to believe that the Lord himself was there, or that the Prophet Joseph Smith came to deliver the revelation, which was one of the possibilities. Well, these things did not happen. The stories that go around to the contrary are not factual or realistic or true, and you as teachers in the Church Educational System will be in a position to explain and to tell your students that this thing came by the power of the Holy Ghost, and that all the Brethren involved, the thirteen who were present, are independent personal witnesses of the truth and divinity of what occurred.

Revelation Incomprehensible to Carnal Mind

There is no way to describe in language what is involved. This cannot be done. You are familiar with the Book of Mormon references where the account says that no tongue could tell and no pen could write what was involved in the experience and that it had to be felt by the power of the Spirit (3 Ne. 19:32; see also 3 Ne. 17:15–17). This was one of those occasions. To carnal people who do not understand the operating of the Holy Spirit of God upon the souls of man, this may sound like gibberish or jargon or uncertainty or ambiguity; but to those who are enlightened by the power of the Spirit and who have themselves felt its power, it will have a ring of veracity and truth, and they will know of its verity. I cannot describe in words what happened; I can only say that it happened and that it can be known and understood only by the feeling that can come into the heart of man. You cannot describe a testimony to someone. No one can really know what a testimony is—the feeling and the joy and the rejoicing and the happiness that come into the heart of man when he gets one—except another person who has received a testimony. Some things can be known only by revelation. "The things of God knoweth no man, except he has the Spirit of God" (JST 1 Cor. 2:11).

This Revelation a Sign of the Times

This is a brief explanation of what was involved in this new revelation. I think I can add that it is one of the signs of the times. It is something that had to occur before the Second Coming. It was something that was mandatory and imperative in order to enable us to fulfill all of the revelations that are involved, in order to spread the gospel in the way that the scriptures say it must spread before the Lord comes, in order for all of the blessings to come to all of the people, according to the promises. It is one of the signs of the times.

All the Brethren United in Testimony

This revelation that came on the first day of June 1978 was reaffirmed by the spirit of inspiration one week later on June 8, when the Brethren approved the document that was to be announced to the world. And then it was reaffirmed the next day, on Friday, June 9, with all of the General Authorities present in the temple, that is, all who were available. All received the assurance and witness and confirmation by the power of the Spirit that what had occurred was the mind, the will, the intent, and the purpose of the Lord.

God Guiding the Church

This is a wondrous thing; the veil is thin. The Lord is not far distant from his church.

President Kimball is a man of almost infinite spiritual capacity —a tremendous spiritual giant. The Lord has magnified him beyond any understanding or expression and has given him His mind and His will on a great number of vital matters that have altered the course of the past—one of which is the organization of the First Quorum of the Seventy. As you know, the Church is being guided and led by the power of the Holy Ghost, and the Lord's hand is in it. There is no question whatever about that. And we are doing the right thing where this matter is concerned.

Great Gratitude Because of This Revelation

There has been a tremendous feeling of gratitude and thanksgiving in the hearts of members of the Church everywhere, with isolated exceptions. There are individuals who are out of harmony on this and on plural marriage and on other doctrines, but for all general purposes there has been universal acceptance; and everyone who has been in tune with the Spirit has known that the Lord spoke, and that his mind and his purposes are being manifest in the course the Church is pursuing.

We talk about the scriptures being unfolded—read again the parable of the laborers in the vineyard (Matt. 20:1–16) and remind yourselves that those who labor through the heat of the day for twelve hours are going to be rewarded the same as those who came in at the third and sixth and eleventh hours. Well, it is the eleventh hour; it is the Saturday night of time. In this eleventh hour the Lord has given the blessings of the gospel to the last group of laborers in the vineyard. And when he metes out his rewards, when he makes his payments, according to the accounts and the spiritual statements, he will give the penny to all, whether it is for one hour or twelve hours of work. All are alike unto God, black and white, bond and free, male and female. (*Priesthood* [Salt Lake City: Deseret Book Co., 1981], pp. 126–37.)

Notes

1. Illustrating the perfect harmony that exists between the doctrine and practice of the Church both here and in the spirit world, Elder McConkie said to a family gathering in Colorado Springs, on July 26, 1978, "This means that the same revelation had to be given to the Brethren in the Church in the spirit world, so that they

can conform their preaching of the gospel to our new system on earth.''

At that same gathering, to dramatize the significance of this revelation, he said, ''This revelation is something in the same category as the revelation which caused Wilford Woodruff to issue the Manifesto.''

The Three Pillars of Eternity: Creation, Fall, and Atonement

INTRODUCTION
TO PART III

In this section Elder McConkie focuses on three interrelated doctrines—the doctrine of the Creation, the doctrine of the Fall, and the doctrine of the Atonement—each one of which must be properly understood in order to understand the others; indeed, so interdependent and so intertwined are these three doctrines that they become one. Their importance cannot be overstated; Elder McConkie calls them the "three pillars of eternity," the three pillars which uphold and sustain life, and upon which the entire plan of salvation rests. Because of the events here considered, everything that is, or that ever will be, has meaning.

This particular analysis is a helpful contribution to the literature of the Restoration for two overriding reasons. First, Elder McConkie adds a number of insights which have escaped our general notice: that the very reason the Lord spends so much scriptural effort to help us to understand the Creation is to enable us to understand the Atonement; that the length of the creative days has not been revealed; that we have no reason to suppose the creative days were of equal length; that we have been given only as much information on the Creation as our understanding and faith will permit; that in some future day the full account (as contained in the sealed portions of the Book of Mormon) will be given us; that the whole earth was Eden, and that Adam and Eve lived in a garden located "eastward in Eden" (Gen. 2:8); that the expression, "the tree of knowledge of good and evil" is figurative (and he points out its meaning); and that the doctrine of the Creation provides important understandings with regard to the theories of men as to the earth's origin and also with regard to other scriptural occurrences such as Noah's experience with the Flood.

Second, and equally important, Elder McConkie's analysis is scriptural, avoiding the foundations of speculation and guesswork, or the effort to harmonize the scientific and worldly accounts of the Creation with what the Lord has revealed, which so often characterize the writings which deal with the Creation, the Fall, and even the Atonement. For this reason, this section is a myth-breaker, couched in the testimony that the things of God—things such as the Creation, the Fall, and the Atonement—are known, understood, and meaningful only to those who come to understand them by the power of the Holy Ghost, a power accessed through the scriptures, not through scientific textbooks and theories, however useful and insightful they are in their own sphere.

In analyzing the Fall and its effects on mankind (chapter 10), Elder McConkie reviews its impacts, points to the differences existing in the pre- and post-Fall earth, and then offers a case study ("Eve and the Fall") in which mother Eve is offered as a pattern through which we understand not only God's purposes with regard to the earth as a whole, but also to us as individuals. As Eve shares with Adam in all his greatness, so do husbands and wives today; his glory is her glory, and his reward hers. In their case, as in that of all mankind, "neither is the man without the woman, neither the woman without the man, in the Lord" (1 Cor. 11:11).

Eve is important not only because of the doctrinal insights we gain from her, and not only because of the eternally important role she played in introducing the Fall and all the blessings that flow therefrom, but also in that she is the perfect role model and example, in her relationship to Adam, for all men and women in their own marital and family ties.

Chapter 11 contains Elder McConkie's last public address, in which he bore a binding witness of the doctrine of Atonement—of the purifying powers of Gethsemane. It is a heaven-inspired overview of the events surrounding the atoning sacrifice. In addition, it provides a doctrinal context for interpreting those events. It is powerful because it is so scriptural, because Elder McConkie's knowledge of the truth of these events was perfect, and because the Spirit of the Lord was so powerfully manifest when it was delivered that few if any remained insensitive to the truths of which he spoke.

Chapter 10

CHRIST
AND THE CREATION

True Doctrine of Creation

The Lord expects us to believe and understand the true doctrine of Creation—the creation of this earth, of man, and of all forms of life. Indeed, as we shall see, an understanding of the doctrine of Creation is essential to salvation. Unless and until we gain a true view of the creation of all things we cannot hope to gain that fulness of eternal reward which otherwise would be ours.

Import of Creation, Fall, and Atonement

God himself, the Father of us all, ordained and established a plan of salvation whereby his spirit children might advance and progress and become like him. It is the gospel of God, the plan of Eternal Elohim, the system that saves and exalts, and it consists of three things. These three are the very pillars of eternity itself. They are the most important events that ever have or will occur in all eternity.

Before we can even begin to understand the temporal creation of all things, we must know how and in what manner these three eternal verities—the Creation, the Fall, and the Atonement—are inseparably woven together to form one plan of salvation. No one of them stands alone; each of them ties into the other two; and without a knowledge of all of them, it is not possible to know the truth about any one of them.

Be it known, then, that salvation is in Christ and comes because of his atoning sacrifice. The atonement of the Lord Jesus Christ is the heart and core and center of revealed religion. It ransoms men from the temporal and spiritual death brought into the world by the fall of Adam. All men will be resurrected because our blessed Lord himself died and rose again, becoming thus the firstfruits of them that slept.

And further: Christ died to save sinners. He took upon himself the sins of all men on conditions of repentance. Eternal life, the greatest of all the gifts of God, is available because of what Christ did in Gethsemane and at Golgotha. He is both the resurrection and the life. Immortality and eternal life are the children of the Atonement. There is no language or power of expression given to man which can set forth the glory and wonder and infinite import of the ransoming power of the great Redeemer.

Fall Necessitates Atonement

But, be it remembered, the Atonement came because of the Fall. Christ paid the ransom for Adam's transgression. If there had been no Fall, there would be no Atonement with its consequent immortality and eternal life. Thus, just as surely as salvation comes because of the Atonement, so also salvation comes because of the Fall.

Mortality and procreation and death all had their beginnings with the Fall (2 Ne. 2:22–25). The tests and trials of a mortal probation began when our first parents were cast out of their Edenic home. "Because that Adam fell, we are," Enoch said, "and by his fall came death; and we are made partakers of misery and woe" (Moses 6:48). One of the most profound doctrinal declarations ever made fell from the lips of mother Eve. She said: "Were it not for our transgression we never should have had seed, and never should have known good and evil, and the joy of our redemption, and the eternal life which God giveth unto all the obedient" (Moses 5:11).

Creation Necessitates Fall

And be it also remembered that the Fall was made possible because an infinite Creator, in the primeval day, made the earth and man and all forms of life in such a state that they could fall. This fall involved a change of status. All things were so created that they could fall or change, and thus was introduced the type and kind of existence needed to put into operation all the terms and conditions of the Father's eternal plan of salvation.

This first temporal creation of all things, as we shall see, was paradisiacal in nature. In the primeval and Edenic day all forms of life lived in a higher and different state than now prevails. The coming fall would take them downward and forward and onward. Death and procreation had yet to enter the world. That death would be Adam's gift to man, and then the gift of God would be eternal life through Jesus Christ our Lord.

Thus, existence came from God; death came by Adam; immortality and eternal life came through Christ. And thus, in Lehi's precise and eloquent language, all men are in "a state of probation" because of the Fall. And "if Adam had not transgressed he would not have fallen, but he would have remained in the garden of Eden." He was then in a state of physical immortality; meaning he would have lived forever because there was as yet no death. "And they [our first parents] would have had no children"; they would have been denied the experiences of a mortal probation and a mortal death; and it is out of these two things—out of death and the tests of mortality—that eternal life comes. But—thanks be to God!— "Adam fell that men might be; and men are, that they might have joy. And the Messiah cometh in the fulness of time, that he may redeem the children of men from the fall." (2 Ne. 2:21–26.)

Knowing all these things about the plan of salvation, we are in a position to consider the creation of this earth, of man, and of all forms of life. Knowing that the Creation is the father of the Fall, and that the Fall made possible the Atonement, and that salvation itself comes because of the Atonement, we are in a position to put the revealed knowledge about the Creation in a proper perspective.

Ours a Limited Understanding of Creation

Our analysis properly begins with the frank recital that our knowledge about the Creation is limited. We do not know the how and why and when of all things. Our finite limitations are such that we could not comprehend them if they were revealed to us in all their glory, fulness, and perfection. What has been revealed is that portion of the Lord's eternal word which we must believe and understand if we are to envision the truth about the Fall and the Atonement and thus become heirs of salvation. This is all we are obligated to study.

In a future day the Lord will expect more of his Saints in this regard than he does of us. "When the Lord shall come, he shall reveal all things," our latter-day revelations tell us—"Things which have passed, and hidden things which no man knew, things of the earth, by which it was made, and the purpose and the end thereof." (D&C 101:32–33.) Pending that millennial day it is our responsibility to believe and accept that portion of the truth about the Creation that has been dispensed to us in our dispensation.

Christ the Creator and the Redeemer

Christ is the Creator and Redeemer of worlds so numerous that they cannot be numbered by man. As to his infinite and eternal creative and redemptive enterprises the divine word attests: "And worlds without number have I created," saith the Father; "and by the Son I created them, which is mine Only Begotten. . . . But only an account of this earth, and the inhabitants thereof, give I unto you." As to all of the other worlds of the Lord's creating we know only that it is his work and his glory "to bring to pass"—through the Redeemer—"the immortality and eternal life" of all their inhabitants. (Moses 1:33, 35, 39.)

In what is probably the most glorious vision given to mortals in this dispensation, Joseph Smith and Sidney Rigdon saw "the Son, on the right hand of the Father," and "heard the voice bearing record that he is the Only Begotten of the Father—That by him, and through him, and of him, the worlds are and were created, and the inhabitants thereof are begotten sons and daughters unto God." (D&C 76:20, 23-24.) Christ is thus the Creator and the Redeemer. By him the worlds were made, and through his infinite atonement the inhabitants of those worlds are adopted into the divine family as heirs with himself. It was of this vision and of this provision whereby the Saints become the sons of God by faith that the Prophet Joseph Smith wrote:

> And I heard a great voice bearing record from heav'n,
> He's the Saviour and Only Begotten of God;
> By him, of him, and through him, the worlds were all made,
>
> Whose inhabitants, too, from the first to the last,
> Are saved by the very same Saviour of ours;
> And, of course, are begotten God's daughters and sons
> By the very same truths and the very same powers.
> (Cited in *Mormon Doctrine*, 2nd ed., p. 66.)

Creation Incomprehensible to Mortal Mind

That the infinite and eternal nature of creation and redemption are beyond mortal comprehension we are frank to admit. We are grateful that the Lord has given us this glimpse of everlasting truth relative to his unending labors; it is a brief view from his eternal perspective. But this earth and all that thereon is are our concern. It is the truths about "our creation," as it were, that will chart the course for us in our enduring efforts to gain eternal life.

Let us, then, with Abraham gaze upon the great host of "noble and great ones" in premortal existence. "Among them" stands one "like unto God." He is the great Jehovah, the Firstborn of the Father. We hear him say "unto those who were with him," unto Michael and a great host of valiant souls: "We will go down, for there is space there, and we will take of these materials, and we will make an earth whereon these may dwell." (Abr. 3:22, 24.)

And as we gaze and hear and ponder, our minds are enlightened and our understanding reaches to heaven. Truly Christ is the creator of the future abode of the spirit children of the Father. But he does not work alone. The Creation is an organized venture; each of the other noble and great spirits plays his part. And the earth is created from matter that already exists. Truly the elements are eternal (D&C 93:33) and to create is to organize (*Teachings,* pp. 350–51).

As the work goes forward we see the fulfillment of that which God spake to Moses in the Ten Commandments: "In six days the Lord made heaven and earth, the sea, and all that in them is, and rested the seventh day" (Ex. 20:11). It is of the creative events that took place on each of these "days" that we shall now speak.

Length of Creative Days

But first, what is a day? It is a specified time period; it is an age, an eon, a division of eternity; it is the time between two identifiable events. And each day, of whatever length, has the duration needed for its purposes. One measuring rod is the time required for a celestial body to turn once on its axis. For instance, Abraham says that according to "the Lord's time" a day is "one thousand years" long. This is "one revolution . . . of Kolob," he says, and it is after the Lord's "manner of reckoning." (Abr. 3:4.)

There is no revealed recitation specifying that each of the "six days" involved in the Creation was of the same duration. Our three accounts of the Creation are the Mosaic, the Abrahamic, and the one presented in the temples. Each of these stems back to the Prophet Joseph Smith. The Mosaic and Abrahamic accounts place the creative events on the same successive days. We shall follow these scriptural recitations in our analysis. The temple account, for reasons that are apparent to those familiar with its teachings, has a different division of events. It seems clear that the "six days" are one continuing period and that there is no one place where the dividing lines between the successive events must of necessity be placed.

Accounts of Physical Creation

The Mosaic and the temple accounts set forth the temporal or physical creation, the actual organization of element or matter into tangible form. They are not accounts of the spirit creation. Abraham gives a blueprint as it were of the Creation. He tells the plans of the holy beings who wrought the creative work. After reciting the events of the "six days" he says: "And thus were their decisions at the time that they counseled among themselves to form the heavens and the earth". (Abr. 5:3).

Then he says they performed as they had planned, which means we can, by merely changing the verb tenses and without doing violence to the sense and meaning, also consider the Abrahamic account as one of the actual creation.

The First Day

Elohim, Jehovah, Michael, a host of the noble and great ones — all these played their parts. "The Gods" created the atmospheric heavens and the temporal earth. It was "without form, and void"; as yet it could serve no useful purpose with respect to the salvation of man. It was "empty and desolate"; life could not yet exist on its surface; it was not yet a fit abiding place for those sons of God who shouted for joy at the prospect of a mortal probation. The "waters" of the great "deep" were present, and "darkness reigned" until the divine decree: "Let there be light." The light and the darkness were then "divided," the one being called "Day" and the other "Night." Clearly our planet was thus formed as a revolving orb and placed in its relationship to our sun. (See Moses 2:1-5; Abr. 4:1-5.)

The Second Day

On this day "the waters" were "divided" between the surface of the earth and the atmospheric heavens that surrounded it. A "firmament" or an "expanse" called "Heaven" was created to divide "the waters which were under the expanse from the waters which were above the expanse." Thus, as the creative events unfold, provision seems to be made for clouds and rain and storms to give life to that which will yet grow and dwell upon the earth. (See Moses 2:6-8; Abr. 4:6-8.)

The Third Day

This is the day when life began. In it "the waters under the heaven" were "gathered together unto one place," and the "dry land" appeared. The dry land was called "Earth," and the assembled waters became "the Sea." This is the day in which "the Gods organized the earth to bring forth" grass and herbs and plants and trees; and it is the day in which vegetation in all its varied forms actually came forth from the seeds planted by the Creators. This is the day when the decree went forth that grass, herbs, and trees could each grow only from "its own seed," and that each could in turn bring forth only after its own "kind." And thus the bounds of the plant and vegetable kingdoms were set by the hands of those by whom each varied plant and tree was made. (See Moses 2:9-13; Abr. 4:9-13.)

The Fourth Day

After seeds in all their varieties had been planted on the earth; after these had sprouted and grown; after each variety was prepared to bring forth fruit and seed after its own kind—the Creators organized all things in such a way as to make their earthly garden a productive and beautiful place. They then "organized the lights in the expanse of the heaven" so there would be "seasons" and a way of measuring "days" and "years." We have no way of knowing what changes took place in either the atmospheric or sidereal heavens, but during this period the sun, moon, and stars assumed the relationship to the earth that now is theirs. At least the light of each of them began to shine through the lifting hazes that enshrouded the newly created earth so they could play their parts with references to life in all its forms as it soon would be upon the new orb. (See Moses 2:14-19; Abr. 4:14-19.)

The Fifth Day

Next came fish and fowl and "every living creature" whose abode is "the waters." Their Creators placed them on the newly organized earth, and they were given the command: "Be fruitful, and multiply, and fill the waters in the sea; and let fowl multiply in the earth." This command—as with a similar decree given to man and applicable to all animal life—they could not then keep, but they soon would be able to do so. Appended to this command to multiply was the heaven-sent restriction that the creatures in the waters could only bring forth "after their kind," and that "every winged fowl" could only bring forth "after his kind." There was no provision for evolvement or change from one species to another. (See Moses 2:20–23; Abr. 4:20–23.)

The Sixth Day

The crowning day of creation is at hand. In its early hours, the great Creators "made the beasts of the earth after their kind, and cattle after their kind, and everything which creepeth upon the earth after his kind." And the same procreative restrictions applied to them that apply to all forms of life; they too are to reproduce only after their kind.

The Creation of Man Also on Sixth Day

All that we have recited is now accomplished, but what of man? Is man found upon the earth? He is not. And so "the Gods," having so counseled among themselves, said: "Let us go down and form man in our image, after our likeness. . . . So the Gods went down to organize man in their own image, in the image of the Gods to form they him, male and female to form they them." They then did as they had counseled, and the most glorious of all the creative acts was accomplished. Man is the crowning creature to step forth according to the divine will. He is in the image and likeness of the Eternal Elohim, and to him is given "dominion" over all things. And, then, finally, that his purposes shall roll everlastingly onward, God blesses the "male and female" whom he has created and commands them: "Be fruitful, and multiply, and replenish the earth, and subdue it, and have dominion over the fish of the sea, and over the fowl of the air, and over every living thing that moveth upon the earth." As the "sixth day" closes, the Creators, viewing their creative labors with satisfaction, see that "all things" which they have "made" are "very good." (See Moses 2:24–31; Abr. 4:24–31.)

Such is the revealed account of the creation of all things. Our summary has combined elements from the Mosaic, the Abrahamic, and the temple accounts. At this point in the Mosaic record the scripture says: "Thus the heaven and the earth were finished, and all the host of them." The Lord then rests on the "seventh day." (Moses 3:1–3.)

Lord's Purpose in Teaching Creation

Having come this far in our analysis of the Creation, we are led to ask: Why did the Lord give us these revealed accounts of the Creation? What purposes do they serve? How does the knowledge in them help us to work out our salvation or to center our affection in him whose we are and by whom all things were made?

It is self-evident that we have received no useless and unneeded revelations. All that the Lord does has a purpose and serves a need. He expects us to treasure up his word, to ponder in our hearts its deep and hidden meanings, and to understand its full import. Those who have done so know that the revealed accounts of the Creation are designed to accomplish two great purposes. Their *general purpose* is to enable us to understand the nature of our mortal probation, a probation in which all men are being tried and tested "to see if they will do all things whatsoever the Lord their God shall command them" (Abr. 3:25). Their *specific purpose* is to enable us to understand the atoning sacrifice of the Lord Jesus Christ, which infinite and eternal atonement is the very foundation upon which revealed religion rests.

It is only fair to say that a mere recitation of what took place during the "six days" and of the Lord's resting on the "seventh day" do not of themselves set forth with clarity the purposes of the creation accounts. And so the Lord, as recorded in chapter 3 of the Mosaic account, proceeds to explain the purpose and nature of the Creation. He comments about the Creation. He reveals some facts and principles without which we cannot envision what the true doctrine of the Creation is. His statements are interpolative; they are inserted in the historical account to give us its true depth and meaning and import. They are not chronological recitations, but are commentary about what he had already set forth in its sequential order.

We Must Understand Premortal Existence to Understand Creation

The Lord introduces his commentary about the Creation by saying that the events of the "six days," which he has just recited, "are the generations of the heaven and of the earth, when they were created, in the day that I, the Lord God, made the heaven and the earth'' (Moses 3:4). Thus, all things have been created; the work is finished; the account is revealed; but it can only be understood if some added truths are set forth. These deal with the premortal existence of all things and with the paradisiacal nature of the earth and of all created things when they first came from their Creator's hand. Both of these concepts are interwoven in the same sentences, and in some instances the words used have a dual meaning and apply to both the premortal life and the paradisiacal creation.

"Spiritual" Creation Precedes Natural

And so the Lord says that he created ''every plant of the field before it was in the earth, and every herb of the field before it grew. . . . And I, the Lord God, had created all the children of men; and not yet a man to till the ground; for in heaven created I them.'' (Moses 3:5.) Clearly he is speaking of the premortal existence of all things. This earth, all men, animals, fish, fowls, plants, all things— all lived first as spirit entities. Their home was heaven, and the earth was created to be the place where they could take upon themselves mortality.

''For I, the Lord God, created all things, of which I have spoken, spiritually, before they were naturally upon the face of the earth.'' Apply these words to the spirit creation, if you will, and they will be true in such a context. But they have a much more pointed and important meaning. They are followed by the statement: ''For I, the Lord God, had not caused it to rain upon the face of the earth; . . . and there was not yet flesh upon the earth, neither in the water, neither in the air; But I, the Lord God, spake, and there went up a mist from the earth, and watered the whole face of the ground.'' (Moses 3:5–6.) The Lord is here telling us about the events of which he has spoken, about the events of ''the six days,'' about the account of the physical or tangible or temporal creation set forth in chapter 2 of Moses. He says the things so made were ''spiritually'' created and were not ''naturally upon the face of the earth,'' for the reasons quoted.

Earth's Edenic Creation

At this point we must insert a statement from our tenth article of faith: ''We believe . . . that the earth will be renewed and receive its paradisiacal glory.'' That is to say, when the earth was first created it was in a paradisiacal state, an Edenic state, a state in which there was no death. And when the Lord comes again, and the millennial era is ushered in, the earth will return to its paradisiacal state and be renewed. It will be made new again; it will become a new heaven and a new earth whereon dwelleth righteousness. In that day, "there shall be no sorrow because there is no death" as we know it (D&C 101:29).

Thus we learn that the initial creation was paradisiacal; death and mortality had not yet entered the world. There was no mortal flesh upon the earth for any form of life. The Creation was past, but mortality as we know it lay ahead. All things had been created in a state of paradisiacal immortality. It was of this day that Lehi said: "And all things which were created must have remained in the same state in which they were after they were created; and they must have remained forever, and had no end" (2 Ne. 2:22). If there is no death, all things of necessity must continue to live everlastingly and without end.

Adam Created "Spiritually" in Eden

Continuing the divine commentary about the Creation, we read: "And I, the Lord God, formed man from the dust of the ground, and breathed into his nostrils the breath of life; and man became a living soul, the first flesh upon the earth, the first man also; nevertheless, all things were before created; but spiritually were they created and made according to my word" (Moses 3:7). How filled with meaning are these words! The physical body of Adam is made from the dust of this earth, the very earth to which the Gods came down to form him. His "spirit" enters his body, as Abraham expresses it (Abr. 5:7). Man becomes a living, immortal soul; body and spirit are joined together. He has been created "spiritually," as all things were because there is as yet no mortality. Then comes the Fall; Adam falls; mortality and procreation and death commence. Fallen man is mortal; he has mortal flesh; he is "the first flesh upon the earth." And the effects of his fall pass upon all created things. They fall in that they too become mortal. Death enters the world; mortality reigns; procreation commences; and the Lord's great and eternal purposes roll onward.

Thus, "all things" were created as spirit entities in heaven; then "all things" were created in a paradisiacal state upon the earth; that is, "spiritually were they created," for there was yet no death. They had *spiritual bodies* made of the elements of the earth as distinguished from the *mortal bodies* they would receive after the Fall when death would enter the scheme of things. Natural bodies are subject to the natural death; spiritual bodies, being paradisiacal in nature, are not subject to death. Hence the need for a fall and the mortality and death that grows out of it.

Adam "First Man" and "First Flesh"

Thus, as the interpolative exposition in the divine word explains, "I, the Lord God, planted a garden eastward in Eden, and there I put the man whom I had formed" (Moses 3:8). Adam, our father, dwelt in the Garden of Eden. He was the first man of all men in the day of his creation, and he became the first flesh of all flesh through the Fall. Because of the Fall "all things" changed from their spiritual state to a natural state. And thus we read: "And out of the ground made I, the Lord God, to grow every tree, *naturally*, that is pleasant to the sight of man; and man could behold it. And it became also a living soul. For it was *spiritual* in the day that I created it." (Moses 3:9; italics added.)

There is no evolving from one species to another in any of this. The account is speaking of "every tree" and of "all things." Considering them as one collective unit, the account continues: "It remaineth in the sphere in which I, God, created it, yea, even all things which I prepared for the use of man; and man saw that it was good for food" (Moses 3:9).

The Lord's commentary about the Creation also says: "Out of the ground I, the Lord God, formed every beast of the field, and every fowl of the air; . . . and they were also living souls; for I, God, breathed into them the breath of life" (Moses 3:19). It also says, speaking figuratively, that Eve was formed from Adam's rib. And in that primeval day, when neither death nor the probationary experiences of mortality had entered the world, "they were both naked, the man and his wife, and were not ashamed." (See Moses 3:21–25.)

Tree of Knowledge of Good and Evil

As to the Fall itself we are told that the Lord planted "the tree of knowledge of good and evil" in the midst of the garden (Moses 3:9). To Adam and Eve the command came: "Of every tree of the garden thou mayest freely eat, But of the tree of the knowledge of good and evil, thou shalt not eat of it, nevertheless, thou mayest choose for thyself, for it is given unto thee; but, remember that I forbid it, for in the day thou eatest thereof thou shalt surely die'' (Moses 3:16–17). Again, the account is speaking figuratively. What is meant by partaking of the fruit of the tree of knowledge of good and evil is that our first parents complied with whatever laws were involved so that their bodies would change from their state of paradisiacal immortality to a state of natural mortality.

Moses 4 gives the actual account of the Fall. Adam and Eve partake of the forbidden fruit and the earth is cursed and begins to bring forth thorns and thistles; that is, the earth falls to its present natural state. Eve is identified as ''the mother of all living'' (Moses 4:27); and she and Adam begin to have ''sons and daughters'' (Moses 5:3).

Man Created to Fall

Thus, man is created in such a way that he can fall. He falls and brings mortality and procreation and death into being so that he can be redeemed by the atoning sacrifice of the Lord Jesus Christ. And he is ransomed from the temporal and spiritual death brought into the world by the fall of Adam so that he can have immortality and eternal life. The Creation, the Fall, and the Atonement are bound together as one.

These revealed verities about the creation of all things run counter to many of the speculations and theoretical postulates of the world. They are, however, what the inspired word sets forth, and we are duty bound to accept them. We are frank to admit that our knowledge of the creation of the universe, of this earth, of man, and of all living things is meager—perhaps almost miniscule—as compared to what there is to learn. But the Lord has revealed to us as much about the mystery of creation as is necessary for us in our probationary estate.

True Doctrine of Creation

He has revealed to us the basic verities which enable us to understand the true doctrine of creation. This doctrine is that the Lord Jesus Christ is both the Creator and Redeemer of this earth and all that on it is, save only man. It is that the Lord God himself, the Father of us all, came down and created man, male and female, in his own image and likeness. It is that the earth and all else were created in a paradisiacal state so there could be a fall. It is that the Great Creator became the Redeemer so he could ransom men from the effects of the Fall, thereby bringing to pass the immortality and eternal life of man. It is that the Creation, the Fall, and the Atonement are the three pillars of eternity. It is that all who accept him as both the Creator and the Redeemer have power to become joint-heirs with him and thereby inherit all that his Father hath.

Truly Christ is both the Creator and the Redeemer, as is portrayed by the marble reproduction of Thorvaldsen's *Christus* that stands in the rotunda of the visitors' center on Temple Square. There we see the Creator in majestic marble standing in the midst of eternity. On the domed ceiling and the encircling walls are paintings of the sidereal heavens with their endless orbs, all moving through an organized cosmos. And as we gaze upon what the hand of mere men has made, our minds are opened to see in a limited manner the miracle of creation.

There we also see the nail marks in those blessed hands, the hands that healed and blessed, and also in the feet that trod the dusty lanes of that earth which his hands had made. We see the gash in his pierced side from whence came the blood and water as a sign that the Atonement had been wrought. And our minds are opened, again in a limited manner, to see the miracle of redemption.

And as we ponder upon the wonder if it all, our gaze and thoughts dwell upon the beatific face and we feel the beckoning power of the outstretched arms. And the marvel in marble seems to breathe the breath of life and say: "I am the way, the truth, and the life" (John 14:6). "Come unto me, all ye that labour and are heavy laden, and I will give you rest" (Matt. 11:28). Come unto me and be saved. Come, inherit the kingdom prepared from the foundation of the world for all who accept me as the Creator and Redeemer. Come, be one with me; I am thy God. ("Christ and the Creation," *Ensign*, June 1982, pp. 9–15.)

Chapter 11

THE FALL OF
ADAM

Fall and Atonement Inseparably Linked

The fall of Adam and the atonement of Christ are linked together—inseparably, everlastingly—never to be parted. They are
as much a part of the same body as are the head and the heart, and
each plays its part in the eternal scheme of things.

Effects of the Fall

The fall of Adam brought temporal and spiritual death into the
world, and the atonement of Christ ransomed men from these two
deaths by bringing to pass the immortality and eternal life of man.
This makes the Fall as essential a part of the plan of salvation as the
very Atonement itself.

There are in fact five things that came into being and continue
to exist because of the Fall. None of these things would have existed
if there had been no fall, and all of them are essential parts of the
divine plan of salvation. They are:

1. Temporal death. This is the natural death; it occurs when body
and spirit separate; it results in corruption and decay. Because of the
atonement of Christ, all men will be raised from corruption to incor-
ruption, from mortality to immortality, thence to live everlastingly
in a resurrected state.

2. Spiritual death. This is death as pertaining to the things of the
Spirit. It is death as pertaining to things of righteousness. It is to be
cast out of the presence of the Lord. It is a way of life which is in opposition to that of the Father of us all. Because of the Atonement,
because the Lord Jesus bore our sins on conditions of repentance,
we have power to gain eternal life, which is spiritual life, which is a
life of righteousness, which is life in the presence of our God.

3. *Mortality.* Mortal life comes because of the Fall. If there had been no fall there would be no mortal life of any sort on earth. Mortal life is life where there is death. Death must enter the world to bring mortality into being.

4. *Procreation.* Before the Fall there was no procreation. I repeat, for thus saith the holy word, before the Fall there was no procreation. Adam and Eve, in their Edenic state, could not have children (2 Ne. 2:22–23; Moses 5:11), nor, as we shall see, could any form of life when first placed on the newly created paradisiacal earth.

5. *A probationary estate.* We are here to be tried and tested, to see if we will believe the truths of salvation and keep the commandments while we walk by faith. After the Fall men became carnal, sensual, and devilish by nature and the plan of salvation calls upon them to put off these worldly snares and to put on Christ (Mosiah 3:19).

Now, lest there be any sliver of misunderstanding about any of this, let us reason together on all these things as did they of old. Indeed, let us use the very words they used as they are found in the holy scriptures.

Fall Introduced Death

"Now is Christ risen from the dead," Paul said as he testified of the Atonement. "For since by man came death, by man came also the resurrection of the dead." Adam brought death, and if he had not fallen there would be no death; and Christ brought the Resurrection, and if there had been no atonement there would be no resurrection. "For as in Adam all die, even so in Christ shall all be made alive." (1 Cor. 15:20–22.)

Atonement Overcomes Death

Moroni linked the Fall and the Atonement together in this way. God, he said, "created Adam, and by Adam came the fall of man. And because of the fall of man came Jesus Christ." It is just that simple; the Fall is the source, and cause, and reason for the Atonement. "And because of Jesus Christ came the redemption of man." Salvation is in Christ!

"And because of the redemption of man, which came by Jesus Christ," men "are brought back into the presence of the Lord; yea, this is wherein all men are redeemed, because the death of Christ bringeth to pass the resurrection, which bringeth to pass a redemption from an endless sleep." (Morm. 9:12–13.)

Atonement Delivers from Spiritual Death

What saith the angel to king Benjamin? He saith: "[Christ's] blood atoneth for the sins of those who have fallen by the transgression of Adam." We are descendants of Adam; we all have a common father.

He saith: "As in Adam, or by nature, they fall, even so the blood of Christ atoneth for their sins." The blessings of the Fall have passed upon all men; all can be redeemed because Adam fell and Christ came.

He saith: "Salvation was, and is, and is to come, in and through the atoning blood of Christ, the Lord Omnipotent." There is no other source of salvation from the Fall than that which comes through Christ.

He saith: "The natural man is an enemy to God, and has been from the fall of Adam, and will be, forever and ever, unless he yields to the enticings of the Holy Spirit, and putteth off the natural man and becometh a saint through the atonement of Christ the Lord." (Mosiah 3:11, 16, 18–19.)

Thus the natural man, which is Adam, is conquered by the perfect man, which is Christ, and thus "all mankind may be saved, by obedience to the laws and ordinances of the Gospel" (third article of faith). And now, what saith our great and good friend Lehi about all these things?

He saith: The "Redeemer . . . cometh to bring salvation unto men. . . . And the way is prepared [for him] from the fall of man, and salvation is free." The Fall is the foundation upon which the Atonement rests.

Fall Introduces Mortality and Procreation

He saith that "after Adam and Eve had partaken of the forbidden fruit they were driven out of the garden of Eden, to till the earth." Their mortal probation and the trials and tests of mortality began after the Fall.

He saith: "And they have brought forth children; yea, even the family of all the earth." Every living soul on earth is a descendant of Adam and Eve. God hath made of one blood all the nations of men.

He saith: "If Adam had not transgressed he would not have fallen, but he would have remained in the garden of Eden." If Adam had not fallen, he would be there today, six thousand years later, in all the glory and beauty of his immortal nature. Such is the word of the holy writ.

And next—marvel of marvels and wonder of wonders—Lehi saith: "And all things which were created"—*all things* means *all* things; it includes animals and fishes and fowls and creeping things and plants; it includes dinosaurs and whales and ants; it means all things—"All things which were created must have remained in the same state in which they were after they were created; and they must have remained forever, and had no end."

There was, we repeat, no death in the world until after the Fall. And there was, we repeat, no procreation until after the Fall. And there was, we repeat, no mortality until after the Fall.

And so, Lehi continues: "And they"—Adam and Eve—"would have had no children."

And then, on the foundation so laid, while filled with light and guided by the Spirit, Lehi acclaimed: "Adam fell that men might be; and men are, that they might have joy. And the Messiah cometh in the fulness of time, that he may redeem the children of men from the fall." (2 Ne. 2:3–4, 19–20, 22–23, 25–26.)

Truly, as Enoch said: "Because that Adam fell, we are; and by his fall came death; and we are made partakers of misery and woe. . . . and men have become carnal, sensual, and devilish, and are shut out from the presence of God." (Moses 6:48–49.)

Truly, as Mother Eve said: "Were it not for our transgression we never should have had seed, and never should have known good and evil, and the joy of our redemption, and the eternal life which God giveth unto all the obedient" (Moses 5:11).

Truly, salvation, comes because of the Fall, and it is just as important to believe in the Fall as it is to believe in the Atonement, and, indeed, it is not possible to believe in the Atonement without believing in the Fall.

Fall Grows Out of Creation

Now, even as the Atonement grows out of the Fall, so the Fall grows out of the Creation. If all things had not been created in the very way in which they were created, there could have been no fall. If created things were to fall they must be created in a higher state than the state they would be in after the Fall. To fall is to go downward, or forward, not upward.

And so it is that the revealed accounts of the creation of this earth and all things on the face thereof are accounts of the paradisiacal creation. They speak of the immortal state in which all things were first made; they are telling of created things in the day before death entered the world.

Our tenth article of faith says: "We believe . . . that the earth will be renewed and receive its paradisiacal glory." When the Lord comes and the millennial era commences, there will be new heavens and a new earth (Isa. 65:17–25; 66:22–24; D&C 101:23–31); the earth will be renewed; it will become new again; and it will return to its paradisiacal state; it will become like it was in the Edenic day. And once again death as we know it will cease.

The accounts of the Creation in Genesis 1 and 2 and Moses 2 are accounts of the paradisiacal or Edenic creation. They are descriptive of a creation that antedated death and mortality and the Fall. They speak of a creation in which—again these are Lehi's words—"All things which were created must have remained in the same state in which they were after they were created; and they must have remained forever and had no end" (2 Ne. 2:22). That is, they would have so remained if there had been no fall.

Now, we are speaking of the three pillars of heaven, of the three greatest events ever to occur in all eternity, of the three doctrines that are woven inseparably together to form the plan of salvation. We are speaking of the Creation, the Fall, and the Atonement. And these three are one. And, be it noted, all things were created; all things fell; and all things are subject to the redeeming power of the Son of God.

I am not conscious of expressing a single thought or concept that has not already been said by the Brethren who have gone before. Almost every sentence I have uttered is a quotation or a paraphrase of something said by Joseph Smith, Brigham Young, John Taylor, Joseph F. Smith, Joseph Fielding Smith, Orson Pratt, or some other of the great theologians of our dispensation.

Fall as Universal as Atonement

Many among us have no difficulty envisioning that the Atonement is infinite and eternal and applies to all forms of life. They know that the revelations say in so many words that all forms of life both lived as spirit entities and will be resurrected—animals, fowls, fishes, all things are eternal in nature.

But some among us have not yet had it dawn upon them that all things fell and became mortal so they could be resurrected. The early Brethren of our dispensation wrote these words: "The word *atonement* signifies deliverance, through the offering of a ransom, from the penalty of a broken law. . . . As effected by Jesus Christ, it signifies the deliverance, through his death and resurrection, of the earth, and everything pertaining to it, from the power which death has obtained over them through the transgression of Adam. . . . Redemption from death, through the sufferings of Christ, is for all men, both the righteous and the wicked; for this earth, and for all things created upon it." (*Compendium*, pp. 8–9, cited in *Mormon Doctrine*, pp. 64–65.)

When we speak of the Creation, the Fall, and the Atonement, we are speaking of the works of Elohim, Jehovah, and Michael. We are talking of the doctrines which are stated or are implicit in our first three articles of faith. We need to come to a unity of the faith as to the labors of each of these glorious beings.

Elohim Is God the Creator

Who is Elohim? He is God the Eternal Father. He is a glorified and exalted personage. He has a body of flesh and bones as tangible as man's. In the language of Adam, Man of Holiness is his name (Moses 6:59). He is omnipotent, omniscient, and omnipresent. He knows all things and has all power—not simply as pertaining to us or in some prescribed sphere or realm—but in the absolute, eternal, and unlimited sense. In the ultimate sense, he is the Creator. And anything you may have heard to the contrary, whether in the creeds of Christendom or the mouthings of intellectuals who, in their own eyes, know more than the Lord, is false.

Michael Is Adam, Who Fell

Who is Michael? He is a spirit son of the great Elohim. Under Christ he led the armies of righteousness when there was war in heaven. Our revelations say he "was the son of God" (Moses 6:22), that he was "the first flesh [the first mortal flesh] upon earth, the first man also" (Moses 3:7), and that he was "the first man of all men" (Moses 1:34). He is Adam our father; he is the presiding high priest over all the earth. Under Christ, who is "the Holy One," he holds "the keys of salvation" (D&C 78:16). He is the one by whom the Fall came. And anything you may have heard to the contrary, from whatever source, is false.

Jehovah Is Christ the Redeemer

Who is Jehovah? He is the Lord Jesus Christ, the Firstborn of the Father, the Savior and Redeemer. He is the Lamb slain from the foundation of the world. He is the Only Begotten in the flesh, the only person ever born with a mortal mother and an immortal Father. He worked out the infinite and eternal atonement, ransomed men and all forms of life from the Fall, and made the purposes of creation operative. Salvation is in him and comes to those who believe and obey. And anything you have heard to the contrary is false.

The truths relative to Elohim, Jehovah, and Michael are the greatest of all eternal verities. They wrap the Creation, the Fall, and the Atonement into one grand plan of salvation. They are the gospel of God who is the Father. And of their truth the Holy Ghost bears witness. ("The Three Pillars of Eternity," BYU Devotional, 17 February 1981.)

Eve and the Fall

Having thus singled out the three most transcendent events of all eternity—the Creation, the Fall, and the Atonement—and having mentioned the intertwined relationship that binds them together, let us now consider under six headings the position of Eve in this eternal scheme of things:

1. Eve Before Eden

Who was Adam and who was Eve when they twain dwelt in the presence of the Father in that premortal life before the foundations of this earth were laid?

They were spirit children of the Father. Adam, a male spirit, then called Michael, stood next in power, might, and dominion to the Lord Jehovah (*Teachings*, p. 157). Eve, a female spirit, whose premortal name has not been revealed, was of like stature, capacity, and intelligence.

Christ and Adam were companions and partners in preexistence. Christ, beloved and chosen of the Father, was foreordained to be the Savior of the world; Adam, as the great Michael, led the armies of heaven when Lucifer and one-third of the spirit hosts rebelled (Rev. 12:1–9; D&C 29:36–38). The Lord Jesus, then reigning as the Lord Jehovah, was the number one Spirit Son; described as being "like unto God" (Abr. 3:24), he then ascended the throne of eternal power; and with him, and by his side, and serving under his direction, was Michael who is Adam, who was then foreordained to be the first man and the head of the human race.

And we cannot doubt that the greatest of all female spirits was the one then chosen and foreordained to be "the mother of the Son of God, after the manner of the flesh" (1 Ne. 11:18). Nor can we do other than suppose that Eve was by her side, rejoicing in her own foreordination to be the first woman, the mother of men, the consort, companion, and friend of mighty Michael.

Christ and Mary, Adam and Eve, Abraham and Sarah, and a host of mighty men and equally glorious women comprised that group of "the noble and great ones," to whom the Lord Jesus said: "We will go down, for there is space there, and we will take of these materials, and we will make an earth whereon these may dwell" (Abr. 3:22–25). This we know: Christ, under the Father, is the Creator; Michael, his companion and associate, presided over much of the creative work; and with them, as Abraham saw, were many of the noble and great ones. Can we do other than conclude that Mary and Eve and Sarah and myriads of our faithful sisters were numbered among them? Certainly these sisters labored as diligently then, and fought as valiantly in the War in Heaven as did the brethren, even as they in like manner stand firm today, in mortality, in the cause of truth and righteousness.

2. Eve in Eden

From the celestial presence to a garden planted eastward in Eden; from life as a spirit in the presence of God to life on this earth in a tabernacle of clay; from the realms of eternal light to the dark recesses of life on planet earth—this was one giant step forward for Adam and Eve. By first obtaining bodies made of the dust of the earth, our first parents commenced the course whereby they could obtain resurrected bodies like those of other exalted beings, including the Exalted Father of us all.

How did Adam and Eve gain their temporal bodies? Our revelations record Deity's words in this way: "And I, God, said unto mine Only Begotten, which was with me from the beginning: Let us make man in our image, after our likeness" (Moses 2:26). Man on earth—Adam and Eve and all their descendants—were to be created in the image of God; they were to be in his image spiritually and temporally, with power to convert the image into a reality by becoming like him. Then the scripture says: "And I, God, created man in mine own image, in the image of mine Only Begotten created I him; male and female created I them" (Moses 2:27). Also: "And I, the Lord God, formed man from the dust of the ground, and breathed into his nostrils the breath of life; and man became a living soul, the first flesh upon the earth, the first man also" (Moses 3:7).

For those whose limited spiritual understanding precludes a recitation of all the facts, the revealed account, in figurative language, speaks of Eve being created from Adam's rib (Moses 3:21–25). A more express scripture, however, speaks of "Adam, who was the son of God, with whom God, himself, conversed" (Moses 6:22). In a formal doctrinal pronouncement, the First Presidency of the Church (Joseph F. Smith, John R. Winder, and Anthon H. Lund) said that "All who have inhabited the earth since Adam have taken bodies and become souls in like manner," and that "the first of our race, began life as . . . the human germ or embryo that became a man" (see *Mormon Doctrine*, 2nd ed., p. 17).

Christ is universally attested in the scriptures to be the Only Begotten. At this point, as we consider the "creation" of Adam, and lest there by any misunderstanding, we must remember that Adam was created in immortality, but that Christ came to earth as a mortal; thus our Lord is the Only Begotten *in the flesh*, meaning into this mortal sphere of existence. Adam came to earth to dwell in immortality until the Fall changed his status to that of mortality.

Those who have ears to hear will understand these things. All of us, however, must know and believe that when Adam and Eve were placed in the Garden of Eden, there was no death. They were immortal. Unless some change occurred they would live forever, retaining all the bloom and beauty and the freshness of youth. Joseph Smith, Brigham Young, Orson Pratt, and our early Brethren preached many sermons on this.

Also, though they had been commanded to multiply and fill the earth with posterity, Adam and Eve, in their then immortal state could not have children. Nor could they be subject to the tests, trials, and probationary experiences of mortality. Hence came the need—the imperative, absolute need—for the Fall, for the change in status that would bring children, death, and testing into the world.

3. The Fall of Adam and Eve

As to the imperative need imposed upon our first parents to undergo that change of status which bears the name the "Fall of Adam" or the Fall of man, and as to the rationale that underlies it, I have written elsewhere (*The Promised Messiah* [Salt Lake City: Deseret Book Co., 1978], pp. 220–21):

"To 'the first man of all men' (Moses 1:34), who is called Adam, and to 'the first of all women,' who is called Eve, 'the mother of all living' (Moses 4:26)—while they were yet immortal and thus incapable of providing mortal bodies for the spirit children of the Father—the command came: 'Be fruitful, and multiply, and replenish the earth' (Moses 4:28).

"Be fruitful! Multiply! Have children! The whole plan of salvation, including both immortality and eternal life for all the spirit hosts of heaven, hung on their compliance with this command. If they obeyed, the Lord's purposes would prevail.

"If they disobeyed, they would remain childless and innocent in their paradisiacal Eden, and the spirit hosts would remain in their celestial heaven—denied the experiences of mortality, denied a resurrection, denied a hope of eternal life, denied the privilege to advance and progress and become like their Eternal Father. That is to say, the whole plan of salvation would have been frustrated, and the purposes of God in begetting spirit children and in creating this earth as their habitat would have come to naught.

" 'Be fruitful, and multiply.' 'Provide bodies for my spirit progeny.' Thus saith thy God. Eternity hangs in the balance. The plans of Deity are at the crossroads. There is only one course to follow: the course of conformity and obedience. Adam, who is Michael—the spirit next in intelligence, power, dominion, and righteousness to the great Jehovah himself—Adam, our father, and Eve, our mother, must obey. They must fall. They must become mortal. Death must enter the world. There is no other way. They must fall that man may be.

"Such is the reality. Such is the rationale. Such is the divine will. Fall thou must, O mighty Michael. Fall? Yes, plunge down from thy immortal state of peace, perfection, and glory to a lower existence; leave the presence of thy God in the garden and enter the lone and dreary world; step forth from the garden to the wilderness; leave the flowers and fruits that grow spontaneously and begin the battle with thorns, thistles, briars, and noxious weeds; subject thyself to famine and pestilence; suffer with disease; know pain and sorrow; face death on every hand—but with it all bear children; provide bodies for all those who served with thee when thou led the hosts of heaven in casting out Lucifer, our common enemy.

"Yes, Adam, fall; fall for thine own good; fall for the good of all mankind; fall that man may be; bring death into the world; do that which will cause an atonement to be made, with all the infinite and eternal blessings which flow therefrom.

"And so Adam fell as fall he must. But he fell by breaking a lesser law — an infinitely lesser law — so that he too, having thereby transgressed, would become subject to sin and need a Redeemer and be privileged to work out his own salvation, even as would be the case with all those upon whom the effects of his fall would come."

4. The Man Adam and the Woman Eve

When we speak of the fall of Adam, do we have reference to the man Adam as an individual? Or to Adam as a generic term for the human race? Or to the term Adam as meaning both the man Adam and the woman Eve? When we speak of the fall of man are we talking about the fall of a male individual? Or of the man in the generic sense that includes women as a part of mankind? What of the woman Eve and her fall?

God, meaning the Father, created Adam and Eve in his own image, "male and female created" he "them" (Moses 2:27). The woman was given to the man in eternal marriage, for there was no death. They were commanded not to partake of the tree of knowledge of good and evil. But "when the woman saw that the tree was good for food, and that it became pleasant to the eyes, and a tree to be desired to make her wise," as the figurative language has it, "she took of the fruit thereof, and did eat, and also gave unto her husband with her, and he did eat. And the eyes of them both were opened." (Moses 4:12-13.)

It is of this event that Paul says: "And Adam was not deceived, but the woman being deceived was in the transgression" (1 Tim. 2:14). Thus we read of the transgression of Eve. Our revelations also say: "The devil tempted Adam, and he partook of the forbidden fruit and transgressed the commandment" (D&C 29:40). Indeed, many scriptures speak of "Adam's transgression" (Rom. 5:14), though we are left to conclude that Eve fell first and then Adam, speaking of these two as individuals.

Our understanding of the Fall comes into true focus when we ponder these words from the book of the generations of Adam: "In the day that God created man, in the likeness of God made he him;

In the image of his own body, male and female, created he them, and blessed them, and called *their* name Adam, in the day when *they* were created and became living souls in the land upon the footstool of God'' (Moses 6:8–9; italics added).

Thus the name of Adam and Eve as a united partnership is Adam. *They,* the two of them together, are named Adam. This is more than the man Adam as a son of God or the woman Eve as a daughter of the same Holy Being. Adam and Eve taken together are named Adam, and the fall of Adam is the fall of them both, for they are one. How aptly did Paul say: "Neither is the man without the woman, neither the woman without the man, in the Lord" (1 Cor. 11:11). The fall of Adam is the fall of the man Adam and the woman Eve.

5. Eve After Eden

We are led to believe that the name Adam means "first father" and reason therefrom that the name Eve means "first mother." We know that Adam was first man of all men and that Eve is "the mother of all living" (Moses 4:26).

Lehi says, "If Adam had not transgressed he would not have fallen, but he would have remained in the garden of Eden." Then he adds: "And they"—meaning Adam and Eve—"would have had no children." Hence the epigrammatic conclusion: "Adam fell that men might be." (2 Ne. 2:22–25.)

Thus it was that "Adam knew his wife, and she bare unto him sons and daughters, and they began to multiply and to replenish the earth. And from that time forth, the sons and daughters of Adam began to divide two and two in the land, and to till the land, and to tend flocks, and they also begat sons and daughters." (Moses 5:2–3.) Eden was behind them and the earth before them. The purposes of the Lord were under way.

While Adam and Eve were yet in Eden, the Lord "gave unto *them*"—meaning the revelation came to *both* of them—"commandments that *they* should love and serve him, the only living and true God, and that he should be the only being whom they should worship" (D&C 20:19; italics added). Then came the Fall.

After the Fall, "Adam and Eve, his wife, called upon the name of the Lord, and *they* heard the voice of the Lord . . . speaking unto *them* . . . and he gave unto *them* commandments, that *they* should worship the Lord *their* God," including the offering of sacrifices. Be it noted that both the man and the woman prayed; both heard the voice of the Lord; and both were commanded to worship him.

Then Adam offered sacrifices, an angel appeared and bore record of Christ, the Holy Ghost fell upon Adam, and he prophesied many things. "And Eve, his wife, heard all these things and was glad, saying: Were it not for our transgression we never should have had seed, and never should have known good and evil, and the joy of our redemption, and the eternal life which God giveth unto all the obedient." Then Adam and Eve "blessed the name of God," taught the gospel to their children, and continued in prayer and devotion. (Moses 5:4–16.)

Again, be it noted, the Lord is not dealing with Adam alone. Both of the eternal partners are glorying in the wonders of the gospel and walking in the light of heaven. Eve is a full partner; she is a helpmeet to her husband in both temporal and spiritual things.

6. *Eve in the Eternal Eden*

In a not far distant day this "earth will be renewed and receive its paradisiacal glory" (tenth article of faith). The Edenic, paradisiacal state which covered the face of the whole earth in a primeval day will be restored, and the millennial era will be ushered in as the Lord Jesus returns in all the glory of his Father's kingdom.

Before that day Adam, who is the Ancient of Days, will preside at a great conference to which all those of every dispensation who have held keys and positions of presidency on earth will come. The appointed place for this assemblage is Spring Hill, Daviess County, Missouri, which is named by the Lord "Adam-ondi-Ahman, because, said he, it is the place where Adam shall come to visit his people, or the Ancient of Days shall sit, as spoken of by Daniel the prophet" (D&C 116).

Daniel's testimony is: "I beheld till the thrones were cast down, and the Ancient of days did sit, whose garment was white as snow, and the hair of his head like the pure wool: his throne was like the fiery flame, and his wheels as burning fire. A fiery stream issued and came forth from before him: thousand thousands ministered unto him, and ten thousand times ten thousand stood before him: the judgment was set, and the books were opened. I saw in the night visions, and, behold, one like the Son of man came with the clouds of heaven, and came to the Ancient of days, and they brought him near before him. And there was given him dominion, and glory, and a kingdom, that all people, nations, and languages, should serve him: his dominion is an everlasting dominion, which shall not pass away, and his kingdom that which shall not be destroyed." (Dan. 7:9–10, 13–14.)

That is to say, after all to whom the keys of God's earthly kingdom have been given have reported their stewardships to Adam; after Adam has received back again the keys delegated to his descendants; then Christ will come, take them unto himself, and reign personally on earth for the space of a thousand years. This is a great initial day of judgment at which Adam presides.

Now, what of Eve? Will she and the sisters play a part in this and other great events which lie ahead? The scriptures are silent on this point. We are left to formulate an answer which accords with the great and eternal principles which have been revealed. We know, to some extent, the part she played — at Adam's side — in the past. We cannot believe that she is other than by his side now, or that she will depart therefrom in future days.

In our hymnbook we have the song, "Sons of Michael, He Approaches," in which we raise our voices in glad acclaim to Adam and sing of what he will do at Adam-ondi-Ahman. One of the verses is a paean of praise to Eve.

> Mother of our generations,
> Glorious by great Michael's side,
> Take thy children's adoration;
> Endless with thy Lord preside;
> Lo, lo, to greet thee now advance,
> Thousands in the glorious dance.
> (*LDS Hymns* No. 51.)

This, of course, assumes that she and other faithful women will continue to stand and serve at the sides of their husbands in the glorious events ahead.[1]

Speaking of the eternal state of exaltation and of those who live in the married state, the Lord says: "Then shall *they* be gods, because *they* have no end; therefore shall *they* be from everlasting to everlasting, because *they* continue; then shall *they* be above all, because all things are subject unto *them*. Then shall *they* be gods, because *they* have all power, and the angels are subject unto *them*." (D&C 132:20; italics added.)

What shall we say, then, of Eve — as an individual and as a generic name for all women who believe and obey as she did? Would we go far astray if we came up with such conclusions as the following:

Eve—a daughter of God, one of the spirit offspring of the Almighty Elohim—was among the noble and great in the preexistence. She ranked in spiritual stature, in faith and devotion, in conformity to eternal law with Michael, who participated in the creation of the earth and who led the hosts of heaven when Lucifer and his rebels were cast out.

As she was at Michael's side before the foundations of the earth, so she came with him into Eden. The two of them there performed for all men the inestimably great service called the fall of man. Thus mortality, and the begetting of children, and the probations of this life, and the hope of eternal life and exaltation—all these—become available to all of the children of the Father of us all.

After the Fall, Eve continued to receive revelation, to see visions, to walk in the Spirit. As Adam became the pattern for all his sons, so did Eve for all her daughters. And as they twain have gone on to exaltation and sit upon their thrones in glorious immortality, so may all, both male and female, who walk as they walked.

As there are no words to extol the greatness of the Ancient of Days unto whom thousands of thousands shall minister and before whom "ten thousand times ten thousand" shall stand in a day of judgment, so there is no language which can do credit to our glorious mother Eve.

Let God be praised for the glorious plan of creation, redemption, and exaltation. And let Adam and Eve be praised for the infinitely great part they played in the eternal plan of the Eternal One. ("Eve and the Fall," *Woman* [Salt Lake City: Deseret Book Co., 1980], pp. 57–68.)

Notes

1. One scriptural hint that righteous women will share the glories of the future with their husbands is found in the account of the premillennial gathering at Adam-ondi-Ahman in which dispensation heads give their keys to Adam, who in turn gives them back to Christ. In naming those who will be present, the Savior identifies many of the great prophets—Moroni, John the Baptist, Elijah,

Joseph, Jacob, Isaac, Abraham, Michael or Adam, Peter, James, John, and ''all those whom my Father hath given me out of the world.'' (D&C 27:5-14.) Surely this number must include, among those given the Savior out of the world, righteous women of every dispensation.

Chapter 12

THE PURIFYING POWER
OF GETHSEMANE

I feel, and the Spirit seems to accord, that the most important doctrine I can declare, and the most powerful testimony I can bear, is that of the atoning sacrifice of the Lord Jesus Christ.

Atonement Most Transcendent Event Ever

His atonement is the most transcendent event that ever has or ever will occur, from Creation's dawn through all the ages of a never-ending eternity.

It is the supreme act of goodness and grace that only a god could perform. Through it, all of the terms and conditions of the Father's eternal plan of salvation become operative.

Through it are brought to pass the immortality and eternal life of man. Through it, all men are saved from death, hell, the devil, and endless torment (2 Ne. 9:7–12).

And through it, all who believe and obey the glorious gospel of God, all who are true and faithful and overcome the world, all who suffer for Christ and his word, all who are chastened and scourged in the cause of him whose we are—all shall become as their Maker and sit with him on his throne and reign with him forever in everlasting glory (Rev. 3:5, 21; 21:7).

In speaking of these wondrous things, I shall use my own words, though you may think they are the words of scripture, words spoken by other Apostles and prophets.

True it is they were first proclaimed by others, but they are now mine, for the Holy Spirit of God has borne witness to me that they are true, and it is now as though the Lord had revealed them to me in the first instance. I have thereby heard his voice and know his word (D&C 18:33–36).

Gethsemane—A Sacred Spot

Two thousand years ago, outside Jerusalem's walls, there was a pleasant garden spot, Gethsemane by name, where Jesus and his intimate friends were wont to retire for pondering and prayer.

There Jesus taught his disciples the doctrines of the kingdom, and all of them communed with him who is the Father of us all, in whose ministry they were engaged, and on whose errand they served.

This sacred spot, like Eden where Adam dwelt, like Sinai from whence Jehovah gave his laws, like Calvary where the Son of God gave his life a ransom for many, this holy ground is where the sinless Son of the Everlasting Father took upon himself the sins of all men on condition of repentance (Alma 11:40–41; D&C 19:2–4, 16–20).

Significance of Atonement Incomprehensible

We do not know, we cannot tell, no mortal mind can conceive, the full import of what Christ did in Gethsemane.

We know he sweat great gouts of blood from every pore (Mosiah 3:7; Luke 22:44) as he drained the dregs of that bitter cup his Father had given him (Matt. 26:38–39).

We know he suffered, both body and spirit, more than it is possible for man to suffer, except it be unto death (D&C 19:18).

We know that in some way, incomprehensible to us, his suffering satisfied the demands of justice, ransomed penitent souls from the pains and penalties of sin, and made mercy available to those who believe in his holy name.

The Atonement an Infinite Burden

We know that he lay prostrate upon the ground as the pains and agonies of an infinite burden caused him to tremble, and would that he might not drink the bitter cup (Matt. 26:39; Mark 14:36; D&C 19:18–19).

We know that an angel came from the courts of glory to strengthen him in his ordeal (Luke 22:43), and we suppose it was mighty Michael, who foremost fell that men might be.

As near as we can judge, these infinite agonies—this suffering beyond compare—continued for some three to four hours.

After this—his body then wrenched and drained of strength—he confronted Judas and the other incarnate devils, some from the very Sanhedrin itself; and he was led away with a rope around his neck, as a common criminal, to be judged by the arch-criminals who as Jews sat in Aaron's seat and who as Romans wielded Caesar's power (Matt. 26:47–57; Luke 22:47–54; John 18:4).

Jesus Scourged, Judged of Men

They took him to Annas, to Caiaphas, to Pilate, to Herod, and back to Pilate. He was accused, cursed, and smitten (Matt. 27:29–33; Luke 22:63–65; Mark 15:17–20). Their foul saliva ran down his face as vicious blows further weakened his pain-engulfed body.

With reeds of wrath they rained blows upon his back. Blood ran down his face as a crown of thorns pierced his trembling brow.

But above it all he was scourged (John 19:1), scourged with forty stripes save one, scourged with a multithonged whip into whose leather strands sharp bones and cutting metals were woven.

Many died from scourging alone, but he rose from the sufferings of the scourge that he might die an ignominious death upon the cruel cross of Calvary.

Then he carried his own cross (John 19:17) until he collapsed from the weight and pain and mounting agony of it all.

On Calvary's Cross

Finally, on a hill called Calvary—again, it was outside Jerusalem's walls—while helpless disciples looked on and felt the agonies of near death in their own bodies, the Roman soldiers laid him upon the cross.

With great mallets they drove spikes of iron through his feet and hands and wrists. Truly he was wounded for our transgressions and bruised for our iniquities (Isa. 53:5).

Then the cross was raised that all might see and gape and curse and deride. This they did, with evil venom, for three hours from 9:00 A.M. to noon.

Then the heavens grew black. Darkness covered the land for the space of three hours, as it did among the Nephites. There was a mighty storm, as though the very God of nature was in agony. (1 Ne. 19:11–12.)

And he truly was, for while he was hanging on the cross for another three hours, from noon to 3:00 P.M., all the infinite agonies and merciless pains of Gethsemane recurred.

And, finally, when the atoning agonies had taken their toll—when the victory had been won, when the Son of God had fulfilled the will of his Father in all things—then he said, "It is finished" (John 19:30), and he voluntarily gave up the ghost (John 10:11–18; Luke 23:46).

As the peace and comfort of a merciful death freed him from the pains and sorrows of mortality, he entered the paradise of God.

Seed of Christ Defined

When he had made his soul an offering for sin, he was prepared to see his seed, according to the messianic word (Isa. 53:10; Mosiah 14:10).

These, consisting of all the holy prophets and faithful Saints from ages past; these, comprising all who had taken upon them his name, and who, being spiritually begotten by him, had become his sons and his daughters, even as it is with us (Mosiah 15:10–18); all these were assembled in the spirit world, there to see his face and hear his voice (D&C 138:11–19).

Entombed in Garden Tomb

After some thirty-eight or forty hours—three days as the Jews measured time—our Blessed Lord came to the Arimathaean's tomb, where his partially embalmed body had been placed by Nicodemus and Joseph of Arimathaea (Matt. 27:57–60; Mark 15:42–46; Luke 23:50–55).

Resurrection Crowns Atonement

Then, in a way incomprehensible to us, he took up that body which had not yet seen corruption and arose in that glorious immortality which made him like his resurrected Father. He then received all power in heaven and on earth, obtained eternal exaltation, appeared unto Mary Magdalene and many others, and ascended into heaven, there to sit down on the right hand of God the Father Almighty and to reign forever in eternal glory.

His rising from death on the third day crowned the Atonement. Again, in some way incomprehensible to us, the effects of his resurrection pass upon all men so that all shall rise from the grave.

As Adam brought death, so Christ brought life; as Adam is the father of mortality, so Christ is the father of immortality (1 Cor. 15:21–22).

And without both, mortality and immortality, man cannot work out his salvation and ascend to those heights beyond the skies where gods and angels dwell forever in eternal glory.

Atonement — The Central Doctrine

Now, the atonement of Christ is the most basic and fundamental doctrine of the gospel, and it is the least understood of all our revealed truths.

Many of us have a superficial knowledge and rely upon the Lord and his goodness to see us through the trials and perils of life.

Atonement Enables Exercise of Faith

May I invite you to join with me in gaining a sound and sure knowledge of the Atonement.

We must cast aside the philosophies of men and the wisdom of the wise and hearken to that Spirit which is given to us to guide us into all truth.

We must search the scriptures, accepting them as the mind and will and voice of the Lord and the very power of God unto salvation.

Creation, Fall, Atonement: One Doctrine

As we read, ponder, and pray, there will come into our minds a view of the three gardens of God — the Garden of Eden, the Garden of Gethsemane, and the Garden of the Empty Tomb where Jesus appeared to Mary Magdalene.

In Eden we will see all things created in a paradisiacal state — without death, without procreation, without probationary experiences (2 Ne. 2:22–23; Moses 5:11).

We will come to know that such a creation, now unknown to man, was the only way to provide for the Fall.

We will then see Adam and Eve, the first man and the first woman, step down from their state of immortal and paradisiacal glory to become the first mortal flesh on earth.

Mortality, including as it does procreation and death, will enter the world. And because of transgression a probationary estate of trial and testing will begin.

Then, in Gethsemane we will see the Son of God ransom man from the temporal and spiritual death that came to us because of the Fall.

And finally, before an empty tomb, we will come to know that Christ our Lord has burst the bands of death and stands forever triumphant over the grave.

Thus, Creation is father to the Fall; and by the Fall came mortality and death; and by Christ came immortality and eternal life.

If there had been no fall of Adam, by which cometh death, there could have been no atonement of Christ, by which cometh life.

And now, as pertaining to this perfect atonement, wrought by the shedding of the blood of God—I testify that it took place in Gethsemane and at Golgotha, and as pertaining to Jesus Christ, I testify that he is the Son of the living God and was crucified for the sins of the world. He is our Lord, our God, and our King. This I know of myself, independent of any other person.

A Perfect Witness

I am one of his witnesses, and in a coming day I shall feel the nail marks in his hands and in his feet and shall wet his feet with my tears.

But I shall not know any better then than I know now that he is God's Almighty Son, that he is our Savior and Redeemer, and that salvation comes in and through his atoning blood and in no other way.

God grant that all of us may walk in the light as God our Father is in the light so that, according to the promises, the blood of Jesus Christ his Son will cleanse us from all sin. (Conference Report, April 1985.)

PART IV

The Written Word

INTRODUCTION
TO PART IV

We study the gospel because of the sanctifying effects it has on our lives: by gospel study we learn the ways of God and can discern whether or not our lives conform to his laws. From such study comes faith.

Moreover, as Elder McConkie observes, gospel study opens the door to the receipt of revelation: through study we learn to think, speak, and act, as it were, as the Apostles and prophets, who have been given to us as examples (James 5:10), thought, spoke, and acted. Such learning is the great preparation for thinking, speaking, and acting as God thinks, speaks, and acts. When we learn to perfectly imitate God in all things, we become exalted; the process of sanctification is nothing more than the process of learning to be godlike in thought and conduct. Knowing this, Joseph Smith said: "The principle of knowledge is the principle of salvation"—and it is a principle which is comprehended only "by the faithful and diligent; and every one that does not obtain knowledge sufficient to be saved will be condemned. The principle of salvation is given us through the knowledge of Jesus Christ." (*Teachings*, p. 297.)

It is not gospel study alone which saves a man, but keeping the commandments. However, as the Prophet Joseph Smith observed, "we cannot keep all the commandments without first knowing them" (*Teachings*, p. 256)—which means we must study. Thus knowledge, obedience, and service are all parts of the same body, joining together to make, as it were, the "whole man in Christ." In short, we study gospel truths to learn how to make a more perfect and more acceptable service in the kingdom of our Father. The more we know of gospel truths, the more penetrating, the more convincing, and the more powerful a testimony we can bear; the more we understand of gospel laws, the more perfectly are we able to administer the programs of the kingdom and the ordinances of salvation; the more fully we understand gospel principles, the more perfectly we are able to counsel and instruct others—particularly in our own families—and thereby earn the rewards of eternal life. Surely, as the Prophet Joseph Smith said, "knowledge saves a man" (*Teachings*, p. 357), for it increases our capacity to do everything God requires of us.

In this context, Elder McConkie explains (chapter 13) that we study the gospel in order to know God; and while much good can and does come from many of the commentaries written about the scriptures, the best writings on God and the things of his kingdom are the things which he himself wrote in the scriptures, as he inspired his prophets. Thus comes the divine command: "Search the scriptures" (John 5:39). For, after all is said and done, the best commentary on the scriptures is the scriptures. The best interpretive explanations of Isaiah, for instance, come from the Book of Mormon (see chapter 20).

Because, as a part of the sifting processes of mortality, heresies constantly rear their ugly heads, and not infrequently disrupt the thought and even sometimes the conduct of the Saints, men and women need the protections which a correct understanding of the gospel can bring. Thus Joseph Smith testified: "In knowledge there is power. God has more power than all other beings, because he has greater knowledge." (*Teachings*, p. 288.) Just as this principle applies to God, even so it applies to men: we gain ascendency over the powers of evil by first knowing, and then living, the laws of God—that is, by studying and obeying. Thus the Prophet warned: "Nothing is a greater injury to the children of men than to be under the influence of a false spirit when they think they have the Spirit of God" (*Teachings*, p. 205). Similarly, few things are as great an injury to the children of men as to be under the influence of a false principle, a false teaching, or a false testimony, for falsity leads but to folly—and sometimes even to the loss of our souls.

Chapter 13 is both a warning against false teaching and an instruction on how to recognize and obtain true teachings. It is in chapter 14, however, that Elder McConkie makes the point more forcefully, first with the "Parable of the Unwise Builder," and then more expressly with his "Finding Answers to Gospel Questions," in which he analyzes the processes of constructive gospel study. This all lays the groundwork for our understanding the value and import of the new LDS editions of the holy scriptures, completed in 1981. These scriptures contain the best teaching aids, and therefore the best learning aids, of any scriptures ever compiled on earth. The section entitled "Holy Writ Published Anew" (chapter 15) is important not only because it teaches about the unique features of the LDS editions of the scriptures but also because it contains an apostolic testimony of the inspiration that was a part of producing these scriptures.

By enlarging our capacity to understand the scriptures, the new LDS scriptures enlarge our ability to get in tune with the Holy Ghost. This is important, for to read the scriptures by the power of the Holy Ghost is to hear, by scriptural definition, the voice of the Lord. In chapter 16 Elder McConkie draws attention to the standard works, noting peculiar strengths of each, and pointing thereby to ways that each helps to bring the Spirit of God into the lives of its readers. Of particular note are the scriptures restored in this dispensation: the Book of Mormon, which Joseph Smith called "the most correct" of any book, and "the keystone of our religion"; the Doctrine and Covenants, a compilation of revelations given specifically and uniquely for our day; and the Pearl of Great Price, which so perfectly teaches that the gospel is eternal, and that it was enjoyed in its fulness long before the meridian of time.

Chapter 17 focuses attention on the specific strengths of the Book of Mormon and invites all men everywhere to take a stand with regard to this great American scripture, for the measure of one's spirituality can be tested by his acceptance or rejection of the Book of Mormon.

Thus, in chapter 17 Elder McConkie dramatizes the power of the Book of Mormon: free from the history which plagued the Bible, it has come to us in a purer form; written to a people who lacked the traditions, the rituals, the synagogues and temples, and the established Church of Christ, it is clearer and plainer in its presentation of gospel truths than is the Bible. Moreover, the Book of Mormon tests the spirituality of all who read it in that its truth can be known only by revelation — it has no long history and religious tradition associated with it which would beguile men into accepting it on intellectual or historical terms. Thus it puts the focus of true religion where it ought to be — on the acceptance of living prophets, and on the ability to receive personal revelation. At the same time, it is in this chapter that we see that the real genius of gospel study — and the strength of the Latter-day position — lies in the Book of Mormon and the revelations of this dispensation. The revelations of this dispensation are the key to Bible interpretation. They are also the key to a true understanding of the gospel, and thus they open the door to salvation. Indeed, the Book of Mormon was revealed with the express purpose of "proving to the world" that the Bible is true, and that Jesus is the Christ.

Building on this foundation, Elder McConkie points his attention to the Bible, which in the past has been a sealed book—sealed by the seals of ignorance and intellectuality. In chapter 18 he outlines twelve keys, the application of which will lift those seals from our understanding. Chapter 18 is important not only because it lays a doctrinal foundation for gospel study but also because it provides such a steady framework for avoiding the errors which control the sectarian world. Here we see that the Bible is not the infallible, inerrant word of God; it is not a revelation from God, but rather the history of revelations given to others. It is not the divine feast, it is the history of the feast, as well as the recipe for obtaining the feast. Salvation comes from receiving revelation, not from reading about the revelations experienced by others. Indeed, to teach inerrancy is to eliminate the need for living prophets, revelation, and ultimately the need for God, as inerrancy not only assumes that the Bible is without error, but also that it contains all the truth we need in order to be saved. It is a doctrine which leads men to worship the Bible, rather than God.

This chapter is also filled with additional insights, such as the content of the sealed portions of the Book of Mormon, that the purpose of the Bible is to prepare men to receive the Book of Mormon, that we have other inspired writings which ought to be studied hand in hand with the scriptural canon, that not all scripture is of equal worth, that the same scriptures may have more than one interpretation, and that the King James Version is deservedly our preferred translation because it is in the language of the Book of Mormon and the Doctrine and Covenants. This is important because an awareness of the linguistic ties between the Bible and modern scriptures enables us to see doctrinal ties between all the scriptures which would be obscured if we relied on a different Bible translation. Moreover, this chapter also shows some of the implications which flow from using latter-day scriptures to interpret ancient ones.

In chapter 19, two pieces, one on the book of Isaiah and the other on the Revelation of John, provide helps on how to understand these books. More important, however, they demonstrate the processes of analysis and study which have given Elder McConkie his understanding of these two books—a process of years of gospel study, of approaching the Lord for understanding in faith and prayer, of using the Book of Mormon and other scriptures to interpret difficult passages, and of learning to listen to the promptings of the Holy Spirit.

But understanding gospel truths is not sufficient. Our commission is to "teach one another the doctrine of the kingdom" (D&C 88:77). And as we are the Lord's agents, gospel teaching, as with all things we do as his agents, "must needs be done in [his] own way" (D&C 104:16). And what is the Lord's way? Elder McConkie, leaning upon the revelations, points to the principles the Lord has outlined: we are to preach the principles of the gospel, as they are found in the standard works of the Church, by the power of the Holy Ghost. These we apply to the lives and circumstances of our hearers, with the testimony that the specific principles we have taught are true. With this outline, he provides a warning against the teaching of false doctrine, notes with particularity some of the most common falsehoods taught in the world and some of those creeping into the Church, and testifies that just as true doctrines build faith and testimony, false doctrines destroy true faith and testimony.

Chapter 13

WHY WE STUDY
THE GOSPEL

Study the Gospel to Know God

Jesus issued this invitation: "Come unto me. . . . Take my yoke upon you and learn of me." (Matt. 11:28–29.) He also said, "This is life eternal, that they might know thee the only true God, and Jesus Christ, whom thou hast sent" (John 17:3).

To know God in that full sense which will enable us to gain eternal salvation means that we must know what he knows, enjoy what he enjoys, experience what he experiences. In New Testament language, we must "be like him" (1 John 3:2).

But before we can become like him, we must obey those laws that will enable us to acquire the character, perfections, and attributes that he possesses. And before we can obey these laws, we must learn what they are (*Teachings*, pp. 255–56); we must learn of Christ and obey his gospel. We must learn "that salvation was, and is, and is to come, in and through the atoning blood of Christ, the Lord Omnipotent" (Mosiah 3:18). We must learn that baptism under the hands of a legal administrator is essential to salvation and that after baptism we must keep the commandments and "press forward with a steadfastness in Christ, having a perfect brightness of hope, and a love of God and of all men" (2 Ne. 31:20).

Our revelation says, "The glory of God is intelligence, or, in other words, light and truth" (D&C 93:36). Joseph Smith taught that "a man is saved no faster than he gets knowledge" of God and his saving truths (*Teachings*, p. 217) and that "it is impossible for a man to be saved in ignorance" of Jesus Christ and the laws of his gospel (D&C 131:6).

We believe in gospel scholarship. We think that devout men everywhere, in and out of the Church, should seek spiritual truth, should come to know God, should learn his laws, and should strive to live in harmony with them. There are no truths as important as those that pertain to God and his gospel, to the pure religion that he has revealed, to the terms and conditions whereby we may gain an inheritance with him in his kingdom.

Thus we find Deity commanding: "Search these command- ments" (D&C 1:37); "Study my word which hath gone forth among the children of men" (D&C 11:22); "Teach the principles of my gos- pel, which are in the Bible and the Book of Mormon, in the which is the fulness of the gospel" (D&C 42:12).

Thus we find Jesus saying: "Search the prophets" (3 Ne. 23:5); "Search the scriptures; for . . . they are they which testify of me" (John 5:39); "Yea, a commandment I give unto you that ye search these things diligently" (3 Ne. 23:1).

Christ is the great exemplar, the prototype of perfection and sal- vation: "He said unto the children of men: Follow thou me" (2 Ne. 31:10). Also: "What manner of men ought ye to be? Verily I say unto you, even as I am." (3 Ne. 27:27.) I know of no better way to respond to Jesus' invitation, "Learn of me" (Matt. 10:29), than to study the scriptures with a prayerful heart.

I know of no better way to heed his counsel, "Follow thou me," than to live in harmony with the truths recorded in the scrip- tures, for as Nephi asked, "Can we follow Jesus save we shall be willing to keep the commandments of the Father?" (2 Ne. 31:10).

Scriptures Reveal Christ

The Old Testament prophets reveal Christ's laws and foretell his messianic ministry. The Doctrine and Covenants records his mind and will and voice as he speaks to men in our day. The Book of Mormon is an American witness of his divine sonship which has come forth "to the convincing of the Jew and Gentile that Jesus is the Christ, the Eternal God, manifesting himself unto all nations" (title page, Book of Mormon). The New Testament contains the wit- ness of the ancient Apostles that he ministered among men and set up his earthly kingdom in the meridian of time. (Conference Re- port, April 1966.)

Knowledge Precedes Testimony

These words were dictated by the Holy Ghost to an inspired man in ancient Israel: "The law of the Lord is perfect, converting the soul: the testimony of the Lord is sure, making wise the simple. The statutes of the Lord are right, rejoicing the heart: the commandment of the Lord is pure, enlightening the eyes. The fear of the Lord is clean, enduring for ever: the judgments of the Lord are true and righteous altogether. More to be desired are they than gold, yea, than much fine gold: sweeter also than honey and the honeycomb. Moreover by them is thy servant warned: and in keeping of them there is great reward." (Ps. 19:7–11.)

Now, if I may be enlightened by the same Spirit that rested upon him who wrote these words, I would like to indicate the great compelling necessity, the overwhelming obligation, that rests upon us as members of this great latter-day kingdom, to come to a knowledge of the law of the Lord, to know the doctrines of the gospel, to understand the principles, requirements, and ordinances which we must comply with in order to be heirs of salvation in the Lord's kingdom.

We believe and advocate that every member of this Church should have a testimony of the divinity of the work; that he should know for himself, independent of any other person, that Jesus Christ is the Son of God, and that salvation is in him; that Joseph Smith is the agent and instrument through whom the knowledge of salvation has come again in our day; and that the mantle of the Prophet rests upon the President of the Church. By first gaining a testimony and then by being valiant in testimony, we can be heirs of salvation.

But no man can have a testimony of this work until he begins to get a knowledge of the gospel. A testimony is based on knowledge; first a man must learn about God and his laws, and then by obedience to these laws he will gain a testimony. Jesus said, "My doctrine is not mine, but his that sent me. If any man will do his will, he shall know of the doctrine, whether it be of God, or whether I speak of myself." (John 7:16–17.)

We believe that all members of this Church should be fully and completely converted, so much so that they are changed from a natural and fallen state into Saints of God, changed into a state where they have in their hearts desires for righteousness. By following such a course they are born again; they are renewed of the Spirit; they are in line for eternal salvation. But no one can attain unto such a state until he knows the laws that govern the process of being converted.

We believe that after we join this Church it is incumbent upon us to press forward in steadfastness and in devotion, living by every word that proceedeth forth from the mouth of God, desiring righteousness, seeking his Spirit, loving him with all our hearts, minds, and strength; and yet we cannot do any of these things until we first learn the laws which govern them. In the full gospel sense, there is no such thing as living a law of which we are ignorant. We cannot worship a God of whom we know nothing, as far as gaining eternal life through that worship is concerned.

Commanded to Search the Scriptures

We have the obligation, the great underlying responsibility, to learn the doctrines of the Church so that we will be able to serve in the kingdom, so that we will be able to carry the message of salvation to our Father's other children, and so that we will be able to live in such a manner as to have peace and joy ourselves, and gain this hope of glorious exaltation and eternal life.

We have been commanded to do this very thing. We say, for instance, that no man can be saved in ignorance (D&C 131:6), and we mean in ignorance of Jesus Christ and the saving truths of the gospel. We say that men are saved no faster than they gain knowledge (D&C 130:18-19), and we mean knowledge of God and the principles and doctrines which he has revealed. We say that the glory of God is intelligence (D&C 93:36), and we mean that his glory is light and truth—including the revealed light of heaven and the truths of salvation.

When Moses was finishing his ministry in ancient Israel, after he had led that people through all their travails in the wilderness, he, being moved upon by the Spirit, took occasion to summarize the laws, the statutes, the judgments, the ordinances, the things that they, Israel, would be required to do; and after having so done, he said this:

"And these words, which I command thee this day, shall be in thine heart: And thou shalt teach them diligently unto the children, and shalt talk of them when thou sittest in thine house, and when thou walkest by the way, and when thou liest down, and when thou risest up. And thou shalt bind them for a sign upon thine hand, and they shall be as frontlets between thine eyes. And thou shalt write them upon the posts of thy house, and on thy gates." (Deut. 6:6-9.)

In other words, Moses was commanding that Israel should center their souls and hearts upon studying and knowing and learning the laws of the Lord so that they would be in the position and have the ability to live them, and thus gain salvation and perform fully the mission appointed to that chosen people.

Saints Need Regular Study

In our day we have the standard works of the Church. We have the Bible, the Book of Mormon, the Doctrine and Covenants, and the Pearl of Great Price. There are in these four books a total of 1579 chapters. I think it would not be too much to say that we could with propriety, day in and day out, consistently, read three chapters in one or the other of these works; and if we pursued such a course, we would read all of the Gospels in less than a month. We would read the entire New Testament in three months. We would read the Old Testament in ten months, and the whole Bible in thirteen months. We would go through the Book of Mormon in two and two-thirds months, the Doctrine and Covenants in a month and a half, and the Pearl of Great Price in five days. Taken altogether, we would read all the standard works in less than eighteen months and be ready to start over again.

The Lord is not viewing us any differently from the way he viewed ancient Israel. Our whole hearts and souls and our continual meditation should be centered on the gospel and the things of the Lord, so that we can work out our salvation and fulfill our missions. By regular, systematic study of the standard works we can go a long way toward keeping in a course that will please the Lord and further our own eternal progression. (Conference Report, October 1959.)

Chapter 14

GUIDELINES TO GOSPEL STUDY

The Parable of the Unwise Builder

The Parable

Hear now the parable of the unwise builder:

A certain man inherited a choice piece of ground whereon to build a house to shelter his loved ones from the storms of the day and the cold of the night.

He began his work with zeal and skill, using good materials, for the need was urgent.

But in his haste, and because he gave no heed to the principles of proper construction, he laid no foundation, but commencing immediately, he built the floor, and raised the walls, and began to cover them with a roof.

Then, to his sorrow, because his house had no foundation, it fell and became a heap of rubble, and those whom he loved had no shelter.

Verily, verily, I say unto you: A wise builder, when he buildeth a house, first layeth the foundation and then buildeth thereon.

The Interpretation of the Parable

Hear now the interpretation of the parable of the unwise builder:

A certain Church officer was called to build a house of faith and righteousness and salvation for the souls entrusted to his care. Knowing he had been called by inspiration and having great zeal, he hastened to strengthen and build up the programs of the Church without first laying the foundation of faith and testimony and conversion.

He spent his time on mechanics and means and programs and procedures and teaching leadership and never laid the great and eternal foundation upon which all things must rest in the Lord's house—the foundation of our theology and our doctrine.

Import of the Proper Foundation

I am told that a high Catholic prelate said to one who held the holy apostleship: "There are two things which you Mormons have which we as Catholics would like to adopt."

"What are they?" he was asked.

"They are tithing and your missionary system," he replied.

"Well, why don't you adopt them?" came the rejoinder.

"We would except for two reasons: our people won't pay tithing, and our people won't go on missions."

How often have well-meaning and sincere people in the world attempted to adopt our youth programs, our family home evening program, our missionary system, and so on, and yet have not been able to operate them in their situations!

Why? Because they do not lay a proper foundation; however inspired the programs may be, they do not stand alone. They must be built on the foundation of faith and doctrine.

The foundation upon which we build our whole Church system is one of testimony and faith and conversion. It is our theology; it is the doctrine God has given us in this day; it is the restored and revealed principles of eternal truth—these are the things that give us the ability to operate our programs and build houses of salvation.

Four Suggestions for a Proper Foundation

I suggest:
1. Learn the doctrines of the gospel; ponder their wondrous import and meaning; and pray continually for wisdom and understanding. Hunger and thirst after righteousness.
2. Search the scriptures; learn the doctrines of salvation; treasure up the Lord's word. Read the scriptures daily.
3. Preach from the scriptures. Always, always, always without fail, quote or paraphrase some appropriate passage of scripture when presenting any program or procedure.

4. Get others to go and do likewise.

Remember, no man buildeth a house which will stand as a safe covert from the storms in the world unless he first lays the proper foundation. (Address, Regional Representatives Seminar, 3 April 1981.)

Finding Answers to Gospel Questions

I receive a flood of letters asking questions about the doctrines, practices, and history of the Church. Several thousand questions are presented to me each year. Recently I received a single letter containing 210 major questions plus numerous lesser ones. To answer the questions in this one letter alone would have taken several hundred pages. Frequently I have a stack of unanswered letters which is six or eight inches high. There are times when weeks go by without an opportunity even to read the letters, let alone attempt to answer them.

Thoughtful persons will realize that if I devoted all my waking hours to the research and work involved in answering the questions which come to me, I still would not be able to answer all of them. But — and this is far more important — if I were able to perform this service it still would not be the right thing to do, nor would it be in the best interests of those who present their problems to me. May I instead make the following general suggestions to those who seek answers to gospel questions:

1. Seek light and truth. All men everywhere, in and out of the Church, without reference to sect, party, or denomination, are obligated to seek light and truth. The Light of Christ comes as a free gift to all men; it enlighteneth every man born into the world (D&C 84:45–46); and those who follow its promptings seek truth, gain knowledge and understanding, and are led to the gospel and its saving truths.

Members of the Church have an added obligation to understand both the laws of nature and the doctrines of salvation (Alma 19:6; D&C 20:37; 84:47). They have the gift of the Holy Ghost, which is the right to the constant companionship of this member of the Godhead based on faithfulness. The Holy Ghost is a revelator. "And by the power of the Holy Ghost ye may know the truth of all things" (Moro. 10:5). In the full and final sense, the only perfect and absolute way to gain a sure knowledge of any truth in any field is to receive personal revelation from the Holy Spirit of God. This heaven-sent boon is reserved for those who keep the commandments and obtain the companionship of the Holy Spirit. Be it remembered that the Spirit will not dwell in an unclean tabernacle (Alma 7:21).

2. Search the scriptures. The answers to nearly all important doctrinal questions are found in the standard works or in the sermons and writings of the Prophet Joseph Smith. If they are not found in these sources, they probably are not essential to salvation and may well be beyond our present spiritual capacity to understand. New revelations will be given when we believe and understand and live in harmony with those truths we have already received.

The way to achieve a high state of gospel scholarship is first to study and ponder and pray about the Book of Mormon and then to follow the same course with reference to the other scriptures. The Book of Mormon contains that portion of the Lord's word which he has given to the world to prepare the way for an understanding of the Bible and the other revelations now had among us. We have been commanded to search the scriptures (John 5:39), all of them; to treasure up the Lord's word, lest we be deceived (D&C 6:20; 43:34; JS—M 1:37); to drink deeply from the fountain of holy writ, that our thirst for knowledge may be quenched.

Paul says the scriptures are able to make us "wise unto salvation through faith which is in Christ Jesus" (2 Tim. 3:15). They lead us to the true Church and the legal administrators whom God has appointed to administer his work on earth. It is far better for us to gain our answers from the scriptures than from something someone else says about them. It is true that we oftentimes need an inspired interpreter to help us understand what Apostles and prophets have written for us in the standard works. But it is also true that many explanations given by many people as to the meaning of scriptural passages are somewhat less than true and edifying.

We are in a far better position if we are able to drink directly from the scriptural fountain without having the waters muddied by others whose insights are not as great as were those of the prophetic writers who first penned the passages found in the accepted canon of holy writ. I am not rejecting proper scriptural commentaries; I know and appreciate their value and have written volumes of them myself; I am simply saying that people with the ability to do it would be far better off to create their own commentaries. There is something sacred and solemn and saving about studying the scriptures themselves. We should train ourselves in this direction.

3. True doctrines are in harmony with the standard works. The standard works are scripture. They are binding upon us. They are the

mind and will and voice of the Lord. He never has, he does not
now, and he never will reveal anything which is contrary to what is
in them. No person, speaking by the spirit of inspiration, will ever
teach doctrine that is out of harmony with the truths God has already revealed.

These words of President Joseph Fielding Smith should guide
all of us in our gospel study: "It makes no difference what is written
or what anyone has said, if what has been said is in conflict with
what the Lord has revealed, we can set it aside. My words, and the
teachings of any other member of the Church, high or low, if they
do not square with the revelations, we need not accept them. Let us
have this matter clear. We have accepted the four standard works
as the measuring yardsticks, or balances, by which we measure
every man's doctrine.

"You cannot accept the books written by the authorities of the
Church as standards of doctrine, only in so far as they accord with
the revealed word in the standard works.

"Every man who writes is responsible, not the Church, for
what he writes. If Joseph Fielding Smith writes something which is
out of harmony with the revelations, then every member of the
Church is duty bound to reject it. If he writes that which is in perfect
harmony with the revealed word of the Lord, then it should be accepted." (Joseph Fielding Smith, *Doctrines of Salvation*, 3 vols. [Salt
Lake City: Bookcraft, 1954–56], pp. 203–4; also cited in *Mormon Doctrine*, p. 609.)

4. Seek to harmonize scriptural and prophetic utterances. Every truth,
in every field, in all the earth, and in all eternity, is in complete and
total harmony with every other truth. Truth is always in harmony
with itself. The word of the Lord is truth, and no scripture ever con-
tradicts another, nor is any inspired statement of any person out of
harmony with an inspired statement of any other person. Paul and
James did not have differing views on faith and works, and everything that Alma said about the Resurrection accords with section 76
in the Doctrine and Covenants. When we find seeming conflicts, it
means we have not as yet caught the full vision of whatever points
are involved.

The Lord expects us to seek for harmony and agreement in the
scriptures and among the Brethren rather than for seeming diver-
gences of views. Those who have faith and understanding always
seek to harmonize into one perfect whole all the statements of the
scriptures and all the pronouncements of the Brethren. The unfor-
tunate complex in some quarters to pounce upon this bit of infor-

mation or that and conclude that it is at variance with what someone else has said is not of God. Over the years I have received thousands of letters saying, "So-and-So said one thing, but Someone-Else said the reverse—who is right?" My experience is that in most instances—nay, in almost all instances—the seeming divergencies can be harmonized, and when they cannot be it is of no moment anyway. The Spirit of the Lord leads to harmony and unity and agreement and oneness. The spirit of the devil champions division and debate and contention and disunity (3 Ne. 11:29).

5. *Are all prophetic utterances true?* Of course they are! This is what the Lord's system of teaching is all about. Anything which his servants say when moved upon by the Holy Ghost is scripture, and his command to his ministers is: "The Spirit shall be given unto you by the prayer of faith; and if ye receive not the Spirit ye shall not teach" (D&C 42:14).

But not every word that a man who is a prophet speaks is a prophetic utterance. Joseph Smith taught that a prophet is not always a prophet, only when he is acting as such (*Teachings*, p. 278). Men who wear the prophetic mantle are still men; they have their own views; and their understanding of gospel truths is dependent upon the study and inspiration that is theirs.

Some prophets—I say it respectfully—know more and have greater inspiration than others. Thus, if Brigham Young, who was one of the greatest of the prophets, said something about Adam which is out of harmony with what is in the book of Moses and in section 78, it is the scripture that prevails. This is one of the reasons we call our scriptures the standard works. They are the standards of judgment and the measuring rod against which all doctrines and views are weighed, and it does not make one particle of difference whose views are involved. The scriptures always take precedence.

6. *Leave the mysteries alone and avoid gospel hobbies.* We do not and in our present state of spiritual progression cannot comprehend all things. We do not have the sealed portion of the Book of Mormon because we are not prepared to understand and live the truths found therein. Some things in the scriptures are hidden from full view in parables, similitudes, and imagery (Matt. 13:10–13; John 16:25; Alma 12:9–11). We are obligated to understand the basic doctrines which lead to eternal life; beyond this, how much we know about the mysteries depends upon the degree of our spiritual enlightenment. It is unwise to swim too far in water over our heads. (Mosiah 4:27; D&C 10:4.) My experience is that people who get themselves ensnared in fruitless contention over the meanings of

deep and hidden passages of scripture are usually those who do not have a sound and basic understanding of the simple and basic truths of salvation.

It is also my experience that people who ride gospel hobbies, who try to qualify themselves as experts in some specialized field, who try to make the whole plan of salvation revolve around some field of particular interest to them—it is my experience that such persons are usually spiritually immature and spiritually unstable. This includes those who devote themselves—as though by divine appointment—to setting forth the signs of the times; or to expounding about the Second Coming; or, to a faddist intepretation of the Word of Wisdom; or, to a twisted emphasis on temple work or any other doctrine or practice. The Jews of Jesus' day made themselves hobbiests and extremists in the field of Sabbath observance, and it colored and blackened their whole way of worship. We would do well to have a sane, rounded, and balanced approach to the whole gospel and all of its doctrines.

7. Be not overly concerned about unimportant matters. There is so much to learn about the great eternal verities which shape our destiny that it seems a shame to turn our attention everlastingly to the minutiae and insignificant things. So often questions like this are asked: "I know it is not essential to my salvation, but I would really like to know how many angels can dance on the head of a pin and if it makes any difference whether the pin is made of brass or bronze?" There is such a thing as getting so tied up with little fly specks on the great canvas which depicts the whole plan of salvation that we lose sight of what the life and the light and the glory of eternal reward are all about. (See, e.g., Matt. 23:23–25.) There is such a thing as virtually useless knowledge, the acquisition of which won't make one iota of difference to the destiny of the kingdom or the salvation of its subjects.

8. Withhold judgment, if need be, on hard questions. To those with full insight and complete understanding there are no hard questions. After a mystery has been solved it is no longer a mystery. But there are some questions which seem to invite intellectual forays into unknown areas, or which seem to ensnare, in endless contention, those who are somewhat less than spiritually literate.

If you cannot believe all of the doctrines of the gospel, withhold judgment in the areas in question. Do not commit yourself to a position which is contrary to that espoused by the prophets and Apostles who preside over the kingdom. Study, pray, work in the Church and await further light and knowledge.

If you are troubled about so-called evolution, and have not learned that Adam was both the first man and the first mortal flesh (Moses 3:7), and that there was no death of any form of life until after the Fall (2 Ne. 2:22) — withhold judgment and do not take a stand against the scriptures.

If you suppose God is progressing and gaining more knowledge and truth, and that he is not really omnipotent, omniscient, and omnipresent as Joseph Smith taught — withhold judgment. Remain silent. Do not lock yourself into a position contrary to the revealed word.

If you think there will be progression from one kingdom of glory to another after resurrection; or that people who reject the gospel in this life will have a second chance to gain salvation in the world to come; or that couples who are married in the temple can commit all manner of sin and still gain salvation; or any of a host of the common heresies of the hour — withhold judgment. Do not commit yourself to the defense of a false cause. Study something else and await the day when you will be prepared for more light on the matter that troubles you.

9. *Ignore, if you can, the endless array of anti-Mormon literature and avoid cults like a plague.* Conversion is not born of contention. He that hath the spirit of contention is not of God (Prov. 18:6; Rom. 2:7–8; 1 Cor. 11:16; James 3:16; 3 Ne. 11:29; D&C 10:63). Our divine commission is to declare glad tidings to the world, not to quarrel with others about the meaning of texts. There are, of course, answers to all of the false claims of those who array themselves against us — I do not believe the devil has had a new idea for a hundred years — but conversion is not found in the dens of debate. It comes rather to those who read the Book of Mormon in the way Moroni counseled. Most members of the Church would be better off if they simply ignored the specious claims of the professional anti-Mormons.

If the false claims about salvation by grace alone, or whatever the anti-Mormon literature is proclaiming, if these claims trouble you, search out the answers. They are in the scriptures. Anyone who cannot learn from the Bible that salvation does not come by simply confessing the Lord with one's lips, without reference to all the other terms and conditions of the true plan of salvation, does not deserve to be saved.

And as to the cults — they are the gate to hell. Members of the Church who espouse the cultish practice of plural marriage, for instance, are adulterers, and adulterers are damned. The common approach of those who propagandize for this practice is to pit the sayings of the dead prophets against those of the living prophets. Anyone who follows a dead prophet rather than a living prophet will follow him to death rather than to life. Again, there are answers to all the specious cultist views, and those who are tainted by false and forlorn fallacies had better find the truth at the peril of their salvation. It is the course of safety and wisdom never to get mixed up in these matters in the first instance.

10. There are no private doctrines. All of the doctrines and practices of the Church are taught publicly. There are no secret doctrines, no private practices, no courses of conduct approved for a few only (Isa. 45:19; 48:16; 2 Ne. 20:16; D&C 1:34). The blessings of the gospel are for all men. Do not be deceived into believing that the General Authorities believe any secret doctrines or have any private ways of living. Everything that is taught and practiced in the Church is open to public inspection, or, at least, where temple ordinances are concerned, to the inspection and knowledge of everyone who qualifies himself by personal righteousness to enter the house of the Lord.

11. Maintain an open mind. The doctrines are the Lord's. He established them; he reveals them; he expects us to accept them. Often those who ask questions are more interested in sustaining a prechosen position than in learning what the facts are. Our concern should be to find and cleave to the truth. It should not matter to us *what* the doctrine is, only that we come to a knowledge of it. Our espousal and defense of a false doctrine will not make it true. Our concern is to come to a knowledge of the truth, not to prove a point to which we may unwisely have committed ourselves.

12. The responsibility to study is a personal one. Now, let us come to the conclusion of this whole matter, a conclusion that will have an important bearing on our eternal salvation. It is that *each person must learn the doctrines of the gospel for himself.* No one else can do it for him. Each person stands alone where gospel scholarship is concerned; each has access to the same scriptures and is entitled to the guidance of the same Holy Ghost; each must pay the price set by a divine Providence if he is to gain the pearl of great price.

The same principle governs both learning truth and living in harmony with its standards. No one can repent for and on behalf of another; no one can keep the commandments in the place and stead of another; no one can be saved in someone else's name. And no one can gain a testimony or press forward in light and truth to eternal glory for anyone but himself. Both the knowledge of the truth and the blessings that come to those who conform to true principles are personal matters. And as a just God offers the same salvation to every soul who lives the same laws, so he offers the same understanding of his eternal truths to all who will pay the truth seeker's price.

The Church system for gaining gospel knowledge is as follows:

(a) The responsibility rests upon each person to gain a knowledge of the truth through his own efforts.

(b) Next, families should teach their own family members. Parents are commanded to bring up their children in light and truth. The home should be the chief teaching center in the life of a Latter-day Saint.

(c) To help families and individuals, the Church, as a service agency, provides many opportunities to teach and learn. We are commanded to "teach one another the doctrine of the kingdom" (D&C 88:77). This is done in sacrament meetings, in conferences and other meetings, by home teachers, in priesthood and auxiliary classes, through seminaries and institutes, and through the Church Educational System.

Opportunities to learn are unlimited. Proper questions may be discussed in any of the classes and schools provided for such purposes.

One final word seems appropriate. There are few joys in life to compare with the joy of coming to a knowledge of truth. How faithful people rejoice in the testimonies that are theirs! And what a spirit of exhilaration and peace comes into the heart of a gospel student each time a new truth is manifest to him! Each time his views expand to catch the full vision of some prophetic passage! Each time his soul both learns and feels the import of what the revelations say about some great principle!

The foregoing expressions are made in an attempt to be helpful; to encourage gospel scholarship; and to guide truth seekers in a wise and proper course.

It is my prayer that all of us may learn and live the gospel and gain an eventual inheritance in the everlasting kingdom of him whose servants we are. (From an open letter directed to "Honest Truth Seekers," 1 July 1980.)

Chapter 15

HOLY WRIT
PUBLISHED ANEW

We are grateful beyond any measure of expression for the excellence of our new editions of the scriptures.

We feel that the three things that have happened in our lifetime which will do more for the spread of the gospel, for the perfecting of the Saints, and for the salvation of men are:

1. The receipt of the revelation which makes the priesthood and the blessings of the temple available to all men without reference to race or ancestry;
2. The organization of the First Quorum of the Seventy as the third great council of the Church; and
3. The publication of the standard works in their new format and with the new teaching aids that accompany them.

We are somewhat saddened, however, that the generality of the Saints have not yet caught the vision of what our new scriptural publications contain and are not using them as they should.

I hope and pray that all of us may have the spiritual maturity, and can attune our souls to the Spirit, so as to both understand and act upon the things I shall say relative to the holy scriptures.

The Gospel—Not Programs—Saves

Our tendency—it is an almost universal practice among most Church members—is to get so involved with the operation of the institutional Church that we never gain faith like the ancients, simply because we do not involve ourselves in the basic gospel matters that were the center of their lives.

We are so wound up in programs and statistics and trends, in properties, lands, and mammon, and in achieving goals that will highlight the excellence of our work, that we "have omitted the weightier matters of the law." And as Jesus would have said: "These [weightier things] ought ye to have done, and not to leave the other undone." (Matt. 23:23.)

Let us be reminded of the great basic verities upon which all Church programs and all Church organization rest.

We are not saved by Church programs as such, by Church organizations alone, or even by the Church itself. It is the gospel that saves. The gospel is "the power of God unto salvation" (Rom. 1:16).

Salvation comes because "Jesus Christ," as Paul said, "hath abolished death, and hath brought life and immortality to light through the gospel" (2 Tim. 1:10). It is the gospel that raises men "in immortality" and "unto eternal life" (D&C 29:43). The gospel is the plan of salvation by which we can change the souls we possess into the kind of souls who can go where God and Christ are.

Church Administers the Gospel

But the Church and the priesthood administer the gospel. There must be an institutional Church so there will be order and system in all things. There neither is nor can be salvation without the Church. The Church is the service agency, the organization, the earthly kingdom which makes salvation available to men.

Paul tells us that the gospel comes to men in two ways—in word and in power (1 Thes. 1:5). The word of the gospel is written in the scriptures; the power of the gospel is written in the lives of those who both receive and enjoy the gift of the Holy Ghost.

Before we can write the gospel in our own book of life we must learn the gospel as it is written in the books of scripture. The Bible, the Book of Mormon, and the Doctrine and Covenants—each of them individually and all of them collectively—contain the fulness of the everlasting gospel (see, e.g., D&C 20:8-9). They contain the words of eternal life which lead to immortal glory.

Commanded to Study

Is it any wonder, then, that we are commanded to search the scriptures (John 5:39) and particularly the commandments that have come to us by revelation in our day (D&C 1:37-39)?

Is it any wonder we are counseled to treasure up the Lord's word (D&C 6:20; 43:34; JS—M 1:37) and to ponder in our hearts how merciful he has been from the creation of Adam to the present time (Moro. 10:3)?

Should it surprise us to read that the Lord commanded Joseph Smith and all the elders, and all the Saints—over and over again—that they were to expound all scriptures unto the Church and the world (D&C 20:42, 46, 50; 68:1)?

Can men be saved without a knowledge of what God has revealed both anciently and in our day?

Gospel study and gospel knowledge and gospel scholarship are highly personal. Every person must learn the doctrines of salvation for himself and in his own way.

My wife and I read out loud to each other every day for years on end until we had been through all of the standard works several times.

May I suggest, based on personal experience, that faith comes and revelations are received as a direct result of scriptural study.

Paul says, "Faith cometh by hearing" the word of God (Rom. 10:17). Joseph Smith taught that to gain faith men must have a knowledge of the nature and kind of being that God is; they must have a correct idea of his character, perfections, and attributes; and they must so live as to gain the assurance that their conduct is in harmony with the divine will.

Scriptural Study Creates Faith

Faith is thus born of scriptural study. Those who study, ponder, and pray about the scriptures, seeking to understand their deep and hidden meanings, receive from time to time great outpourings of light and knowledge from the Holy Spirit. This is what happened to Joseph Smith and Sidney Rigdon when they received the vision of the degrees of glory (D&C 76, superscription).

However talented men may be in administrative matters; however eloquent they may be in expressing their views; however learned they may be in worldly things—they will be denied the sweet whisperings of the Spirit that might have been theirs unless they pay the price of studying, pondering, and praying about the scriptures.

Import of New LDS Scriptures

All of this brings us to the new editions of holy writ which have just been published by the Church.

Never since the day of Joseph Smith; never since the translation of the Book of Mormon; never since the receipt of the revelations in the Doctrine and Covenants and the inspired writings in the Pearl of Great Price—never has there been such an opportunity to increase gospel scholarship as has now come to us.

This opportunity arises for two reasons: One is the new teaching aids that have been made a part of each one of the standard works. The other is the imperative need, because of textual and other changes, for all members of the Church to reread and re-mark for reference all of our four volumes of scripture as they are now constituted and in their new format.

Unique Features of New Scriptures

For the first time, chapter headings have been included for the Bible and the Pearl of Great Price. These summarize the contents of the chapters and set forth a correct view of the prophetic word. The stick of Joseph mentioned in Ezekiel 37, for instance, is identified by name as the Book of Mormon.

There are new and greatly improved section and chapter headings for the Doctrine and Covenants and the Book of Mormon. Numerous historical corrections have been made in the headings in the Doctrine and Covenants and Pearl of Great Price.

Running heads at the top of each page in all four of the standard works name both the book and the chapters and verses.

There is a six-hundred-page Topical Guide and Concordance with references to all of the standard works and also a two-hundred-page Bible Dictionary prepared from a Latter-day Saint standpoint.

There are 24 pages of colored maps in the Bible, 4 pages of maps in the Doctrine and Covenants, and a 416-page index for the Triple Combination. This index is in effect a concordance.

A new footnoting system has been devised by chapters and verses with the cross-references running to all of the standard works. It also points the student to the appropriate headings in the Topical Guide, shows the meaning of words in Hebrew and other languages, and records changes made by inspiration and found in the Joseph Smith Translation of the Bible.

Changes too extensive to be included in the footnotes are contained in a seventeen-page supplement. As every student knows, these inspired changes made by the Prophet throw a marvelous flood of light on a host of doctrines and are one of the great evidences of his divine calling.

There are also numerous important textual changes in the Book of Mormon and the Pearl of Great Price. All of these hark back to the original manuscripts or to corrections made by the Prophet. Two new sections and a second official declaration have been added to the Doctrine and Covenants.

Without question our latter-day scriptures are in a more nearly perfect form now than they have ever been since the beginning.

We have many things to do to work out our salvation and to succeed in our ministries. Nephi gives this summary: "Ye must press forward with a steadfastness in Christ, having a perfect brightness of hope, and a love of God and of all men.'

Then he gives this promise: "If ye shall press forward, *feasting upon the word of Christ*, and endure to the end, behold, thus saith the Father: Ye shall have eternal life" (2 Ne. 31:20; italics added).

Feasting upon the word of Christ. What a banquet of choice food is laid before us in holy writ! Feasting upon the word of Christ. How we ought to partake of the good word of God, and feast upon the bread from heaven which if men eat they shall never hunger more (John 6:35, 51)!

A Pattern for Gospel Study

May I suggest, for you and your families and all those with whom you labor in the kingdom, the following:
1. Study the scriptures daily. Drink directly from holy writ. Learn the word as it is found in the scriptures.
2. Mark a new set of the standard works. Learn to use the footnotes and teaching aids in our new editions of the scriptures. Pay particular attention to the inspired changes made by the Prophet Joseph Smith in the Bible. Be sure any quotations you make include the new textual changes.
3. Apply what you learn to your life and to your administrative assignments in the Church. Act and live as the scriptures decree.
4. Use the scriptures in all your sermons and teaching. Rely on the scriptures. Quote the scriptures. Believe the scriptures. Choose your illustrations from them.
5. Ponder the revealed word in your hearts. Pray about its deep and hidden meanings. Let the things of eternity be your constant meditation.

6. Expound the scriptures. Explain their meanings. Let others know what you know. Raise your voice in testimony.
7. Get others to go and do likewise with reference to all of these things.

Every stake president and every bishop should receive the counsel I am now giving. And from them, it should go to the end of the row.

Remember: "The law of the Lord is perfect, converting the soul: the testimony of the Lord is sure, making wise the simple. The statutes of the Lord are right, rejoicing the heart: the commandment of the Lord is pure, enlightening the eyes. The fear of the Lord is clean, enduring for ever: the judgments of the Lord are true and righteous altogether. More to be desired are they than gold, yea, than much fine gold: sweeter also than honey and the honeycomb. Moreover by them is thy servant warned: and in keeping of them there is great reward." (Ps. 19:7–11.)

The Lord Directed and Guided Work on New Editions of Scripture

I feel very strongly, and have rejoiced individually, in the testimony that has been borne of the productiveness, of the spirit, the wonder and the glory that has attended this near-ten-year project [i.e. the work of issuing the new LDS scriptures] that involves all of the standard works of the Church. I have no language which indicates how strongly I feel or how much I am assured that the work that has been done will benefit the members of the Church and the hosts of people who yet will hear the message of the Restoration. These brethren — Robert Matthews, Ellis Rasmussen, Robert Patch, James Mortimer — have just literally been raised up by the Lord at this time and season to do the particular, difficult, and technical work that has been required. The Lord's hand has been in it.

Engaged in Our Father's Business

Our work as bearers of the priesthood of God is unique. There is much that we can do which none others can. To use Jesus' manner of expression, we are engaged in our Father's business (see Luke 2:46–52). It is the same identical business in which he himself works on a full-time basis. His work is "to bring to pass the immortality and eternal life of man" (Moses 1:39). We are in the business of saving souls. He has commanded us to preach his gospel, and also to send it forth by the hands of others (D&C 42:6; 43:15; 49:11–14; 133:8, 38). Salvation is available for all who believe and obey. Paul said that "it pleased God, by the foolishness of preaching to save them that believe" (1 Cor. 1:21).

We hold the keys of salvation. It is within our power to open the door of salvation to all of our Father's other children, and we do it by proclaiming the gospel of salvation ourselves, and by arranging for others to go and do likewise.

Three Tools of the Ministry

The Lord has given us certain tools to use in doing this work. After all, it is his business and he knows what he wants done and how he wants us to do it. Whether we use the tools he provides is up to us. To the extent that we use his tools in the manner and way that he expects, we shall succeed in the work. To the extent that we use other tools, or work slothfully or indifferently with his tools, we shall fail. Now, the Lord's chief tools—tools we must use if we work in his business; tools which if we use properly will result in the salvation of precious souls—are three in number.

Our first tool is the power and authority and majesty of the holy priesthood, without which we could not preach the gospel or save a single soul. It is the priesthood which administers the gospel, and the gospel is the plan of salvation.

Our second tool is the revelations of heaven as recorded in the holy scriptures, without which we would have no source material, no standards of reference, no divinely approved accounts of what we should say in preaching the gospel. It is the standard works of the Church that chart our course and set forth the doctrines we must preach to save souls.

Our third tool is the gift and guidance and power of the Holy Ghost, without which there would never be the fires of testimony nor the cleansing power that sanctifies the human soul. Conversion comes when we speak, and when an attuned truth seeker hears, by the power of the Holy Ghost.

Hear now the voice of the Lord as he speaks to all those who hold his holy priesthood. The time is February, 1831. Thus saith the Lord: "The principles of my gospel, which are in the Bible and the Book of Mormon . . . these shall be their teachings, as they shall be directed by the Spirit . . . until the fulness of my scriptures is given" (D&C 42:12–13, 15).

Since that day the Doctrine and Covenants and the Pearl of Great Price have been added to that holy canon of revealed writ which one day will be ours and will be known as "the fulness of my scriptures."

Hear also this word from the Lord, given to all who are called to the ministry. In preaching the word, they are to say "none other things than that which the prophets and apostles have written" (meaning in the standard works) "and that which is taught them by the Comforter through the prayer of faith" (D&C 52:9; see also v. 36). Our divine commission is to teach the principles of the gospel as they are found in the standard works, by the power of the Holy Ghost. Our commission—and there is none greater—deals with the doctrines of the gospel, with the standard works of the Church, and with the Holy Spirit of God.

Gospel Preached and Administered by Revelation

If there is anything we need above all other things to succeed in the work, to successfully carry on our Father's business, to save the souls he has entrusted to us, if there is anything we need, it is revelation—it is the guidance of the Holy Spirit, it is to learn the mind and will of the Lord on all things that it is expedient for us to understand.

Scripture Study Leads to Revelation

As we all know, revelation comes from the Revelator; he is the Holy Ghost, and he will not dwell in an unclean tabernacle. Hence we strive eternally to keep the commandments so we may be in tune with the Lord and always have his Spirit to be with us. But I sometimes think that one of the best-kept secrets of the kingdom is that the scriptures open the door to the receipt of revelation. Those who, in the spirit of faith, read, ponder and pray about the Book of Mormon, come to know by the power of the Holy Ghost that the ancient Nephite record is true. They learn also, at one and the same time by the power of the same Spirit, that Jesus is the Lord, that Joseph Smith is a prophet and that The Church of Jesus Christ of Latter-day Saints is the kingdom of God on the earth.

I would hope that all those called to teach and preach the gospel have had the same experience that has been mine on many occasions. In the spirit of prayer, while reading and pondering the holy word, new views, added concepts, truths theretofore un-known, have suddenly dawned upon me. Doctrines that were dim and hidden and little known, have, in an instant, been shown forth with a marvelous clarity and in wondrous beauty. This is exactly what happened to President Joseph F. Smith when he received the vision of the redemption of the dead (D&C 138:1–11).

I would hope that our gospel teachers and priesthood leaders throughout the Church would have the experience, while preach-ing upon scriptural passages, of having a sudden rush of ideas which gives them a far greater comprehension of the doctrine they teach. We are all entitled to this spirit of prophecy and revelation.

Some are sustained as prophets, seers, and revelators to the Church. Others will be in due course. But all of us are entitled to the spirit of prophecy and of revelation in our lives, both for our per-sonal affairs and in our ministry. The prayerful study and ponder-ing of the holy scriptures will do as much, or more than any other single thing, to bring that spirit, the spirit of prophecy and the spirit of revelation, into our lives.

High Quality of New Scriptures

More has been done in the last ten years to make all the stand-ard works available for intelligent use by us and by our fellow la-borers, than at any time since their original publication. The new footnotes, the new chapter and section headings, the other concord-ance-type indexes are all better than any like material ever before published by us or by anyone else.

Again, I repeat, there is no question in my mind that the Lord has raised up those who have been engaged in this work—he has had them in the right places at the right times. And there is no ques-tion that major decisions were made by the spirit of inspiration, and that the conclusions reached accord with the mind and will of the Lord. I have been close enough to the work to be aware of the inspi-ration that has attended it, and I want you to hear me bear my testi-mony to that effect.

New LDS Scripture Will Improve Gospel Scholarship

The publication of all of the standard works as now consti-tuted, with the changes, additions, and teaching aids, opens a new day of gospel scholarship in the Church. Priesthood leaders, above all others, engaged as they are in our Father's business, having the tools he has given us, seeking as we should be to save souls, we above all others should lay aside the candles of the past and pick up the heaven-sent light of the present. Then we will be able to say to all others in the Church, "Come, follow thou us, and we will lead you to new heights of light and knowledge and truth."

Saints Must Learn to Use New Editions of Scriptures

I own an 1879 edition of the Doctrine and Covenants. It is the copy of Julina Lambson Smith, who is my wife's grandmother; she was the wife of President Joseph F. Smith. I also have, in this same edition, the copy used by President Joseph F. Smith himself. From a standpoint of sentiment and of feeling, I could make a good case in my mind for using these books, because of the heritage, as it were, that they have. But the revelations in these editions do not have one single footnote; there is not a single cross-reference. There are no teaching aids. There are some brief, single sentences at the head of the sections which simply say, "Revelation given through Joseph the Seer at Kirtland, Ohio, June 1831."

I also have the copy my wife gave me when I went on my mission; it has been rebound and recovered three times. It has been in every state of the union, and in many of the nations of the earth. I could make a good case for using that book—but again, the improvement in the teaching aids that are a part of the new LDS editions of the scriptures are so great that by using them I can increase the rate with which I learn about the gospel.

The Best Teaching Aids

We have in these new editions the best teaching aids that have ever been devised to include in any set of scriptures. And we have them because we have as much, or more, of the scholarship of the world than is found anywhere else. Far more important than that, however, we have them because we are members of the Lord's Church, and we are his agents and his representatives and we are in his business, and he has given us the spirit of inspiration so that the right things can be done.

Far-Reaching Impact of New LDS Editions

I am very grateful to have been a part of the work that has made these standard works available. I just paraphrase Brother

Packer's language when I say I don't think there will be anything in my ministry among men that I will do that will have a more far-reaching effect than what is involved in preparing and disseminating these new LDS editions of the standard works. And I would like to offer a prayer of thanksgiving to the Lord for the inspiration that he has given and that has attended this work. It was commissioned in the days of President Harold B. Lee; it has come into fruition under the guiding hand and with the approval and encouragement of President Kimball. It will rank supreme, in a sense, and superlative above almost anything else as the periods of time roll on. (Address, Regional Representatives Seminar, 2 April 1982.)

Chapter 16

COME: HEAR THE VOICE
OF THE LORD

Holy Scriptures Contain Word of God

We have been given the holy scriptures—those compilations of the divine word—by a gracious God to guide us back into his eternal presence. These volumes are of infinite worth. They contain "the will of the Lord, . . . the mind of the Lord, . . . the voice of the Lord, and the power of God unto salvation" (D&C 68:4).

Indeed, it was Paul, our apostolic colleague of old, who told his beloved Timothy: "The holy scriptures . . . are able to make thee wise unto salvation through faith which is in Christ Jesus" (2 Tim. 3:15). Truly, salvation, the greatest of all gifts (1 Ne. 15:36; D&C 6:13; 14:7), is available to those Saints who live the Lord's law as recorded in his holy word!

Paul continues: "All scripture is given by inspiration of God, and is profitable for doctrine, for reproof, for correction, for instruction in righteousness: That the man of God may be perfect, throughly furnished unto all good works" (2 Tim. 3:16–17).

Another marvelous passage, one filled with divine wisdom and insight, extols the scriptures in these poetic words: "The law of the Lord is perfect, converting the soul: the testimony of the Lord is sure, making wise the simple. The statutes of the Lord are right, rejoicing the heart: the commandment of the Lord is pure, enlightening the eyes. The fear of the Lord is clean, enduring for ever: the judgments of the Lord are true and righteous altogether. More to be desired are they than gold, yea, than much fine gold: sweeter also than honey and the honeycomb. Moreover by them is thy servant warned: and in keeping of them there is great reward." (Ps. 19:7–11.)

As we are all aware, the revealed word which has come to us in our day conforms to the ancient standard. As the Lord's law, it is perfect; through it, testimonies are received and souls are converted.

How precious is the divine word revealed anew to modern men to meet modern needs, to guide anew in all the circumstances, unknown to our ancestors, that now exist in the last days! What great rewards await us if we learn that which has come forth in our day and if we live as therein decreed!

Let us then, consider our latter-day volumes of scripture — first, the Book of Mormon, then the Doctrine and Covenants, and after that the Pearl of Great Price.

The Book of Mormon

What is the Book of Mormon? In many respects it is the most marvelous book ever prepared by prophetic hands. Call it an American Bible if you will, for it goes hand in hand with the Bible itself in announcing the mind and will of the Lord and in proclaiming the eternal plan of salvation.

As all members of the Church know, the Book of Mormon is a history of God's dealings with the ancient inhabitants of the Americas. It is the history of fallen peoples. Some of them came from the Tower of Babel when the Lord confounded the tongues of all people. Others were led by divine hand from their Jerusalem home to a promised land, lest they be taken captive into Babylon with the rest of rebellious Israel in the days of Nebuchadnezzar.

These two groups — known generally as Jaredites and Lehites, after their first leaders — inhabited the Western Hemisphere for thousands of years. They had the fulness of the everlasting gospel (D&C 20:6–12), received revelations, saw visions, entertained angels, performed miracles, and heard the words of their prophets — prophets who saw the Lord, knew of his goodness and grace, and taught of Christ and the salvation that comes through his atoning blood.

As with the Bible in the Old World, so with the Book of Mormon in the New. Both record the teachings of holy men of God who spake as they were moved upon by the Holy Ghost. (2 Pet. 1:21.)

Book of Mormon Plainer Than the Bible

Thus, the Book of Mormon is a volume of holy scripture. It speaks of God, of Christ, and of the gospel. It records the terms and conditions whereby salvation comes. And it does it all with a plainness, clarity, and perfection that far surpasses the Bible.

The Bible of the Old World has come to us from the manuscripts of antiquity—manuscripts which passed through the hands of uninspired men who changed many parts to suit their own doctrinal ideas (JST Luke 11:53). Deletions were common and, as it now stands, many plain and precious portions and many covenants of the Lord have been lost (1 Ne. 13:20–40). As a consequence, those who rely upon it alone stumble and are confused and divide themselves among many churches, all based on this or that interpretation of the Bible.

On the other hand, the Bible of the New World, as I choose to designate the Book of Mormon, has been preserved for us by a divine providence which kept the ancient record in prophetic hands. Written by inspiration on plates of gold, it was hidden in the soil of Cumorah, to come forth in modern times by angelic ministration and then be translated by the gift and power of God (D&C 1:29; 3:12; 5:4; 135:3).

After the translation, the voice of God, speaking from heaven to witnesses chosen beforehand by him, declared two things—that the translation was correct and that the book was true (D&C 17:6). We, of course, believe the Bible as far as it has been translated correctly, but we place no such restriction on the Book of Mormon (eighth article of faith). And so it is that there has come into our hands a book that is as perfect, or near perfect, as mortal hands can make it. It is a divine book, a book like none other ever written, translated, or published.

In telling what transpired at a meeting of the leaders of the Church in his day, Joseph Smith, who under God stands as the translator of this holy book, said: "I told the brethren that the Book of Mormon was the most correct of any book on earth, and the keystone of our religion, and a man would get nearer to God by abiding by its precepts, than by any other book" (*Teachings*, p. 194).

New Scriptural Study Aids

Now, what of our study and use of such a book? Certainly we want to read and ponder this divine word so as to get near to the Lord, so as to gain testimonies of the truth and divinity of the Lord's great latter-day work, so as to learn the doctrines of salvation, so as to place our feet firmly on the strait and narrow path leading to eternal life.

Would it help if we were guided in our study of the Book of Mormon? Truly it would, and hence the helps and aids offered to us in the newly published edition of this divine book. Let us note some of them.

First, the name of the book itself. It now reads, "The Book of Mormon: Another Testament of Jesus Christ." This change was made in the wisdom of the Brethren and with the approval of the Holy Spirit.

Its purpose—in this godless age, when many who oppose the truth cry out that the Latter-day Saints are not Christians—is to send forth the signal that Christ is the center of that revealed religion which has come to us (2 Ne. 31:21; Mosiah 3:17; 4:8; 3 Ne. 9:17).

Just as truly as the New Testament, sent forth from the Old World, proclaims the divinity of God's Son, so does this testament preserved in the New World. Indeed, it would not be amiss to say there are five gospels: Matthew, Mark, Luke, John, and Third Nephi. And the witness is as sure—the testimony as fervent, the doctrine as sound—in the new word that comes from the Western Hemisphere as in the old word from Palestine.

Second, there is a new introduction which succinctly and carefully sets forth the purpose and nature of the book and has the effect of inviting all men to read and ponder its truths.

Third, there are new chapter headings, plus helpful running heads at the top of the pages. The chapter headings, for the first time, summarize the content of each chapter and thus guide students in their search for truth. For instance, Mosiah 3 is introduced with these words: "King Benjamin continues his address—The Lord Omnipotent shall minister among men in a tabernacle of clay —Blood shall come from every pore as he atones for the sins of the world—His is the only name whereby salvation comes—Men can put off the natural man and become saints through the atonement —The torment of the wicked shall be as a lake of fire and brimstone."

Fourth, new footnotes of inestimable worth are included. For instance, 40 percent of pages 152 and 153 contain footnotes, which verse by verse cross-reference the scriptural content to other like passages of the standard works and to the Topical Guide, where extended references are found on all of the subjects involved.

Fifth, there is an extensive new index of 416 pages, covering the Book of Mormon, the Doctrine and Covenants, the Pearl of Great Price, and the Articles of Faith. The comprehensive nature of this index is seen from the fact that these books themselves contain only a total of **886** pages. Truly the index is a work of art.

Sixth, and perhaps of greater interest than all else, come the textual changes. Except for a few technical corrections in spelling and the like, which clearly were the mistakes of men, all of the changes hark back to the original manuscripts and editing of the Prophet Joseph Smith.

Textual Changes in New Scriptures

Such changes as the following are of special interest:

Speaking of the Lamanites, 2 Nephi 30:6 heretofore read: "Their scales of darkness shall begin to fall from their eyes; and many generations shall not pass away among them, save they shall be a *white* and delightsome people."

Now it says: "They shall be a *pure* and delightsome people."

Heretofore 1 Nephi 13:6 said: "I beheld this great and abominable church: and I saw the devil that he was the *foundation* of it."

Now it reads: "I saw the devil that he was the *founder* of it."

Second Nephi 29:4, which heretofore read, "Do they remember the *travels*, and the labors, and the pains of the Jews?" now reads, "Do they remember the *travails*, and the labors, and the pains of the Jews?" And so it goes.

The Doctrine and Covenants

It is now our privilege to speak of the Doctrine and Covenants, another unique book, a book written in effect by the Lord Jesus Christ himself, a book of revealed truth sent forth for the salvation of all who will believe and obey in these last days.

May we ask these questions:

If we could have only one book of scripture, what would it be?

If we hunger and thirst after righteousness, and desire to know the mind and will of the Lord for those now living, to what book shall we turn?

If there is a book of truly modern scripture that records the mind and will and voice of the Lord as given in the nineteenth and twentieth centuries, what is it?

If I, for one, were called upon to answer these questions, my answer would be the Doctrine and Covenants, that volume of holy writ that reaffirms the scriptures of the past, charts our course of the present, and foretells that which will yet be when the Lord returns and the Millennium is ushered in.

In the new explanatory introduction to the Doctrine and Covenants, the book is defined as "a collection of divine revelations and inspired declarations given for the establishment and regulation of the kingdom of God on the earth in the last days. . . . In the revelations one sees the restoration and unfolding of the gospel of Jesus Christ and the ushering in of the dispensation of the fulness of times."

The first Quorum of Twelve Apostles called in this dispensation gave this testimony to the truth of the book of Doctrine and Covenants: "We . . . bear testimony to all the world of mankind, to every creature upon the face of the earth, that the Lord has borne record to our souls, through the Holy Ghost shed forth upon us, that these commandments were given by inspiration of God, and are profitable for all men and are verily true."

This same testimony is anchored with a sure certainty in the hearts of the Apostles who now serve as special witnesses of the name of the Lord who has redeemed us with his blood. And I, as one among them, bear this witness: I know by the revelations of the Holy Spirit to my soul, as certainly as did my predecessors, that the Doctrine and Covenants — as also the Book of Mormon and the Pearl of Great Price — are true; that they are the voice of the Almighty to all men now living, and that the Saints are bound, by eternal covenant, to learn that which is in them and to conform their lives thereto.

Is it any wonder, thus, that we find the Lord himself saying: "Search these commandments, for they are true and faithful, and the prophecies and promises which are in them shall all be fulfilled" (D&C 1:37).

To aid us in our search, we now have two new styles of chapter headings, new cross-references and footnotes, two new sections, and supportive material for the official declarations — one of which declarations announces the receipt of the revelation offering the blessing of the priesthood and the temple to those of all races, solely on the basis of righteousness.

Let us take section 76 as an illustration of how the section heads guide us in our study of the revelation itself.

First, there is the usual heading setting forth the time and place and circumstances surrounding the receipt of the revelation. In this instance this heading includes a statement from the Prophet Joseph Smith telling why the term *heaven* must include more kingdoms than one.

Then comes the supplemental section heading. In it the revealed word is segregated by verses and a definitive statement is made about the content of each series of verses. Thus we read:

"1–4, The Lord is God; 5–10, Mysteries of the kingdom will be revealed to all the faithful; 11–17, All shall come forth in the resurrection of the just or the unjust; 18–24, Inhabitants of many worlds are begotten sons and daughters unto God through the atonement of Jesus Christ;" and so on.

The footnotes and cross-references follow the same pattern found in the other standard works. The two new sections, numbered 137 and 138, are included, together with maps showing where places of import in Church history are found.

The great advantage of all this to the student is self-evident.

The Pearl of Great Price

Now let us say a word about the Pearl of Great Price. This priceless pearl of divine wisdom consists of a selection from the revelations, translations, and narrations of the Prophet Joseph Smith. The purpose of selecting and publishing them in one volume is to make them readily available to the Saints and the world, and to show that they came by the spirit of inspiration, and are true, and should be accepted by all truth seekers.

The first portion of the Pearl of Great Price is entitled, "Selections from the Book of Moses," rather than simply "The Book of Moses," as heretofore. It is, in fact, an extract from the translation of the Bible as revealed to the Prophet Joseph Smith.

As all of us should know, the Joseph Smith Translation, or Inspired Version as it is sometimes called, stands as one of the great evidences of the divine mission of the Prophet. The added truths he placed in the Bible and the corrections he made raise the resultant work to the same high status as the Book of Mormon and the Doctrine and Covenants. It is true that he did not complete the work, but it was far enough along that he intended to publish it in its present form in his lifetime.

These selections from the book of Moses, as also the twenty-fourth chapter of Matthew, now cited as "Joseph Smith—Matthew," rather than "Writings of Joseph Smith," as heretofore, are of course complete and perfect and are included in our canonized word. Other Inspired Version changes are found in the footnotes of our new edition of the Bible. Those too lengthy for inclusion in the footnotes are published in a seventeen-page section at the back of this Bible edition. All of these changes and additions are scripture and have the same truth and validity as if they were in the Pearl of Great Price itself. It is important that this is clearly understood by all who seek to learn the law of the Lord and to be in tune with that which has been revealed by the great seer of latter days.

As to the selections from Moses that are now in the Pearl of Great Price, they are divided into eight chapters and contain 356 verses, many of which are rather long and complex and have more than one thought in them. The comparable material in Genesis is 151 verses, most of which are short and confined to a single thought.

What is important to us about the writings of Moses, as we now have them in the Pearl of Great Price, is that they completely revolutionize the concept of a Christian Era growing out of a patriarchal past. They show that Adam and those before the Flood had the fulness of the everlasting gospel, the same gospel in all its parts that we have (Moses 5:58–59). They worshipped the Father in the name of Christ by the power of the Spirit, as we do (see, e.g., Moses 5:8–9, 14). They held the holy priesthood (Moses 6:7; Abr. 1:2–4, 18, 26–27, 31; 2:9–11; *Teachings*, p. 157), were married for time and all eternity (Moses 3:18–25; 4:22; 8:21; Abr. 5:14–19), and by faith wrought many mighty miracles.

The book of Abraham is also holy writ of wondrous worth. As with the Mosaic word, and all else with which we are dealing, it has new chapter headings, new footnotes, and its contents are newly identified in a modern index.

One minor textual change in Abraham is significant. A single letter is changed and a whole new doctrinal meaning is revealed. Heretofore the text read, "the first man, who is Adam, *our* first father," which is a simple recitation of the fact, also set forth in other scriptures, that Adam, the first man, is also our first father. If he is the first man he is obviously the first father of other men. The new rendition, according with the ancient manuscript, reads, "Adam, *or* first father," making the word *Adam* a synonym for "first father." That is, the name *Adam* means first father. (See Abr. 1:3; italics added.)

Fruits of Scripture Reading

Scripture Reading Brings Blessings

There are certain blessings that attend the study of the scriptures which are denied those whose studies and interests are in different fields. It is the study of the scriptures that enables men to gain revelations for themselves. Those who read the Book of Mormon, in the way Moroni specifies, gain a testimony of its truth and divinity, of the divine sonship of Christ, and of the prophetic call of Joseph Smith.

Scripture Reading Led to First Vision

Joseph Smith himself read in the book of James the famous words known to us all: "If any of you lack wisdom, let him ask of God, that giveth to all men liberally, and upbraideth not; and it shall be given him" (James 1:5).

In describing his feelings at the time, he said: "Never did any passage of scripture come with more power to the heart of man than this did at this time to mine. It seemed to enter with great force into every feeling of my heart. I reflected on it again and again." (JS—H 1:12.)

Then, because the hour had come for the ushering in of the dispensation of the fulness of times, and because he was the one chosen and foreordained from eternity to commence the work, the Great God and his Beloved Son, descending in eternal splendor from the courts of glory, manifested themselves to this guileless and believing youth.

But, be it remembered, the scripture was the guidepost leading to the receipt of the First Vision, a vision equalled by few in import and glory in all the history of the world.

Scripture Study Invites Revelation

I have spent many hours poring over and pondering the scriptures. In seeking to learn the doctrines of salvation, I have studied, weighed, and compared what the various prophets have said about the same subjects.

Time and again, after much praying and pondering about a given point, new and added concepts have burst upon me, showing

deep and hidden truths that I had never before known. It can be so
with all of us if we will read, ponder, and pray about the holy
word.

Jesus said: "Ask, and it shall be given unto you; seek, and ye
shall find; knock, and it shall be opened unto you: For every one
that asketh receiveth; and he that seeketh findeth; and to him that
knocketh it shall be opened" (Matt. 7:7-8).

"But let him ask in faith, nothing wavering. For he that
wavereth is like a wave of the sea driven with the wind and tossed.
For let not that man think that he shall receive any thing of the
Lord." (James 1:6-7.)

His voice comes to us in many ways. He may speak audibly to
attuned ears. His voice may come by the power of the Spirit. It
may also be given by the mouths of his servants as they recite the
words revealed to them. All of the Saints are entitled to hear his
voice in each of these ways.

But there is another way to hear the voice of the Lord, and,
almost universally, it should be our first approach in seeking revelation. It is available to us all, but sadly is overlooked or ignored by
many of us.

After revealing certain truths through Joseph Smith to his
modern Apostles, the Lord, continuing to speak to Joseph Smith,
said:

"And I, Jesus Christ, your Lord and your God, have spoken it.
These words are not of men nor of man, but of me; wherefore, you
shall testify they are of me and not of man; For it is my voice which
speaketh them unto you; for they are given by my Spirit unto you,
and by my power you can read them one to another; and save it
were by my power you could not have them; Wherefore, you can
testify that you have heard my voice, and know my words." (D&C
18:33-36.)

If the Spirit bears record to us of the truth of the scriptures, then
we are receiving the doctrines in them as though they had come to
us directly. Thus, we can testify that we have heard his voice and
know his words.

Let us now highly resolve that we will search the scriptures and
make them a part of all that we do.

And if such be our course, we shall surely receive peace and joy
in this life and inherit eternal life in the realms ahead. ("Come: Hear
the Voice of the Lord," *Ensign*, December 1985, pp. 54-59.)

Chapter 17

WHAT THINK YE OF THE BOOK OF MORMON?

Two ministers of one of the largest and most powerful Protestant denominations came to a Latter-day Saint conference to hear me preach.

After the meeting I had a private conversation with them, in which I said they could each gain a testimony that Joseph Smith was the Prophet through whom the Lord had restored the fulness of the gospel for our day and for our time.

I told them they should read the Book of Mormon, ponder its great and eternal truths, and pray to the Father in the name of Christ, in faith, and he would reveal the truth of the book to them by the power of the Holy Ghost.

As every gospel scholar knows, the Book of Mormon proves that Joseph Smith was called of God to minister in the prophetic office and to restore the truths of salvation in plainness and perfection.

The Book of Mormon is a volume of holy scripture comparable to the Bible. It contains a record of God's dealings with the ancient inhabitants of the Americas. It is another testament of Jesus Christ.

How Book of Mormon Contains the Fulness of the Gospel

The Book of Mormon contains the fulness of the gospel, meaning that it is a record of the Lord's dealings with a people who had the fulness of the gospel, and meaning also that in it is found a summary and a recitation of what all men must believe and do to gain an inheritance in the heavenly kingdom reserved for the Saints.

Bible and Book of Mormon Are Twin Witnesses

As the teachings and testimonies of Moses and Isaiah and Peter find place in the Bible, so the parallel preaching and the same Spirit-guided testimonies of Nephi and Alma and Moroni have come down to us in the Book of Mormon.

This American witness of Christ was written upon gold plates which were delivered to Joseph Smith by an angelic ministrant. This ancient record was then translated by the gift and power of God and is now published to the world as the Book of Mormon.

Book of Mormon Proves Divinity of the Work

If this book is what it purports to be; if the original record was revealed by a holy angel; if the translation was made by the power of God and not of man; if Joseph Smith was entertaining angels, seeing visions, and receiving revelations—all of which is an established verity—if the Book of Mormon is true, then the truth and divinity of the Book of Mormon proves the truth of this great latter-day work in which we are engaged.

All of this I explained to my two Protestant friends. One of them, a congenial and decent sort of fellow, said somewhat casually that he would read the Book of Mormon. The other minister, manifesting a bitter spirit, said: "I won't read it. We have experts who have read the Book of Mormon, and I have read what our experts have to say about it."

Must Read Book of Mormon

This account dramatizes one of our problems in presenting the message of the Book of Mormon to the world. There are sincere and devout people everywhere who have heard what other people say about this volume of holy writ, and so they do not read it themselves.

Instead of drinking from that fountain from whence clear streams of living water flow, they prefer to go downstream and drink from the roily, muddy, poison-filled streams of the world.

Book of Mormon the Standard by Which Salvation Is Judged

The plain fact is that salvation itself is at stake in this matter. If the Book of Mormon is true—if it is a volume of holy scripture, if it contains the mind and will and voice of the Lord to all men, if it is a divine witness of the prophetic call of Joseph Smith—then to accept it and believe its doctrines is to be saved, and to reject it and walk contrary to its teachings is to be damned.

Let this message be sounded in every ear with an angelic trump; let it roll round the earth in resounding claps of never-ending thunder; let it be whispered in every heart by the still, small voice. Those who believe the Book of Mormon and accept Joseph Smith as a prophet thereby open the door to salvation; those who reject the book outright or who simply fail to learn its message and believe its teachings never so much as begin to travel that course along the strait and narrow path that leads to eternal life.

Illustrative Experience with Ministers

Shortly after my experience with these two ministers, two other ministers from the same denomination came to another of our conferences to hear me preach. And, once again, after the meeting I had a private discussion with them.

My message was the same. Taking the Book of Mormon as their guide, they must read, ponder, and pray in order to gain a witness from the Spirit as to the truth and divinity of this great latter-day work.

I told them of my prior experience with their two colleagues and how one of them had refused to read the Book of Mormon, saying that they had experts who had read the book and he had read what their experts had said.

I then said, "What is it going to take to get you gentlemen to read the Book of Mormon and find out for yourselves what is involved, rather than relying on the views of your experts?"

One of these ministers, holding my copy of the Book of Mormon in his hands, let the pages flip past his eyes in a matter of seconds. As he did so, he said, "Oh, I've read the Book of Mormon."

I had a momentary flash of spiritual insight that let me know that his reading had been about as extensive as the way he had just flipped the pages. In his reading he had done no more than scan a few of the headings and read an isolated verse or two.

A lovely young lady, a convert to the Church, whose father was a minister of the same denomination as my four Protestant friends, was listening to my conversation with the second two. At this point she spoke up and said, "But Reverend, you have to pray about it."

He replied, "Oh, I prayed about it. I said, 'O God, if the Book of Mormon is true, strike me dead'; and here I am."

My unspoken impulse was to give this rejoinder: "But Reverend, you have to pray in faith!"

This account dramatizes another of our problems in teaching those who read the Book of Mormon how to read it in order to gain the promised witness by the power of the Holy Ghost.

Oliver Cowdery Experience Illustrates Pattern for Gaining Testimony

The pattern for this was set in the experience of Oliver Cowdery. He desired not only to act as a scribe to Joseph Smith but also to translate directly from the plates. After much importuning, the Lord permitted Brother Cowdery to try.

The divine authorization contained these provisos: "Remember that without faith you can do nothing; therefore ask in faith. Trifle not with these things; do not ask for that which you ought not. . . . And according to your faith shall it be done unto you." (D&C 8:10–11.)

Oliver tried to translate and failed. Then came the divine word. "Behold, you have not understood; you have supposed that I would give it unto you, when you took no thought save it was to ask me." That is, he had not done all that in his power lay; he had expected the Lord to do it all merely because he asked.

"But, behold, I say unto you," the divine word continued, "that you must study it out in your mind; then you must ask me if it be right, and if it is right I will cause that your bosom shall burn within you; therefore, you shall feel that it is right." (D&C 9:7–8.)

Now, if the Book of Mormon is true, our acceptance of it will lead to salvation in the highest heaven. On the other hand, if we say it is true when in fact it is not, we are thereby leading men astray and surely deserve to drop down to the deepest hell.

Pivotal Doctrinal Role of Book of Mormon

The time is long past for quibbling about words and for hurling unsavory epithets against the Latter-day Saints. These are deep and solemn and ponderous matters. We need not think we can trifle with sacred things and escape the wrath of a just God.

Either the Book of Mormon is true, or it is false; either it came from God, or it was spawned in the infernal realms. It declares plainly that all men must accept it as pure scripture or they will lose their souls (2 Ne. 27:14; 33:4–5, 10–15; W of M 1:11; 3 Ne. 29:1–5). It is not and cannot be simply another treatise on religion; it either came from heaven or from hell. And it is time for all those who seek salvation to find out for themselves whether it is of the Lord or of Lucifer.

A Test for Honest Truth Seekers

May I be so bold as to propose a test and issue a challenge. It is hoped that all who take this test will have a knowledge of the Holy Bible, because the more people know about the Bible, the greater their appreciation will be of the Book of Mormon.

This test is for Saint and sinner alike; it is for Jew and Gentile, for bond and free, for black and white, for all our Father's children. We have all been commanded to search the scriptures (John 5:39), to treasure up the Lord's word (D&C 6:20; 43:34; 84:85), to live by every word that proceedeth forth from the mouth of God (Deut. 8:3; Matt. 4:4; D&C 84:44; 98:11).

Let every person make a list of from one hundred to two hundred doctrinal subjects, making a conscious effort to cover the whole field of gospel knowledge. The number of subjects chosen will depend on personal inclination and upon how broad the spectrum will be under each subject.

Then write each subject on a blank piece of paper. Divide the paper into two columns; at the top of one, write ''Book of Mormon,'' and at the top of the other, ''Bible.''

Then start with the first verse and phrase of the Book of Mormon, and continuing verse by verse and thought by thought, put the substance of each verse under its proper heading. Find the same doctrine in the Old and New Testaments, and place it in the parallel columns.

Ponder the truths you learn, and it will not be long before you know that Lehi and Jacob excel Paul in teaching the Atonement; that Alma's sermons on faith and on being born again surpass anything in the Bible; that Nephi makes a better exposition of the scattering and gathering of Israel than do Isaiah, Jeremiah, and Ezekiel combined; that Mormon's words about faith, hope, and charity have a clarity, a breadth, and a power of expression that even Paul did not attain; and so on and so on.

A Second Test

There is another and simpler test that all who seek to know the truth might well take. It calls for us simply to read, ponder, and pray — all in the spirit of faith and with an open mind. To keep ourselves alert to the issues at hand—as we do read, ponder, and pray —we should ask ourselves a thousand times, "Could any man have written this book?"

And it is absolutely guaranteed that sometime between the first and thousandth time this question is asked, every sincere and genuine truth seeker will come to know by the power of the Spirit that the Book of Mormon is true, that it is the mind and will and voice of the Lord to the whole world in our day.

We ask, then: What think ye of the Book of Mormon? Who can tell its wonder and worth? How many martyrs have suffered death in the flesh to bring it forth and carry its saving message to a wicked world?

We answer: It is a book, a holy book, a book of sacred, saving scripture. It is a voice from the dust, a voice that whispers low out of the earth (Isa. 29:1-4, 18), telling of a fallen people who sank into an endless oblivion because they forsook their God.

It is truth springing out of the earth as righteousness looks down from heaven (Ps. 85:11; Moses 7:62). It is the stick of Joseph in the hands of Ephraim, which will guide all Israel, the ten tribes included, to return to him whom their fathers worshipped (Ezek. 37:15-28). It contains the word that will gather the whole house of Israel and make them once again one nation upon the mountains of Israel, as it was in the days of their fathers.

It is an account of the ministry of the Son of God to his other sheep in the day they saw his face and heard his voice and believed his word (John 10:1-28; 3 Ne. 15:15-24).

It is the divine evidence, the proof, that God has spoken in our day. Its chief purpose is to convince all men, Jew and Gentile alike, that Jesus is the Christ (Introduction to the Book of Mormon; 2 Ne. 30:3-5; 33:10), the Eternal God, who manifests himself, by faith, in all ages and among all peoples.

It came forth in our day, proving to the world that the Bible is true (1 Ne. 13:39-40; D&C 20:6-11); that Jesus, by whom the Atonement came, is Lord of all; that Joseph Smith was called of God, as were the prophets of old; that The Church of Jesus Christ of Latter-day Saints is the one place on earth where salvation is found.

It is the book that will save the world and prepare the sons of men for joy and peace here and now and everlasting life in eternity. (Conference Report, October 1983.)

The Keystone of Our Religion

Bible and Book of Mormon Summarize Doctrines of Salvation

The Book of Mormon, like the Bible, with which it is in complete conformity, contains a record of God's dealings with a people who had the fulness of the everlasting gospel. Thus both the Book of Mormon and the Bible present a summary of the doctrines of salvation, of the truths men must accept and live by to gain the celestial heaven; and both record the wondrous blessings poured out by Deity upon those in former days who walked in the light of the Lord and who kept his commandments.

Both of these books shed forth a flood of light and knowledge about those truths which must be believed and obeyed to gain salvation, to gain peace in this life and eternal life in the world to come. And none now living can gain that salvation which is the greatest of all the gifts of God without conforming to those truths of which both books testify.

Salvation in Christ, Not Books

But salvation is not found in a book, any book, either the Book of Mormon or the Bible. Salvation is in Christ; it comes because of his atoning sacrifice; his is the only name given under heaven whereby men can be saved (2 Ne. 31:21; Mosiah 3:17; 4:8; 3 Ne. 9:17; Acts 4:10–12). Salvation comes by the grace of God, through the shedding of the blood of his Son. As a Book of Mormon prophet said, "Salvation was, and is, and is to come, in and through the atoning blood of Christ, the Lord Omnipotent" (Mosiah 3:18).

Salvation Administered by Legal Administrators

However, salvation is made available to men because the Lord calls prophets and Apostles to testify of Christ and to teach the true doctrines of his gospel. Salvation is available only when there are legal administrators who can teach the truth and who have power to perform the ordinances of salvation so they will be binding, and have efficacy, virtue, and force on earth and in heaven.

Joseph Smith a Legal Administrator

The Book of Mormon was brought forth in our day by such a legal administrator, one Joseph Smith by name. This man was called of God by His own voice and by angelic administration. To him was given the ancient record whereon was inscribed the words of prophets and seers who dwelt on the American continent in ages past, holy men who ministered among the land's inhabitants in much the same way that biblical prophets represented the Lord in the lands of their labors.

Book of Mormon Part of "Restitution of All Things"

With the setting up of the true Church, there came once again a restoration of the fulness of the everlasting gospel, a restoration of the fulness of those truths, keys, powers, and authorities which again enable men to gain a fulness of salvation in the heaven of God our Father.

Thus the coming forth of the Book of Mormon, the call of Joseph Smith to represent God as a prophet on earth, the restoration of the gospel of salvation, and the setting up anew of the earthly Church and kingdom of God—all these are tied together; they are all woven into one pattern; either all of them are realities or none of them are.

Book of Mormon an Added Witness

Men in this day are as much obligated as men have been in any age to hearken to the voice of the prophets, to lend a listening ear to their sayings, to open their hearts to the truths of heaven which fall from their lips. But today we also have the Book of Mormon to bear record of the truth of the message that has come from a loving Heavenly Father to us his erring children.

Joseph Smith said the Book of Mormon was "the keystone of our religion" (*Teachings*, p. 194), meaning that the whole structure of restored truth stands or falls depending on its truth or falsity.

Joseph Smith also wrote, "by the spirit of prophecy and revelation," that the Book of Mormon came forth to prove "to the world that the holy scriptures are true, and that God does inspire men and call them to his holy work in this age and generation, as well as in generations of old; Thereby showing that he is the same God yesterday, today and forever" (D&C 20:11–12).

In the Book of Mormon is found the Lord's promise to all men that if they will read the record and ponder it in their hearts, and then ask the Father in the name of Christ if it is true—asking with a sincere heart, with real intent, having faith in Christ—he will manifest the truth of it unto them by the power of the Holy Ghost (Moro. 10:4).

Book of Mormon Proves Many Truths

I am one who knows by the power of the Spirit that this book is true, and as a consequence I also know, both by reason and by revelation from the Spirit, of the truth and divinity of all the great spiritual verities of this dispensation. For instance:

I know the Father and the Son appeared to Joseph Smith—because the Book of Mormon is true.

I know the gospel has been restored and that God has established his Church again on earth—because the Book of Mormon is true.

I know Joseph Smith is a prophet, that he communed with God, entertained angels, received revelations, saw visions, and has gone on to eternal glory—because the Book of Mormon is true.

I know the Bible is the word of God as far as it is translated correctly—because the Book of Mormon is true.

I know The Church of Jesus Christ of Latter-day Saints is the kingdom of God on earth, the one kingdom with legal administrators who can seal men up unto eternal life—because the Book of Mormon is true.

To my testimony of the Book of Mormon I add that of the Lord God himself, who said: Joseph Smith "has translated the book, . . . and as your Lord and your God liveth it is true" (D&C 20:6). (Conference Report, April 1968.)

The Book of Mormon—Its Eternal Destiny

Books That Shake the Earth

Who can measure the worth of a single book? Is it merely a roll of papyrus on which a Grecian slave has copied the sayings of Socrates? Or a Hebrew scroll on which a scribe has dutifully recorded the messianic words of Isaiah—words which Jesus will one day read in a synagogue in Nazareth and then say to his own townfolk: "This day is this scripture fulfilled in your ears" (Luke 4:21)? Or is it only an Egyptian Amarna tablet on which we read in clear cuneiform characters the words of Amenhotep? What would we give today to read the whole book of Enoch or to have a copy of the book of remembrance kept by Adam our father (Moses 6:4–5, 46), the first man of all men?

Import of the Written Word

Adam and his children were taught "to write by the spirit of inspiration; And by them their children were taught to read and write, having a language which was pure and undefiled" (Moses 6:5–6). From that day to this, in one form or another, men have preserved their history, their culture, their civilization, by means of the written word. Even today, with all our vaunted wisdom and learning, if all the books of the earth were burned and written language ceased, our civilization would die. In scarcely more than a generation we would be living again in the Dark Ages. Airplanes would no longer fly or factories run; surgery would cease, medical help would die out, a black plague would desolate the world. Religion and doctrine and ethics and ordinances and true worship would soon become things of the past. Indeed the great apostasy of centuries past gained its evil hold when men were no longer able to read the words of the Apostles and prophets of the past (1 Ne. 13:20–40).

Nephi slew Laban and took the brass plates to America as a means of preserving the culture and civilization and religion of the Hebrews (1 Ne. 3:3–4, 19–20). The Mulekites came to America without their scriptures and soon lost their heritage (Omni 15–17).

There are no words to describe the power of a single book.

The Old Testament contains many of the covenants of the Lord, given to his people anciently, and by means of it they were kept more or less in the line of their duty for four thousand years.

The New Testament contains fragments of the teachings of Jesus and his prophetic associates in their day. From it we learn of the life of him who came to bring life and immortality to light through the gospel (2 Tim. 1:10); from it we learn the doctrines of salvation as they were taught by those to whom the heavens were an open book; and in it is recorded such of the Christian ethic as remained available on earth for nearly eighteen hundred years.

Bible of Inestimable Influence

During all this long period the Bible did more to mellow the souls of men, more to keep such light and truth alive as was then found on earth, more to prepare men for a day when new revelation would come, than any other book. Because of it wars were fought, nations overrun, and the whole history of western civilization channeled one way after another. The King James Version of the Bible has done more than any other book to preserve the English language and culture. And, even more important, it is the book which the Lord preserved to prepare men for the restoration of all things and the coming forth of the Book of Mormon in the latter days to be a second witness of his holy name.

No one has ever improved upon the King James Version of the Bible except the Prophet Joseph Smith as he was moved upon by the spirit of prophecy and revelation. As you know, "We believe the Bible to be the word of God as far as it is translated correctly" (eighth article of faith); and as you also know, many "plain and precious things," and "many covenants of the Lord," were taken from this sacred record when it passed through the hands of that great church which is not the Lord's church (1 Ne. 13:26–29). As you also know, Joseph Smith restored many of these "plain and precious things" in his New Translation, which is commonly called among us the Joseph Smith Translation. This version, as now published, accurately records the inspired corrections of the Prophet and can be used by us with great profit. It is in fact one of the great evidences of the divine mission of the greatest of our prophets.

I have unbounded appreciation for both the King James Version and the Joseph Smith Translation. I stand in reverential awe as I read and ponder the wondrous words they contain. I do not believe there is a person on earth who has a greater respect for or appreciation of the Holy Bible than I do.

Book of Mormon Superior to the Bible in Many Ways

Now, I say all this as a prelude to making these flat and unequivocal declarations:
1. Most of the doctrines of the gospel, as set forth in the Book of Mormon, far surpass their comparable recitation in the Bible.
2. This Nephite record bears a plainer and purer witness of the divine sonship of Christ and the salvation which comes in and through his holy name than do the Old World scriptures.
3. Men can get nearer to the Lord; can have more of the spirit of conversion and conformity in their hearts; can have stronger testimonies; and can gain a better understanding of the

doctrines of salvation through the Book of Mormon than they
can through the Bible.

4. More people will flock to the gospel standard; more souls will
be converted; more of scattered Israel will be gathered; and
more people will migrate from one place to another because of
the Book of Mormon than was or will be the case with the Bible
(Ezek. 15–28).

5. There will be more people saved in the kingdom of God— ten
thousand times over—because of the Book of Mormon than
there will be because of the Bible. (Address, Book of Mormon
Symposium, BYU, 18 August 1978.)

Scriptural Records Fragmentary

The standard works contain just fragmentary portions of the
eternal truths that our Father has and desires that we have as rapidly as we get into a position to receive them. This is particularly
true of the Bible. Both the Bible and the Book of Mormon, in my
judgment, are that portion of the Lord's word that he feels the
people in the world are able to receive. They do not pretend to give
all of the word of the Lord.

In order to get a perspective of what is involved in the Book of
Mormon, we of necessity have to contrast it and compare it to what
we have in the Bible. The effect of that comparison, in some
people's minds, might be interpreted as downgrading the Bible. It is
not. We have unbounded appreciation and respect for the Bible; it
is a marvelous reservoir of scriptural truth.

Multiple Translations of Same Verses

The Bible in no single passage gives all the facts about what it is
talking about. We sometimes get the idea that things get translated
and that the translation is what the Lord originally revealed. That is
not quite right. There is more than one translation for some passages and both translations are correct. The classical illustration of
this comes from the passages in Malachi dealing with the coming of
Elijah (Mal. 4:5–6). When Moroni appeared to the Prophet Joseph
Smith, he changed the wording. He talked about restoring the
priesthood by the hand of Elijah the prophet. (JS—H 1:38–39; D&C
2:1.) The Prophet Joseph Smith, with full knowledge that this was
the correct meaning of the passage, proceeded to translate the Book

of Mormon and copy the King James language (3 Ne. 25:5–6). He then proceeded to quote the King James Version in an inspired epistle in the Doctrine and Covenants, adding that he "might have rendered a plainer translation" except that the King James Translation was sufficient for his purposes (D&C 128:17b–18). This shows that it is possible to have a passage of scripture translated in two ways, one having a lesser meaning and one having a much higher meaning. Certainly we have a much higher and better meaning in these passages in the way they were quoted by Moroni. We see this concept repeatedly applied in the Joseph Smith Translation of the Bible, which too, in the language of the Prophet Joseph Smith, is "a plainer translation."

The things in the forepart of the book of Genesis are true. But the forepart of Genesis is virtually rewritten in the book of Moses and there is a tremendous added flood of light and knowledge because of what the Prophet added by the spirit of inspiration. I do not know whether he added all of it because it was in the original record or whether some of it is inspired interpolation by him, but that doesn't matter. The point is that when he gives us the book of Moses, he is giving a book that contains the sense and meaning of the early chapters in Genesis. So we have two translations, as it were, of the same thing and both of them are true.

I suppose the best New Testament illustration of this is in the first chapter of John. Our New Testament account says, "In the beginning was the Word, . . ." and so on. That, of course, is true. Yet after the Prophet Joseph Smith translated that same verse, it read: "In the beginning was the gospel preached through the Son. And the gospel was the word, and the word was with the Son," and so on, giving it an entirely new perspective. (Compare KJV John 1:1 and JST John 1:1.)

These are illustrations of the fact that there can be two translations of the same thing and both of them can be true. One translation is designed as a translation to present the gospel to people who have limited understanding and the other translation is for a people who have grown in the things of the Spirit and are prepared and capable of receiving more.

I say this about the Bible. It is not complete in any instance. If Mormon could have just had the records of ancient Israel, and done unto them what he did to the records of the Nephites, and given us an account of Israel's history by inspiration, and then if we could receive it in translation the way he gave it, the Old Testament would read just exactly the way the Book of Mormon reads. It

would speak about atonement, faith and repentance, gifts of the
Spirit, the fall of Adam, and so on, the same way that the Book of
Mormon does.

But the Old Testament has not come to us in that way. It has
come to us in a degenerated form, with many of the plain and precious things, as the angel told Nephi (1 Ne. 13:23–29), taken out of
the original text. Thus, even with the corrections in the Joseph
Smith Translation, we do not have the Bible the way it once was.
There are many more corrections that could be made. We have
many places where the Bible speaks of the restoration of the gospel
and the gathering of Israel—as, for instance, in the thirty-seventh
chapter of Ezekiel or the twenty-ninth chapter of Isaiah—that I
could take and rewrite and make them twice as long as they are.
They would then conform to the doctrine that was being taught by
Ezekiel and Isaiah in each instance, which has only been preserved
for us in fragmentary form.

Corrections in the Book of Mormon Text

We have no such reservations about the translation of the Book
of Mormon. There have been some minor errors in it over the years
—as evidenced by the fact that we have made corrections by going
back to the original manuscript. In some instances we have not
gone back to original manuscripts, but have simply corrected something that was obviously wrong. For instance, the spelling of the
word "straight" in the thirty-first chapter of 2 Nephi. It is spelled
"s-t-r-a-i-g-h-t" in the old edition, and "s-t-r-a-i-t" in the new. Very
simply, the scholarship wasn't available at the time of the Book of
Mormon publication to distinguish between "straight" and
"strait," which sound the same but have slightly different meanings.

Salvation Not Available Through Dead Prophets

Suppose all you had was the Bible, and you taught the gospel so
far as you could interpret it out of the Bible. What would you have?
You would have the sectarian world, would you not? You would
have the Catholics and the Protestants, and all varieties and
branches and types of churches. That is inevitable if what you are
trying to do is give the Lord's word through dead prophets. All you
can do, where a dead prophet is concerned, is call on his words to
sustain or to amplify or to explain something that has come by

latter-day revelation. The word of the Lord must come through a living oracle, a legal administrator, one who on the one hand can preach by inspiration and on the other has the power to perform the ordinances of salvation.

This Generation Receives Gospel Through Joseph Smith

That is why the Lord said to Joseph Smith, "This generation shall have my word through you" (D&C 5:10). But let us note the context in which the Lord so speaks:

"And in addition to your testimony, the testimony of three of my servants, whom I shall call and ordain, unto whom I will show these things, and they shall go forth with my words that are given through you.

"Yea, they shall know of a surety that these things are true, for from heaven will I declare it unto them.

"I will give them power that they may behold and view these things as they are; [that is, the plates and so on]

"And to none else will I grant this power, to receive this same testimony among this generation, in this the beginning of the rising up and the coming forth of my church out of the wilderness — clear as the moon, and fair as the sun, and terrible as an army with banners.

"And the testimony of three witnesses will I send forth of my word.

"And behold, whosoever believeth on my words, them will I visit with the manifestation of my Spirit; and they shall be born of me, even of water and of the Spirit." (D&C 5:11–16.)

Now, these amplifying words show that when the Lord says to Joseph Smith — "this generation shall have my word through you" — he is in large measure talking about the Book of Mormon.

Book of Mormon Proves the Bible Is True

We call section 20 in the Doctrine and Covenants the constitution of the Church, meaning it is the document that sets forth what the basic doctrines, organizational structure, and procedures of the Church are. It contains some of the most persuasive reasoning that there is in any revelation. Having spoken of the rise of the Church and the call of Joseph Smith, it says:

"After it was truly manifested unto this first elder that he had received a remission of his sins, he was entangled again in the vanities of the world [which simply means, as we know from our histor-

ical accounts, there was too much levity in his life. He was not talking about serious moral sins.];

"But after repenting, and humbling himself sincerely, through
faith, God ministered unto him by an holy angel, whose counte-
nance was as lightning, and whose garments were pure and white
above all other whiteness [this refers to Moroni];

"And gave unto him commandments which inspired him;
[meaning God, not Moroni, gave him commandments]

"And [God] gave him power from on high, by the means
which were before prepared, to translate the Book of Mormon;

"Which [meaning the Book of Mormon] contains a record of a
fallen people, and the fulness of the gospel of Jesus Christ to the
Gentiles and to the Jews also."

While the Book of Mormon is a record of the Nephites and Jaredites, it is primarily a volume of scripture containing the mind and
will and voice of the Lord to people in that day and in our day.

"Which [meaning the Book of Mormon] was given by inspiration [meaning to Nephi, Alma, Moroni and the other ancient
prophets] and is confirmed to others by the ministering of angels
[that is, the record was given by angelic ministrants to people in our
day], and is declared unto the world by them [that is, by the three
witnesses and Joseph Smith and the people who got the message
from them]—

"Proving to the world that the holy scriptures are true [the holy
scriptures spoken of here means the Bible; so the Book of Mormon
was given to prove the Bible is true], and that God does inspire men
and call them to his holy work in this age and generation, as well as
in generations of old;

"Thereby showing that he is the same God yesterday, today
and forever. Amen." (D&C 20:5–12.)

Thus, the Book of Mormon came to prove the truthfulness of
the Bible and the divine mission of Joseph Smith. That is what it is
for. Anyone who reads the Book of Mormon with real intent and
ponders its truth will come to know it is inspired. Sometimes we
say, "Read the Book of Mormon and you will gain a testimony."
But that is not what the scripture says. You cannot just read it and
think to yourself that it is true and then get an answer. You must
ponder its truths. After pondering its truths, then comes the testimony of the Holy Spirit.

When you know the Book of Mormon is true, what else do you
know? Automatically you have a testimony, and a testimony consists in three things: a knowledge of the divine sonship of Christ, a

knowledge of the prophetic mission of Joseph Smith, and a knowledge that the Church is true. Those three things are synonymous with the message of the Restoration—and the purpose of the Book of Mormon is to prove the message of the Restoration. It also proves that Jesus is the Christ because it so repeatedly testifies that he is.

The Book of Mormon proves and establishes the whole system of religion that we're engaged in. The Lord says that those who praise and defend this work shall receive "a crown of eternal life," while those who condemn it shall in turn be condemned (D&C 20:14–16). In short, the world is judged by its acceptance or rejection of the Book of Mormon.

Warning to Use Book of Mormon

The Lord said: "Your minds in times past have been darkened because of unbelief, and because you have treated lightly the things you have received." Now, we ask, what are the things which we have received? We have received latter-day revelations and the Book of Mormon. We have treated lightly the things we have received, "which vanity and unbelief have brought the whole church under condemnation."

In other words, the Church was looking back to former dispensations; they treated lightly the revelations of this dispensation. "And this condemnation resteth upon the children of Zion, even all. And they shall remain under this condemnation until they repent and remember the new covenant, even the Book of Mormon and the former commandments which I have given them, not only to say, but to do according to that which I have written." (D&C 84:54–56.)

The Old Testament reads as the "old covenant" and the New Testament reads as the "new covenant," as far as the world is concerned. That simply means that one is a covenant the Lord made with older generations and the other is the covenant he made with a new generation. But from our standpoint, both of them are an old covenant. They were made with dead people. Now, the new covenant, as this revelation says, is the Book of Mormon and "the things" received or revealed in this day.

Forgiveness Comes from Testifying of Restoration

The Lord further decrees, "I will forgive you of your sins with this commandment [in other words, with this proviso]—that you remain steadfast in your minds in solemnity and the spirit of prayer, in bearing testimony to all the world of those things which are communicated unto you'' (D&C 84:61).

Thus, forgiveness of sins is given to those who in the right spirit bear testimony not of what was revealed anciently to Peter, James, and John, but of that which has been ''communicated unto you''— meaning us—in this dispensation. Our entire perspective in teaching should be based on latter-day revelations. In fact, it is because we receive revelations in this day, and because we are different from the world, that people in this day are attracted to and joining the Church.

New Scripture Grows Out of Inspired Application of Older Scripture

It is a fascinating thing to see what is in the Bible once you already know what is in the Book of Mormon. For instance, the Book of Mormon speaks of faith, hope, and charity (Moro. 7:25–48) and does it better than Paul does (1 Cor. 13), though in many instances uses the same language as Paul. I don't know if I can categorically state why, but a probable answer is that both Paul and Mormon had before them what a previous prophet had written and they just picked it up and repeated what he had said.

The Book of Mormon also talks about things that are in the book of Malachi, about the earth burning and so on (compare 1 Ne. 22:15 and Mal. 4:1; also 1 Ne. 22:24 with Mal. 4:2), and attributes them to a prophet named Zenos. Now, these portions of the Book of Mormon were written before Malachi was written. This must mean that Nephi (with the brass plates) and Malachi (using Old Testament records) had before them the writings of Zenos and they paraphrased them in the things they were writing. This process of one prophet making an inspired application of the writings of an earlier prophet, and of integrating it into his own testimony, illustrates one of the ways in which scripture is developed.

Book of Mormon Contains Deep Truths

As I left the building this morning I said to Dallin Oaks, ''I'm going down to the BYU to talk to a symposium about the Book of Mormon. What should I tell them?'' He said, ''You tell them Dallin Oaks is reading the Book of Mormon again and finding truths he never dreamed were there.''

Inevitably, that happens. I said to Dallin, ''I was reading in Church history somewhere and the Prophet Joseph Smith said, 'I spent the afternoon reading the Book of Mormon.' '' It really doesn't make any difference whether it is Joseph Smith, Spencer Kimball, Dallin Oaks, me, or anybody else. You get in tune with the Spirit of God and get an understanding of the gospel when you center your interest and attention on the Book of Mormon and latter-day revelation. You fall short if you think you are going to be a great biblical scholar and go along with the people in the world. (Address, BYU Religion Faculty, 13 June 1984.)

Chapter 18

THE BIBLE—
A SEALED BOOK

I am pleased and honored to be here, and pray for a rich outpouring of the Holy Spirit upon all of us as we now consider some matters of surpassing import where our work as teachers is concerned.

I shall speak about the sealed book, which contains many of the mysteries of the kingdom. These are things which are of great worth unto all who teach the gospel. My specific subject is, "The Bible—A Sealed Book," but my approach and handling of this subject may not fit the normal pattern.

There are many things that need to be said, and I shall speak plainly, hoping to edify and not to offend.

Seals on the Holy Word

Both Isaiah and John tell us about a book that is sealed. Isaiah's prophecy speaks of taking words from the unsealed portion of the book to one of great learning, to a mighty tower of intellectual power, who asked to receive the book itself.

Being told that some two-thirds of the book was sealed, the intellectual giant, skilled in all the linguistic learning of the world, said: "I cannot read a sealed book." This prophecy was fulfilled when Martin Harris took some of the characters copied from the Book of Mormon plates to Professor Charles Anthon in New York City. (Isa. 29; 2 Ne. 27; JS—H 1:63–65.)

John the Revelator saw in the hands of the Great God a book sealed with seven seals. "It contains," as our revelation tells us, "the revealed will, mysteries, and the works of God; the hidden things of his economy concerning this earth during the seven thousand years of its continuance, or its temporal existence," each seal covering a period of one thousand years. As John saw, no one but the Lord Jesus—"the Lion of the tribe of Juda, the Root of David" —had power to loose these seven seals. (Rev. 5:5; D&C 77:6.)

Content of Sealed Portion of Book of Mormon

This same or like knowledge is contained in the sealed portion of the Book of Mormon. For aught we know the two sealed books are one and the same. Of this much we are quite certain: When, during the Millennium, the sealed portion of the Book of Mormon is translated, it will give an account of life in preexistence; of the creation of all things; of the Fall and the Atonement and the Second Coming; of temple ordinances in their fulness; of the ministry and mission of translated beings; of life in the spirit world, in both paradise and hell; of the kingdoms of glory to be inhabited by resurrected beings, and many such things (see, e.g., Ether 1:3–5).

As of now, the world is not ready to receive these truths. For one thing these added doctrines will completely destroy the whole theory of organic evolution as it is now almost universally taught in the halls of academia. For another they will set forth an entirely different concept and time frame of the Creation, both of this earth and all forms of life, and of the sidereal heavens themselves, than is postulated in all the theories of men. And, sadly, there are those who, if forced to make a choice at this time, would select Darwin over Deity.

Our purpose in referring to the sealed book or books spoken of by Isaiah and John is to set the stage for a consideration of the sealed book—the Holy Bible—that is now in our hands. As the Lord Jesus alone has power to loose the seven seals on John's book, so the coming forth of the sealed portion of the Book of Mormon depends upon the faith and righteousness of us men.

When we rend the damning veil of unbelief that now shuts us out from perfect communion with Gods and angels, and when we gain faith like the brother of Jared, then we will gain the knowledge that was his. This will not occur until after the Lord comes. (Ether 4.)

Understanding Comes by Inspiration, Not Intellectuality

The Book of Mormon came forth and was translated by the gift and power of God. The scholarship and learning of wise men was not involved. It was not brought forth by intellectual giants who had been trained in all the linguistic wisdom of the world. It came forth by the power of the Holy Ghost. The translator said: "I am not learned." The Lord replied: "The learned shall not read" the account on the plates. (2 Ne. 27.)

There is a great key in this. The Book of Mormon is translated correctly because an unlearned man did it by the gift and power of God. It took him less than sixty translating days. The Bible abounds in errors and mistranslations, in spite of the fact that the most learned scholars and translators of the ages labored years on end over the manuscripts of antiquity to bring it forth.

The key to an understanding of holy writ lies not in the wisdom of men; not in cloistered halls; not in academic degrees; not in a knowledge of Greek and Hebrew—though special intellectual insights may result from all of these—but the things of God are known and understood only by the power of the Spirit of God (1 Cor. 2). Thus saith the Lord: "I call upon the weak things of the world, those who are unlearned and despised" to do my work (D&C 35:13).

How well Paul said: "Where is the wise? where is the scribe? where is the disputer of this world? hath not God made foolish the wisdom of this world? Because the foolishness of God is wiser than men; and the weakness of God is stronger than men. For ye see your calling, brethren, how that not many wise men after the flesh, not many mighty, not many noble, are called: But God hath chosen the foolish things of the world to confound the wise." (1 Cor. 1:20, 25–27.)

Of course we should learn all we can in every field; we should sit with Paul at the feet of Gamaliel; we should gain a knowledge of kingdoms and countries and languages (D&C 88:76–81; 90:15). "To be learned is good," Jacob tells us, if we "hearken unto the counsels of God" (2 Ne. 9:29).

But above all this—more important than all of it combined; more important than all the wisdom ever gained by the power of the intellect by all the wise men of all the ages—above it all is the need for the guidance of the Spirit in our study and in our teaching. The way the Book of Mormon came forth—by the power of God who used an unlearned man—sets the tone for all of us in all our work in the kingdom. The Lord can do his work through us if we will let him.

The Bible a Sealed Book

Now, it is my considered judgment and I firmly believe that the Bible as we now have it is a sealed book. It does not have the Jaredite seal which can only be removed by faith and righteousness; the

Bible is for men in our day, both the righteous and the wicked. And it is not sealed with seven seals, but with two. These we shall name and show how they can be removed. The Bible should become an open book, a book that is read and believed and understood by all men on earth.

What the Bible Is

But first we must tell what the Bible is and show its relationship to gaining salvation and to other inspired writings. Everyone knows that the Bible is the book of books; that it is a volume of holy scripture; that it contains the mind and will and voice of the Lord to all men on earth; and that it has had a greater impact on the civilization of the world, up to this time, than any other book ever written.

There are no people on earth who hold the Bible in such high esteem as we do. We believe it; we read and ponder its sayings; we rejoice in the truths it teaches; and we seek to conform our lives to the divine standard it proclaims. But we do not believe, as does evangelical Christianity, that the Bible contains all things necessary for salvation, nor do we believe that God has now taken upon himself the tongue of the dumb which no longer speaks, or reveals, or makes known his will to his children.

Not All Truth in the Bible

Indeed, we know that the Bible contains only a sliver, a twig, a leaf, no more than a small branch at the most, from the great redwood of revelation that God has given in ages past. There has been ten thousand times ten thousand more revelation than has been preserved to us in our present Bible. It contains a bucket, a small pail, a few draughts, no more than a small stream at most, out of the great ocean of revealed truth that has come to men in ages more spiritually enlightened than ours.

Bible an Imperfect Record

And even the small portion of truth preserved for us in our present Bible has not come down to us in its original plainness and perfection. An angel told Nephi, with repetitive emphasis, that the Bible—including both the Old and the New Testament—contained the knowledge of salvation when first written; that it then went through the hands ''of that great and abominable church, which is most abominable above all other churches''; that many plain and precious parts and many covenants of the Lord were taken away; and that as a result an exceedingly great many did stumble and did not know what to believe and how to act (1 Ne. 13).[1]

And yet, with all this, we cannot avoid the conclusion that a divine providence is directing all things as they should be. This means that the Bible, as it now is, contains that portion of the Lord's word that a rebellious, wicked, and apostate world is entitled and able to receive.

Bible to Prepare Men for the Book of Mormon

We doubt not also that the Bible, as now constituted, is given to test the faith of men. It prepares men for the Book of Mormon. Those who truly believe the Bible accept the Book of Mormon; those who believe the Book of Mormon accept the Doctrine and Covenants and Pearl of Great Price; and those so enlightened strive so to live that they can receive the greater light and knowledge in those sealed books that are yet to come to light—those books, we repeat, which shall come forth from unlearned men as they are guided by the Holy Ghost.

Providentially, the Bible is so written that all men, however slight their spiritual endowment may be, can gain truth and enlightenment from it, while those who have the power of discernment can learn from it the deep and hidden things reserved for the Saints alone.

Modern Scripture Superior to Bible

By way of perspective, as far as gaining salvation is concerned, the Bible is far excelled—immeasurably so—by the Book of Mormon and the other latter-day revelations. These modern scriptures are in fact the ones that must be believed and accepted in order to be saved. If it came right down to it, those of us who live in the dispensation of the fulness of times could be saved if there were no Bible at all, because the gospel truths and powers have all been given anew to us by direct revelation.

Uncanonized Scriptural Companions

Also, by way of having all things in perspective, we should be aware that there are approved and inspired writings that are not in the standard works. These also are true and should be used along with the scriptures themselves in learning and teaching the gospel. Next to the standard works the five greatest documents in our literature are:

1. The Wentworth Letter

Written by the Prophet Joseph Smith, it contains an account of the coming forth of the Book of Mormon, of the ancient inhabitants of the Americas, of the organization of the Church in this dispensation, and of the persecutions suffered by the early Latter-day Saints. The thirteen Articles of Faith are a part of this letter. (*History of the Church*, 4:535–39.)

2. The Lectures on Faith

These lectures were prepared by and under the direction of the Prophet Joseph Smith and were taught by him and by others in the School of the Prophets. The Prophet said they embraced "the important doctrines of salvation." (*Lectures on Faith.*)

3. The Father and the Son: A Doctrinal Exposition by the First Presidency and the Twelve

This exposition sets forth the status and relationship of the Father and the Son, shows those ways in which Christ is the Father, and through its various recitations lays to rest the false and heretical view that Adam is our Father and our God (James E. Talmage, *The Articles of Faith* [Salt Lake City: Deseret Book Co., 1955], p. 466.)

4. The King Follett Discourse and the Sermon in the Grove

These two sermons, one in thought and content, set forth the doctrine of the plurality of Gods and of becoming joint-heirs with Christ. They show that man may become as his Maker and reign in celestial exaltation forever. (*Teachings*, pp. 342–60, 369–76.)

5. The Origin of Man, by the First Presidency of the Church

This inspired writing sets forth the official position of the Church on the origin of man and therefore impinges on the evolutionary fantasies of biologists and their fellow travelers. As might be expected it arouses great animosity among intellectuals whose testimonies are more ethereal than real. (Joseph Fielding Smith, *Man, His Origin and Destiny* [Salt Lake City: Deseret Book Co., 1973], pp. 348–55.)

Two Seals upon the Bible

Now to our modern sealed book—the Holy Bible—the book that prepares men for the further light and knowledge the Lord has in store for them. What are the seals that hide its wonders from the world?

They are two in number and are the opposite extremes of a swinging pendulum. They are the seals of Satan and have been forged with devilish cleverness. In fact, I cannot think of two seals that could more effectively destroy the value and use of the Bible than these two.

They are: the seal of *ignorance*, and—please hold on to your seats—the seal of *intellectuality*. A word about each is in order.

The Seal of Ignorance

This seal kept the Bible away from almost every living soul on earth for nearly fifteen hundred years. If ever there was a sealed book it was the Bible all during the Dark Ages. The dominant church neither used it nor taught it, but followed instead the traditions of the fathers. Hence such doctrines as the three-in-one spirit God; the worship of Mary and images; the intercession of saints; masses for the salvation of the living and the dead; the sale of indulgences; purgatory; infant baptism; the justifying of the persecution and slaying of heretics, as in the Spanish Inquisition; and so on—for none of which is there one shred of proper scriptural justification.

The Renaissance and the Reformation that grew out of it were in large measure movements to translate and use the Bible. Many is the truth seeker who was burned at the stake for the mere possession of an unauthorized Bible. We need not dwell more on this. There are shelves of books in every good library that tell the dire and dark story.

Today the seal of ignorance remains only insofar as the generality of Christendom, and the rest of the world in general, have no real interest in studying the Bible. Modern ministers are sociologists, not theologians. And in Catholic nations there is almost no encouragment or incentive to own or read the biblical word.

The Seal of Intellectuality

As to the seal of intellectuality—this is quite another matter. It is imposed, no doubt unwittingly in many cases, by "the wise, and the learned, . . . who are puffed up because of their learning, and their wisdom"—these are Jacob's words—and who do not know they are thereby numbered with those "whom" the Holy One of Israel "despiseth" (2 Ne. 9:42).

We shall now show the fallacy of relying on learning and intellectuality, rather than upon the Spirit and upon an overall understanding of the plan of salvation, as we now set forth the keys of understanding that will enable us to remove the seals from the sealed Bible.

Some of these keys of understanding are of almost infinite import, others are so insignificant that if they are ignored, no one will ever miss them. Even these, however, must be mentioned so as to keep the important items in perspective. We shall take the liberty of rating each key on a scale of one to ten.

And so we say of the Bible, as Parley P. Pratt said of the Book of Mormon:

> Remove the seals; be wide unfurled
> Its light and glory to the world.
> ("An Angel from on High,"
> *LDS Hymns* No. 13.)

Keys to Understanding the Bible

Key One: Read the Bible

Could anything be more obvious than this? Simply read the book itself. Unless and until we do, nothing else will fall into place. We cannot do other than rate this as a ten on our scale. All biblical scholarship and understanding begins with reading the basic source material.

One of our problems is that we read what others have said about the Bible; we read a book of Old Testament stories; we get something the *Reader's Digest* publishes under the biblical name which leaves out the genealogies and supposedly hard parts.

Read the book itself. "Search the scriptures" (John 5:39). Treasure up the Lord's word. Go to the source. The words are sacred. Insofar as they have come down to us as originally penned, they were inspired by the Holy Ghost. They are to be read over and over again as long as we live.

But they are not all of equal worth. The Gospels, particularly the Gospel of John, are worth their weight in gold. Acts is not far behind them. Paul's epistles, Romans being the chief and Philemon the least, are treasure houses of doctrine and wise counsel. The writings of Peter and James, plus First John, rank as though written by angels. Second and Third John are of no special moment; Jude is worthwhile at least; and for those with gospel understanding, Revelation is a foundation of divine wisdom that expands the mind and enlightens the soul.

In the Old Testament, Genesis is the book of books—a divine account whose worth cannot be measured. Exodus and Deuteronomy are also of surpassing worth. Numbers, Joshua, Judges, the Samuels, the Kings, and the Chronicles are all essential history, interwoven with deeds of faith and wonder that form a background for an understanding of the Christian faith. Leviticus has no especial application to us, and except for a few passages need not give us permanent concern. Ruth and Esther are lovely stories that are part of our heritage. The Psalms contain marvelous poetry and the portions that are messianic and that speak of the last days and the Second Coming are of great import. Proverbs, Ecclesiastes, and Lamentations are interesting books; Job is for people who like the book of Job; and the Song of Solomon is biblical trash; it is not inspired writing. Ezra, Nehemiah, Obadiah, and Jonah are the least of the prophets; and all the rest of the prophets—Isaiah above them all—each in his place and order set forth the doctrinal and prophetic word that must be studied in depth.

Key Two: Know Hebrew and Greek

There is certainly no objection to this, but it does have some hazards. Joseph Smith and some of our early Brethren studied Hebrew. When a knowledge of ancient languages is used properly—as a means of gaining inspiration about particular passages—it merits a rating of, say, one or one and two-tenths. Improperly used, as an end in itself, its value sinks off the scale to a minus five or a minus ten, depending upon the attitude and spiritual outlook of the user.

Those who turn to the original tongues for their doctrinal knowledge have a tendency to rely on scholars rather than prophets for scriptural interpretations. This is perilous; it is a sad thing to be numbered with the wise and the learned who know more than the Lord.

Certainly none of us should be troubled or feel inferior if we do not have a working knowledge of the languages in which the Bible was first written. Our concern is to be guided by the Spirit and to interpret the ancient word in harmony with latter-day revelations.

Key Three: Use Biblical Commentaries and Dictionaries

Anything to be said under this heading is more of a warning than an endorsement. As to historical and geographical matters they drop off the scale to a minus ten, a minus one hundred, a minus one thousand, depending on the doctrine.

The wise and the learned know so infinitesimally little about doctrine that it is almost a waste of time to read them. All their creeds are an abomination in the Lord's sight. They teach for doctrines the commandments of men. They twist and pervert the scriptures to conform to their traditions, and if they get anything right it is an accident.

One says Jesus did not walk on the water, for that is impossible; rather, he waded in the surf.

Another says he did not feed the five thousand by multiplying loaves and fishes, for that is contrary to all nature; rather, many in the congregation carried food in their knapsacks, but were afraid to take it out lest they would have to share it with others. Jesus merely taught them to share.

Yet another says we need not look for the Second Coming in the literal sense, for surely Christ is no longer a man who can dwell among men; rather, the Second Coming takes place whenever Christ dwells in the heart of a man.

Worldly commentaries inadequate. What can the commentaries of the world teach us about the personal nature of God; about preexistence, the War in Heaven, and the eternal plan of salvation; about the fall of man with its temporal and spiritual death; about the paridisiacal creation that is to be restored during the Millennium; about the Melchizedek Priesthood and its various offices; about the literal gathering of Israel and the restoration of the Ten Tribes upon the mountains of Israel; about the preaching to the spirits in prison and the doctrine of salvation for the dead; about temples and celestial marriage and the continuation of the family unit in eternity; about gifts and signs and miracles; about a universal apostasy, a glorious day of restoration, and the coming forth of the Book of Mormon;

about the atonement of Christ which makes salvation available on conditions of obedience; about the three degrees of glory; about exaltation in the highest heaven of the celestial world where men will be joint-heirs with Christ; about almost every basic doctrine of salvation?

My fellow teachers: All these things, and ten thousand more, have come from God in heaven to us in this final dispensation of grace by direct revelation. They are the truths that make salvation available; and they are not to be found in the tomes of the scholars of the world.

Key Four: Learn of Local Customs and Traditions

This has some considerable advantage. It rates a two or a three. The words of scripture often take on a new and added meaning when read in the light of the local conditions that called them forth.

When we learn that the counsel of Jesus to beware of false prophets (Matt. 7:15), who come to us in sheep's clothing but inwardly are ravening wolves, had reference to the rabbis and scribes and Pharisees of his day, we realize that its modern application is to the ministers of false churches who teach false doctrines.

When we learn that the call of the meek Nazarene to come unto him, take his yoke upon them, and learn of him, for his yoke was easy and his burden light, and he would give them rest to their souls (Matt. 11:28–29), was an invitation to leave the ritualistic, formalistic, burdensome performances of the Mosaic law and accept the simplicity of gospel worship, it places an entirely new light on the call to leave the sin-laden burdens of the world and accept the holy gospel.

When we learn that every group of travelers in Palestine camped out at caravanserais, in which rooms called inns surrounded a courtyard where their animals were tethered, we get an entirely new vision of the place where the Lord Jesus was born.

When Jesus excoriated the Jewish teachers because their traditions made the law of God of none effect (Matt. 15:6 [Mark 7:13]); when he arraigned them for their utterly inane Sabbath restrictions (see, e.g., Matt. 12; Mark 2; Luke 6); when he condemned them for their ceremonial acts of washings and purifyings (Matt. 6:16–18) — it is of considerable help to know what the traditions, the restrictions, and the ceremonial acts were.

Nephi quotes "the words of Isaiah" and says "they are plain unto all those that are filled with the spirit of prophecy." As a supplemental way of understanding the words of the prophets he says men must be "taught after the manner of the things of the Jews." (2 Ne. 25:4–5.)

Such authors as Edersheim (Edersheim, Alfred, *The Life and Times of Jesus the Messiah* [Grand Rapids, Mich.: Eerdmans Pub. Co., 1971]; *Sketches of Jewish Social Life in the Days of Christ* [New York: F. H. Revell, 1876]), Farrar (Farrar, Frederick William, *The Life of Christ* [Portland, Oregon: Fountain Publications, 1972]), and Geikie (Geikie, Cunningham, *The Life and Words of Christ* [London: H. S. King, 1886]), writing more than a hundred years ago, when men had more faith and when they believed in the divine sonship, give us much good data on these ancient customs and ways of life.

Key Five: Study All Scripture in Context

The context of every passage of scripture is important; let us rate it as a two or three on our scale. God is no respecter of persons. Anything he has or will say to one person, he will say to another who is similarly situated. And he may give what seem to be conflicting commands to different persons differently situated.[2]

If the scripture says, "Thou shalt not kill" (Ex. 20:13; Deut. 5:17; Mosiah 13:21), what is to stop the Lord from telling Nephi to slay Laban as that Jewish leader lies in a drunken stupor (1 Ne. 4:7–19)? If the scripture says members of the Church who commit murder are denied eternal life (compare 1 John 3:15 and D&C 42:19 with 3 Ne. 30:2, for example), does this apply also to the heathen nations? If we need a passage to teach the separation of church and state, will we find it in the Old Testament when the people were ruled theocratically, or in the New Testament when they were required to render unto Caesar the things that were his? If we are studying Levitical performances, will we turn to the Book of Mormon among which people there were no Levites? And so on and so on. Obviously scriptures have limited or general application according to the context.

Key Six: Rightly Divide Between Literal and Figurative Passages

This is difficult to do; it requires considerable experience and discernment; and it surely rates as a three or a four. In general we are safer in taking things literally, although the scriptures abound in figurative matters.

Literal occurrences include speaking with God face to face as a man speaketh with his friend (Ex. 33:11; Moses 7:4); that man was made in the image of God both physically and spiritually (Gen.

1:26–27; 5:1; James 3:9); the coming of Christ as the Only Begotten
in the flesh (Moses 1:6, 17, 33; 2:1, 26–27; 3:18; 4:1; Jacob 4:5, 11;
Alma 12:33–34; 13:5; D&C 20:21; 29:42; 49:5; 76:13, 25; John
3:16); the Lord Jesus himself dwelling in Enoch's Zion (Moses 7:16,
21, 69); his personal reign during the Millennium (Joel 3:17, 21;
Zech. 2:10–13; Rev. 20:4; D&C 29:11; 43:29; 133:25); the resurrection of all men from the dead with corporeal bodies of flesh and
bones (1 Cor. 15:21–22; Alma 11:40–41, 44; 42:23; Rev. 20:13);
and so on.

Figurative matters include Enoch's walking with God (Moses
6:34, 39; 7:69); the Lord Jehovah dwelling with ancient Israel;
Christ being the living bread that came down from heaven (John
6:29–59); eating his flesh and drinking his blood in the sacramental
ordinance (Matt. 26:26–29; Mark 14:22–25; Luke 22:19–20; 1 Cor.
11:23–29); and so on.

Key Seven: Use the King James Version of the Bible

As far as the Bibles of the world are concerned, the King James
Version is so far ahead of all others that there is little comparison. It
rates as an item of five or six on our scale. It is the Bible that came
into being to prepare the way for the translation of the Book of Mormon and to set a literary pattern and standard for the revelations in
the Doctrine and Covenants.[3] It is the official Bible of the Church.
Reference might well be made to President J. Reuben Clark's *Why
the King James Version?* (Salt Lake City: Deseret Book Co., 1956) for an
extensive consideration of this matter.

Key Eight: What of the Other Translations of the World?

In answer we say: Forget them; they are of so little value that it
is almost a waste of time to delve into them. We take a liberal view
to even rate them as one on our scale. They are not binding upon
us, and in general they simply set forth the religious predilections of
their translator. Some, for instance, have Christ born of a young
woman rather than a virgin.[4]

There may be an occasional instance in which one of these
alien translations throws some light on a particular point; they are
not all bad; but there are so many things to study and learn that I
question the wisdom of treasuring up the translation views of the
wise and the learned who really have nothing in the inspired sense
to contribute to an understanding of eternal truth.

Key Nine: Use and Rely on the Joseph Smith Translation, the So-called Inspired Version

This counsel rates an eight or a nine. It can scarcely be stated with too great an emphasis. The Joseph Smith Translation, or Inspired Version, is a thousand times over the best Bible now existing on earth. It contains all that the King James Version does, plus pages of additions and corrections and an occasional deletion. It was made by the spirit of revelation, and the changes and additions are the equivalent of the revealed word in the Book of Mormon and the Doctrine and Covenants.

For historical and other reasons, there has been among some members of the Church in times past some prejudice and misunderstanding of the place of the Joseph Smith Translation. I hope this has now all vanished away. Our new Church Bible footnotes many of the major changes made in the Inspired Version and has a seventeen-page section which sets forth excerpts that are too lengthy for inclusion in the footnotes.

Reference to this section and to the footnotes themselves will give anyone who has spiritual insight a deep appreciation of this revelatory work of the Prophet Joseph Smith. It is one of the great evidences of his prophetic call.

And I am pleased to say that here at Brigham Young University we have the world's foremost authority on the Joseph Smith Translation. His contributions in this field of gospel scholarship rank with the best works published in our dispensation. He is of course Elder Robert J. Matthews, the dean of the school of religion. His published work, *Joseph Smith's Translation of the Bible* (Provo, Utah: Brigham Young University Press, 1975), is deserving of your careful study.

Key Ten: Use the Teaching Aids in Our New Editions of the Scriptures

I received a letter from a seminary teacher in which he criticized our new scriptural publications because they had footnotes, cross-references, and teaching aids. He argued that these were crutches which kept people from that intensive study in which they would make their own cross-references.

Well, I for one need these crutches and recommend them to you. They include the Joseph Smith Translation items, the chapter headings, Topical Guide, Bible Dictionary, footnotes, the Gazeteer, and the maps.

None of these are perfect; they do not of themselves determine doctrine; there have been and undoubtedly now are mistakes in them. Cross-references, for instance, do not establish and never were intended to prove that parallel passages so much as pertain to the same subject. They are aids and helps only. Certainly they rate a four or five in importance. Use them consistently.

Key Eleven: Use Inspired and Interpreting Translations of the Scriptures

It seems to me that most of us are almost unaware of the great enlightenment that is available to us from inspired and interpreting translations of biblical passages. For those with spiritual insight these inspired interpretations rate an eight or nine on our scale; for those with less spiritual maturity all they do is raise doubts and questions.

As all of you know, almost every New Testament quotation of an Old Testament scripture varies from the original Hebrew text as it has been translated in our Bible. Why? There are two reasons. One reason is that many quotations came from the Greek Septuagint and not from the Hebrew text that has become our Old Testament. The Septuagint had many deficiencies because it incorporated the doctrinal views of the translators.

But, more important, the Jews in the days of Jesus spoke Aramaic and not Hebrew, but their scriptures were written in Hebrew. Hence, it was the practice in their synagogue worship for one teacher to read texts from the Hebrew and for another to translate, paraphrase, or, as they said, targum these passages into Aramaic so they could be understood by the people.

When these targums were made by Jesus and the Apostles, all of whom taught regularly and consistently in the synagogues, they were inspired, and hence they throw great floods of light upon whatever scripture is involved. Many Old Testament passages take on new meanings because of the way they are quoted in the New Testament.

For all practical purposes Nephi often did much the same thing when quoting Isaiah or Zenos. He gave, not a literal, but an inspired and interpreting translation. And in many instances his words give either a new or greatly expanded meaning to the original prophetic word.

As a matter of fact Moroni did this same thing in his 1823 appearances to Joseph Smith. For instance, he so improved upon the promise of Elijah's return that it is like stepping from a pleasant twilight into the brilliance of the noonday sun. And yet, years later, with a full knowledge of the more perfect translation, Joseph smith retained the King James language in the Book of Mormon and the Doctrine and Covenants and his inspired rendition of the Bible.

Surely there is a message here. For one thing it means that the same passage of scripture can be translated correctly in more ways than one and that the translation used depends upon the spiritual maturity of the people.

Similarly, the Sermon on the Mount in the Book of Mormon preserves, with a few improvements, the language of the King James Version. But, later, the Joseph Smith Translation renders much of this sermon in a way that excels even the Book of Mormon.

So simple a passage as John 17:3 has a limited meaning for all men, but it is a celestial beacon of blazing light to us.[5] From it we learn that to know God and Christ is to be like them—thinking what they think, speaking what they speak, doing what they do, all of which knowledge is beyond the capacity of an unenlightened mind to receive.

As rapidly as we learn the plan of salvation and get ourselves in tune with the Holy Spirit, the scriptures will take on an entirely new meaning for us. No longer will we be limited, as are the small minds of the worldly wise, but our whole souls will be filled with light and understanding beyond anything of which we can now conceive.

Key Twelve: Modern Scripture Unveils the Ancient Scripture

I cannot lay too much stress on this key.[6] It rates a ten or more. In the real and true sense of the word the only way to understand the Bible is first to gain a knowledge of God's dealings with men through latter-day revelation.

We could be saved without the Bible, but we cannot be saved without latter-day revelation. Ours is a restored kingdom. The doctrines, laws, ordinances, and powers were all restored. God and angels gave them anew. We believe what we believe, and have the truths we possess, and exercise the keys and powers in us vested, because they have come by the opening of the heavens in our day. We do not look back to a dead day or a past people for salvation.

As it happens—it could not be otherwise with an unchangeable God—what we have conforms to what the ancient Saints had. Any agreeing truths and practices they had stand as a second and supplemental witness of gospel verities. But our knowledge and powers come directly from heaven.

Hence, the imperfect and partial accounts of the Lord's dealings with his ancient Saints, as found in the Bible, must conform to and be read in harmony with what we have received. It is time we learned, not that the Book of Mormon is true because the Bible is true, but just the reverse. The Bible is true, insofar as it is, because the Book of Mormon is true.

The everlasting gospel; the eternal priesthood; the identical ordinances of salvation and exaltation; the never-varying doctrines of salvation; the same Church and kingdom; the keys of the kingdom, which alone can seal men up unto eternal life—all these have always been the same in all ages; and it shall be so everlastingly on this earth and all earths to all eternity. These things we know by latter-day revelation.

Once we know these things the door is open to an understanding of the fragmentary slivers of information in the Bible. By combining the Book of Mormon, the Doctrine and Covenants, and the Pearl of Great Price, we have at least a thousand passages which let us know what prevailed among the Lord's people in the Old World.

Did they have the fulness of the everlasting gospel at all times? Yes. There was not a period of ten minutes from the days of Adam to the appearing of the Lord Jesus in the land Bountiful when the gospel—as we have it in its eternal fulness—was not on earth.

Do not let the fact that the performances of the Mosaic law were administered by the Aaronic Priesthood confuse you on this matter. Where the Melchizedek Priesthood is, there is the fulness of the gospel, and all of the prophets held the Melchizedek Priesthood (*Teachings*, pp. 180–81).

Was there baptism in the days of ancient Israel? The answer is in the Joseph Smith Translation of the Bible (see, e.g., JST Gen. 17:3–7; JST Matt. 9:18–21) and in the Book of Mormon. The first six hundred years of Nephite history is simply a true and plain account of how things were in ancient Israel from the days of Moses downward.

Was there a Church anciently, and, if so, how was it organized and regulated? There was not so much as the twinkling of an eye during the whole so-called pre-Christian Era when the Church of Jesus Christ was not on earth, organized basically in the same way it now is. Melchizedek belonged to the Church (D&C 107:1–4); Laban was a member (1 Ne. 4:7–28, especially v. 22, 26); so also was Lehi, long before he left Jerusalem.

There was always apostolic power (see, e.g., *Teachings*, p. 157). The Melchizedek Priesthood always directed the course of the Aaronic Priesthood. All of the prophets held a position in the hierarchy of the day. Celestial marriage has always existed. Indeed, such is the heart and core of the Abrahamic covenant (see D&C 132:29–38). Elias and Elijah came to restore this ancient order and to give the sealing power which gives it eternal efficacy (D&C 110:12–16).

People ask: Did they have the gift of the Holy Ghost before the day of Pentecost? As the Lord lives they were so endowed; such is part of the gospel; and those so gifted wrought miracles and sought and obtained a city whose builder and maker is God (see, e.g., Heb. 11:8–10).

I have often wished the history of ancient Israel could have passed through the editing and prophetic hands of Mormon. If so, it would read like the Book of Mormon; but I suppose that was the way it read in the first instance anyway.

General Key: Ponder, Pray, and Seek the Spirit

This is the conclusion of the whole matter. This is the key that removes the seal. This is the only way the pure and sweet and hidden truths of the Bible may be known in full. And it is rated above all others.

We all know that we must treasure up the words of life (D&C 6:20; 43:34; 83:85); that we must live by every word that proceedeth forth from the mouth of God (Deut. 8:3; Matt. 4:4; D&C 84:44); that we must ponder the things of righteousness by day and, with Nephi, water our pillows by night (2 Ne. 33:3)—all as we let the solemnities of eternity sink into our souls.

We all know we must ask the Lord for guidance and enlightenment. Ask and ye shall receive; knock and it shall be opened (Matt. 7:7–8). "If any of you lack wisdom, let him ask of God, that giveth to all men liberally, and upbraideth not; and it shall be given him" (James 1:5).

"And the Spirit shall be given unto you by the prayer of faith; and if ye receive not the Spirit ye shall not teach" (D&C 42:14). For, "No prophecy of the scripture is of any private interpretation. For the prophecy came not in old time by the will of man: but holy men of God spake as they were moved by the Holy Ghost." (2 Pet. 1:20–21.)

Now, much more might be said; we have but opened the door to investigation. However great the darkness may be in the world among the wise and the learned, we need not be confused or uncertain. The gospel trump sounds no uncertain tones. We have power to remove the seals from the sealed book and to bask in the light that shines forth from its pages.

May I, by way of conclusion, doctrine and testimony, give you four simple directions:

1. Teach from the source. Use the scriptures themselves; our tendency often is to study texts about the Bible, rather than to take the divine word in its purity.

Streams of living water flow from the Eternal Fountain, and they flow in scriptural channels prepared by the prophets. Here is a bit of wisdom most of you will understand: Don't drink below the horses, particularly the horses of sectarianism.

2. Teach doctrine in preference to ethics. Read again your instructions as given by President J. Reuben Clark in "The Chartered Course of the Church in Education."[7] As he sets forth, if we teach ethics and nothing more, we fail; if we teach the great and eternal doctrines of salvation, we succeed, and the ethical principles will thereby take care of themselves.

3. Teach by the Spirit. This is axiomatic. It has been true from the beginning and will be so everlastingly. Have you caught the vision of that great proclamation made in the Adamic day as to how and in what manner the gospel must be preached?

The scripture saith: "Believe on his Only Begotten Son, even him whom he declared should come in the meridian of time, who was prepared from before the foundation of the world." That is, believe in Christ and conform to the great and eternal plan of salvation.

Then come these words: "And thus the Gospel began to be preached, from the beginning, being declared by holy angels sent forth from the presence of God, and by his own voice, and by the gift of the Holy Ghost" (Moses 5:57–58).

The gospel is and must be and can only be taught by the gift of the Holy Ghost. That gift is given to us as the Saints of the Most High and to none others. We stand alone and have a power the world does not possess. Our views on religious and spiritual matters are infinitely better than theirs because we have the inspiration of heaven.

This is the reason the call to teach, the call to be a teacher—and I speak now of teachers of both sexes—is the third greatest position in the Church. Truly Paul said: "God hath set some in the church, first apostles, secondarily prophets, thirdly teachers, after that miracles, then gifts of healings, helps, governments, diversities of tongues" (1 Cor. 12:28). Apostles, prophets, teachers—in that order. Then the moving of mountains and the raising of the dead.

Apostles and prophets are also teachers, and what greater commission can anyone have from the Lord than to stand in his place and stead, saying what he would say if he personally were present, and doing it because the words uttered flow forth by the power of the Holy Ghost?

4. Become a gospel scholar. With such a great commission, how can we do other than become gospel scholars and then so live as to enable the Spirit to draw from our acquired treasures of truth those portions needed in the very hour?

Gospel Teaching Is Scriptural Interpretation

In the very nature of things every teacher becomes an interpreter of the scriptures to his hearers. It could not be otherwise. We are to preach, teach, expound, and exhort. But our explanations must be in harmony with prophetic and apostolic utterances, and they will be if they are guided by the Spirit. Remember that these are the chief officers placed in the Church to see that we are not "tossed to and fro, and carried about with every wind of doctrine" (Eph. 4:14).

Now, one final word: In the Church we are all brethren; the Lord is no respecter of persons; it is not Church position that saves, but obedience and personal righteousness.

The gospel has been restored so "that every man might speak in the name of God the Lord, even the Savior of the world" (D&C 1:20). We are all entitled to the spirit of inspiration. As the Prophet Joseph Smith said: "God hath not revealed anything to Joseph, but what he will make known unto the Twelve, and even the least Saint may know all things as fast as he is able to bear them" (*Teachings*, p. 149).

The gifts of the Spirit are available to all of us. Indeed, it is our privilege—the privilege of every elder in the kingdom—to strip ourselves from jealousies and fears, and to humble ourselves before the Lord, until "the veil shall be rent" and we shall see him and know that he is (D&C 67:10).

The work is true; the Lord's hand is in it; it will come off triumphant. And all of us who do our part will receive peace and joy in this life and be inheritors of eternal life in the world to come. ("The Bible—A Sealed Book," Church Education Symposium, BYU, 17 August 1984.)

Notes

1. The world, over the past few centuries, has seen repeated efforts on the part of scholars and theologians to come closer to the original intent of the ancient prophets by giving us new and different translations of the Bible. Typically, they reason to the effect that the Bible was written in "King James" English, which has largely fallen into disuse. Consequently, they conclude, modern translations are more helpful. In addition, they insist that the linguistics skills of the modern translators are equal to those of the earlier translators, and that since they are translating into modern English, and sometimes with the comparative help of manuscripts unavailable in 1611, their translations are certainly as good and maybe better.

We generally have no squabble with their translation skills. The problems, however, are at least twofold: first, as Nephi indicates, "plain and precious" parts of the text have been removed; and, second, there was clear tampering with the text *before* it got to the hands of the translators. This is serious, because from a faulty text comes a faulty translation. In reproving those of his day, the Savior said: "Woe unto you, lawyers! for ye have taken away the key of knowledge, the fulness of the scriptures; ye enter not in yourselves into the kingdom; and those who were entering in, ye hindered" (JST Luke 11:53). Yet the text-tampering took place even before the days of Jesus, as is suggested by Jeremiah 8:8, which the New English Translation renders thus: "How can you say, 'We are wise, and the law of the Lord is with us?' When lying scribes with their pens have falsified it!"

2. In this connection, Joseph Smith said: "Happiness is the object and design of our existence; and will be the end thereof, if we pursue the path that leads to it; and this path is virtue, uprightness, faithfulness, holiness, and keeping all the commandments of God. But we cannot keep all the commandments without first knowing

them, and we cannot expect to know all, or more than we now know, unless we comply with or keep those we have already received. That which is wrong under one circumstance, may be, and often is, right under another.

"God said, 'Thou shalt not kill'; at another time He said, 'Thou shalt utterly destroy.' This is the principle on which the government of heaven is conducted—by revelation adapted to the circumstances in which the children of the kingdom are placed. Whatever God requires is right, no matter what it is, although we may not see the reason thereof till long after the events transpire." (*Teachings*, pp. 255–56.)

3. That the King James Version of the Bible set the literary pattern for both the Book of Mormon and the Doctrine and Covenants is a point not to be passed over lightly, for a familiarity with the King James English is very important if we are to see the literary ties and doctrinal connections between verses in the different scriptures. Moreover, it is an important help in our learning how scriptures are given. Much of the scripture we have came when one prophet, having his mind filled with the language and expression of an earlier scripture, by the power of the Holy Ghost applied it to a new and different setting, and thus enlarged our understanding. Thus, some of the marvelous expressions in Isaiah 65 and 66, for example, when applied anew and enlarged in meaning, are found in Doctrine and Covenants 133; similarly, Doctrine and Covenants 132 consists in part of the inspired enlargement and thus interpretation of passages in the New Testament (Matt. 22:23–33; Mark 12:18–27; Luke 20:27–38). There are dozens of such illustrations in both the Doctrine and Covenants and the Book of Mormon, most if not all of which would escape our notice if those two books were not written in the same King James style as our Bible. The harmony in style helps us see how one scripture builds upon and grows out of another.

4. Note how from what appears to be but a slight mischief comes serious error. By changing the meaning of a verse, and doing away with the doctrine of the virgin birth, we destroy at the same time the doctrine of the divine sonship of Christ, and hence the doctrine of the Atonement, without which we have no gospel and life has no meaning.

5. One inspired and scriptural interpretation of John 17:3 is found in Doctrine and Covenants 132:24, which, as Elder Mc-Conkie notes, teaches us that in the full and complete sense we must be like God and Christ in order to know them. This verse is also im-

portant because of what it teaches about the eternal offspring of those who so come to know the Father and the Son.

6. Critics of the Latter-day Saints occasionally accuse us of reading "Mormonism" into the Old Testament in our interpretations of it. To this charge we plead guilty, at least in the sense that because the gospel is eternal, what *we* have is exactly what *they* had. Indeed, as Elder McConkie notes, it was they who in good measure came to restore it to us: many of the ancient messengers who gave Joseph Smith priesthood keys came from the Old Testament Church —Adam, Gabriel, Raphael (D&C 128:20–21), Moses, a man named Elias from Abraham's day, and Elijah (D&C 110:11–13), for instance. In truth, one of the better ways of understanding the Old Testament is to read the eternal gospel—"Mormonism" so-called —into it. The same may be said of the New Testament.

7. President Clark's speech, "The Chartered Course of the Church in Education," was given 8 August 1938 to Church Seminary and Institute leaders in summer school, at Aspen Grove, Utah. It is also found as an appendix in Boyd K. Packer, *Teach Ye Diligently* (Salt Lake City: Deseret Book Co., 1975), pp. 307–21. In this speech President Clark teaches that there are "two prime things which may not be overlooked, forgotten, shaded, or discarded." These are the testimony of Jesus and his atoning mission and ministry, and the testimony of Joseph Smith and his mission and ministry of restoration. In preference to the teaching of ethics or the theories of men, it is the teaching of these great truths and the doctrines that flow out of them that inspires men with the desire to keep the commandments. Similarly, Elder McConkie taught that any doctrine we teach ties into and bears testimony of both Jesus and Joseph Smith.

Chapter 19

SEARCHING
THE SCRIPTURES

The Book of Isaiah

"Great Are the Words of Isaiah"

If our eternal salvation depends upon our ability to understand the writings of Isaiah as fully and truly as Nephi understood them —and who shall say such is not the case!—how shall we fare in that great day when with Nephi we shall stand before the pleasing bar of him who said: "Great are the words of Isaiah" (3 Ne. 23:1)?

To Laman and Lemuel, the words of Isaiah were as a sealed book. The older brothers of Nephi could read the words and understand the language written by Israel's great seer, but as for envisioning their true prophetic meaning, it was with them as though they read words written in an unknown tongue.

Commanded to Study Isaiah

The risen Lord commanded the Nephites and all the house of Israel, including us, and, for that matter, all the nations of the Gentiles, to "search . . . diligently . . . the words of Isaiah. For surely he spake," the Lord said, "as touching all things concerning my people which are of the house of Israel; therefore it must needs be that he must speak also to the Gentiles. And all things that he spake have been and shall be, even according to the words which he spake." (3 Ne. 23:1-3.)

Laman and Lemuel are but prototypes of most of modern Christendom. They were almost totally unable to understand the difficult doctrines of this ancient prophet, and for their lack of spiritual discernment they found themselves on the downward path leading to everlasting destruction.

When father Lehi "spake many great things unto them, which were hard to be understood, save a man should inquire of the Lord," they rebelled against his teachings and refused to "look unto the Lord," they rebelled against his teachings and refused to "look unto the Lord" to learn their true meaning. Asked by Nephi, "Have ye inquired of the Lord?" to learn the true meaning of the prophetic utterances, they responded, "We have not; for the Lord maketh no such thing known unto us."

Then Nephi quoted to them—in the language of the Lord God himself—the great promise and law whereby any man can come to know the true meaning of the revealed word: "If ye will not harden your hearts, and ask me in faith, believing that ye shall receive, with diligence in keeping my commandments, surely these things shall be made known unto you." (See 1 Ne. 15:1-11.)

Nephi said: "My soul delighteth in the words of Isaiah" (2 Ne. 25:5). Personally, I feel about Isaiah and his utterances the same way Nephi felt and think that if I expect to go where Nephi and Isaiah have gone, I had better speak their language, think their thoughts, know what they knew, believe and teach what they believed and taught, and live as they lived.

It just may be that my salvation (and yours also!) does in fact depend upon our ability to understand the writings of Isaiah as fully and truly as Nephi understood them.

For that matter, why should either Nephi or Isaiah know anything that is withheld from us? Does not that God who is no respecter of persons treat all his children alike? Has he not given us his promise and recited to us the terms and conditions of his law pursuant to which he will reveal to us what he has revealed to them?

If the Lord Jehovah revealed to Isaiah that "a virgin shall conceive, and bear a son," whose very name shall be "God is with us" (Isa. 7:14); if this "child" shall be "The mighty God, The everlasting Father," who shall reign "with judgment and with justice" forever (Isa. 9:6-9); if he is to "make his soul an offering for sin," and place his "grave with the wicked" (Isa. 53:9-10); if his redemptive promise to all men is: "Thy dead men shall live, together with my dead body shall they arise" (Isa. 26:19); if he shall gather Israel in the last days and bring "the ransomed of the Lord . . . to Zion with songs and everlasting joy upon their heads" (Isa. 35:10); if his people "shall see eye to eye, when the Lord shall bring again Zion" (Isa. 52:8); if these and a great host of other glorious truths were known to Isaiah and Nephi, should they be hidden from us? Why should either of these prophets know what we do not know? Is not the Lord Jehovah our God also?

Isaiah Sometimes Hard to Understand

Let us freely acknowledge that many people find Isaiah hard to understand. His words are almost totally beyond the comprehension of those in the churches of the world. Nephi said, "Isaiah spake many things which were hard for many of my people to understand" (2 Ne. 25:1). Even in the true Church, among those who should be enlightened by the gift of the Holy Ghost, there are those who skip the Isaiah chapters in the Book of Mormon as though they were part of a sealed book, which perhaps they are to them. If, as many suppose, Isaiah ranks with the most difficult of the prophets to understand, his words are also among the most important for us to know and ponder. Some Latter-day Saints have managed to open the seal and catch a glimpse of the prophetic wonders that came from his pen, but even among the Saints there is little more than a candle glow where this great treasure trove is concerned.

But the seeric vision of Isaiah need not be buried under a bushel; his prophetic words can and should shine brightly in the heart of every member of the Church. If there are those who truly desire to enlarge and perfect their knowledge of the plan of salvation and of the Lord's dealings with latter-day Israel—all in harmony with his command to search diligently the words of Isaiah (3 Ne. 23:1)—I can give them the key which opens the door to that flood of light and knowledge that flowed from the pen of that witness of Christ and his laws who in many respects was Israel's greatest prophet.

Ten Keys to Understanding Isaiah

1. Gain an overall knowledge of the plan of salvation and of God's dealings with his earthly children. The book of Isaiah is not a definitive work that outlines and explains the doctrines of salvation, as do 2 Nephi and Moroni in the Book of Mormon, for instance. Rather, it is written to people who already know—among other things—that Jesus is the Lord through whose atoning blood salvation comes, and that faith, repentance, baptism, the gift of the Holy Ghost, and righteous works are essential to an inheritance in his Father's kingdom. To illustrate, it takes a prior knowledge of preexistence and the War in Heaven to recognize in Isaiah 14 the account of Lucifer and his host being cast down to earth without ever gaining mortal bodies.

2. Learn the position and destiny of the house of Israel in the Lord's eternal scheme of things. Isaiah's love and interests center in the chosen race. His most detailed and extensive prophecies portray the latter-day triumph and glory of Jacob's seed. He is above all else the prophet of the Restoration.

As foretold by all the holy prophets since the world began, the Lord's program calls for a restitution of all things (Acts 3:19–21). That is, every truth, doctrine, power, priesthood, gift, grace, miracle, ordinance, and mighty work ever possessed or performed in any age of faith shall come again. The gospel enjoyed by Adam shall dwell in the hearts of Adam's descendants before and during the great millennial era. Israel—the Lord's chosen and favored people—shall once again possess the kingdom; they shall dwell again in all the lands of their inheritance. Even the earth shall return to its paradisiacal state, and the peace and perfection of Enoch's city shall dwell on the earth for a thousand years.

These are the things of which Isaiah wrote. Of all the ancient prophets, he is the one whose recorded words preserve for us the good news of the Restoration, of the gospel coming again, of the everlasting covenant once more being established, of the kingdom being restored to Israel, of the Lord's triumphant return, and of a reign of millennial splendor.

3. Know the chief doctrines about which Isaiah chose to write. His chief doctrinal contributions fall into seven categories: (a) restoration of the gospel in latter days through Joseph Smith, (b) latter-day gathering of Israel and her final triumph and glory, (c) coming forth of the Book of Mormon as a new witness for Christ and the total revolution it will eventually bring in the doctrinal understanding of men, (d) apostate conditions in the nations of the world in the latter days, (e) messianic prophecies relative to our Lord's first coming, (f) second coming of Christ and the millennial reign, and (g) historical data and prophetic utterances relative to his own day.

In all of this, once again, the emphasis is on the day of restoration and on the past, present, and future gathering of Israel.

It is our habit in the Church—a habit born of slovenly study and a limited perspective—to think of the restoration of the gospel as a past event and of the gathering of Israel as one that, though still in process, is in large measure accomplished. It is true that we have the fulness of the everlasting gospel in the sense that we have those doctrines, priesthoods, and keys which enable us to gain the fulness of reward in our Father's kingdom. It is also true that a remnant of

Israel has been gathered; that a few of Ephraim and Manasseh (and some others) have come into the Church and been restored to the knowledge of their Redeemer.

But the restoration of the wondrous truths known to Adam, Enoch, Noah, and Abraham has scarcely commenced. The sealed portion of the Book of Mormon is yet to be translated. All things are not to be revealed anew until the Lord comes. The greatness of the era of restoration is yet ahead. And as to Israel herself, her destiny is millennial; the glorious day when "the kingdom and dominion, and the greatness of the kingdom under the whole heaven, shall be given to the people of the saints of the most High" (Dan. 7:27) is yet ahead. We are now making a beginning, but the transcendent glories and wonders to be revealed are for the future. Much of what Isaiah—prophet of the Restoration—has to say is yet to be fulfilled.

Isaiah is everywhere known as the messianic prophet because of the abundance, beauty, and perfection of his prophetic utterances foretelling the first coming of our Lord. And truly such he is. No Old World prophet whose inspired sayings have come down to us can compare with him in this respect. Moreover, the first coming of the Messiah is past, and so even those among us who are not overly endowed with spiritual insight can look back and see in the birth, ministry, and death of our Lord the fulfillment of Isaiah's forecasts.

But if we are to truly comprehend the writings of Isaiah, we cannot overstate or overstress the plain, blunt reality that he is in fact the prophet of the Restoration, the mighty seer of Jacob's seed who foresaw our day and who encouraged our Israelite fathers, in their spiritually weary and disconsolate state, with assurances of glory and triumph ahead for those of their descendants who would return to the Lord in the last days and at that time serve him in truth and righteousness.

4. *Use the Book of Mormon.* In the book of Isaiah, as recorded in the King James Version of the Bible, there are 66 chapters composed of 1,292 verses. Isaiah's writings, in an even more perfect form than found in our Bible, were preserved on the brass plates, and from this source the Nephite prophets quoted 414 verses and paraphrased at least another 34. (In a half a dozen or so instances duplicate verses are quoted or paraphrased.) In other words, one-third of the book of Isaiah (32 percent, to be exact) is quoted in the Book of Mormon and about another 3 percent is paraphrased.

And the Book of Mormon prophets—note this carefully and let its significance dawn upon you—the Book of Mormon prophets interpreted the passages they used, with the result that this volume of latter-day scripture becomes the witness for and the revealer of the truths of this chief book of Old Testament prophecies. The Book of Mormon is the world's greatest commentary on the book of Isaiah.

And may I be so bold as to affirm that no one, absolutely no one, in this age and dispensation has or does or can understand the writings of Isaiah until he first learns and believes what God has revealed by the mouths of his Nephite witnesses as these truths are found in that volume of holy writ of which he himself swore this oath: "As your Lord and your God liveth it is true" (D&C 17:6). As Paul would have said, "Because he could swear by no greater, he sware by himself" (Heb. 6:13), saying in his own name that the Book of Mormon, and therefore the writings of Isaiah recorded therein, are his own mind and will and voice. The Saints of God know thereby that the sectarian speculations relative to Deutero-Isaiah and others being partial authors of the book of Isaiah are like the rest of the vagaries to which the intellectuals in and out of the Church give their misplaced allegiance.

5. *Use latter-day revelation.* The Lord by direct revelation has also taken occasion in our day to interpret, approve, clarify, and enlarge upon the writings of Isaiah.

When Moroni came to Joseph Smith on 21 September 1823, that holy messenger "quoted the eleventh chapter of Isaiah, saying that it was about to be fulfilled" (JS—H 1:40). Section 113 in the Doctrine and Covenants contains revealed interpretations of verses in chapters 11 and 52 of Isaiah. Section 101 holds the key to an understanding of chapter 65 of the ancient prophet's writings, while chapters 35, 51, 63, and 64 are opened plainly to our view because of what the Lord has to say in section 133. As reference to the footnotes in the Doctrine and Covenants will show, there are around one hundred instances in which latter-day revelation specifically quotes, paraphrases, or interprets language used by Isaiah to convey those impressions of the Holy Spirit born in upon his soul some twenty-five hundred years before.

There are also, of course, numerous allusions to and explanations of the great seer's words in the sermons of Joseph Smith and the other inspired teachers of righteousness of this dispensation. So often it takes only a prophetically uttered statement, revealing the age or place or subject involved in a particular passage in the writings of any prophet, to cause the whole passage and all related ones to shine forth with their true meaning and import.

It truly takes revelation to understand revelation, and what is more natural than to find the Lord Jehovah, who revealed his truths anciently, revealing the same eternal verities today and so tying his ancient and modern words together that we may be blessed by our knowledge of what he has said in all ages.

6. *Learn how the New Testament interprets Isaiah.* Isaiah is a prophet's prophet; his words live in the hearts of those who themselves are authoring holy writ. He is quoted at least fifty-seven times in the New Testament. Paul is his chief disciple, calling upon his word some twenty times in his various epistles. Peter uses him as authority in seven instances. He is also quoted seven times in Matthew, five times each in Mark, Luke, and Acts, and four times in both John and Revelation. Some of these quotations are duplicates, some are messianic in nature, and all establish the revealed meaning of the original writing.

7. *Study Isaiah in its Old Testament context.* Other Old Testament prophets preached the same doctrines and held out the same hopes to Israel that were the burden of Isaiah's own expressions. To know what Isaiah meant, it is essential to know what his fellow prophets had to say in like circumstances and on the same matters. For instance, Isaiah 2:2–4 is quoted in Micah 4:1–3. After Isaiah gives this great prophecy about all nations flowing to the temple built by gathered Israel in the latter days, he describes certain millennial events that will follow this gathering. Micah does the same thing in principle, except that his list of millennial events refers to other matters and thus enlarges our understanding of the matter. And so that we shall be sure of these things, the risen Lord quotes from chapters 4 and 5 of Micah, as will be seen by references to 3 Nephi, chapters 20 and 21.

8. *Learn the manner of prophesying used among the Jews in Isaiah's day.* One of the reasons many of the Nephites did not understand the words of Isaiah was that they did not know "concerning the manner of prophesying among the Jews" (2 Ne. 25:1). And so it is with all Christendom, plus many Latter-day Saints.

Nephi chose to couch his prophetic utterances in plain and simple declarations. But among his fellow Hebrew prophets it was not always appropriate so to do. Because of the wickedness of the people, Isaiah and others often spoke in figures, using types and shadows to illustrate their points. Their messages were, in effect, hidden in parables. (2 Ne. 25:1–8.)

For instance, the virgin birth prophecy is dropped into the midst of a recitation of local historical occurrences so that to the spiritually untutored it could be interpreted as some ancient and unknown happening that had no relationship to the birth of the Lord

Jehovah into mortality some seven hundred years later (Isa. 7). Similarly, many chapters dealing with latter-day apostasy and the second coming of Christ are written relative to ancient nations whose destruction was but a symbol, a type, and shadow of that which would fall upon all nations when the great and dreadful day of the Lord finally came. Chapters 13 and 14 are an example of this. Once we learn this system and use the interpretive keys found in the Book of Mormon and through latter-day revelation, we soon find the Isaiah passages unfolding to our view.

9. *Have the spirit of prophecy.* In the final analysis there is no way, absolutely none, to understand any scripture except to have the same spirit of prophecy that rested upon the one who uttered the truth in its original form. Scripture comes from God by the power of the Holy Ghost. It does not originate with man. It means only what the Holy Ghost thinks it means. To interpret it, we must be enlightened by the power of the Holy Spirit (2 Pet. 1:20–21). It takes a prophet to understand a prophet, and every faithful member of the Church should have "the testimony of Jesus" which "is the spirit of prophecy" (Rev. 19:10). "The words of Isaiah," Nephi said, ". . . are plain unto all those that are filled with the spirit of prophecy" (2 Ne. 25:4). This is the sum and substance of the whole matter and an end to all controversy where discovering the mind and will of the Lord is concerned.

10. *Devote yourself to hard, conscientious study.* Read, ponder, and pray—verse by verse, thought by thought, passage by passage, chapter by chapter! As Isaiah himself asks: "Whom shall he teach knowledge? and whom shall he make to understand doctrine?" His answer: "Them that are weaned from the milk, and drawn from the breasts. For precept must be upon precept, precept upon precept; line upon line, line upon line; here a little, and there a little." (Isa. 28:9–10).

Let us then glance hastily through the sixty-six chapters that comprise the writings of this man, who according to tradition was sawn asunder for the testimony of Jesus which was his, and outline enough to guide us in a more detailed analysis.

Keys to the Interpretation of Isaiah

Chapters	Events
1	Apostasy and rebellion in ancient Israel; call to repentance; promise of restoration and then of the destruction of the wicked.

Chapters	Events
2–14	Quoted by Nephi in 2 Ne. 12–24. General interpretation of 2 Nephi 11, 19, 25, 26.
2	2 Nephi 12. Gathering of Israel to the temple in our day; latter-day state of Israel; millennial conditions and second coming of Christ. Micah 4 and 5; 3 Nephi 20 and 21.
3	2 Nephi 13. Status of Israel in her scattered and apostate condition before the Second Coming.
4	2 Nephi 14. Millennial.
5	2 Nephi 15. Apostasy and scattering of Israel; her dire state; restoration and gathering.
6	2 Nephi 16. Isaiah's vision and call. Verses 9 and 10 are messianic.
7	2 Nephi 17. Local history except verses 10–16, which are messianic. 2 Nephi 11.
8	2 Nephi 18. Local wars and history; counsel on identifying true religion. Verses 13–17 are messianic.
9–10	2 Nephi 19–20. Local history: destruction of wicked Israel by Assyrians to typify destruction of all wicked nations at Second Coming. 9:1–7 is messianic.
11	2 Nephi 21. Restoration; gathering of Israel; millennial era. JS—H 1:40; D&C 101:26; 113:1–6. Verses 1–5 are messianic and apply also to the Second Coming. 2 Nephi 30:9–15.
12	2 Nephi 22. Millennial.
13	2 Nephi 23. Overthrow of Babylon typifying Second Coming. D&C 29 and 45.
14	2 Nephi 24. Millennial gathering of Israel; fall of Lucifer in War in Heaven; destruction preceding Second Coming.
15–17	Local prophecies and history; fate of those who oppose Israel in day of restoration. 16:4–5 is messianic.
18	Restoration; gathering of Israel; sending of missionaries from America.
19	Local; salvation for Egypt in day of restoration.
20	Local.
21–22	Local, but typifying Second Coming. 22:21–25 is messianic.
23	Local.
24	Latter-day apostasy and Second Coming. D&C 1.
25	Second Coming. Verse 8 is also messianic.
26	Second Coming; Resurrection; Millennium.
27	Millennial triumph of Israel.

Chapters   Events

28   Desolations incident to Second Coming. Verse 16 is mes-
        sianic.

29   2 Nephi 26:14–20, 27. Nephites, last days, Book of Mor-
        mon, and restoration. This Book of Mormon account is
        one of the best illustrations of an inspired interpretation
        of a chapter that is difficult to understand.

30   Israel, rebellious and worldly, to be saved in day of
        restoration; apostasy, restoration, and resultant blessings;
        Second Coming.

31   The world vs. the Second Coming.

32   Apostasy of Israel until the restoration. Verse 1–4 are
        messianic.

33   Apostasy followed by restoration.

34   Second Coming and attendant desolations. D&C 1 and
        133

35   Restoration; gathering; Second Coming. D&C 133.

36–39   Local history of inspiration and beauty.

40   Second Coming. Verses 1–11 are messianic.

41   God reasons with Israel, ancient and modern, and
        speaks of the era of restoration. Verse 27 is messianic.

42   Verses 1–8 and 16 are messianic; the balance of the
        chapter praises God and bemoans Israel's troubles.

43–44   Restoration and gathering.

45   Israel to be gathered and saved; salvation is in Christ.
        Verses 20–25 are messianic.

46   Idols vs. true God, both anciently and now.

47   Babylon, symbol of our modern world.

48–49   1 Nephi 20; 21. Scattering and gathering of Israel. 1
        Nephi 22; 2 Nephi 6.

50–51   2 Nephi 7; 8. Scattering, gathering, restoration, Second
        Coming. 2 Nephi 9:1–3; 10. 50:5–6 is messianic.

52   Restoration and gathering. Mosiah 12:20–25; 15:13–18;
        3 Nephi 16, 20, 21; Moroni 10:30–31; D&C 113:7–10.
        Verses 13–15 are messianic.

53   Mosiah 14. Probably the greatest single Old Testament
        messianic prophecy. Mosiah 15–16.

54   Restoration and gathering; millennial. 3 Nephi 22;
        23:1–6, 14.

55–62   Apostasy; restoration; gathering; glory of latter-day Zion.
        61:1–3 is messianic.

63–64   Second Coming. D&C 133.

Chapters	Events
65	Israel and false religionists in latter days; Millennium. D&C 101:22–38.
66	Restoration and Second Coming.

For our purposes now, two things only need to be added to our recitations relative to Isaiah the seer, Isaiah the prophet of the Restoration, Isaiah the messianic prophet:

1. Scriptural understanding and great insight relative to the doctrines of salvation are valuable only insofar as they change and perfect the lives of men, only insofar as they live in the hearts of those who know them; and

2. What Isaiah wrote is true; he was God's mouthpiece in his time and season; the glories and wonders he promised for our day will surely come to pass; and if we are true and faithful we will participate in them, whether in life or in death. This is my witness. ("Ten Keys to Understanding Isaiah," *Ensign*, October 1973, pp. 78–83.)

The Book of Revelation

Uniqueness of Book of Revelation

One of our most fascinating exercises in scriptural interpretation is to study the book of Revelation, to ponder its truths, and to discover—to our surprise and amazement—what this commonly misunderstood work is all about.

If you have already fallen in love with John's presentation of the plan of salvation as it is set out in the Apocalypse, you are one of the favored few in the Church. If this choice experience is yet ahead of you, the day and hour is here to launch one of the most intriguing and rewarding studies in gospel scholarship in which any of us ever engage.

Our purpose in this article is to lay a foundation and generate an interest in what is probably the most unique of all our books of scripture. The real joys of gospel learning will come to us when we begin to drink from the fountain of truth as here recorded by the ancient Revelator.

In my judgment the Gospel of John ranks far ahead of those of Matthew, Mark, or Luke; at least, John's record of the life of our Lord is directed to the Saints; it deals more fully with those things that interest people who have received the gift of the Holy Ghost, and who have the hope of eternal life. But even ahead of his gospel account stands this wondrous work, the book of Revelation; or at least so it seems to those who are prepared to build on the foundations of the Gospels and Epistles and to go forward forever in perfecting their knowledge of the mysteries of the kingdom.

For our purposes now, let us use the question and answer method to give an overview of what this unknown book, Revelation, is all about.

What Is the Book of Revelation?

Before we can understand this book we must have one thing clearly lodged in our minds—it is a book of holy scripture. It is the mind and will and voice of the Lord. It came by revelation. The Lord spoke, his servant heard, the word was written, and we now have the written record for our profit and blessing.

In our study of the book of Revelation, we must start out with the clear understanding that—aside from changes and errors of translation—it is as though the same words were written in the Book of Mormon or the Doctrine and Covenants. That is, they are true and are the very words the Lord wants us to have on the matters with which they deal. Such is the view of the Latter-day Saints relative to this most misunderstood of all scriptural accounts.

How Is This Book Viewed by Other Christians?

There is no uniformity of belief whatever, except that none of those outside the Church envision it for what it truly is. It is commonly classed with a great mass of apocalyptic writings, by which is meant that it is considered to be a symbolical presentation designed to encourage the early Christians in their days of spiritual depression, by setting forth the ultimate triumph of God and his cause over the manifest evils of the day.

Many theologians doubt its canonicity. Some even consider it to be apocryphal in nature. All concede insurmountable difficulties in its interpretation. As Dummelow says: "Its reception in modern times has not been so unqualified as that of the rest of the New Testament. Luther was at first strongly averse from the book, though, later, he printed it with Hebrews, James, and Jude in an appendix to his New Testament. Zwingli regarded it as non-biblical, and Calvin did not comment upon it.'' (J. R. Dummelow, *The One Volume Bible Commentary* [New York: Macmillan Publishing Co., 1975, 35th printing], p. 1069.)

Who Is the Author of the Book of Revelation?

To this there is an unqualified answer. It was John—John the Beloved, he who wrote the Gospel of John and the three Epistles that bear his name. This runs counter to the conclusion of most Christian intellectuals, but it is a verity which has been confirmed to us by latter-day revelation.

More than six centuries before John was born, the Lord revealed to Nephi many of the things in the book of Revelation. Nephi saw John in vision, and an angel identified him as ''one of the twelve apostles of the Lamb.'' Nephi heard and bore record ''that the name of the apostle of the Lamb was John,'' and that he was the one appointed and foreordained to write the very visions now found in the book of Revelation. (1 Ne. 14:19–28.)

Have Other Prophets Seen and Written What John Saw and Wrote?

Yes! And their accounts shall be revealed to us in due course. When Nephi saw many of the same things, he was commanded not to write them, and was told by the angel:

''The Lord God hath ordained the apostle of the Lamb of God that he should write them. And also others who have been, to them hath he shown all things, and they have written them; and they are sealed up to come forth in their purity, according to the truth which is in the Lamb, in the own due time of the Lord, unto the house of Israel.'' (1 Ne. 14:25–26.)

We suppose that many of these things are preserved on the brass plates, and we know that when the sealed portion of the Book of Mormon comes forth, ''all things shall be revealed unto the children of men which ever have been among the children of men, and which ever will be even unto the end of the earth'' (2 Ne. 27:11).

How Was the Book of Revelation Given?

John was on the isle of Patmos. It was Sunday. The promised hour had come. The heavens opened, angelic ministrants attended, voices were heard, and visions were seen. John was overshadowed by the power of the Holy Ghost. Under that holy influence he wrote:

"The Revelation of John, a servant of God, which was given unto him of Jesus Christ. . . . who hath sent forth his angel from before his throne, to testify unto those who are the seven servants over the seven churches. Therefore, I, John, the faithful witness, bear record of the things which were delivered me of the angel." (JST Rev. 1:1–5.)

Was the Account Clear and Plain When It Was First Written?

Yes, as much so as any scripture. As the angel said to Nephi:

"The things which he [John] shall write are just and true; and behold they are written in the book which thou beheld proceeding out of the mouth of the Jew; and at the time they proceeded out of the mouth of the Jew, or, at the time the book proceeded out of the mouth of the Jew, the things which were written were plain and pure, and most precious and easy to the understanding of all men" (1 Ne. 14:23).

In this connection, however, we must always remember that prophecy, visions, and revelations come by the power of the Holy Ghost and can only be understood in their fulness and perfection by the power of that same Spirit.

Are We Expected to Understand the Book of Revelation?

Certainly. Why else did the Lord reveal it? The common notion that it deals with beasts and plagues and mysterious symbolisms that cannot be understood is just not true. It is so far overstated that it gives an entirely erroneous feeling about this portion of revealed truth. Most of the book—and it is no problem to count the verses so included—is clear and plain and should be understood by the Lord's people. Certain parts are not clear and are not understood by us—which, however, does not mean that we could not understand them if we would grow in faith as we should.

The Lord expects us to seek wisdom, to ponder his revealed truths, and to gain a knowledge of them by the power of his Spirit. Otherwise he would not have revealed them to us. He has withheld the sealed portion of the Book of Mormon from us because it is beyond our present ability to comprehend. We have not made that spiritual progression which qualifies us to understand its doctrines.

But he has not withheld the book of Revelation, because it is not beyond our capacity to comprehend; if we apply ourselves with full purpose of heart, we can catch the vision of what the ancient Revelator recorded. The Apostles in Palestine did not know about the Nephites because they did not seek such knowledge (see 3 Ne. 15:11-24). We would have many additional revelations and know many added truths if we used the faith that is in our power to exercise.

What, Then, of the Beasts and Plagues and Hard Portions of the Book?

An answer to this question gives rise to an interesting point. It is our observation that those who concern themselves about these hidden and mysterious things, generally speaking, are the ones who have not yet come to an understanding of the many plain and clear doctrines found in this and in all other books of scripture.

As to these difficult portions of the book of Revelation, Joseph Smith said: "I make this broad declaration, that whenever God gives a vision of an image, or beast, or figure of any kind, He always holds Himself responsible to give a revelation or interpretation of the meaning thereof, otherwise we are not responsible or accountable for our belief in it. Don't be afraid of being damned for not knowing the meaning of a vision or figure, if God has not given a revelation or interpretation of the subject." (*Teachings*, p. 291.)

Also: "It is not very essential for the elders to have knowledge in relation to the meaning of beasts, and heads and horns, and other figures made use of in the revelations; still, it may be necessary, to prevent contention and division and do away with suspense. If we get puffed up by thinking that we have much knowledge, we are apt to get a contentious spirit, and correct knowledge is necessary to cast out that spirit.

"The evil of being puffed up with correct (though useless) knowledge is not so great as the evil of contention. Knowledge does away with darkness, suspense and doubt; for these cannot exist where knowledge is." (*Teachings*, pp. 287-88.)

As a matter of fact, the Prophet, acting by the spirit of inspiration, did give some rather extensive interpretations of many of these difficult passages. An examination of these interpretations is far beyond the purview of this article, but they are set out in extenso in my *Doctrinal New Testament Commentary*, vol. 3, pp. 429-595.

In this connection we may well note the Prophet's declaration, to those properly endowed and enlightened, that the book of Revelation ''is one of the plainest books God ever caused to be written'' (*Teachings*, p. 290).

How Can We Understand the Book of Revelation?

Our position in this respect is strong. The path of understanding is clearly marked. Here are seven basic guidelines:

1. Know that the book of Revelation deals with things that are to occur after New Testament times, particularly in the last days. John is not writing of events of his time. He is not concerned with ancient history. The initial pronouncement in the book is that it concerns things that must shortly come to pass (Rev. 1:1; 4:1), things that are to happen after New Testament times, things that shall transpire in the last days. To give an overall perspective, some past events are mentioned, but all such presentations are clearly labeled. In discussing the war on earth between good and evil, it is mentioned that there was also a War in Heaven of a similar kind. In opening the successive seals of a book, to set forth what is to be, brief mention is of necessity made of what has transpired in past days. But the whole thrust of the book pertains to future events.

Joseph Smith said: ''The things which John saw had no allusion to the scenes of the days of Adam, Enoch, Abraham or Jesus, only so far as is plainly represented by John, and clearly set forth by him. John saw that only which was lying in futurity and which was shortly to come to pass.'' (*Teachings*, p. 289.) Also: ''John had the curtains of heaven withdrawn, and by vision looked through the dark vista of future ages, and contemplated events that should transpire throughout every subsequent period of time, until the final winding up scene'' (*Teachings*, p. 247).

2. Have an overall knowledge of the plan of salvation and of the nature of God's dealings with men on earth. We find in the book either passing allusions, brief commentary, or fairly extended consideration of such doctrines as preexistence and the War in Heaven, the creation of the earth, the Lord's dealings with men in successive generations, our Lord's atonement and glorious resurrection, what is required to overcome the world and gain exaltation, the gross darkness of the apostasy which followed New Testament times, the setting up of the church of the devil and the reign of the anti-Christs, the restoration of the gospel and the latter-day gathering of Israel, concourses of plagues and desolations to be poured out in the last days, final destruction of the great and abominable church, the Second Coming and millennial reign, resurrection and eternal judgment, and final celestialization of the earth.

These are but a part of the great events described and of the doctrines taught. Manifestly, those who already know the prophetic mind relative to such things will be able to focus the added light found in the book of Revelation on them and thus perfect their understanding of the Lord's doings.

3. *Use various latter-day revelations which expand upon the same subjects in similar language.* For instance:

Section 45 of the Doctrine and Covenants contains comparable truths relative to latter-day plagues and the Second Coming.

Section 76 expands upon the doctrines relative to salvation and exaltation.

Section 77 contains revealed answers to specific questions raised in otherwise incomprehensible portions of John's writings.

Section 88 speaks of some of the same angels and sounding trumpets of which John wrote.

Section 101 has considerable data relative to the Second Coming and the Millennium.

Ether 13 sets forth analogous truths relative to the New Jerusalem and the new heaven and new earth.

4. *Study the sermons of Joseph Smith relative to the book of Revelation.* As already noted, the Prophet preached rather extensively about this book, giving inspired commentary and interpretation as led by the Spirit.

5. *Use the Joseph Smith Translation of the Bible.* Acting by the spirit of prophecy and revelation, Joseph Smith corrected portions, but not all, of what is amiss in the King James Version of the Bible. In the book of Revelation corrections, for instance, the angels of the various earthly churches become the servants (presiding officers) of those units. The lamb with seven horns and seven eyes becomes a lamb with twelve eyes and twelve horns, thus perfecting the symbolism to identify Christ and his Apostles. Chapter 12 is so revised as to identify the woman as the Church of God and the child that she brought forth as the kingdom of our God and of his Christ. And so forth.

6. *Reserve judgment on those things for which no interpretation is given.* An example of this is the so-called number of the beast, which is stated to be the number of a man, which, if it could be identified, would show who was involved in the great deceptions imposed upon mankind. This is an answer that we do not know. The wise

course is to avoid being entangled in the specious speculation of an uninspired world.

7. *Seek the Spirit.* This is the crowning counsel. The things of God are known only by the power of his Spirit. Prophecy and revelation come by the power of the Holy Ghost. Only those endowed by the same power are able to understand the full meaning of the inspired accounts.

What Is the Chief Message of the Book of Revelation?

There can be no question about the answer to this query. It has the same purpose as all the scriptures, though the approach is different and the setting original. The message is that Jesus is Lord of all; that he descended from his Father's throne to dwell among men; that he worked out the infinite and eternal atonement and has now returned in glory to that throne from whence he came; and that he will raise all men to a kindred glory and a like dominion if they will overcome the world and walk as he walked.

A Book for the Maturing Scholar

But why this particular book? What does it add to the reservoir of revealed truth which is not found elsewhere?

In answer to these queries we find the real genius of John's apocalyptic writing. Gospel truths are and should be variously adorned with literary attraction—all to the end that they will appeal, in one form or another, to every heart that can be touched. The book of Revelation takes an approach to the plan of salvation that is found nowhere else in all of our inspired writings. The language and imagery is so chosen as to appeal to the maturing gospel scholar, to those who already love the Lord and have some knowledge of his goodness and grace.

After the baptism of water, after being born of the Spirit, after charting a course of conformity and obedience, the true Saint is still faced with the need to overcome the world. Nowhere in any scripture now had among men are there such pointed and persuasive explanations as to why we must overcome the world, and the attendant blessings that flow therefrom, as in this work of the Beloved John.

As the Saints pursue the course of progression and perfection, they look for a better world. Amid the evils and downdrafts of this life they have a need to look upward and ahead, to look at the overall course ordained by their Creator; they need to think in terms of millennial and celestial rewards. Where is all this set forth so effectively as in the latter part of these writings of John?

Nowhere else do we find the detailed data relative to the plagues and scourges of a sick and dying world. Nowhere is the overflow of satanic power so pitilessly described. Truly the teachings of this inspired work are some of the greatest incentives to personal righteousness now found in holy writ.

Has not the day come when the maturing gospel scholar can dip into this great treasury of revealed truth and come up with a knowledge of those things that will assure him of peace and joy in this life and eternal life in the world to come? ("Understanding the Book of Revelation," *Ensign*, September 1975, pp. 85–89.)

Chapter 20

TEACHING THE GOSPEL

The Foolishness of Teaching

The Significance of Gospel Teaching

I take as my subject "the foolishness of teaching." I do not say "the foolishness of teachers." There may be some of that, but I am not aware of any. I take this expression, "the foolishness of teaching," from a similar statement made by Paul (1 Cor. 1:17–29, especially v. 21). But first, I think we ought to set forth the dignity and preeminence of gospel teaching, and the eternal worth and everlasting value that comes because of those who teach the gospel in the way the Lord intended that it should be taught.

Yours [Seminary and Institute teachers] is a high and a glorious work. It was of you, as some of the chief gospel teachers in the Church, that President J. Reuben Clark said (I am going to read several quotations from President Clark and all of them are taken from a document which each of you has, "The Chartered Course of the Church in Education"):

"You teachers have a great mission. As teachers you stand upon the highest peak in education, for what teaching can compare in priceless value and in far-reaching effect with that which deals with man as he was in the eternity of yesterday, as he is in the mortality of today, and as he will be in the forever of tomorrow? Not only time but eternity is your field. Salvation of yourself not only, but of those who come within the purlieus of your temple, is the blessing you seek, and which, doing your duty, you will gain. How brilliant will be your crown of glory, with each soul saved an encrusted jewel thereon." (J. Reuben Clark, Jr., "The Chartered Course of the Church in Education," 8 August 1938; reprinted ed., 1980, p. 10.)

Paul Ranks Teachers Second to Apostles

Now, with that statement setting the tone and conveying the spirit for what, if I am properly guided, I hope to say, I shall turn to that wondrous verse in the twelfth chapter of 1 Corinthians in which Paul speaks of the kind of teachers who are involved in proclaiming the message of salvation to the world. He is identifying the true Church. He is giving some of the essential identifying characteristics of the kingdom that has power to save men. He says: "And God hath set some in the Church, first apostles, secondarily prophets, thirdly teachers, after that miracles, then gifts of healings, helps, governments, diversities of tongues." (1 Cor. 12:28.)

That verse tells you some of the proofs or evidences or witnesses that the work is true. It names some of the essential identifying characteristics of the true Church. Where there are Apostles and prophets and teachers of the sort and kind of whom Paul is speaking, there will be found the true Church and kingdom of God on earth. And where any of these are not found, there the Church and kingdom of God is not. That makes the President of the Church, as a prophet of God, an evidence and a witness that this work is true. The fact we are guided by a prophet shows we have the true Church. That makes all of the Apostles who have been called in this dispensation witnesses and evidences and proofs to the world that the work is true. True Apostles are always found in the true Church. I think this order of priority is perfect: Apostles, prophets, teachers. And that places you, because you are the kind of teachers that Paul is talking about, that makes you the third great group whose very existence establishes the truth and divinity of the work. This means that if you learn how to present the message of salvation, and in fact do it in the way that the Lord intends that it be presented, then you stand to all the world as an evidence that this is God's kingdom. As we go forward in this presentation, I think it will be evident to all that no one is or can be a teacher in the divine sense, in the eternal sense of which President Clark is speaking, except a legal administrator in The Church of Jesus Christ of Latter-day Saints—except someone who is so living that he is endowed with the gift and power of the Holy Ghost.

Role of Secular Teachers

We are not talking about worldly teachers. We do not concern ourselves a great deal about those in the various academic or scientific disciplines. What they do is meritorious and appropriate as long as it conforms to the standards of truth and integrity and virtue. Their work is in no sense to be demeaned. But the kind of teaching that is involved where the Church and kingdom of God on earth is concerned, the kind of teaching that you do is as the heavens above the earth when compared to the intellectual type of teaching and learning that is to be had out in the world.

Gospel Teachers Are God's Agents

All of us are agents of the Lord. We are the servants of the Lord. In the law there is a branch that is called the law of agency. And in the law of agency there are principals and there are servants. These are something akin to master and servant. An agent represents a principal and the acts of the agent bind the principal, provided they are performed within the proper scope and authorization, within the authority delegated to the agent. Now, the Lord said to us: "Wherefore, as ye are agents, ye are on the Lord's errand; and whatever ye do according to the will of the Lord is the Lord's business" (D&C 64:29).

We are engaged in our Father's business. Our Father's business is to bring to pass the immortality and eternal life of man (Moses 1:39). We do not have anything to do with bringing to pass immortality. That comes as a free gift to all men because of the atoning sacrifice of the Lord Jesus. (1 Cor. 15:22.) But we have a very great deal to do with bringing to pass eternal life for ourselves and for our brethren and sisters and in offering it to our Father's other children (Philip. 2:12; Morm. 9:27). Eternal life is the kind of life that God our Father lives. It is the name of the life he lives. It is to have exaltation and glory and honor and dominion in his presence everlastingly. And it comes by obedience to the laws and ordinances of the gospel. It is full and complete salvation. And so we bring to pass, in a sense, the eternal life of men by persuading them to conform to the standards that the Lord has set.

Eternal life and immortality both come by the grace of God. They are made available through the Atonement but in the case of the great gift of eternal life, which is the greatest of all the gifts of God (D&C 14:7), it comes by conformity, and obedience, and sacrifice; by doing all of the things that are counseled and required in the inspired word.

Gospel Taught by Weak and Humble

Now, let me point to the source of my text and my title, "The Foolishness of Teaching." It is a paraphrase of Paul's words. "For

Christ sent me not to baptize, but to preach the gospel'' (1 Cor. 1:17). And I will use *preach* and *teach*, for our purposes, as synonyms. Preaching is teaching and teaching, in many respects, is a perfected form of preaching.

"[He] sent me . . . to preach [teach] the gospel: not with wisdom of words, lest the cross of Christ should be made of none effect. For the preaching [and I insert teaching] of the cross is to them that perish foolishness; but unto us which are saved it is the power of God. For it is written, I will destroy the wisdom of the wise, and will bring to nothing the understanding of the prudent. Where is the wise? where is the scribe? where is the disputer of this world? hath not God made foolish the wisdom of this world? For after that in the wisdom of God the world by wisdom knew not God, it pleased God by the foolishness of preaching to save them that believe." (1 Cor. 1:17–21.)

Now I turn to the teaching aspect:

"It pleased God by the foolishness of [teaching] to save them that believe. For the Jews require a sign, and the Greeks seek after wisdom: But we preach [meaning we teach] Christ crucified, unto the Jews a stumblingblock, and unto the Greeks foolishness; But unto them which are called, both Jews and Greeks, Christ the power of God, and the wisdom of God. Because the foolishness of God is wiser than men; and the weakness of God is stronger than men." (1 Cor. 1:21–25.)

Now, think of yourselves as I read this next scripture. Think of Wilford Woodruff and Lorenzo Snow. Think of the men who have presided over this dispensation. Think of them as they have been viewed by the worldly wise and the aristocrats and the highly intellectual and by those with great mental capacities. Paul says:

"For ye see your calling, brethren, how that not many wise men after the flesh, not many mighty, not many noble, are called: But God hath chosen the foolish things of the world to confound the wise; and God hath chosen the weak things of the world to confound the things which are mighty; And base things of the world, and things which are despised, hath God chosen, yea, and things which are not, to bring to nought things that are. That no flesh should glory in his presence." (1 Cor. 1:26–29.)

Teaching a Gift of the Spirit

We are the weak and the simple and the unlearned as far as the intellectual giants of the world are concerned, but our teaching is not in the intellectual field. It is pleasing if we have some intellectual attainments. But basically and fundamentally, as teachers, we are dealing with the things of the Spirit.

A Personal Experience: The Worldly Wise Lack Understanding

At this last general conference, in April, I was doing what we are pretty much required to do now. I was reading the expressions I was making. And then at the end I said a few sentences extemporaneously. As I said them I had in my mind the document that had recently come to light purporting to be an account of a blessing given by the Prophet Joseph to one of his sons.[1] And so I felt impressed, after my formal remarks were concluded, to bear a witness of what was involved in succession in the presidency. And I named all of the Presidents from Joseph Smith to Spencer W. Kimball and said that down that line the power and authority and keys of the kingdom had come. Then I said something that highly offended all the intellectuals. I said, "What I am saying is what the Lord would say if he were here" (Conference Report, April 1981, p. 104). Now, the only way you can say a thing like that is to be guided and prompted by the power of the Holy Spirit because the Spirit is a revelator and places in your mind the thoughts that the Lord wants expressed.

Our intellectual friends reading that in the account were offended and annoyed. And in decrying the stand I had taken, one of the chief among them said, "Well, what can you expect when they have incompetents like Bruce R. McConkie running loose?" (See Fred Esplin, "The Saints Go Marching On: Learning to Live with Success," *Utah Holiday,* vol. 10, no. 9, June 1981, p. 47.) I read about it in one of the semi-anti-Mormon publications. And when I read it, it gave me a great feeling of personal satisfaction. I thought, "This is marvelous. It is just as important to know who your enemies are as your friends." And of course, the intellectuals in the world view our teachings as foolishness, or as Paul calls it, "the foolishness of God" (1 Cor. 1:25).

Secular and Gospel Teaching Differ

There is worldly teaching and there is gospel teaching. There is teaching by the power of the intellect alone, and there is teaching by the power of the intellect when quickened and enlightened by the power of the Holy Spirit.

"O that cunning plan of the evil one! [Jacob is speaking] O the vainness, and the frailties, and the foolishness of men! When they are learned they think they are wise, and they hearken not unto the counsel of God, for they set it aside, supposing they know of themselves, wherefore, their wisdom is foolishness and it profiteth them not. And they shall perish. But to be learned is good if they hearken unto the counsels of God.'' (2 Ne. 9:28–29.)

That is our stand in the Church and kingdom.

The Teacher's Divine Commission

I suggest to you five things that compose and comprise the teacher's divine commission. We are talking about divine, inspired, heavenly, Church teaching, the type and kind in which we are, or should be, involved.

1. We Are Commanded to Teach the Principles of the Gospel

Our revelation says:

''And again, the elders, priests and teachers of this church [this language is mandatory] shall teach the principles of my gospel, which are in the Bible and the Book of Mormon, in the which is the fulness of the gospel. And they shall observe the covenants and church articles to do them, and these shall be their teachings, as they shall be directed by the Spirit.'' (D&C 42:12–13.)

We are to teach the principles of the gospel. We are to teach the doctrines of salvation. We have some passing interest in ethical principles but not a great deal as far as emphasis in teaching is concerned. If we teach the doctrines of salvation, the ethical concepts automatically follow. We do not need to spend long periods of time or make elaborate presentations in teaching honesty or integrity or unselfishness or some other ethical principle. Any Presbyterian can do that. Any Methodist can do that. But if we teach the doctrines of salvation, which are basic and fundamental, the ethical concepts automatically follow. It is the testimony and knowledge of the truth that causes people to reach high ethical standards in any event. And so our revelation says:

''And I give unto you a commandment [again we are using mandatory language; the Lord is talking] that you shall teach one another the doctrine of the kingdom. Teach ye diligently and my grace shall attend you, that you may be instructed more perfectly in theory, in principle, in doctrine, in the law of the gospel, in all things that pertain unto the kingdom of God, that are expedient for you to understand." (D&C 88:77-78.)

Avoid the mysteries. That last modifying phrase indicates that we are to leave the mysteries alone. There are some things that are not given us in clarity, and, as of now, do not need to be fully comprehended in order to work out our salvation. We stay away from these; we stay with the basic concepts. Now President Clark's words:

Our students prepared to learn. "These students are prepared to believe and understand that all these matters are matters of faith, not to be explained or understood by any process of human reason, and probably not by any experiment of known physical science.

"These students (to put the matter shortly) are prepared to understand and to believe that there is a natural world and there is a spiritual world; that the things of the natural world will not explain the things of the spiritual world; that the things of the spiritual world cannot be understood or comprehended by the things of the natural world; that you cannot rationalize the things of the spirit, because first, the things of the spirit are not sufficiently known and comprehended, and secondly, because finite mind and reason cannot comprehend nor explain infinite wisdom and ultimate truth.

"These students already know that they must be honest, true, chaste, benevolent, virtuous, and do good to all men, and that 'if there is anything virtuous, lovely, or of good report or praiseworthy, we seek after these things' — these things they have been taught from very birth. They should be encouraged in all proper ways to do these things which they know to be true, but they do not need to have a year's course of instruction to make them believe and know them.

"These students fully sense the hollowness of teaching which would make the Gospel plan a mere system of ethics, they know that Christ's teachings are in the highest degree ethical, but they also know they are more than this. They will see that ethics relate primarily to the doings of this life, and that to make of the Gospel a mere system of ethics is to confess a lack of faith, if not a disbelief, in the hereafter. They know that the Gospel teachings not only touch this life, but the life that is to come, with its salvation and exaltation as the final goal.

"These students hunger and thirst, as did their fathers before them, for a testimony of the things of the spirit and of the hereafter, and knowing that you cannot rationalize eternity, they seek faith, and the knowledge which follows faith.[2] They sense by the spirit they have, that the testimony they seek is engendered and nurtured by the testimony of others." (Clark, *Chartered Course*, pp. 5–6.)

Now, notice this. I have never heard this better expressed by anyone than President Clark gives it:

"[They know that] one living, burning, honest testimony of a righteous God-fearing man that Jesus is the Christ and that Joseph was God's prophet, is worth a thousand books and lectures aimed at debasing the Gospel to a system of ethics or seeking to rationalize infinity" (Clark, *Chartered Course*, p. 6).

Conversion comes through testimony. We must teach it that way, as I will subsequently, with some particularity, point out.

We teach gospel truths—not ethics. "There is neither reason nor is there excuse for our Church religious teaching and training facilities and institutions, unless the youth are to be taught and trained in the principles of the Gospel, embracing therein the two great elements that Jesus is the Christ and that Joseph Smith was God's prophet. The teaching of a system of ethics to the students is not a sufficient reason for running our seminaries and institutes. The great public school system teaches ethics. The students of seminaries and institutes should of course be taught the ordinary canons of good and righteous living, for these are part of the Gospel. But there are the great principles involved in eternal life, the Priesthood, the resurrection, and many like other things, that go way beyond these canons of good living. These great fundamental principles also must be taught to the youth; they are the things the youth wish first to know about." (Clark, *Chartered Course*, pp. 6–7.)

We teach as Jesus taught. From all this I conclude that we should do as Jesus did. We should teach the gospel. We should teach the gospel only. We should teach nothing but the gospel. Ethics are a part of the gospel, but they will take care of themselves if we preach the gospel. Teach doctrine. Teach sound doctrine. Teach the doctrines of the kingdom. You say, What did Jesus teach? Well, of course we have the great accounts of his teachings about ethical problems, but notice this:

"Now after that John was put in prison, Jesus came into Galilee, preaching the gospel of the kingdom of God, And saying, The time is fulfilled, and the kingdom of God is at hand: repent ye, and believe the gospel" (Mark 1:14–15).

Jesus taught the gospel. Now, what did Jesus teach? Jesus taught the gospel. Unfortunately, from our standpoint, there is not very much preserved in the New Testament account of what he taught. I say from our standpoint because we as a people, having the Restoration and the light of heaven, would be able to recognize and glory in the gospel truths he taught had they been recorded and preserved for us. But obviously, in the wisdom of him who knoweth all things and doeth all things right, it was the intent and design that only the portion of his teachings that are found in Matthew, Mark, Luke, and John should have been preserved for men in this day.

But with our background and understanding, when the revelation says that Jesus preached the gospel, we know thereby what he preached. And we know it simply by answering the questions, What is the gospel? What is the eternal plan of salvation? What truths has God given us which we must believe and understand and obey to gain peace in this life, and glory and honor and dignity in the life to come?

What is "the gospel which Jesus preached"? The gospel can be defined from two perspectives. We can talk about it in the eternal sense as it was in the mind of God when he ordained and established all things. And we can talk about it in a more restricted sense as it is involved in the lives of people here.

Now, in the eternal and unlimited sense, the gospel that Jesus taught was itself infinite and eternal. It included the creation of all things, the nature of this probationary estate, and the great and eternal plan of redemption. He taught that God was the creator of all things, that he created this earth and all things that on it are. He taught that there was a fall of Adam; that Adam and all forms of life fell, or changed, from their original paradisiacal state to the mortal state that now prevails; and that as a consequence of that fall, which brought temporal and spiritual death into the world, an atonement of a divine being was required. Someone had to come and ransom men from the effects of the Fall and bring to pass temporal life, which is immortality, and make available spiritual life again, which is eternal life.

The great and eternal plan of salvation, from God's viewpoint, is the Creation, the Fall, and the Atonement. If there had been no creation, there would be nothing. If things had not been created in the manner and form and way that they were, there could have been no fall of Adam, and, as a consequence, no procreation and no mortality and no death. And if there had been no fall of Adam which brought temporal and spiritual death into the world, there would be no need for the redemption of the Lord Jesus.

Jesus taught the plan of salvation. The plan of salvation, to us, is the atoning sacrifice of the Lord Jesus by which immortality and eternal life come. When you talk about the gospel from the standpoint of men, you are talking about the things men must do to work out their own salvation with fear and trembling before the Lord. And what is involved here is faith in the Lord Jesus Christ; repentance from sin; baptism by immersion under the hands of a legal adminis- trator for the remission of sins; the receipt of the gift of the Holy Ghost, which is the right to the constant companionship of that member of the Godhead; and then, finally, enduring in righteous- ness and integrity and devotion and obedience all of one's days. That is the plan of salvation as far as acts on our part are concerned. But that plan of salvation rests on the greater eternal concept of the atoning sacrifice which grew out of the Fall, which Fall grew out of the Creation.

Jesus preached the gospel. Jesus was a theologian. There has never been a theologian on earth to compare with him. In this field, as in all others, no man ever spake as he did. I grant you that his teachings are not preserved for us. In his providences, he let Paul and Peter and some of the others present to us the theological con- cepts that had to be known in order for people to gain salvation. But Jesus preached the gospel. That, of course, is what we are expected to do; that is the first great concept. Here is the second:

2. We Are to Teach the Principles of the Gospel as They Are Found in the Standard Works

"And let them [the elders of the kingdom] journey from thence preaching the word by the way, saying none other things than that which the prophets and apostles have written, and that which is taught them by the Comforter through the prayer of faith" (D&C 52:9).

We have a multitude of passages that talk about searching the scriptures, about searching "these commandments." We have counsel to "ponder" the things of the Lord, to "treasure up" the words of truth. He told the Nephites, "Great are the words of Isaiah" (3 Ne. 23:1). He said to them, "Search the prophets" (3 Ne. 23:5).

"Differences of administration" in gospel teaching. These and other passages show we should study the standard works of the Church. The scriptures themselves present the gospel in the way that the Lord wants it presented to us in our day. I do not say that it is always presented to men in the same way.[3] There have been civili- zations of a higher spiritual standing than ours. I think he did some different kind of teaching among the people in Enoch's day and in

that golden Nephite era when for two hundred years everyone was conforming to principles of light and truth and had the Holy Spirit for a guide. We know perfectly well that during the Millennium the teaching processes will change. One of the revelations says of that day: "And they shall teach no more every man his neighbour, and every man his brother, saying, Know the Lord: for they shall all know me, from the least of them unto the greatest of them" (Jer. 31:34).

For our day: teach from the standard works. But for *our* day and *our* time and *our* hour, the time of *our* mortal probation, we are to teach in the way things are recorded in the standard works that we have. And if you want to know what emphasis should be given to gospel principles, you simply teach the whole standard works and, automatically, in the process, you will have given the Lord's emphasis to every doctrine and every principle. As far as learning the gospel and teaching the gospel is concerned, the Book of Mormon, by all odds, is the most important of the standard works, because in simplicity and in plainness it sets forth in a definitive manner the doctrines of the gospel. If you would like to test that sort of thing, just arbitrarily choose a hundred or so gospel subjects and then put in parallel columns what the Bible says about them and what the Book of Mormon says about them. And in about 95 percent of the cases, the clarity and perfection and superlative nature of the Book of Mormon teaching will be so evident that it will be perfectly clear that that is the place to learn the gospel.

Learn and teach from the Book of Mormon. I think in many respects the literature and the language and the power of expression that is in Paul's writings and Isaiah's writings is superior to what is in the Book of Mormon. But we understand the Bible because we have the knowledge gained out of the Book of Mormon. The epistles of Paul, for instance, were written to members of the Church. I do not think he has any epistles that are intended to be definitive explanations of gospel doctrines. He was writing the portion of the Lord's word that the Corinthians or the Hebrews or the Romans needed, he being aware of the problems and questions and difficulties that confronted them. In effect, he is writing to people who already had the knowledge that is in the Book of Mormon. That means, obviously, that there are no people on earth who can understand the epistles of Paul and the other brethren in the New Testament until they first get the knowledge that we as Latter-day Saints have.

The Book of Mormon is a definitive, all-embracing, comprehensive account. Our scriptures say it contains the fulness of the everlasting gospel (D&C 20:8-9). What that means is that it is a record of God's dealings with a people who had the fulness of the gospel. It means that in it are recorded the basic principles which men must believe to work out their salvation. After we accept and believe and comprehend the principles therein recorded, we are qualified and prepared to take another step and to begin to acquire a knowledge of the mysteries of godliness.

After somebody gets the basic understanding that is in the Book of Mormon about salvation, for instance, then he is in a position to envision and comprehend what section 76 is all about. When that section was first given in our dispensation, the Prophet forbade the missionaries to talk about it when they went out into the world and told them that if they did they would heap persecution upon their heads because it was something that was beyond the spiritual capacity of those to whom they were sent. We do not have that type of religious climate today, but it was one that prevailed in that day.

"The law of the Lord is perfect." I think this language in the Psalms is about as good as anything that has been written about the scriptures:

"The law of the Lord is perfect, converting the soul: the testimony of the Lord is sure, making wise the simple. The statutes of the Lord are right, rejoicing the heart; the commandment of the Lord is pure, enlightening the eyes. The fear of the Lord is clean, enduring for ever: the judgments of the Lord are true and righteous altogether. More to be desired are they than gold, yea, than much fine gold: sweeter also than honey and the honeycomb. Moreover by them is thy servant warned: and in keeping of them there is great reward." (Ps. 19:7-11.)

I love these words also that Paul wrote to Timothy:

"And that from a child thou hast known the holy scriptures, which are able to make thee wise unto salvation through faith which is in Christ Jesus. All scripture is given by inspiration of God, and is profitable for doctrine, for reproof, for correction, for instruction in righteousness: That the man of God may be perfect, throughly furnished unto all good works." (2 Tim. 3:15-17.)

President Clark said on this point:

"You do have an interest in matters purely cultural and in matters of purely secular knowledge; but I repeat again for emphasis, your chief interest, your essential and all but sole duty, is to teach the Gospel of the Lord Jesus Christ as that has been revealed in these latter days. You are to teach this Gospel using as your sources and authorities the Standard Works of the Church, and the words of those whom God has called to lead His people in these last days. You are not, whether high or low, to intrude into your work your own peculiar philosophy, no matter what its source or how pleasing or rational it seems to you to be. To do so would be to have as many different churches as we have seminaries—and that is chaos." (Clark, *Chartered Course*, pp. 10–11.)

3. We Are to Teach by the Power of the Holy Ghost

There are some passages on this matter of teaching by the power of the Holy Ghost that are so strong and so blunt and so plain that unless we understand what is involved, it almost makes us fear ever to teach. And a couple of them I shall read.

"And the Spirit shall be given unto you by the prayer of faith; and if ye receive not the Spirit ye shall not teach" (D&C 42:14).

This is a mandatory thing, a prohibition.

"And all this ye shall observe to do as I have commanded concerning your teaching, until the fulness of my scriptures is given. And as ye shall lift up your voices by the Comforter, ye shall speak and prophesy as seemeth me good; For, behold, the Comforter knoweth all things, and beareth record of the Father and of the Son." (D&C 42:15–17.)

Teach by the Spirit to speak the voice of God. We are talking about Church teaching, gospel teaching, teaching spiritual things, teaching by the power of the Holy Ghost. And if you teach by the power of the Holy Ghost, you say the things that the Lord wants said, or you say the things the Lord would say if he himself were here. The Holy Ghost is a revelator, and you are speaking words of revelation. And that kind of preacher or teacher, as we have seen, is the third great essential identifying officer of God's kingdom.

"First apostles, secondarily prophets, thirdly teachers" (1 Cor. 12:28).

"And now come, saith the Lord, by the Spirit, unto the elders of his Church, and let us reason together, that ye may understand; Let us reason even as a man reasoneth one with another face to face. Now, when a man reasoneth he is understood of man, because he reasoneth as a man; even so will I, the Lord, reason with you that you may understand." (D&C 50:10–12.)

Have in mind as we consider these matters from section 50 the law pertaining to principals and agents, to masters and servants. Consider how these apply to a divine being who gives direction to someone else, letting him know what he should teach and what he should say.

Have in mind also that it really does not make a particle of difference to any of you what we teach. I often think as I go around the Church and preach in various meetings that it just does not make a snap of the fingers difference to me what I am talking about. I do not care what I talk about. All I am concerned with is getting in tune with the Spirit and expressing the thoughts, in the best language and way that I can, that are implanted there by the power of the Spirit. The Lord knows what a congregation needs to hear, and he has provided a means to give that revelation to every preacher and every teacher.

Teach what God wants taught. We do not create the doctrines of the gospel. People who ask questions about the gospel, a good portion of the time, are looking for an answer that sustains a view they have expressed. They want to justify a conclusion that they have reached instead of looking for the ultimate truth in the field. Once again, it does not make one snap of the fingers difference to me what the doctrines of the Church are. I cannot create a doctrine. I cannot originate a concept of eternal truth. The only thing I ought to be concerned with is learning what the Lord thinks about a doctrine. If I ask a question of someone to learn something, I ought *not* to be seeking for a confirmation of a view that I have expressed. I ought to be seeking knowledge and wisdom. It should not make any difference to me whether the doctrine is on the right hand or on the left. My sole interest and my sole concern should be to find out what the Lord thinks on the subject.

Inspired teaching is "the mind of Christ." And we have the power to do that. I suppose that is part at least of what Paul had in mind when he said of the Saints, "We have the mind of Christ" (1 Cor. 2:16).

If we have the mind of Christ, we think what Christ thinks and we say what Christ says; and out of those two things come our acts, and so we do what Christ would have done in an equivalent situation. Well, back to section 50 in which the Lord is reasoning with us. "Wherefore, I the Lord ask you this question—unto what were ye ordained?" (D&C 50:13.) That is, "What agency did I give you? What commission have I conferred upon you? What authorization is yours? What divine commandment came from me to you?" And then he answers, and his answer tells us what we are ordained to do.

"To preach my gospel by the Spirit, even the Comforter which was sent forth to teach the truth. And then received ye spirits which ye could not understand, and received them to be of God; and in this are ye justified?" (D&C 50:14-15.)

I'd like to try that again. "And then received ye spirits [doctrines, tenets, views, theories] which ye could not understand" (D&C 50:15). Then you received something that you could not understand and thought it came from God. And are you justified?

"Behold ye shall answer this question yourselves; nevertheless, I will be merciful unto you; he that is weak among you hereafter shall be made strong" (D&C 50:16).

Now, here is some very strong language. If you can italicize words in your mind as it were, when they are read, do it with these words.

"Verily I say unto you, he that is ordained of me and sent forth to preach the word of truth by the Comforter [that is our commission], in the Spirit of truth, doth he preach it by the Spirit of truth or some other way? And if it be by some other way it is not of God." (D&C 50:17–18.)

Even truth, if uninspired, is "not of God." Now let me pick up that last verse again and give you the antecedent of the pronoun. It said, "If it be by some other way it is not of God" (D&C 50:18).

What is the antecedent of *it*? It is *the word of truth*. That is to say, if you teach the word of truth—now note, you are saying what is true, everything you say is accurate and right—by some other way than the Spirit, it is not of God. Now, what is the other way to teach than by the Spirit? Well, obviously, it is by the power of the intellect.

Suppose I came here tonight and delivered a great message on teaching, and I did it by the power of the intellect without any of the Spirit of God attending. Suppose that every word that I said was true, no error whatever, but it was an intellectual presentation. This revelation says: "If it be by some other way it is not of God" (D&C 50:18).

That is, God did not present the message through me because I used the power of the intellect instead of the power of the Spirit. Intellectual things—reason and logic—can do some good, and they can prepare the way, and they can get the mind ready to receive the Spirit under certain circumstances. But conversion comes and the truth sinks into the hearts of people only when it is taught by the power of the Spirit.

We teach and learn by the power of the Holy Ghost. "And again, he that receiveth the word of truth, doth he receive it by the Spirit of truth or some other way?" (D&C 50:19).

And the answer is: "If it be some other way it is not of God. Therefore, why is it that ye cannot understand and know, that he that receiveth the word by the Spirit of truth receiveth it as it is preached by the Spirit of truth? Wherefore, he that preacheth and he that receiveth, understand one another, and both are edified and rejoice together.'' (D&C 50:20–22.)

We worship by the power of the Holy Ghost. That is how you worship. Real, true, genuine, Spirit-born worship, in a sacrament meeting for instance, comes when a speaker speaks by the power of the Holy Ghost, and when a congregation hears by the power of the Holy Ghost. So the speaker gives the word of the Lord, and the congregation receives the word of the Lord. Now, that is not the norm, I think, in our sacrament meetings. At least it does not happen anywhere nearly as often as it ought to happen. What happens is this: the congregation comes together in fasting and prayer, pondering the things of the Spirit, desiring to be fed. They bring a gallon jug. The speaker comes in his worldly wisdom and he brings a little pint bottle and he pours his pint bottle out and it rattles around in the gallon jug. Or else, as sometimes happens, the preacher gets his errand from the Lord and gets in tune with the Spirit and comes with a gallon jug to deliver a message, and there is not anybody in the congregation that brought anything bigger than a cup. And he pours out the gallon of eternal truth and people get just a little sample, enough to quench a moment's eternal thirst, instead of getting the real message that is involved. It takes teacher and student, it takes preacher and congregation, both of them uniting in faith, to have a proper preaching or teaching situation.

Both teacher and student must be in tune. I suspect that many of you sometime or other, probably in high school, took a course in physics and had laboratory experiments and used a tuning fork. You remember an occasion when two tuning forks were selected which were calibrated on the same wavelength, and one of them was set up in one part of the room and the other thirty or forty feet away. Someone struck the first tuning fork, and people put their ear to the second, and it vibrated and made the same sound that came from the first one. This is an illustration. It is what is involved in speaking by the Spirit.

Somebody who is in tune with the Spirit speaks words that are heard by the power of the Spirit, where righteous people are concerned.

4. We Are to Apply the Gospel Principles Taught to the Needs and Circumstances of Our Hearers

The principles are eternal. They never vary. World conditions and personal problems vary. We apply the divine teachings to the present need. Nephi said: ''I did liken all scriptures unto us, that it might be for our profit and learning'' (1 Ne. 19:23).

What he did was quote Isaiah who was talking about the whole house of Israel. And he, Nephi, applied it to the Nephite portion of Israel. Now President Clark says: ''Our youth are not children spiritually; they are well on towards the normal spiritual maturity of the world. To treat them as children spiritually, as the world might treat the same age group, is therefore and likewise an anachronism. I say once more there is scarcely a youth that comes through your seminary or institute door who has not been the conscious beneficiary of spiritual blessings, or who has not seen the efficacy of prayer, or who has not witnessed the power of faith to heal the sick, or who has not beheld spiritual outpourings, of which the world at large is today ignorant.'' (Clark, *Chartered Course*, p. 10.)

We must not dilute or disguise gospel teachings. Now, this next expression pleases me to no end.

''You do not have to sneak up behind this spiritually experienced youth and whisper religion in his ears; you can come right out, face to face, and talk with him. You do not need to disguise religious truths with a cloak of worldly things; you can bring these truths to him openly, in their natural guise. Youth may prove to be not more fearful of them than you are. There is no need for gradual approaches, for 'bed-time' stories, for coddling, for patronizing, or for any other childish devices used in efforts to reach those spiritually inexperienced and all but spiritually dead.'' (Clark, *Chartered Course*, p. 10.)

I suppose that has some bearing on games and parties and entertainments and gimmicks, which really are poor substitutes for teaching the doctrines of salvation to the students that you have.

5. *We Must Testify That What We Teach Is True*

We are a testimony-bearing people. Everlastingly we are bearing testimony. You pay particular attention to the testimonies that are borne in sacrament meeting. A lot of them will just be expressions of thanksgiving or of appreciation for parents or this or that. Sometimes there will be a testimony that says in words that the work is true and that Jesus is the Lord and Joseph Smith is a prophet. And that raises the level. Now I am going to talk about something different from that.

Testify not only of gospel but also of specific doctrine. There are two fields in which we are expected to bear testimony, if we perfect our testimony bearing. Of course we are to bear testimony of the truth and divinity of the work. We are to say that we know by the power of the Holy Spirit that the work is the Lord's, that the kingdom is his. We get a revelation and it tells us that Jesus is the Lord and Joseph Smith is a prophet, and we ought to say it. That is testimony bearing. But we are obligated also to bear testimony of the truth of the doctrine that we teach, not simply that the work is true, but that we have taught true doctrine, which of course we cannot do unless we have taught by the power of the Spirit.

The fifth chapter of Alma is a very expressive sermon on being born again. Alma teaches the great truths incident to that doctrine in some language and with some expressions that are not found anywhere else in the revelations. And after he has taught his doctrine about being born again, he says this: "For I am called to speak after this manner" (Alma 5:44). In effect: "I've been called to preach this doctrine I just preached to you."

"According to the holy order of God, which is in Christ Jesus; yea, I am commanded to stand and testify unto this people the things which have been spoken by our fathers concerning the things which are to come" (Alma 5:44). He is using the scriptures. He is using the revelations that came to the fathers.

"And this is not all. Do ye not suppose that I know of these things myself? Behold, I testify unto you that I do know that these things whereof I have spoken are true." (Alma 5:45.)

He is testifying of the truth of the doctrine that he taught.

"And how do ye suppose that I know of their surety? Behold, I say unto you they [the doctrines he has taught] are made known unto me by the Holy Spirit of God. I have fasted and prayed many days that I might know these things of myself. And now I do know of myself that they are true; for the Lord God hath made them manifest unto me by his Holy Spirit' and this is the spirit of revelation which is in me." (Alma 5:45–46.)

The foolishness of teaching! The foolishness of teaching after the manner we have been describing! The teacher's divine commission!

The teacher's commission: a recapitulation. I repeat: I have no power to create a doctrine. I have no power to manufacture a theory or a philosophy or choose a way in which we must go or a thing we must believe to gain eternal life in our Father's kingdom. I am an agent, a servant, a representative—an ambassador, if you will. I have been called of God to preach what? To preach *his* gospel, not mine. It doesn't matter what I think. The only commission I have is to proclaim *his* word. And if I proclaim *his* word by the power of the Spirit, then everyone involved is bound. People are bound to accept it, or if they reject it, it is at their peril.

Now, my divine commission and your divine commission is, number one, to teach the principles of the gospel; number two, to teach them out of the standard works; number three, to teach them by the power of the Holy Ghost; number four, to apply them to the situation at hand; and number five, to bear a personal witness, a witness born of the Spirit that the doctrine that is taught is true. That is the teacher's divine commission.

Struggle and labor for the Spirit. I do not always measure up to that by any means. I guess the Brethren of whom I am one do as much preaching and speaking in Church congregations as anyone, unless it is the seminary and institute teachers. There are times when I struggle and strive to get a message over and just do not seem to myself to be getting in tune with the Spirit. The fact is, it is a lot harder for me to choose what ought to be said, what subject ought to be considered, than it is for me to get up and preach it. I am always struggling and trying to get the inspiration to know what ought to be said at general conference, or in a stake conference, or whatever. If we labor at it and if we struggle, the Spirit will be given by the prayer of faith. If we do our part, we will improve and grow in the things of the Spirit until we get to a position where we can, being in tune, say what the Lord wants said. That is what is expected of us. And that is foolishness in the eyes of the world, in the disciplines of science, and sociology, and so on. But it is the foolishness of God, and the foolishness of God which is wiser than men is what brings salvation.

Avoid False Doctrines

Let me say just a word about false doctrine. Pitfalls we are supposed to avoid are the teaching of false doctrine, teaching ethics in preference to doctrine, compromising our doctrines with the philosophies of the world, entertaining rather than teaching, and using games and gimmicks rather than sound doctrine — "coddling students," as President Clark expressed it.

Judge All Teachings by Gospel Standards

We ought to judge everything by gospel standards, not the reverse. Do not take a scientific principle, so-called, and try to make the gospel conform to it. Take the gospel for what it is, and, insofar as you can, make other things conform to it, and if they do not conform to it, forget them. Forget them; do not worry. They will vanish away eventually. In the true sense of the word, the gospel embraces all truth. And everything that is true is going to conform to the principles that God has revealed.

"O the wise, and the learned, and the rich, that are puffed up in the pride of their hearts, and all those who preach false doctrines, and all those who commit whoredoms, and pervert the right way of the Lord, wo, wo, wo be unto them, saith the Lord God Almighty, for they shall be thrust down to hell!" (2 Ne. 28:15).

I want to say something about this. That scripture is talking about people who have a form of godliness, as Paul expressed it, but who deny the power thereof (see 2 Tim. 3:5). And the Lord quoted Paul in the First Vision, using this very language. He is talking about those people of whom Paul said: They are "ever learning, and never able to come to the knowledge of the truth" (2 Tim. 3:7).

President Clark said: "You are not to teach the philosophies of the world, ancient or modern, pagan or Christian, for this is the field of the public schools. Your sole field is the Gospel, and that is boundless in its own sphere.

"We pay taxes to support those state institutions whose function and work is to teach the arts, the sciences, literature, history, the language, and so on through the whole secular curriculum. These institutions are to do this work. But we use the tithes of the Church to carry on the Church school system, and these are impressed with a holy trust. The Church seminaries and institutes are to teach the Gospel." (Clark, *Chartered Course*, p. 11.)

List of Prominent False Doctrines

You talk about teaching false doctrine and being damned. Here is a list of false doctrines that if anyone teaches he will be damned. And there is not one of these that I have ever known to be taught in the Church, but I am giving you the list for a perspective because of what will follow. Teach that God is a Spirit, the sectarian trinity. Teach that salvation comes by grace alone, without works. Teach original guilt, or birth sin, as they express it. Teach infant baptism. Teach predestination. Teach that revelation and gifts and miracles have ceased. Teach the Adam-God theory (that does apply in the Church). Teach that we should practice plural marriage today. Now, any of those are doctrines that damn. They are what I just read about from the twenty-eighth chapter of 2 Nephi.

List of Faith-Destructive Doctrines

Now, here are some doctrines that weaken faith and may damn. It depends on how inured a person gets to them, and how much emphasis he puts on them, and how much the doctrine begins to govern the affairs of his life. Evolution is one of them. Somebody can get so wrapped up in so-called organic evolution that he ends up not believing in the atoning sacrifice of the Lord Jesus. Such a course leads to damnation.

Somebody can teach that God is progressing in knowledge. And if he begins to believe it, and emphasizes it unduly, and it becomes a ruling thing in his life, then, as the *Lectures on Faith* say, it is not possible for him to have faith unto life and salvation. He is required to believe, in the Prophet's language, that God is omnipotent, omniscient, and omnipresent, that he has all power and he knows all things.

If you teach a doctrine that there is a second chance for salvation, you may lose your soul. You will, if you believe that doctrine to the point that you do not live right and if you go on the assumption that someday you will have the opportunity for salvation even though you did not keep the commandments here.

And so it is with the paradisiacal creation, with progression from one degree of glory to another, with figuring out what the beasts in the book of Revelation are about, or the mysteries in any field. If you get talking about the fact that the sons of perdition are not resurrected, or where the ten tribes are, or if you make a mistake on the true doctrine of the gathering of Israel, or some of the events incident to the Second Coming, or millennial events and the like, these false doctrines can lead to the kinds of behaviors, such as rejecting the living prophets in preference for the dead, that damn.

False Teachings Create False Faith

I am not saying that those doctrines will damn in the sense that the first list that I read will, but they may. They certainly will lead people astray, and they will keep you from perfecting the kind of faith that will enable you to do good and work righteousness and perform miracles. I do not get very troubled about an honest and sincere person who makes a mistake in doctrine, provided that it is a mistake of the intellect or a mistake of understanding, and provided that it is not on a great basic and fundamental principle. If he makes a mistake on the atoning sacrifice of Christ, he will go down to destruction. But if he errs in a lesser way—in a nonmalignant way if you will—he can straighten himself out without too much trouble. Joseph Smith tells us of an experience he had with a man by the name of Brown in the early days. This man was taken before the high council for teaching false doctrine. He had been explaining the beasts in the book of Revelation. And he came to the Prophet, and the Prophet, with him present in the congregation, then preached a sermon on the subject, and in fact told us what the beasts mean. In the sermon he said:

"I did not like the old man being called up for erring in doctrine. It looks too much like the Methodist, and not like the Latter-day Saints. Methodists have creeds which a man must believe or be asked out of their church. I want the liberty of thinking and believing as I please. It feels so good not to be trammelled. It does not prove that a man is not a good man because he errs in doctrine." (*History of the Church*, 5:340.)

Danger in Even "the Lesser Errors"

That statement applies to doctrines of the lesser sort. If you err in some doctrines, and I have, and all of us have, what we want to do is get the further light and knowledge that we ought to receive and get our souls in tune and clarify our thinking. Now, obviously, if you preach one of these great basic doctrines and it is false, and you adhere to it, you will lose your soul.

The Book of Mormon account says that a man goes to hell if he dies believing in infant baptism (Moro. 8:14, 16, 21). He is denying the atoning sacrifice of Christ and the goodness of God if he supposes that infant baptism is needed. It is my hope, obviously, that we will teach sound, true doctrine. And we shall do that if we confine ourselves to the scriptures, and if we leave the mysteries alone.

Personal Witness

In addition to the fact that the kingdom is true, the doctrine I have been teaching tonight is true. The points I have made under the heading, "The Teacher's Divine Commission," are true. If we can conform to them and follow them we shall rise to a standard of teaching that will change the lives of people. You do not change anybody's life by teaching them mathematics, but as Brigham Young told Karl G. Maeser, he was not even to teach the multiplication tables except by the Spirit of God. That is a lesser thing. But you do change the lives of people when you teach them the doctrines of salvation.

"It [pleases] God by the foolishness of preaching to save them that believe" (1 Cor. 1:21).

We save ourselves by our teaching and we save those who will get in tune with the same Spirit that we have, when we teach those truths. What a glorious and wondrous thing it is not to have to worry about the doctrines of the kingdom, not to have to defend them and support them and uphold them. They are true, and they sustain and defend and uphold themselves. ("The Foolishness of Teaching," Address to Seminary and Institute personnel. Published by The Church of Jesus Christ of Latter-day Saints, 1981.)

Notes

1. The document, or purported blessing to which Elder Mc-Conkie refers, called the "Joseph Smith III Blessing" (see Dean C. Jessee, *The Personal Writings of Joseph Smith* [Salt Lake City: Deseret Book Co., 1984], pp. 565–66), is one of the forgeries fabricated and sold by Mark Hoffman. The conference experience alluded to here is one in which the simple promptings of the Holy Spirit led a man to say something which offends the wisdom of the worldly wise but which reaffirms a gospel truth. Elder McConkie was uncomfortable with this particular document from the moment it surfaced. Shortly after it first appeared, in a conversation with his brother, Oscar W. McConkie, Jr., Elder McConkie said: "Joseph never gave that blessing. I know what Joseph taught on doctrine, and Joseph didn't make doctrinal errors—and this blessing has mistakes in doctrine." One of the bothersome doctrinal errors was the failure to mention priesthood keys.

2. One reason that students of the gospel hunger and thirst after gospel knowledge is, in the words of Elder McConkie, that "schooling in nothing new to us here. We went to school in preexistence. There were occasions when Adam taught the classes, and when Abraham taught the classes, and when Joseph Smith did. And the classes were so numerous and so extensive that the whole house of Israel—that group of spirits who were foreordained to be-

come Israelites—were teachers; and they taught classes. And the witness of truth was borne and we were given the opportunity to advance and progress. When the time came for us to come down to mortality, we ended a course of instruction that had been going on for an infinitely long period of time and commenced a new course of instruction—a mortal course. In effect, this mortal course is the final examination for all of the life that we lived through in this infinite premortal period." Thus, after having learned gospel truths in the preexistence, gospel instruction in mortality is but a remembering of that which we knew prior to birth—we brought with us an appetite for gospel truths from the premortal sphere.

3. The phrase "differences in administration" is perplexing to some. It refers not only to a spiritual gift dealing with the ability to manage or administer the Lord's programs, but also to the fact that the same gift may be administered in different ways. Moroni explains that all spiritual gifts come from God and operate through the agency of the Spirit of Christ. There are, he says, many gifts, but "different ways that these gifts are administered" (Moro. 10:8), meaning that the same gift may be manifest, experienced, or exercised in different ways. Consider, for example, the gift of healing. In one instance, Jesus heals a man's blindness by mixing his spittle with the dust and then anointing the eyes of the blind with the clay made therefrom (John 9:1–7); in another, he simply "put forth his hand and touched" a leper, making him clean (Matt. 8:1–4); in yet a third, a centurion's servant is healed when the Savior promises that he will be (Matt. 8:5–13); and he heals Peter's wife by touching her hand (Matt. 8:14). The gift of healing, in our day in particular, is most frequently exercised by the laying on of hands, but as the Savior's experience illustrates, it can be administered in different ways.

The same is true of the gift of teaching, as Elder McConkie here observes. The way in which a spiritual gift is exercised, or administered, we assume is a function of different things, such as the degree of faith possessed by those involved or some specific instruction from the Lord, such as the directive to lay on hands in administering the gift of healing (D&C 42:44).

Overcoming the World

INTRODUCTION TO PART V

Mortality is a testing ground — a probationary estate. Will men choose to repent, to be baptized, to marry, to have children, to live in the family unit? Will they learn the lessons of pain, anguish, toil, and tears? Will they worship the true and living God, serve in his kingdom, honor and sustain his prophets, testify of gospel truths, love their fellowmen, and learn obedience, humility, and charity? Will they "do all things whatsoever the Lord their God shall command them" (Abr. 3:25)? Will men yield to the enticings of the Holy Spirit, and therein put off the natural man and become a Saint? Will they, in short, overcome the world?

To overcome the world — meaning sin, evil, and all that is worldly — men must repent of their sins and thereafter "hold fast," in the language of Paul, "that which is good" (chapter 21). Forgiveness, of course, is a gift of the Spirit; it comes when men have the companionship of the Holy Ghost, which companionship comes as men repent, keep the commandments, and submit to the ordinances of forgiveness, such as baptism and the sacrament. Thereafter, spiritual growth is a continued step-by-step process of perfecting one's self, first in one thing, then in another, until finally, in that great eternal day, men are perfect in all things, even as are Jesus and his Father (Matt. 5:48; 3 Ne. 12:48).

We are thus at war with worldliness, and every man's sword is unsheathed — there are no neutrals. Applying this principle, President Joseph Fielding Smith said: "We are all missionaries; some are missionaries for the Church, and some are missionaries against the Church." President Smith, of course, had reference not only to what men say but to what they do, for it is not sufficient simply to obtain testimony. Valiance in testimony is the eternal measure (chapter 22).

Another easily ignored, but particularly important principle in overcoming the world is that of charity, that "pure love of Christ" which is both a cause and consequence of having the companionship of the Holy Ghost, or of overcoming the world (chapter 24).

Chapter 21

HOLD FAST
THAT WHICH IS GOOD

Defining That Which Is Good

In considering the subject "Hold fast that which is good," two queries naturally arise: first, what is meant by "that which is good"? and second, what course must we pursue, with full purpose of heart, in order to cleave unto the thing that is designated as good?

We should note first, in setting the course of our investigation, that this exhortation was written by the Apostle Paul specifically to members of the Church. He was addressing the Saints at Thessalonica. He was speaking to people who had gained citizenship in the kingdom of God, who had come out of darkness into the marvelous light of Christ—people such as we are supposed to be. He is not speaking to people of the world, but to the Saints.

We should also note the context in which the exhortation is found. He writes these words: "Rejoice evermore. Pray without ceasing. In every thing give thanks. . . . Quench not the Spirit. Despise not prophesyings. Prove all things; hold fast that which is good. Abstain from all appearances of evil." (1 Thes. 5:16–21.)

Hold Fast to the Faith

Now, taking these things together it seems evident to me that the Apostle Paul was directing the members of the Church to hold fast to the faith. He was saying: "Cleave unto that which is good. Hold fast to the iron rod. Be valiant in testimony. Work out your salvation." That is, "Now that you are members of the Church, that you have come in at the gate of repentance and baptism, press forward to the end and do the things that will enable you to be saved in the everlasting kingdom of the Father."

To build on this foundation, suppose we turn to some of the revelations that the Lord has given and see if we can get at the heart of the matter. I choose to read first some words that the resurrected Lord spoke to the Nephites in which he outlined to them the plan of salvation.

Plan of Salvation Summarized

The Savior said that no unclean thing can enter into his Father's kingdom:

"Therefore nothing entereth into his rest save it be those who have washed their garments in my blood, because of their faith, and the repentance of all their sins, and their faithfulness unto the end. Now this is the commandment: Repent, all ye ends of the earth, and come unto me and be baptized in my name, that ye may be sanctified by the reception of the Holy Ghost, that ye may stand spotless before me at the last day. Verily, verily, I say unto you, this is my gospel." (3 Ne. 27:19–21.)

That is a perfect summary of the plan of salvation.

Requirements of Salvation

We seek an inheritance in the kingdom of God, that is, the celestial kingdom, and these words show the course that we must follow if we are to obtain it. We can be saved in that world, providing that first we have faith in Christ. Necessarily that must be faith based on knowledge. We must have an understanding of the nature and kind of being that he is and also the assurance in our hearts that our lives are in conformity with his will.

After faith, we must repent of our sins. We must be washed clean in the waters of baptism. Those who have come into the Church and have repented initially, have yet to repent of the added sins that they commit, or of the things that they do that are not in harmony with the divine will.

Then comes baptism, the third requirement, it being necessary that such be performed under the hands of a legal administrator so that it will be binding on earth and sealed eternally in the heavens.

And after this comes the laying on of hands for the gift of the Holy Ghost. The gift of the Holy Ghost is the right to the constant companionship of that member of the Godhead, based on righteousness. When hands are laid upon our heads and a legal administrator says, "Receive the Holy Ghost," that gives us the right, provided that we are faithful and seek the Lord with all our hearts, to have revelation and guidance, direction and inspiration from that member of the Godhead.

That ordinance gives us the right to have the Holy Ghost speak to the spirit that is within us and thereby give truth with a certainty and assurance that cannot be refuted.

Then, after having received this great gift of the Holy Ghost — and it is by this great gift that we will have power to sanctify and cleanse ourselves and do all the things that are necessary to be saved — then after all that we have to endure to the end.

Enduring to the End

I would like to read one scripture on that subject, a scripture given by the Holy Ghost speaking through the mouth of Nephi, the son of Lehi. He speaks so plainly that, having read his words, we would be able to draw a picture of the things that we must do. He says:

"The gate by which ye should enter is repentance and baptism by water; and then cometh a remission of your sins by fire and by the Holy Ghost. And then are ye in this strait and narrow path which leads to eternal life; yea, ye have entered in by the gate; ye have done according to the commandments of the Father and the Son; and ye have received the Holy Ghost, which witnesses of the Father and the Son, unto the fulfilling of the promise which he hath made, that if ye entered by the way ye should receive." (2 Ne. 31:17–18.)

Now, note this, which is addressed to members of the Church: "And now, my beloved brethren, after ye have gotten into this strait and narrow path, I would ask if all is done?" (2 Ne. 31:19). That is, after you have joined the Church, is your salvation assured or have you only started out on the course that will enable you to gain salvation? Have you then done all that is necessary?

"Behold, I say unto you, Nay; for ye have not come thus far save it were by the word of Christ with unshaken faith in him, relying wholly upon the merits of him who is mighty to save. Wherefore, ye must press forward with a steadfastness in Christ, having a perfect brightness of hope, and a love of God and of all men. Wherefore, if ye shall press forward, feasting upon the word of Christ, and endure to the end, behold, thus saith the Father: Ye shall have eternal life. And now, behold, my beloved brethren, this is the way; and there is none other way nor name given under heaven whereby man can be saved in the kingdom of God.'' (2 Ne. 31:19–21.)

We should desire with all our hearts to go to the celestial kingdom of God.

Purposes of Mortality

We are here in this life with the gospel so that we can have peace and happiness, solace, joy, contentment; and then gain eternal life hereafter. The greatest gift that a person can have in mortality, without any exception, is the gift of the Holy Ghost, the actual guidance, the actual enjoyment of the companionship of that member of the Godhead. Those who have it have peace and solace and joy here. Then the greatest gift that a person can have in eternity is to have eternal life, which is to go where God is and have the kind of existence and kind of life that he has.

Baptism the Gate

Those who come in at this gate of repentance and baptism and have their sins washed away in the blood of Christ because of his atonement, and who then go up the strait and narrow path—that is, those who press forward holding fast that which is good—in the end receive an inheritance in the celestial kingdom of heaven and that inheritance is named eternal life.

If you wanted to draw a picture of the plan of salvation, you could draw a gate and then write by the side of that gate the name, "Repentance and Baptism." Then, from the gate a long, long distance upward you could draw a path, a narrow course, and you could write the name, "The Strait and Narrow Path," by this path. And then at the end of the path you could write the words, "The Kingdom of God," or "Eternal Life."

Salvation an Outgrowth of Church Membership

The process of gaining eternal life is the process of coming in at the gate of repentance and baptism, that is, we must join The Church of Jesus Christ of Latter-day Saints, because such is the kingdom of God on earth, and the only true and living Church on the face of the earth.

But then, having joined the Church, we have but opened the door to our possibilities. Church membership is not an end in itself. Baptism is not an end in itself. When we are baptized we take the covenant of salvation upon ourselves and we covenant in a most solemn and formal manner to keep the commandments of God and to endure to the end; and the Lord on his part covenants that if we do keep his commandments and endure to the end, he will pour out his Spirit more abundantly upon us in this life; that we will come forth in the morning of the first resurrection and will inherit eternal life.

This gospel covenant, of course, takes two parties—man, on his part, obeying the Lord's commandments, and the Lord, on his part, rewarding man for that obedience, rewarding him with an eternal inheritance in his kingdom.

That is a summary of the plan of salvation. That is what lies ahead of us; and all of the activities that go on in this Church, without any exception, are designed and intended to encourage the members of the Church to hold fast to the gospel of Christ. They are designed and intended to help us catch the vision of eternal life, and of eternal glory, so that we will want in our hearts, with all the desire and capacity that we have, to do the things which will enable us, eventually, to go where God and Christ are in the celestial world.

I will read another passage from the revelations, and then inquire, specifically and concretely, what some of the things are that we should do in order to endure to the end. This time I read words written by the great prophet Moroni as he closed the Book of Mormon account: He says:

"Come unto Christ, and be perfected in him, and deny yourselves of all ungodliness; and if ye shall deny yourselves of all ungodliness, and love God with all your might, mind and strength, then is his grace sufficient for you, that by his grace ye may be perfect in Christ; and if by the grace of God ye are perfect in Christ, ye can in nowise deny the power of God. And again, if ye by the grace of God are perfect in Christ, and deny not his power, then are ye sanctified in Christ by the grace of God, through the shedding of the blood of Christ, which is in the covenant of the Father unto the remission of your sins, that ye become holy, without spot." (Moro. 10:32–33.)

There again the plan of salvation is summarized.

Salvation Comes by Purifying the Soul

As we stand here in mortality, we have human souls. A soul is made up of body and spirit. These two are connected together temporarily, which gives us a mortal status. Now, in this status of mortality all of us are imperfect and unclean and impure, some to a great extent, some to a lesser extent. We have read that no unclean thing can inherit the kingdom of God. The process of salvation for each of us consists in doing the things which will enable us to take this soul that we possess, in its present unclean, carnal, imperfect state, and transform it into the kind of a soul that is clean and spotless and pure, and that has overcome all things, and is thereby eligible and able to go where God and Christ are.

God and Christ are perfect beings; they have the fulness of all virtues and all good things dwelling in them independently; and if other beings are to associate with them, they have to go from the present circumstances in which they find themselves up the ladder of progression and advancement until, enduring to the end, they create for themselves the kind of bodies and the kind of souls that the eternal beings in the eternal world have. If they gain that kind of body, they can go where God and Christ are.

The door and the gate that enables us to make this change in the human soul is the door and gate of repentance and baptism, but after we have entered the gate, we then have to travel the distance that is required to the great goal of salvation. The Holy Ghost opens up the way for Church members, provided Church members do the things that the revelations and the living oracles counsel that they should do.

All Commanded to Be Perfect

We have an injunction in the scripture, the word of Christ, that says: "Be ye therefore perfect, even as your Father which is in heaven is perfect" (Matt. 5:48). When the Lord spoke to the Nephites he said: "I would that ye should be perfect even as I, or your Father who is in heaven is perfect" (3 Ne. 12:48). This he said, of course, after he had been resurrected and glorified and obtained the power and glory of the Father.

Perfection Obtained Step by Step

This perfection is not something that is relative; it is something that we are able to attain; and we can now go up this strait and narrow path toward perfection, step by step and degree by degree, perfecting and cleansing our souls. No man in mortality can become wholly perfect; that is, he cannot have his exaltation here in this state of frailty and uncertainty. Amid the vicissitudes of this life he cannot attain unto the state of perfection that our Eternal Father has. That can be his ultimate goal. But here in life he can do the things that will give him perfection, step by step and degree by degree, until eventually he will have the kind of perfection that the Eternal Father has.

One might paint many simple illustrations of this principle.

Perfection in Moral Purity

Consider the basic law of morality. The Lord has commanded without any qualification or reservation whatever, "Thou shalt not commit adultery" (Ex. 20:14). He has decreed without any reservation or qualification: "He that looketh upon a woman to lust after her shall deny the faith, and shall not have the Spirit; and if he repents not he shall be cast out" (D&C 42:23).

There is no more basic law in the gospel than the law of personal morality. Can we be perfect in the law? I say that we can. And we can be perfect here in mortality. If an individual has absolute, total and complete control of himself, or of his appetites and passions, and does not commit sex sin and under no circumstances would, and so controls himself that he governs his desires and his appetites in that field, then in that sphere he has become perfect, because he has completely abided the particular law.

Perfection in Tithe Paying

The same thing applies to the law of tithing. The Lord says to us that we are to pay one-tenth of our interest annually into the tithing funds of the Church. If an individual believes that with all his heart, and does in fact, year in and year out, pay one-tenth of his interest into the tithing funds of the Church, and if he would rather forsake food and clothing and go hungry and naked than not comply with that law, he attains unto a state in which he is perfect in that thing and to that extent, because he is keeping the fulness of the law.

Perfection in Word of Wisdom Observance

We have a law that tells us that we are to abstain completely from tea, coffee, tobacco, and liquor. That is the negative side of the Word of Wisdom. If we govern and bridle our appetites and passions so that we can abstain completely from these things which are forbidden, and if we have such complete control over ourselves that under no circumstances would we partake of them, then as far as that portion of the Word of Wisdom is concerned, we are abiding the law in perfection. If the Lord says, "Thou shalt not use tobacco," and the angels of heaven comply and do not use tobacco, then the angels of heaven are living that law perfectly; and if you and I abide by the same law, then we are living that particular law just as perfectly and just as well as the angels of God in heaven could live it. And so perfection could come degree by degree and step by step.

These things that I have mentioned as illustrations are the concrete and specific things. They are things where we have a measuring rod and can determine whether we are complying with the law. We can divide ten into the income that we have and thereby figure out what our tithing is, and give it to the bishop as tithing, and if we do we have paid a tithing. If we have fallen short in any respect and have not paid one-tenth of our interest then we have just made a contribution to the tithing funds of the Church; or to say it as the street corner conversations would be, we have given the Lord a tip.

Obedience Increases Ability to Further Obey

We can learn to live these concrete things; we can measure whether we do these things. We have a lot of other things that we have to do which are abstract in nature, and which are things that we live only relatively. No man in mortality completely attains unto perfection where they are concerned. We are commanded to love our brethren, to have charity in our hearts, to be humble, to have devotion with full purpose and without reservation to the cause of Christ. These things are done in a relative sense; that is, we do not attain an absolute perfection in this life where they are concerned. But we have the assurance and we have the promise that if we do all the things that we should do, if we keep all the specific laws, we will thereby grow in power and capacity to obey other laws. We will thereby grow in grace and in stature; we will, as the revelation says, go from "grace to grace" (D&C 93:20), that is, climb the ladder, go up the strait and narrow path, and eventually be entitled to have eternal life.

Men Have Ability to Become Perfect

To my mind this is the plan of salvation. This is the course that we should be following and I think that every member of this Church, unless there is someone who has committed the unpardonable sin and done away for himself with the power to repent, by the agency that the Almighty has given him, has the power and capacity to gain salvation in the celestial kingdom of heaven.

The Lord has not been unjust or inequitable; he has not held out to us the promise of a glorious reward which we cannot obtain. It would be an unkind, ill-disposed, and unjust Father who would offer his children something which he knew they could not gain.

It is true that we have to abide in the truth; we have to increase in the attributes of godliness. This may sound strict. It is a strait course and a narrow way, but on the other hand, the Lord knows we have the capacity and the ability, the power and the strength to keep the commandments of God, and have eternal life in his kingdom. There is no soul here, not one, who, if from this hour, he will turn to the Lord with all his heart, but what can be saved in the celestial kingdom of heaven. If we will do the things that we already know we should, we can gain an eternal inheritance. All of us have the agency and power and ability, if we will keep the commandments, to gain eternal salvation in the presence of God. ("Hold Fast That Which Is Good," BYU Devotional, 24 June 1954.)

OVERCOMING THE WORLD

Love Not the World

For my text I take the words of the Beloved Apostle, John: "Love not the world, neither the things that are in the world. If any man love the world, the love of the Father is not in him. For all that is in the world, the lust of the flesh, and the lust of the eyes, and the pride of life, is not of the Father, but is of the world. And the world passeth away, and the lust thereof: but he that doeth the will of God abideth for ever." (1 John 2:15–17.)

Overcome the World by Obeying Christ

No one has overcome the world, the world of carnality and corruption, until he has given his heart to Christ, until he uses his talents, abilities, and strength in keeping the commandments of God, and in causing this great work to roll forth.

The Lord has given us the agency, the talent, and the ability to achieve in this field. He sent his Son into the world to be the great Exemplar, to be a pattern, to mark the way whereby we, like him, might attain glory and eternal reward.

It was Christ who said: "I have overcome the world" (John 16:33), and it was also Christ who promised, "To him that overcometh will I grant to sit with me in my throne, even as I also overcame, and am set down with my Father in his throne" (Rev. 3:21).

The Savior Is the Standard

As members of The Church of Jesus Christ of Latter-day Saints, we seek salvation. We desire peace in this life and eternal life in the realms ahead. We have taken upon ourselves the name of Christ, rejoice in the sure knowledge that he is the Son of God, and seek with all our hearts to be like him. He is the great prototype of saved beings.

Joseph Smith propounded this question: "Where shall we find a saved being? for if we can find a saved being, we may ascertain without much difficulty what all others must be in order to be saved."

His answer: "It is Christ: . . . he is the prototype or standard of salvation; . . . he is a saved being."

Then the Prophet gave this inspired pronouncement: "And if we should continue our interrogation, and ask how it is that he is saved? the answer would be—because he is a just and holy being; and if he were anything different from what he is, he would not be saved; for his salvation depends on his being precisely what he is and nothing else; . . . for salvation consists in the glory, authority, majesty, power and dominion which Jehovah possesses and in nothing else; and no being can possess it but himself or one like him." (*Lectures on Faith*, pp. 63–64.)

Speaking of the mortal probation of this holy and perfect being, who is the prototype of all saved beings, Paul said: "Though he were a Son, yet learned he obedience by the things which he suffered; And being made perfect, he became the author [that is, the cause] of eternal salvation unto all them that obey him" (Heb. 5:8–9).

Now, it was this Jesus who said, "I am not of the world" (John 17:14).

> He marked the path and led the way,
> And every point defines
> To light and life and endless day
> Where God's full presence shines.
> (*LDS Hymns* No. 68.)
> (Stockholm Area Conference, August
> 1979, pp. 119–20.)

Wickedness Prevails Throughout the World

I suppose that in our day—in this age, with all the pressures of advertising, made possible by the use of all the modern inventions —that the enticements and pressures of the world exceed anything that has existed or prevailed in any age past.

Our Lord, in speaking to his ancient disciples about the lusts of the world, said that both he and they had overcome the world. He told them that they would be hated by the world because they were not of the world. (Mark 13:13; Luke 21:17; JS—M 1:7.) In his great intercessory prayer he prayed that the Father would keep the disciples free from sin. He said: "I pray not for the world, but for them which thou has given me; . . . I pray not that thou shouldst take them out of the world, but that thou shouldst keep them from the evil." (See John 15:18–19; 17:6–18.)

Mortality a Probationary Experience

Well, then, an omnipotent God has deliberately and advisedly placed us in the circumstances in which we now find ourselves, with enticements and lusts of every sort around us, for the very purpose of determining whether we will overcome the world, whether we will turn to spiritual things rather than be engulfed in carnal things. (Conference Report, April 1958.)

Overcoming the World

It is Jesus who says to his Saints: "In me ye might have peace. In the world ye shall have tribulation: but be of good cheer; I have overcome the world." (John 16:33.)

As here used, "the world" is not the earth or planet on which we now live. Rather, it is the social circumstances which prevail among the wicked and ungodly. It is the type of life lived by those who are carnal and sensual, who have not put off "the natural man" and become Saints "through the atonement of Christ the Lord" (see Mosiah 3:19). It is the course of conduct pursued by those who walk after the manner of the flesh rather than in the light of the Spirit.

Paul lists the "works of the flesh," the works found among those who are of the world, as follows: "Adultery, fornication, uncleanness, lasciviousness, idolatry, witchcraft, hatred, variance, emulations, wrath, strife, seditions, heresies, envyings, murders, drunkenness, revellings, and such like." Of these, and all other worldly lusts, he says, "They which do such things shall not inherit the kingdom of God." (Gal. 5:19–21.)

In contrast, Paul names as among the fruits of the Spirit, which are the attributes of those who forsake the world and accept the gospel, the following: "Love, joy, peace, longsuffering, gentleness, goodness, faith, Meekness, [and] temperance." Then Paul gives the test whereby the Saints of God can be identified. He says, "They that are Christ's have crucified the flesh with the affections and lusts.'' (Gal. 5:22–24.) That is, they have overcome the world; they have put off the natural man and put on the yoke of Christ; they have become Saints in fact as well as in name.

We Reap as We Sow

How sure and undeviating is God's eternal law: ''Be not deceived; God is not mocked: for whatsoever a man soweth, that shall he also reap. For he that soweth to his flesh shall of the flesh reap corruption; but he that soweth to the Spirit shall of the Spirit reap life everlasting.'' And how comforting and reassuring is his voice to his Saints: ''Let us not be weary in well doing: for in due season we shall reap, if we faint not.'' (Gal. 6:7–9.)

We live in a time of great wickedness. Satan rages in the hearts of his followers. He has restored every evil practice ever known to worldly men of old. And conditions among the generality of mankind are not going to get better until the second coming of the Son of Man. When that day arrives, it will be the end of the world, meaning the wicked and ungodly shall be destroyed and the worldly conditions in which they now live will cease (D&C 19:3).

It is true we must forsake the world if we are to be saved. It is true we must bridle our passions and appetites and overcome every carnal and sensual desire if we are to dwell with the Saints eternally. But that is why we are here in mortality—to be tried and tested, to see if we will stand valiantly in the cause of truth and righteousness in spite of the allurements of the world. (Stockholm Area Conference, August 1974, p. 121.)

There is an eternal law, ordained by God himself before the foundations of the world, that every man shall reap as he sows (Gal. 6:7–8). If we think evil thoughts our tongues will utter unclean sayings. If we speak words of wickedness, we shall end up doing the works of wickedness. If our minds are centered on the carnality and evil of the world, worldliness and unrighteousness will seem to us to be the normal way of life. If we ponder things related to sex immorality in our minds, we will soon think everybody is immoral and unclean and it will break down the barrier between us and the world. And so with every other unwholesome, unclean, impure, and ungodly course. And so it is that the Lord says he hates and esteems as an abomination ''an heart that deviseth wicked imaginations'' (Prov. 6:18).

On the other hand, if we are pondering in our hearts the things of righteousness, we shall become righteous. If virtue garnishes our thoughts unceasingly, our confidence shall wax strong in the presence of God and he in turn will rain down righteousness upon us. Truly as Jacob said, "To be carnally-minded is death, and to be spiritually-minded is life eternal" (2 Ne. 9:39). And as Paul said, "Whatsoever things are true, whatsoever things are honest, whatsoever things are just, whatsoever things are pure, whatsoever things are lovely, whatsoever things are of good report; if there be any virtue, and if there be any praise, think on these things" (Philip. 4:8). (Conference Report, October 1973.)

No Neutrals in War with Evil: Valiance Required of Saints

The Mighty Conflict with Sin

As members of the Church, we are engaged in a mighty conflict. We are at war. We have enlisted in the cause of Christ to fight against Lucifer and all that is lustful and carnal and evil in the world. We have sworn to fight alongside our friends and against our enemies, and we must not be confused in distinguishing friends from foes. As another of our ancient fellow Apostles wrote: "Know ye not that the friendship of the world is enmity with God? whosoever therefore will be a friend of the world is the enemy of God." (James 4:4.)

The great war that rages on every side and which unfortunately is resulting in many casualties, some fatal, is no new thing. There was war even in heaven, when the forces of evil sought to destroy the agency of man, and when Lucifer sought to lead us away from the path of progression and advancement established by an all-wise Father.

That war is continuing on earth, and the devil is still wroth with the Church and goes forth "to make war with the remnant of her seed, which keep the commandments of God, and have the testimony of Jesus Christ" (Rev. 12:17).

And it is now as it has always been. The Saints can only overcome him and his forces "by the blood of the Lamb, . . . by the word of their testimony," and if they love "not their lives unto the death" (Rev. 12:11).

No Neutral Side

Now, there neither are nor can be any neutrals in this war. Every member of the Church is on one side or the other. The soldiers who fight in its battles will either, with Paul, come off victorious and win "a crown of righteousness," or they shall, in Paul's language, "be punished with everlasting destruction from the presence of the Lord, and from the glory of his power" in that day when he comes to take "vengeance on them that know not God, and that obey not the gospel of our Lord Jesus Christ" (2 Thes. 1:8–9).

In this war all who do not stand forth courageously and valiantly are by that fact alone aiding the cause of the enemy. "They who are not for me are against me, saith our God" (2 Ne. 10:16; Matt. 12:30).

We are either for the Church or we are against it. We either take its part or we take the consequences. We cannot survive spiritually with one foot in the Church and the other in the world. We must make the choice. It is either the Church or the world. There is no middle ground. And the Lord loves a courageous man who fights openly and boldly in his army.

To certain members of his ancient church, he said: "I know thy works, that thou art neither cold nor hot: I would thou wert cold or hot. So then because thou art lukewarm, and neither cold nor hot, I will spue thee out of my mouth." (Rev. 3:15–16.) The summer patriot and the sunshine saint retreat when the battle wages fiercely around them. Theirs is not the conqueror's crown. They are overcome by the world.

Valiance in Testimony Required

Members of the Church who have testimonies and who live clean and upright lives, but who are not courageous and valiant, do not gain the celestial kingdom. Theirs is a terrestrial inheritance. Of them the revelation says, "These are they who are not valiant in the testimony of Jesus; wherefore, they obtain not the crown over the kingdom of our God" (D&C 76:79).

As Jesus said, "No man, having put his hand to the plough, and looking back, is fit for the kingdom of God" (Luke 9:62).

What is the testimony of Jesus? And what must we do to be valiant therein?

"Be not . . . ashamed of the testimony of our Lord," Paul wrote to Timothy, ". . . but be thou partaker of the afflictions of the gospel'' (2 Tim. 1:8). And to the Beloved John came this divine message: ''The testimony of Jesus is the spirit of prophecy'' (Rev. 19:10).

What It Means to Be Valiant in Testimony

Now, what does it mean to be valiant in the testimony of Jesus?

It is to be courageous and bold; to use all our strength, energy, and ability in the warfare with the world: to fight the good fight of faith. ''Be strong and of a good courage,'' the Lord commanded Joshua, and then specified that this strength and courage consisted of meditating upon and observing to do all that is written in the law of the Lord (see Josh. 1:6–9). The great cornerstone of valiance in the cause of righteousness is obedience to the whole law of the whole gospel (Eccles. 12:13–14).

To be valiant in the testimony of Jesus is to ''come unto Christ, and be perfected in him''; it is to deny ourselves ''of all ungodliness,'' and ''love God'' with all our ''might, mind and strength'' (Moro. 10:32).

To be valiant in the testimony of Jesus is to believe in Christ and his gospel with unshakable conviction. It is to know of the verity and divinity of the Lord's work on earth.

But this is not all. It is more than believing and knowing. We must be doers of the word and not hearers only (James 1:22). It is more than lip service; it is not simply confessing with the mouth the divine sonship of the Savior. It is obedience and conformity and personal righteousness. ''Not every one that saith unto me, Lord, Lord, shall enter into the kingdom of heaven; but he that doeth the will of my Father which is in heaven'' (Matt. 7:21).

To be valiant in the testimony of Jesus is to ''press forward with a steadfastness in Christ, having a perfect brightness of hope, and a love of God and of all men.'' It is to ''endure to the end.'' (2 Ne. 31:20.) It is to live our religion, to practice what we preach, to keep the commandments. It is the manifestation of ''pure religion'' in the lives of men; it is visiting ''the fatherless and widows in their affliction'' and keeping ourselves ''unspotted from the world'' (James 1:27).

To be valiant in the testimony of Jesus is to bridle our passions, control our appetites, and rise above carnal and evil things. It is to overcome the world as did he who is our prototype and who himself was the most valiant of all our Father's children. It is to be morally clean, to pay our tithes and offerings, to honor the Sabbath day, to pray with full purpose of heart, to lay our all upon the altar if called upon to do so.

Some Measures of Individual Valiance

To be valiant in the testimony of Jesus is to take the Lord's side on every issue. It is to vote as he would vote. It is to think as he thinks, to believe what he believes, to say what he would say and do what he would do in the same situation. It is to have the mind of Christ and be one with him as he is one with his Father.

Our doctrine is clear: its application sometimes seems to be more difficult. Perhaps some personal introspection might be helpful. For instance:

Am I valiant in the testimony of Jesus if my chief interest and concern in life is laying up in store the treasures of the earth rather than the building up of the kingdom?

Am I valiant if I have more of this world's goods than my just needs and wants require and I do not draw from my surplus to support missionary work, build temples, and care for the needy?

Am I valiant if my approach to the Church and its doctrines is intellectual only, if I am more concerned with having a religious dialogue on this or that point than I am on gaining a personal spiritual experience?

Am I valiant if I use a boat, live in a country home, or engage in some other recreational pursuit on weekends that takes me away from my spiritual responsibilities?

Am I valiant if I engage in gambling, play cards, go to pornographic movies, shop on Sunday, wear immodest clothes, or do any of the things that are the accepted way of life among worldly people?

The Kingdom of God or Nothing

If we are to gain salvation, we must put first in our lives the things of God's kingdom. With us it must be the kingdom of God or nothing. We have come out of darkness; ours is the marvelous light of Christ (1 Pet. 2:9). We must walk in the light.

Now, I don't pretend to be able to read the future, but I have a very strong feeling that conditions in the world are not going to get better. They are going to get worse until the coming of the Son of Man, which is the end of the world, when the wicked will be destroyed.

I think the world is going to get worse, and the faithful portion of the Church, at least, is going to get better. The day is coming, more than ever has been the case in the past, when we will be under the obligation of making a choice, of standing up for the Church, of adhering to its precepts and teachings and principles, of taking the counsel that comes from the Apostles and prophets whom God has placed to teach the doctrine and bear witness to the world. The day is coming when this will be more necessary than has ever been the case in our day or at any time in our dispensation. (Conference Report, October 1974.)

Saints Instructed to Be Positive

Latter-day Saints should take an affirmative, wholesome attitude toward world and national conditions; turn their backs on everything that is evil and destructive; look for that which is good and edifying in all things; praise the Lord for his goodness and grace in giving us the glories and wonders of his everlasting gospel.

In view of all that prevails in the world, it might be easy to center our attention on negative or evil things, or to dissipate our energies on causes and enterprises of doubtful worth and questionable productivity.

Support Good Causes

I am fully aware of the divine decree to be actively engaged in a good cause (D&C 58:26–29); of the fact that every true principle which works for the freedom and blessing of mankind has the Lord's approval (D&C 98:4–9); of the need to sustain and support those who espouse proper causes and advocate true principles (D&C 98:10) — all of which things we also should do in the best and most beneficial way we can. The issue, I think, is not *what* we should do but *how* we should do it; and I maintain that the most beneficial and productive thing which Latter-day Saints can do to strengthen every good and proper cause is to live and teach the principles of the everlasting gospel.

There may be those who have special gifts and needs to serve in other fields, but as far as I am concerned, with the knowledge and testimony that I have, there is nothing I can do for the time and season of this mortal probation that is more important than to use all my strength, energy, and ability in spreading and perfecting the cause of truth and righteousness, both in the Church and among our Father's other children.

I think the Latter-day Saints have a great obligation pressing in upon them to rejoice in the Lord, to praise him for his goodness and grace, to ponder his eternal truths in their hearts, and to set their hearts on righteousness.

Isaiah's Counsel: Work Righteousness

I take these words of Isaiah, words which he addressed to us, to the house of Israel, to the members of the Lord's kingdom. He asked: "Who among us shall dwell with the devouring fire? who among us shall dwell with everlasting burnings?" (Isa. 33:14).

That is, who in the Church shall gain an inheritance in the celestial kingdom? Who will go where God and Christ and holy beings are? Who will overcome the world, work the works of righteousness, and enduring in faith and devotion to the end hear the blessed benediction, "Come, and inherit the kingdom of my Father"?

Isaiah answers: "He that walketh righteously, and speaketh uprightly; he that despiseth the gain of oppressions, that shaketh his hands from holding of bribes, that stoppeth his ears from hearing of blood, and shutteth his eyes from seeing evil; He shall dwell on high" (Isa. 33:15–16).

Applying Isaiah to Our Day

Now, if I may, I shall take these words of Isaiah, spoken by the power of the Holy Ghost in the first instance, and give some indication as to how they apply to us and our circumstances.

First, "he that walketh righteously, and speaketh uprightly." That is, building on the atoning sacrifice of the Lord Jesus Christ, we must keep the commandments. We must speak the truth and work the works of righteousness. We shall be judged by our thoughts, our words and our deeds (Alma 12:14).

Second, "he that despiseth the gain of oppressions." That is, we must act with equity and justice toward our fellowmen. It is the Lord himself who said that he, at the day of his coming, will be a swift witness against those that oppress the hireling in his wages (Mal. 3:5; 3 Ne. 24:5).

Third, "he that shaketh his hands from holding of bribes." That is, we must reject every effort to buy influence, and instead deal fairly and impartially with our fellowmen. God is no respecter of persons (Acts 10:34). He esteemeth all flesh alike; and those only who keep his commandments find special favor with him. Salvation is free; it cannot be purchased with money; and those only are saved who abide the law upon which its receipt is predicated. Bribery is of the world.

Fourth, he "that stoppeth his ears from hearing of blood, and shutteth his eyes from seeing evil." That is, we must not center our attention on evil and wickedness. We must cease to find fault and look for good in government and in the world. We must take an affirmative, wholesome approach to all things.

Concentrate on Righteousness

To enable us to keep our minds centered on righteousness, we should consciously elect to ponder the truths of salvation in our hearts. Brother [Boyd K.] Packer yesterday pleaded with eloquence that we sing the songs of Zion in order to center our thoughts on wholesome things. I would like to add that we can also—after we have had the opening song—call on ourselves to preach a sermon. I have preached many sermons walking along congested city streets, or tramping desert trails, or in lonely places, thus centering my mind on the Lord's affairs and the things of righteousness; and I might say they have been better sermons than I have ever preached to congregations.

If we are going to work out our salvation, we must rejoice in the Lord. We must ponder his truths in our hearts. We must rivet our attention and interests upon him and his goodness to us. We must forsake the world and use all our strength, energies, and abilities in furthering his work. (Conference Report, October 1973.)

Rewards of Overcoming the World

In seeking to rivet upon the hearts of the Saints the eternal importance of keeping the commandments and of thereby overcoming the world, the scriptures use words and imagery of an incomparable nature. For instance:

"To him that overcometh will I give to eat of the tree of life, which is in the midst of the paradise of God" (Rev. 2:7). That is, he shall find peace and joy in paradise and then shall come forth to an inheritance of eternal life, which is the greatest of all the gifts of God (D&C 14:7).

Next: "He that overcometh shall not be hurt of the second death" (Rev. 2:11). That is, he shall have eternal life, which is to dwell in the presence of God forever. He shall not die spiritually, meaning he shall not be cast out of the presence of God and die as pertaining to things of righteousness.

Further: "To him that overcometh will I give to eat of the hidden manna" (Rev. 2:17). That is, he shall partake of the bread of life, of the good word of God, of the doctrines of him who is the bread of life—all of which are hidden from the carnal mind. He shall never hunger more, and eternal life is his inheritance.

Again: "He that overcometh, and keepeth my works unto the end, to him will I give power over the nations: . . . even as I received of my Father. And I will give him the morning star." (Rev. 2:26–28.) That is, in a state of glory and exaltation he shall be made ruler over many kingdoms and shall be even as the Lord, who is the bright and morning star.

Again: "He that overcometh, the same shall be clothed in white raiment; and I will not blot out his name out of the book of life, but I will confess his name before my Father, and before his angels" (Rev. 3:5). Who is there among us who does not desire to keep his name forever in the Lamb's book of life and to hear the Lord Jesus confess it before his Father's throne? So shall it be with all those who overcome the world.

Again: "Him that overcometh will I make a pillar in the temple of my God, and he shall go no more out: and I will write upon him the name of my God" (Rev. 3:12). That is, he shall have exaltation and godhood. As Deity now is, he shall become. He shall have eternal life.

Again: "To him that overcometh will I grant to sit with me in my throne, even as I also overcame, and am set down with my Father in his throne" (Rev. 3:21). That is, as a joint-heir with our Lord, he shall inherit the fulness of the Father's kingdom.

And finally: "He that overcometh shall inherit all things; and I will be his God, and he shall be my son" (Rev. 21:7). Again, it is eternal life which is his. He shall be saved. As we quoted from the Prophet: "Salvation consists in the glory, authority, majesty, power and dominion which Jehovah possesses and in nothing else; and no being can possess it but himself or one like him" (*Lectures on Faith*, pp. 63–64). He is our prototype. As he was in the world but not of the world, so must we be.

The Nephites Overcame Worldliness

Now, what more need we say? All things are ours on conditions of obedience! Is it any wonder he said, "Be of good cheer; I have overcome the world" (John 16:33)?

Perhaps one illustration will suffice, an illustration of a whole nation which kept the commandments and overcame the world. I speak of the Nephites during their noblest hour. "There was no contention in the land," the Book of Mormon account says, "because of the love of God which did dwell in the hearts of the people. And there were no envyings, nor strifes, nor tumults, nor whoredoms, nor lyings, nor murders, nor any manner of lasciviousness; and surely there could not be a happier people among all the people who had been created by the hand of God. There were no robbers, nor murderers, neither were there Lamanites, nor any manners of -ites; but they were in one, the children of Christ, and heirs to the kingdom of God. And how blessed were they! For the Lord did bless them in all their doings." (4 Ne. 15–18.)

The Lord's Promise to the Faithful

Now, let us conclude with this promise, revealed through Joseph Smith and addressed by the Lord to "all those whom my Father hath given me out of the world":

"Lift up your hearts and rejoice, and gird up your loins, and take upon you my whole armor, that ye may be able to withstand the evil day, having done all, that ye may be able to stand. Stand, therefore, having your loins girt about with truth, having on the breastplate of righteousness, and your feet shod with the preparation of the gospel of peace, which I have sent mine angels to commit unto you; Taking the shield of faith wherewith ye shall be able to quench all the fiery darts of the wicked; And take the helmet of salvation, and the sword of my Spirit, which I will pour out upon you, and my word which I reveal unto you, and be agreed as touching all things whatsoever ye ask of me, and be faithful until I come, and ye shall be caught up, that where I am ye shall be also." (D&C 27:14–18.) (Stockholm Area Conference Report, August 1974, pp. 122–23.)

Chapter 23

HOW TO WORSHIP

The Importance of True Worship

I desire to give some rather plain and affirmative counsel as to how to worship the Lord. There is probably more misinformation and error in this field than in any other area in the entire world, and yet there is no other thing as important as knowing who and how we should worship.

Worship of God

When the Lord created men and placed them on earth, he gave "them commandments that they should love and serve him, the only living and true God, and that he should be the only being whom they should worship" (D&C 20:19).

Jesus confirmed this most basic of all commands when he said: "Thou shalt worship the Lord thy God, and him only shalt thou serve" (Luke 4:8); and the constant cry of all the prophets of all the ages is: "O come, let us worship and bow down; let us kneel before the Lord our maker. For he is our God; and we are the people of his pasture, and the sheep of his hand." (Ps. 95:6–7.)

As the spirit children of the Eternal Father, we have been placed on earth to be tried and tested, to see if we will keep his commandments and do those things which will qualify us to return to his presence and be like him.

And he has planted in our hearts an instinctive desire to worship, to seek salvation, to love and serve a power or being greater than ourselves. Worship is implicit in existence itself.

Worship in Spirit and Truth

The issue is not whether men shall worship, but who or what is to be the object of their devotions and how they shall go about paying their devotions to their chosen Most High.

And so, at Jacob's well, when the Samaritan woman said to Jesus, "Our fathers worshipped in this mountain; and ye say that in Jerusalem is the place where men ought to worship," we find him answering: "Woman, believe me, the hour cometh, when ye shall neither in this mountain, nor yet at Jerusalem, worship the Father. Ye worship ye know not what; we know what we worship; and salvation is of the Jews. And the hour cometh, and now is, when the true worshippers shall worship the Father in spirit and in truth; for the Father seeketh such to worship him, For unto such hath God promised his Spirit. And they who worship him, must worship in spirit and in truth." (JST John 4:22–26.)

Thus our purpose is to worship the true and living God and to do it by the power of the Spirit and in the way he has ordained. The approved worship of the true God leads to salvation; devotions rendered to false gods and which are not founded on eternal truth carry no such assurance.

Truth Essential to True Worship

A knowledge of truth is essential to true worship. We must learn that God is our Father; that he is an exalted and perfected personage in whose image we are created; that he sent his Beloved Son into the world to redeem mankind; that salvation is in Christ, who is the revelation of God to the world; and that Christ and his gospel laws are known only by revelation given to those Apostles and prophets who represent him on earth.

There is no salvation in worshipping a false god. It does not matter one particle how sincerely someone may believe that God is a golden calf, or that he is an immaterial, uncreated power that is in all things; the worship of such a being or concept has no saving power. Men may believe with all their souls that images or powers or laws are God, but no amount of devotion to these concepts will ever give the power that leads to immortality and eternal life.

If a man worships a cow or a crocodile, he can gain any reward that cows and crocodiles happen to be passing out this season.

If he worships the laws of the universe or the forces of nature, no doubt the earth will continue to spin, the sun to shine, and the rains to fall on the just and on the unjust.

But if he worships the true and living God, in spirit and in truth, then God Almighty will pour out his Spirit upon him, and he will have power to raise the dead, move mountains, entertain angels, and walk in celestial streets.

The Specifics of Divine Worship

May I now illustrate some of the specifics of that divine worship which is pleasing to him whose we are?

To worship the Lord is to follow after him (2 Ne. 31:10; 3 Ne. 27:21; Matt. 4:19), to seek his face (D&C 93:1; 130:3), to believe his doctrine, and to think his thoughts.

It is to walk in his paths, to be baptized as Christ was, to preach that gospel of the kingdom which fell from his lips, and to heal the sick and raise the dead as he did.

To worship the Lord is to put first in our lives the things of his kingdom, to live by every word that proceedeth forth from the mouth of God, to center our whole hearts upon Christ and that salvation which comes because of him.

It is to walk in the light as he is in the light, to do the things that he wants done, to do what he would do under similar circumstances, to be as he is.

To worship the Lord is to walk in the Spirit, to rise above the carnal things, to bridle our passions, and to overcome the world.

It is to pay our tithes and offerings, to act as wise stewards in caring for those things which have been entrusted to our care, and to use our talents and means for the spreading of truth and the building up of his kingdom.

To worship the Lord is to be married in the temple, to have children, to teach them the gospel, and to bring them up in light and truth.

It is to perfect the family unit, to honor our father and our mother; it is for a man to love his wife with all his heart and to cleave unto her and none else (D&C 42:22).

To worship the Lord is to visit the fatherless and the widows in their affliction and to keep ourselves unspotted from the world (James 1:27).

It is to work on a welfare project, to administer to the sick, to go on a mission, to go home teaching, and to hold family home evening.

To worship the Lord is to study the gospel, to treasure up light and truth, to ponder in our hearts the things of his kingdom, and to make them part of their lives.

It is to pray with all the energy of our souls, to preach by the power of the Spirit, to sing songs of praise and thanksgiving.

To worship is to work, to be actively engaged in a good cause, to be about our Father's business, to love and serve our fellowmen.

It is to feed the hungry, to clothe the naked, to comfort those that mourn, and to hold up the hands that hang down and to strengthen the feeble knees.

To worship the Lord is to stand valiantly in the cause of truth and righteousness, to let our influence for good be felt in civic, cultural, educational, and governmental fields, and to support those laws and principles which further the Lord's interests on earth.

To worship the Lord is to be of good cheer, to be courageous, to be valiant, to have the courage of our God-given convictions, and to keep the faith.

Living the Whole Law

To worship the Lord is ten thousand times ten thousand things. It is keeping the commandments of God. It is living the whole law of the whole gospel.

To worship the Lord is to be like Christ until we receive from him the blessed assurance: "Ye shall be even as I am."

These are sound principles. As we ponder them in our hearts, I am sure we shall know increasingly of their verity.

True and perfect worship is in fact the supreme labor and purpose of man. God grant that we may write in our souls with a pen of fire the command of the Lord Jesus: "Thou shalt worship the Lord thy God, and him only shalt thou serve" (Luke 4:83); and may we in fact and with living reality worship the Father in spirit and in truth, thereby gaining peace in this life and eternal life in the world to come. (Conference Report, October 1971.)

Christ Is the Prototype

I take this verse from the great intercessory prayer as a text. Jesus said, "And this is life eternal, that they might know thee the only true God, and Jesus Christ, whom thou hast sent" (John 17:3). It is one thing to know about God; to have information relative to his character, perfection, and attributes; and to know what he has done and is doing for men and all created things. But it is quite another thing to know God in the real, full, and accurate sense of the word. We do not know the Lord unless and until we think what he thinks, say what he says, and experience what he experiences. In other words, we know God when we become like him.

Salvation Defined as Being Like Christ

A statement taught by Joseph Smith and recorded in the *Lectures on Faith*, is, in my judgment, the most perfect and excellent definition of salvation that we have in our literature. This record states: "Where shall we find a prototype into whose likeness we may be assimilated, in order that we may be made partakers of life and salvation? or, in other words, where shall we find a saved being? for if we can find a saved being, we may ascertain without much difficulty what all others must be in order to be saved. We think that it will not be a matter of dispute, that two beings who are unlike each other cannot be saved; for whatever constitutes the salvation of one will constitute the salvation of every creature which will be saved; and if we find one saved being in all existence, we may see what all others must be, or else not be saved.

"We may ask, then, where is the prototype? or where is the saved being? We conclude, as to the answer of this question, there will be no dispute among those who believe the Bible, that it is Christ: all will agree in this, that he is the prototype or standard of salvation; or, in other words, that he is a saved being. And if we should continue our interrogation and ask how it is that he is saved? the answer would be—because he is a just and holy being; and if he were anything different from what he is, he would not be saved; for his salvation depends on his being precisely what he is and nothing else; for if it were possible for him to change, in the least degree, so sure he would fail of salvation and lose all his dominion, power, authority and glory, which constitute salvation; [this next phrase may be singled out as the heart of the whole matter] for salvation consists in the glory, authority, majesty, power and dominion which Jehovah possesses and in nothing else; and no other being can possess it but himself or one like him."

The *Lectures on Faith* then quotes numerous passages from the Bible concerning this subject and continues with these words: "These teachings of the Saviour most clearly show unto us the nature of salvation, and what he proposed unto the human family when he proposed to save them—that he proposed to make them like unto himself, and he was like the Father, the great prototype of all saved beings; and for any portion of the human family to be assimilated unto their likeness is to be saved; and to be unlike them is to be destroyed; and on this hinge turns the door of salvation." (*Lectures on Faith*, pp. 63–67.)

True Worshippers Obtain "the Mind of Christ"

Let us consider what is involved in becoming like Christ. This will help us to know him in the full, complete, and accurate sense of experiencing, believing, and knowing as he experiences, believes, and knows. Paul said that the Saints "have the mind of Christ" (1 Cor. 2:16). If we have the Lord's mind, we think what he thinks, say what he says, and do what he would do under the same circumstances.

Joseph Smith said: "Everlasting covenant was made between three personages before the organization of this earth, and relates to their dispensation of things to men on the earth; these personages, according to Abraham's record, are called God the first, the Creator; God the second, the Redeemer; and God the third, the witness or testator" (*Teachings*, p. 190).

With these words to aid us in our analysis and understanding, I now couple those which Moses spoke in summarizing the law to Israel: "Hear, O Israel: The Lord our God is one Lord: And thou shalt love the Lord thy God with all thine heart, and with all thy soul, and with all thy might" (Deut. 6:4–5). Eternal principles are involved. We believe in three gods: the Father, the Son, and the Holy Ghost. God the first is the Creator; God the second is the Redeemer; and God the third is the Revelator, the Witness, and the Testator.

The Deities United in Perfect Harmony

We can accordingly single out three great eternal principles as the three most important things in all eternity. The first is creation; the second is redemption; and the third is revelation. We announce with Moses that these three gods are one God. That is, they are perfectly united together as one in a sense which I shall further define.

We Worship the Creator

We worship the great God who created the universe. He is our Father in Heaven. We came into being because of him; we are his spirit children. We dwelt with him in a premortal life in a family relationship. We knew him as intimately and as well as we know our mortal fathers in this sphere of existence. This holy and perfected

Being has "a body of flesh and bones as tangible as man's" (D&C 130:22). He is a glorified, exalted, perfected personage. He has all power, all might, all knowledge, all dominion. There is no good characteristic or attribute that does not dwell in him in its entirety. There is no truth that he does not know.

We are his spirit offspring, and he has ordained a plan whereby we might become like him and be exalted. The Prophet Joseph said: "God himself, finding he was in the midst of spirits and glory, because he was more intelligent, saw proper to institute laws whereby the rest could have a privilege to advance like himself" (*Teachings,* p. 354).

These laws are named the gospel of God, the plan of salvation. This is God's gospel. It originated with him; he created it. This system saves all men, Christ included. Christ is the author in the sense that he adopted, espoused, and advocated the plan. This plan is named after him in our ordinary conversation to give honor and dignity to the work that he performs — the work of redemption.

The Importance of Creation in Our Worship

Without the Creation, we would not exist. The earth would not be; there would be no universe (2 Ne. 2:11-13). There would be nothing if it were not for God, our Heavenly Father, by whom all things originated. Consequently, we are in a position in which we ought to give praise, glory, adoration, thanksgiving, and worship to him for the creation of all things, for our existence, and for the very being that we possess. Without God, we are not. He deserves all the worship that we are able to give him. Our problem is to learn how to worship and what we should do to repay him for the great, glorious, and infinite fact of existence and creation.

God the second is the Redeemer, and his great, infinite, and eternal work is to ransom men from the temporal and spiritual death which was brought into the world by the fall of Adam. He is the Savior of the world, the Redeemer of men. He was the firstborn spirit child of the Eternal Father, and in that premortal life he advanced and progressed until he "was like unto God" (Abr. 3:24). He served under the Father, using Deity's power to create all things.

Atonement Enables Perfect Worship — or Becoming Like God

Christ's assignment and work in the eternal scheme is redemption (3 Ne. 27:13-17; D&C 76:40-42). This he accomplished in the meridian of time as the son of Mary and the son of God. He ransomed men from temporal death so that, as a free gift, all men without works or effort can come forth in immortality to a resurrected state. He ransoms men from the effects of spiritual death by making available the hope of eternal life. Eternal life is to dwell in the presence of God and in its fullest signification to be like him — knowing, believing, understanding, possessing, inheriting, and experiencing as he does.

If there had been no creation, there would be nothing. If there had been no redemption, the purpose of creation would have faded away into utter nothingness. There would have been no resurrection, no immortality; there would have been no salvation or eternal life; there would have been no reason or purpose of creation. It would have been impossible for the spirit offspring of our Eternal Father to advance and progress to become like him.

We Hold Reverential Feelings for Christ

According to the Prophet's definition, to be like God is to be saved, to have eternal life, or to fill the full measure and purpose of our creation. With reference to Christ, we are expected to give him love, honor, adoration, and worship; we are expected to pour out our hearts in thanksgiving because of the Atonement he made. If it were not for him, there would be nothing for us. Creation and redemption, then, are the first two great considerations.

True Worship Grows Out of Revelation

The third consideration is revelation. This is more practical and closer to us as individuals. If there were no revelation, there would be no knowledge of God, Christ, or the laws of salvation (Jacob 4:8). None of the information that enables us, as Paul expressed it, to work out our salvation with fear and trembling before God would exist (Philip. 2:12). It is one thing to know about God and another thing to know God. It is one thing to know about religion and another thing to experience religion — to actually know in one's heart what is involved. In the realm of revelation the Lord sends prophets to the earth to reveal the plan of life and salvation. They write this plan in the scriptures; they proclaim it from the pulpits; they herald it to the world. They announce this plan so that men will begin to know about religion, God, and the laws of salvation. Salvation is available to mankind because the Lord sends prophets whose missions are to all men. The prophets in our day, in this dispensation, are sent to the ends of the earth. The ears of every nation, kindred, tongue, and people are expected to be in tune with the prophets' voices.

It is one thing to know about religion and another to know religion — to experience it, to make it become a reality in your life. Revelation is first for the benefit of men generally. But secondly, and far more important, revelation is a personal matter that rests with individuals. If I am going to be saved in the kingdom of God, I have to receive personal revelation. I have to do more than just know about God or religion as it has been revealed to and taught by someone else. I have to receive a personal witness and knowledge in my soul that the gospel is true and that if I live righteously, I can have peace in this life and eternal life in the world to come.

We Worship by Working Out Our Salvation

In this existence, in time or in eternity, nothing is more personal than working out our own salvation. Every living person stands alone and independent in doing the things that will sanctify his soul and enable him to have the enlightening, interpreting, and guiding power of the Holy Spirit in his life. Of course, we must be sealed in the new and everlasting covenant of marriage; we must operate through families. (Salvation is a family affair.) But in the ultimate and final analysis, we are saved on our own. I have to be saved by my own works, if I ever gain such an inheritance; my wife must do precisely the same. But it takes the two of us, united as one, to gain the eternal fulness. If both of us work out our salvation, we will in fact be united as one and go on everlastingly in the family unit, which is a requisite for obtaining eternal life in our Father's kingdom.

As I have said, we have creation, redemption, and revelation; they are the three fields in which the members of the eternal Godhead operate. Without creation, without redemption, and without revelation, there would be nothing for us as mortals. These three things center our mind upon what is important and point to the course we should pursue.

The Way to Worship

Our concern is, How do we worship? How do we do the things that will enable us to become like him? What bearing does the passage "Hear, O Israel: The Lord our God is one Lord" have on us? Let me read from section 93, verses 6 to 20, in the Doctrine and Covenants. This revelation, containing some of the most explicit language we have, tells what Jesus Christ did in principle (not in detail) to work out his salvation. These words, first written by John the Baptist, were then taken by John the Revelator and paraphrased, quoted, and preserved in his gospel. Some of his words were recorded in this revelation; others were not. We await the day when our spiritual capacity will qualify us to receive the added things that these ancient prophets had. The Lord Jesus is speaking:

"And John saw and bore record of the fulness of my glory, and the fulness of John's record is hereafter to be revealed. And he bore record, saying, I saw his glory, that he was in the beginning, before the world was; Therefore, in the beginning the Word was, for he was the Word, even the messenger of salvation—The light and the Redeemer of the world; the Spirit of truth, who came into the world, because the world was made by him, and in him was the life of men and the light of men.

"The worlds were made by him; men were made by him, and through him, and of him. And I, John, bear record that I beheld his glory, as the glory of the Only Begotten of the Father, full of grace and truth, even the Spirit of truth, which came and dwelt in the flesh, and dwelt among us. And I, John, saw that he received not of the fulness at first, but received grace for grace; And he received not of the fulness at first, but continued from grace to grace, until he received a fulness." (D&C 93:6-13.)

This is a matter of advancement and progression. Christ the Lord was with God and like him in intelligence and knowledge. Under God's direction Christ was the creator of all things while yet a spirit being. Like all the spirit hosts of our Father, he then came to earth to undergo a mortal probation and go from grace to grace. The Prophet described this as going from a small degree of intelligence to a greater degree, as going from grace to grace until he gains a fulness of all things.

We read about prototypes. Christ is the prototype of salvation. In principle, then, we are reading what we have to do, as the following words explicitly show: "And thus he was called the Son of God, because he received not of the fulness at first. And I, John bear record, and lo, the heavens were opened, and the Holy Ghost descended upon him in the form of a dove, and sat upon him, and there came a voice out of heaven saying: This is my beloved Son."

That is how we know who the original author of these words is.

"And he received all power, both in heaven and on earth, and the glory of the Father was with him, for he dwelt in him. And it shall come to pass, that if you are faithful you shall receive the fulness of the record of John."

This is in the future. We have not been quite that faithful yet.

"I give unto you these sayings that you may understand and know how to worship [I wonder if we caught the vision of how to worship in the words just revealed], and know what you worship [perhaps we did catch the vision of what we worship. There cannot be much question: it is God the first, the Creator; God the second, the Redeemer, and God the third, the Witness, Testator, or Revelator], that you may come unto the Father in my name, and in due time receive of his fulness." (D&C 93:14–19.)

That is exactly what the Lord Jesus did — received of the fulness of the Father. The revelation continues, giving a promise that we can do the same. "For if you keep my commandments you shall receive of his fulness, and be glorified in me as I am in the Father; therefore, I say unto you, you shall receive grace for grace" (D&C 92:20).

What did we learn from this passage concerning worship? When we talk about worship, the thing that enters our minds is that we pray, preach sermons, or attend church; that we become actively engaged in the religious cause which has been revealed in our day. Like the dictionary, we think of worship as the matter of religious reverence and homage, the act of praying. Although it is a little beyond human ability, we think of worship as giving honor to Deity. This is all true, and in a sense we worship when we do these things. We probably worship more effectively, within the definition here involved, when we strive and struggle within ourselves to keep the commandments.

We Worship by Emulating Christ

These definitions of how to worship, however, are not in the revelation I just read. Read the revelation; meditate upon its principles; and see if you do not reach the same conclusion. The Lord is saying to us, "Here is how to worship. You worship by emulation. You worship by imitation. You worship by patterning your life after mine. You worship by magnifying me and following my course, by doing what I have done." We read a revelation which states that Christ went from grace to grace until he eventually received the fulness and had all power in heaven and on earth. We read that we can do precisely the same if we know how to worship. To my mind, then, the process of worshipping becomes the process of working out our salvation, as the Lord Jesus did, to gain glory, honor, and dominion—to attain a fulfillment of the promise of becoming like the Father.

Oneness of Deity Illustrates Spirit of True Worship

We now come back to our text statement, "Hear, O Israel: The Lord our God is one Lord." I think this single sentence is a summary of the greatest teaching device that has ever been given in the entire history of the world. It tells us how to worship. This concept that the Father, the Son, and the Holy Ghost are perfectly united as one is the most important truth that man can know. Out of its application in our lives comes the hope of eternal life. God has said to all the world, as have his prophets everlastingly and repetitiously, that the Father, the Son, and the Holy Ghost are one. He drills this concept into us. They are one in plan, one in purpose, one in power, one in the possession of the attributes of godliness, and one in every good thing. The whole system of salvation is so ordained that we may become one with Deity. If we do not, we are not like him. In declaring that the Father, the Son, and the Holy Ghost are one God, the revelations are bearing record that we must be one as they are one. We must go from grace to grace until we inherit an eternal fulness.

"Be one; and if ye are not one ye are not mine" (D&C 38:27). This is latter-day revelation. Jesus declared: "And whoso believeth in me believeth in the Father also; and unto him will the Father bear record of me, for he will visit him with fire and with the Holy Ghost. And thus will the Father bear record of me, and the Holy Ghost will bear record unto him of the Father and me; for the Father, and I, and the Holy Ghost are one." (3 Ne. 11:35–36.)

Added to this is the idea that "you must be one with us, if you are going to be like us and possess the same glory and dominion." On this hinge swings the door of salvation. In the Book of Mormon Jesus said: "Ye shall have fulness of joy [this was spoken to certain people but it applies in principle to every saved being]; and ye shall sit down in the kingdom of my Father; yea, your joy shall be full, even as the Father hath given me fulness of joy; and ye shall be even as I am, and I am even as the Father; and the Father and I are one (3 Ne. 28:10).

Salvation—and Worship—Means Being Like God

The greatest teaching device ever used in the entire history of the world is what God Almighty uses to teach man that salvation comes by being like him. This device is the eternal proclamation that the Father, Christ, and the Holy Ghost are one. As Moses declared, "Hear, O Israel: The Lord our God is one Lord." The one Lord consists of God the Creator, God the Redeemer, and God the Revelator. These three fields—creation, redemption, and revelation —signify the particular realms of assignment of the members of the eternal Godhead.

Our Duty Is to Emulate God

Our commission, our assignment, our goal in life is to believe the truth—to let it become a living reality in our souls. It is to have in our hearts the power of the Holy Spirit. No one can be one with God unless he receives revelation from the Holy Ghost. What the Holy Ghost speaks is what the Father and the Son would speak, and he bears witness and testimony of them (2 Ne. 32:3).

True Worship Is Experiential

We must let religion operate in our lives. We must do more than just learn about it. Religion must be a living, operating thing. The glorious and wondrous thing about this doctrine and work is that it is true; we have the truth of heaven. God has spoken in this day. The dispensation of the fulness of his everlasting truth has been restored and revealed anew for the last time. The gospel has been revealed to prepare a people for the second coming of the Son of Man so that they can sit down everlastingly in the kingdom of God with Abraham, Isaac, Jacob, and all the prophets.

Our problem is to learn how to do more than just learn about God and religion. It is to have God in our souls, to have the love of Christ in our hearts. It is to have the mind of Christ—to think what he thinks, say what he says, believe what he believes, and ultimately to do what he does. We must live the kind of life that Christ lives. We must become like him and his Father and thereby have everlasting glory in the eternal realms. ("How to Worship," BYU Devotional, 20 July 1971.)

Consecration and Sacrifice:
Forms of True Worship

Principles of Consecration and Sacrifice

I shall now set forth some of the principles of sacrifice and consecration to which the true Saints must conform if they are ever to
go where God and Christ are and have an inheritance with the faithful Saints of ages past.

It is written: "He who is not able to abide the law of a celestial
kingdom cannot abide a celestial glory" (D&C 88:22). The law of
sacrifice is a celestial law; so also is the law of consecration. Thus, to
gain that celestial reward which we so devoutly desire, we must be
able to live these two laws.

Sacrifice and consecration are intertwined. The law of consecration is that we consecrate our time, our talents, and our money
and property to the cause of the Church; such are to be available to
the extent they are needed to further the Lord's interests on earth.

The law of sacrifice is that we are willing to sacrifice all that we
have for the truth's sake—our character and reputation; our honor
and applause; our good name among men; our houses, lands, and
families: all things, even our very lives if need be.

Joseph Smith said, "A religion that does not require the sacrifice of all things never has power sufficient to produce the faith necessary [to lead] unto life and salvation" (*Lectures on Faith*, p. 58).

Saints Must Be Able to Live the Law

We are not always called upon to live the whole law of consecration and give all of our time, talents, and means to the building
up of the Lord's earthly kingdom. Few of us are called upon to sacrifice much of what we possess, and at the moment there is only an
occasional martyr in the cause of revealed religion.

But what the scriptural account means is that to gain celestial
salvation we must be able to live these laws to the full if we are
called upon to do so. Implicit in this is the reality that we must in
fact live them to the extent we are called upon so to do.

How, for instance, can we establish our ability to live the full
law of consecration if we do not in fact pay an honest tithing? Or
how can we prove our willingness to sacrifice all things, if need be,
if we do not make the small sacrifices of time and toil, or of money
and means, that we are now asked to make?

As a young man, serving at the direction of my bishop, I called upon a rich man and invited him to contribute a thousand dollars to a building fund. He declined. But he did say he wanted to help, and if we would have a ward dinner and charge five dollars per plate, he would take two tickets. About ten days later this man died unexpectedly of a heart attack, and I have wondered ever since about the fate of his eternal soul.

Beware of Covetousness

Wasn't there someone who once said, "Beware of covetousness: for a man's life consisteth not in the abundance of the things which he possesseth"? Didn't this same person then speak this parable: "The ground of a certain rich man brought forth plentifully: And he thought within himself, saying, What shall I do, because I have no room where to bestow my fruits? And he said, This will I do: I will pull down my barns, and build greater; and there will I bestow all my fruits and my goods. And I will say to my soul, Soul, thou hast much goods laid up for many years; take thine ease, eat, drink, and be merry. But God said unto him, Thou fool, this night thy soul shall be required of thee: then whose shall those things be, which thou hast provided?''

And then did he not conclude the matter by saying, "So is he that layeth up treasure for himself, and is not rich toward God"? (Luke 12:15–21.)

When the prophet Gad commanded David to build an altar and offer a sacrifice on property owned by a certain man, that man offered to provide the land, the oxen, and all things for the sacrifice, without cost. But David said: "Nay; but I will surely buy it of thee at a price: neither will I offer burnt offerings unto the Lord my God of that which doth cost me nothing" (2 Sam. 24:24).

When it costs us but little to give, the treasure laid up in heaven is a small one. The widow's mite, given in sacrifice, weighs more heavily in the eternal scales than the bulging granaries of the rich man.

Parable of the Rich Young Man

There came to Jesus, on a certain occasion, a rich young man who asked: "What good things shall I do, that I may have eternal life?''

Our Lord's answer was the obvious one, the one given by all the prophets of all ages. It was: "If thou wilt enter into life, keep the commandments."

The next question was: "Which" commandments?

Jesus listed them: "Thou shalt do no murder, Thou shalt not commit adultery, Thou shalt not steal, Thou shalt not bear false witness, Honour thy father and thy mother: and, Thou shalt love thy neighbour as thyself."

Then came this response and query—for the young man was a good man, a faithful man, one who sought righteousness: "All these things have I kept from my youth up: what lack I yet?"

We might well ask, "Isn't it enough to keep the commandments? What more is expected of us than to be true and faithful to every trust? Is there more than the law of obedience?"

In the case of the rich young friend there was more. He was expected to live the law of consecration, to sacrifice his earthly possessions, for the answer of Jesus was: "If thou wilt be perfect, go and sell that thou hast, and give to the poor, and thou shalt have treasure in heaven: and come and follow me."

The young man went away sorrowful, "for he had great possessions." (Matt. 19:16–22.) And we are left to wonder what intimacies he might have shared with the Son of God, what fellowship he might have enjoyed with the Apostles, what blessings he might have received, if he had been *able* to live the law of the celestial kingdom.

Much Is Expected

Now, I think it is perfectly clear that the Lord expects far more of us than we sometimes render in response. We are not as other men. We are the Saints of God and have the revelations of heaven. Where much is given much is expected (D&C 82:3; Luke 12:48). We are to put first in our lives the things of his kingdom (Matt. 6:33; Luke 12:31; 3 Ne. 13:33; D&C 11:23).

We are commanded to live in harmony with the Lord's laws, to keep all his commandments, to sacrifice all things if need be for his name's sake, to conform to the terms and conditions of the law of consecration (Matt. 19:16–29).

We have made covenants so to do—solemn, sacred, holy covenants, pledging ourselves before gods and angels.

We are under covenant to live the law of obedience.

We are under covenant to live the law of sacrifice.

We are under covenant to live the law of consecration.

With this in mind, hear this word from the Lord: "If you will that I give unto you a place in the celestial world, you must prepare yourselves by doing the things which I have commanded you and required of you" (D&C 78:7).

A Privilege to Sacrifice

It is our privilege to consecrate our time, talents, and means to build up his kingdom. We are called upon to sacrifice, in one degree or another, for the furtherance of his work. Obedience is essential to salvation; so, also, is service; and so, also, are consecration and sacrifice.

It is our privilege to raise the warning voice to our neighbors and to go on missions and offer the truths of salvation to our Father's other children everywhere. We can respond to calls to serve as bishops, as Relief Society presidents, as home teachers, and in any of hundreds of positions of responsibility in our various Church organizations. We can labor on welfare projects, engage in genealogical research, perform vicarious ordinances in the temples.

We can pay an honest tithing and contribute to our fast offering, welfare, budget, building, and missionary funds. We can bequeath portions of our assets and devise portions of our properties to the Church when we pass on to other spheres.

We can consecrate a portion of our time to systematic study, to becoming gospel scholars, to treasuring up the revealed truths which guide us in paths of truth and righteousness.

Sacrifice and Consecration: Evidence of True Church

The fact that faithful members of the Church do all these things is one of the great evidences of the divinity of the work. Where else do the generality of the members of any church pay a full tithing? Where is there a people whose congregations have 1 and 2 and 3 percent of their number out in volunteer, self-supporting missionary work at all times? Where does any people as a whole build temples or operate welfare projects as we do? And where is there so much unpaid teaching and church administration?

In the true Church we neither preach for hire nor divine for money (Micah 3; 1 Pet. 5:2; 2 Ne. 26:29, 31). We follow the pattern of Paul and make the gospel of Christ available without charge, lest we abuse or misuse the power the Lord has given us. Freely we have received and freely we give (Matt. 10:8), for salvation is free. All who thirst are invited to come and drink of the waters of life (John 6), to buy corn and wine without money and without price.

All our service in God's kingdom is predicated on his eternal law which states: "The laborer in Zion shall labor for Zion; for if they labor for money they shall perish" (2 Ne. 26:31).

We know full well that the laborer is worthy of his hire (Luke 10:7; D&C 23:7; 31:5; 84:79; 106:3), and that those who devote all their time to the building up of the kingdom must be provided with food, clothing, shelter, and the necessaries of life. We must employ teachers in our schools, architects to design our temples, contractors to build our synagogues, and managers to run our businesses. But those so employed, along with the whole membership of the Church, participate also on a freewill and voluntary basis in otherwise furthering the Lord's works. Bank presidents work on welfare projects. Architects leave their drafting boards to go on missions. Contractors lay down their tools to serve as home teachers or bishops. Lawyers put aside *Corpus Juris* and the Civil Code to act as guides on Temple Square. Teachers leave the classroom to visit the fatherless and widows in their afflictions. Musicians who make their livelihood from their artistry willingly direct Church choirs and perform in Church gatherings. Artists who paint for a living are pleased to volunteer their services freely.

The Lord's Work Must Go Forward

But the work of the kingdom must go forward, and the members of the Church are and shall be called upon to bear off its burdens. It is the Lord's work and not man's. He is the one who commands us to preach the gospel in all the world, whatever the cost. It is his voice that decrees the building of temples, whatever the cost. He is the one who tells us to care for the poor among us, whatever the cost, lest their cries come up to his throne as a testimony against those who should have fed the hungry and clothed the naked but who did not.

And may I say also—both by way of doctrine and of testimony —that it is his voice which invites us to consecrate our time, our talents, and our means to carry on his work. It is his voice that calls for service and sacrifice. This is his work. He is at the helm guiding and directing the destiny of his kingdom.

And every member of his Church has this promise: That if he remains true and faithful—obeying, serving, consecrating, sacrificing, as required by the gospel—he shall be repaid in eternity a thousandfold and shall have eternal life (D&C 75:5). What more can we ask? (Conference Report, April 1975.)

Chapter 24

CHARITY WHICH NEVER FAILETH

Penetrating Influence of Relief Society

I have been brought up on Relief Society and I still receive that diet and it is good. I stand in awe and in amazement at this great organization.

Let us consider this great field of service, this field of service that, in my judgment, enables the sisters of the Church to grow in the attributes of godliness, to perfect their souls in this life, to lay up those treasures in heaven which will multiply, in due course, to eternal reward in our Father's kingdom.

With regard to the Relief Society, questions like this come to mind: What does the Relief Society mean to me? What does it mean to and what has it done for my wife and for my mother and for their ancestors in considerable numbers? And what will it do for my children and my children's children?

The fact is that the Relief Society lives in my wife and in my mother and in their ancestors. My wife is a different person today than she ever possibly could have been except for the influence and guidance of the Relief Society. Long service in a heaven-originated, a priesthood-led, and a gospel-oriented organization changes the lives of people and, providentially for me, it has changed the lives of those who are nearest and dearest to me. What it has done for them it can do and has done for great hosts of others.

Serve God by Serving Others

For a text I shall read to you a brief statement from the journal of my father in which he speaks of his mother and of my grandmother. My grandmother, Emma Sommerville McConkie, was a ward Relief Society president in Moab, Utah, many years ago. At the time of this experience, she was a widow.

My father writes this:

"Mother was president of the Moab Relief Society. J_____ B_____ [a nonmember who opposed the Church] had married a Mormon girl. They had several children; now they had a new baby. They were very poor and Mother was going day by day to care for the child and to take them baskets of food, etc. Mother herself was ill, and more than once was hardly able to get home after doing the work at the J_____ B_____ home.

"One day she returned home especially tired and weary. She slept in her chair. She dreamed she was bathing a baby which she discovered was the Christ Child. She thought, Oh, what a great honor to thus serve the very Christ! As she held the baby in her lap, she was all but overcome. She thought, who else has actually held the Christ Child? Unspeakable joy filled her whole being. She was aflame with the glory of the Lord. It seemed that the very marrow in her bones would melt. Her joy was so great it awakened her. As she woke, these words were spoken to her, 'Inasmuch as ye have done it unto one of the least of these my brethren, ye have done it unto me.' "

Faith Precedes the Blessing

Now, I think that the Lord first tried her faith. When she had proved worthy by manifesting that charity which never faileth, he gave her a glimpse within the veil.

Charity of the Widow of Zarephath

Next, I shall read the experience of another widow, the widow of Zarephath. This woman lived in the day of Elijah, the day when the Tishbite had sealed the heavens. There was no rain, and as a consequence, a great famine fell upon all the land. The record says:

"The word of the Lord came unto him [that is, Elijah] saying, Arise, get thee to Zarephath, which belongeth to Zidon, and dwell there: Behold, I have commanded a widow woman there to sustain thee. So he arose and went to Zarephath. And when he came to the gate of the city, behold, the widow woman was there gathering of sticks: and he called to her, and said, Fetch me, I pray thee, a little water in a vessel, that I may drink. And as she was going to fetch it, he called to her, and said, Bring me, I pray thee, a morsel of bread in thine hand.

"And she said, As the Lord thy God liveth, I have not a cake, but a handful of meal in a barrel, and a little oil in a cruse: and behold, I am gathering two sticks, that I may go in and dress it for me and my son, that we may eat it, and die. And Elijah said unto her, Fear not; go and do as thou hast said: but make me thereof a little cake first, and bring it unto me, and after make for thee and for thy son. For thus saith the Lord God of Israel, The barrel of meal shall not waste, neither shall the cruse of oil fail, until the day that the Lord sendeth rain upon the earth.

"And she went and did according to the saying of Elijah: and she, and he, and her house, did eat many days. And the barrel of meal wasted not, neither did the cruse of oil fail, according to the word of the Lord, which he spake by Elijah." (1 Kgs. 17:8–16.)

Shortly after this Elijah raised the woman's son from death (1 Kgs. 17:17–23).

Here again, I think the Lord first tried her faith. When she had proved herself worthy by manifesting that charity which never faileth, she gained the preserving care of the Almighty for herself and her household.

Opportunities to Serve Are Available

The fields of compassionate service have not all been plowed. Members of the Relief Society over the years have done wondrous work in this respect—the naked have been fed; the sick have been cared for and healed—but there are many occasions ahead for added service.

We live in a perilous world situation. Things are not going to get better. They are going to get worse until the day of the coming of the Son of Man. And the tests that are being given to the members of the Lord's Church will, in my judgment, increase in severity and intensity. And because of this there will be more opportunities than there hitherto have been to labor on the Lord's errands, to render service to our fellowmen, and to do the things, patterned after these two examples that I have read, which will enable us to work out our salvation.

Now, what is it that the Relief Society does for the women of the Church? What did it do for my grandmother, the widow of Moab? What did it or its equivalent organization in ancient Israel do for the widow of Zarephath? It is perfectly clear to me that the Relief Society was given of God for the temporal and spiritual blessing of the members of his kingdom, not alone of his daughters, but of his sons, and that it is the divine agency which aids in bringing the members of his Church to full salvation in his kingdom. May I remind you of what James said?

"Pure religion and undefiled before God and the Father is this, To visit the fatherless and widows in their affliction, and to keep himself unspotted from the world" (James 1:27).

Service: An Attribute of Godliness

We build on the atoning sacrifice of Christ. We know that by the grace and goodness of the Lord, salvation is available. But then, in order to reap the blessings of eternal life, we have to do two things, both indicated in the revelations. First, we have to keep the commandments of God, and second, we have to serve our fellowmen. There is something more than the general theme of obedience that is involved in acquiring the attributes of godliness here and reaping eternal reward hereafter. That something is service to our fellowmen.

Christ the Lord was himself the perfect pattern in this thing; he said, "I am among you as he that serveth" (Luke 22:27). It is true that a woman's chief and most important work is in the home and with her family, and that, as President McKay says, "No success compensates for failure in the home." But it is also true that every woman needs outside interests, that she needs a God-given way to use the charitable talent with which she is endowed, that service to one's fellowmen is essential to salvation, and that the Relief Society is the organization God has established to enable women to serve and to be guided in those channels wherein they can fill the full measure of their creation.

Mortality Designed to Teach Service

When we talk about gaining salvation, about acquiring the attributes of godliness in this life so that they can be multiplied and perfected and given to us in full in the life to come, we are talking about the family unit. God, our Heavenly Father, lives and presides in the family unit. We are literally his offspring. We are his children. We are members of his family. And he ordained the laws and the system whereby we could advance, progress, and become like him. To become like him, we have to have the same character, perfections, and attributes that he possesses. And we have to live in the family unit as he lives in the family unit. And so he has given us, in this life, eternal family units, units that begin here with the potential and the possibility of continuing hereafter in the same relationship that exists where he, himself, is involved.

And he has given us the opportunity to experiment and labor and struggle and work and try in our relationships with our fellowmen to acquire those capabilities, those attributes, that measure of integrity and honesty and charity and decency and uprightness that will enable us eventually to become like him. Paul's expression is that we have to work out our salvation with fear and trembling before God (Philip. 2:12).

The process of working out our salvation is one of acquiring the attributes of godliness, and this grows out of service and obedience. The matter of obedience is simply a matter of keeping the standards of personal righteousness that are involved; but the matter of service is a matter of getting out of ourselves and getting into the lives of other people, of touching the hearts of men, of taking to them the principles of the everlasting gospel, of helping them perfect and cleanse their lives after they join the Church, of offering them temporal as well as spiritual blessings.

It is just as essential that man eat temporal food as that he eat spiritual food. Without temporal food we will die physically, and without spiritual food we will die spiritually. The Relief Society organization is so geared, and so ordained as to work ably in both of these fields.

> When I leave this frail existence,
> When I lay this mortal by,
> Father, Mother, may I meet you
> In your royal courts on high?
>
> Then at length, when I've completed
> All you sent me forth to do,
> With your mutual approbation
> Let me come and dwell with you.
> (*LDS Hymns* No. 138.)

Words of your great Relief Society poetess, Sister Eliza R. Snow!

In connection with this matter of salvation, since there will be more women who will inherit full salvation than there will be men, it follows automatically that there are more women in the world

who have spiritual talent than there are men, and that women, accordingly, are in a position to labor and work in the compassionate
service field in a far more effective and able manner than men ever
could work.

Scriptures Use Women as Examples

I take just a moment to mention to you that we have some great
illustrations in the revelations where sisters are concerned. Mainly
the scriptures talk about what men have done because they deal
with the organization of the kingdom and its general operation.
But, providentially, the Lord has left us in the revelations enough
scriptures to give us patterns for living. The patterns for living
where women are concerned are such as these: We have the record
of Mary, the mother of Christ. Gabriel ministered unto her. She was
overshadowed by the power of the Holy Ghost. She bore the Son of
God. Her psalm of praise ranks with the greatest psalms ever uttered, and, in my judgment, she is the perfect example of complete
submission to the will of the Lord.

Her statement to Gabriel when the annunciation occurred was:
"Behold, the handmaid of the Lord, be it unto me according to thy
word" (Luke 1:38). And that ranks with what Christ himself said in
the preexistent sphere—"Father, thy will be done, and the glory be
thine forever" (Moses 4:2).

Eve is another. She is, in fact, the pattern for all women. She
knew the plan of salvation; she preached the gospel; she prayed for
blessings; she bore children; she taught the gospel. And one of the
greatest single-sentence sermons that we have in all our revelations
was spoken by Eve: "Were it not for our transgression we never
should have had seed, and never should have known good and
evil, and the joy of our redemption, and the eternal life which God
giveth unto all the obedient" (Moses 5:11).

In the light of our knowledge is the plan of salvation. Is it any
wonder that our hymn says:

> Mother of our generations,
> Glorious by great Michael's side,
> Take thy children's adoration;
> Endless with thy seed abide.
> (*LDS Hymns* No. 163.)

Women Receive Revelation

Now, we might go on with Sarah, with Rebecca, with Rachel, with others, but time does not permit. But out of it all we come to the conclusion that everything that it is possible for man on earth to have—of a spiritual, ennobling, edifying, sanctifying nature—has been and is available for the women of the Lord's kingdom. They can become daughters of Jesus Christ. They take upon them the Lord's name. They are entitled to personal revelation. They can get all of the visions and guidance that men receive. When Rebecca had a problem, she went out and took it up with the Lord. And the record says, "And the Lord said unto her" (Gen. 23:23), and she received the answer.

I would just like to ask this question as I come back now to the theme that I mentioned and the expressions that were read relative to these two widows: Of whom think ye that this revelation speaks?

"Then shall the King say unto them on his right hand, Come, ye blessed of my Father, inherit the kingdom prepared for you from the foundation of the world.

"For I was an hungred, and ye gave me meat: I was thirsty, and ye gave me drink: I was a stranger, and ye took me in:

"Naked, and ye clothed me: I was sick, and ye visited me: I was in prison, and ye came unto me.

"Then shall the righteous answer him, saying, Lord, when saw we thee an hungred, and fed thee? or thirsty, and gave thee drink?

"When saw we thee a stranger, and took thee in? or naked, and clothed thee?

"Or when saw we thee sick, or in prison, and came unto thee?

"And the King shall answer and say unto them, Verily I say unto you, Inasmuch as ye have done it unto one of the least of these my brethren, ye have done it unto me." (Matt. 25:34–40.) ("Charity Which Never Faileth," *Relief Society Magazine,* March 1970, pp. 168–73.)

SUBJECT INDEX

SCRIPTURE INDEX

OLD TESTAMENT

5:13	73	8	307
5:18–20	62	8:13–17	307
7:3, 6	73	9:1–7	307
7:12	32	9–10	307
13:5	116	9:6–9	300
18:18	32	11	304, 307
		11:1–5	307
Ezra		12	307
3:11	73	12:2	84
		13	306, 307
Job		14	301, 306, 307
11:7	11	15–17	307
38:1–7	11	16:4–5	307
		16:9–10	307
Psalms		18	307
19:7–11	223, 241, 247, 329	19	307
		20	307
23	12	21–22	307
31:5	23	22:21–25	307
82:6	49	23	307
83:18	84	24	307
85:11	262	24:5	109
90:2	18	25	307
95:6–7	369	25:8	307
102:26–27	18	26	307
103:6–8, 17, 18	23	26:4, 19	84
106:11	73	26:19	300
107:1	73	27	307
118:1–4	73	28	308
136	73	28:9–10	165, 306
139:7–10	27	28:16	308
146:10	18	29	270, 276, 308
147:4–5	18	29:1–4, 18	262
		30	308
Proverbs		31	308
7:18	359	32	308
18:6	233	32:1–4	308
		33	308
Ecclesiastes		33:14	365
12:13	76	33:15–16	365
12:13–14	362	34	308
		35	304, 308
Isaiah		35:10	300
1	307	36–39	308
2	307	40	308
2–14	307	40:1–11	308
2:2–4	305	41	308
3	307	41:27	308
4	307	42	308
5	307	42:1–8, 16	308
6	307	43–44	308
6:1, 5	9	45	308
6:9–10	307	45:19	234
7	306, 307	45:20–25	308
7:10–16	307	46	308
7:14	300	47	308

48–49	308	Ezekiel	
48:16	234	15–28	268
50–51	308	37	239, 270
50:5–6	308	37:15–28	262
51	304		
52	304, 308	Daniel	
52:8	300	7:9–10, 13–14	204
52:13–15	308	7:13	32
53	48, 308	7:27	303
53:5	209		
53:9–10	300	Hosea	
53:10	210	4:1	70
54	308		
55–62	308	Joel	
61:1–3	308	3:17, 21	288
63	304		
63–64	308	Micah	
64	304	3	385
65	297, 304, 307	4	305
65:17–25	195	4–5	307
66	297, 307	4:1–3	305
66:22–24	195	5	305
Jeremiah		Zechariah	
1:5	11	2:10–13	288
2:13	70		
3:14	72	Malachi	
8:8	296	3:5	365
16:19–21	58	4:1	274
31:9	80	4:2	274
31:34	101, 328	4:5–6	268
32:17	26	4:6	23

NEW TESTAMENT

Matthew		8:5–13	341
3:11	103	8:14	341
4:4	93, 261, 293	9:10	163
4:19	371	9:18–21 (JST)	292
5:13–16	89	9:35	51
5:44	146	10:6	163
5:48	26, 54, 345, 352	10:8	385
		10:29	25, 222
6:9	10	10:40–41	81
6:11	145	11:28	190
6:16–18	286	11:28–29	221, 286
6:19	64	12	286
6:33	384	12:30	361
7:7–8	256, 293	13:10–13	231
7:13	72	15:6	286
7:13–14	80	15:28	163
7:15	286	16:13, 15–17	130
7:21	52, 76, 77, 362	16:13–18	115
		16:13–20	115
8:1–4	341	16:16	100

BOOK OF MORMON

PEARL OF GREAT PRICE